MW01691886

Taste of Home

MOST REQUESTED RECIPES

TASTE OF HOME BOOKS • RDA ENTHUSIAST BRANDS, LLC • MILWAUKEE, WI

SERVE NOTHING BUT THE BEST!

Potluck party pleasers, bake-sale favorites, busy-day dinners, holiday staples, family recipes that have been passed down through generations...find all these and more inside this brand-new edition of ***Taste of Home Most Requested Recipes.*** With 379 innovative recipes to choose from, this book keeps the perfect meal at your fingertips.

What sets these gems apart? Each comforting and flavorful dish in this collection is from the recipe boxes of real family cooks just like you. So you can trust that they're easy to prepare and made with the right combination of wholesome ingredients and affordable everyday items.

They also feature smart tips from our Test Kitchen pros, convenient prep/cook times, nutritional facts and first-person reviews from ***Tasteofhome.com.***

In addition, each recipe was reviewed and approved by our experts in the ***Taste of Home*** Test Kitchen, and step-by-step instructions and vibrant full-color photos make it easy to cook with confidence.

And when life gets busy, refer to these at-a-glance icons to make the most of your time:

Quick-to-fix recipes that are table-ready in 30 minutes or less.

5i Dishes that require no more than five items (not counting water, oil, salt, pepper and optional ingredients). What could be easier?

Recipes that can be made ahead and frozen so you have ready-to-rock dishes that will save the day!

Winners and runners-up in one of our popular ***Taste of Home*** recipe contests.

Whether you're creating a holiday feast with all the trimmings, in need of an extra-special appetizer for a game-day party or simply looking for a weeknight meal that will become a new family favorite, you'll always have a winner when you turn to the stellar recipes inside ***Most Requested Recipes.***

© 2022 RDA Enthusiast Brands, LLC.
1610 N. 2nd St., Suite 102, Milwaukee WI 53212-3906
All rights reserved. Taste of Home is a registered trademark of RDA Enthusiast Brands, LLC.
Visit us at ***tasteofhome.com*** for other *Taste of Home* books and products.

International Standard Book Number:
D 978-1-62145-816-6
U 978-1-62145-817-3

Serial Number: 2166-0522

Component Number:
D 119200108H
U 119200110H

Executive Editor: Mark Hagen
Senior Art Director: Raeann Thompson
Editor: Amy Glander
Art Director: Courtney Lovetere
Deputy Editor, Copy Desk: Dulcie Shoener
Senior Copy Editor: Ann Walter
Contributing Designer: Jennifer Ruetz

Cover Photography
Photographer: Mark Derse
Set Stylist: Stacey Genaw
Food Stylist: Josh Rink

Pictured on front cover: Apple Pie, p. 165
Pictured on title page: Pan-Roasted Chicken & Vegetables, p. 91

Pictured on back cover: Turkey Leg Pot Roast, p. 141; Spinach & Cheese Lasagna Rolls, p. 122; Bacon Avocado Salad, p. 71

INSTANT POT® is a trademark of Double Insight Inc. This publication has not been authorized, sponsored or otherwise approved by Double Insight Inc.

Printed in USA
1 3 5 7 9 10 8 6 4 2

TABLE OF CONTENTS

To find a recipe: tasteofhome.com
To submit a recipe: tasteofhome.com/submit
To find out about other *Taste of Home* products: shoptasteofhome.com

LIKE US facebook.com/tasteofhome

TWEET US twitter.com/tasteofhome

FOLLOW US @tasteofhome

PIN US pinterest.com/taste_of_home

Appetizers, Snacks & Beverages

With hot and cheesy dips, juicy wings and meatballs, grilled party toasts, must-try beverages and other stellar snacks, impressing guests has never been easier. It's time to celebrate—bite by bite!

STICKY MAPLE PEPPER GLAZED CHICKEN WINGS

Here's one of my favorite holiday appetizers. The coarse ground pepper cuts the sweetness of the maple syrup by adding just the right amount of heat. I enjoy these wings best when they are hot and crispy right out of the oven, but they are also delicious when made ahead and kept warm in a slow cooker.
—Shannon Dobos, Calgary, AB

PREP: 25 MIN. • **BAKE:** 40 MIN.
MAKES: ABOUT 40 PIECES

- **4 lbs. chicken wings**
- **¼ cup all-purpose flour**
- **½ Tbsp. baking powder**
- **1 tsp. coarsely ground pepper**
- **1 tsp. kosher salt**
- **½ tsp. garlic powder**

GLAZE

- **⅔ cup maple syrup**
- **2 tsp. coarsely ground pepper**
- **2 tsp. soy sauce**
- **1 garlic clove, minced**
- **Chopped green onions, optional**

1. Preheat the oven to 425°. Line two 15x10x1-in. baking pans with foil and coat with cooking spray; set aside.

2. Using a sharp knife, cut through the 2 wing joints; discard wing tips. In a shallow bowl, combine flour, baking powder, pepper, salt and garlic powder. Add wing pieces, a few at a time, and toss to coat; shake off excess.

3. Place on prepared baking sheets. Bake until no longer pink, 40-50 minutes, turning once. Meanwhile, in a small saucepan, combine glaze ingredients. Bring to a boil. Reduce the heat; simmer until thickened, 5-7 minutes, stirring frequently. Drizzle over wings; toss to coat. If desired, top wings with chopped green onions.

1 PIECE: 66 cal., 3g fat (1g sat. fat), 14mg chol., 63mg sod., 4g carb. (3g sugars, 0 fiber), 5g pro.

WATERMELON SPRITZER

Beverages don't get much easier than this bright spritzer! Watermelon blended with limeade is cool and refreshing. It's a wonderful thirst quencher on a hot summer day.
—Geraldine Saucier, Albuquerque, NM

PREP: 5 MIN. + CHILLING
MAKES: 5 SERVINGS

- 4 cups cubed seedless watermelon
- ¾ cup frozen limeade concentrate, thawed
- 2½ cups carbonated water
- Lime slices

1. Place watermelon in a blender. Cover and process until blended. Strain and discard pulp; transfer juice to a pitcher. Stir in limeade concentrate. Refrigerate for 6 hours or overnight.
2. Just before serving, stir in carbonated water. Garnish servings with lime slices.
1 CUP: 140 cal., 0 fat (0 sat. fat), 0 chol., 4mg sod., 38g carb. (36g sugars, 1g fiber), 0 pro.

TEST KITCHEN TIP
If you want to add an extra kick to this beverage, use champagne or sparkling wine instead of carbonated water. You can also use lemonade concentrate in place of the limeade.

BUFFALO CHICKEN SLIDERS

I came up with the idea for these sliders from my mom and dad, who'd made a similar recipe for a family get-together. To make it special, I sometimes use several different styles of Buffalo sauce and let guests mix and match their favorites.
—Christina Addison, Blanchester, OH

PREP: 20 MIN. • **COOK:** 3 HOURS
MAKES: 6 SERVINGS

- 1 lb. boneless skinless chicken breasts
- 2 Tbsp. plus ⅓ cup Louisiana-style hot sauce, divided
- ¼ tsp. pepper
- ¼ cup butter, cubed
- ¼ cup honey
- 12 Hawaiian sweet rolls, warmed
- Optional: Lettuce leaves, sliced tomato, thinly sliced red onion and crumbled blue cheese

1. Place chicken in a 3-qt. slow cooker. Toss with 2 Tbsp. hot sauce and pepper; cook, covered, on low 3-4 hours or until chicken is tender.
2. Remove chicken; discard the cooking juices. In a small saucepan, combine the butter, honey and remaining hot sauce; cook and stir over medium heat until blended. Shred chicken with 2 forks; stir into sauce and heat through. Serve on rolls with desired optional ingredients.
FREEZE OPTION: Freeze cooled chicken mixture in freezer containers. To use, partially thaw in refrigerator overnight. Microwave chicken, covered, on high in a microwave-safe dish until heated through, stirring occasionally; add water or broth if necessary.
2 SLIDERS: 396 cal., 15g fat (8g sat. fat), 92mg chol., 873mg sod., 44g carb. (24g sugars, 2g fiber), 24g pro.

ASHLEY LECKER
Green Bay, WI

PRESSURE-COOKER CHEDDAR BACON ALE DIP

My tangy, smoky dip won the top prize at our office party recipe contest. Use whatever beer you like, but steer clear of dark varieties.
—Ashley Lecker, Green Bay, WI

TAKES: 25 MIN. • **MAKES:** 4½ CUPS

- **18 oz. cream cheese, softened**
- **¼ cup sour cream**
- **1½ Tbsp. Dijon mustard**
- **1 tsp. garlic powder**
- **1 cup beer or nonalcoholic beer**
- **1 lb. bacon strips, cooked and crumbled**
- **2 cups shredded cheddar cheese**
- **¼ cup heavy whipping cream**
- **1 green onion, thinly sliced**
- **Soft pretzel bites**

1. In a greased 6-qt. electric pressure cooker, combine cream cheese, sour cream, mustard and garlic powder until smooth. Stir in beer; add bacon crumbles, reserving 2 Tbsp. for topping. Lock the lid; close the pressure-release valve. Adjust to pressure-cook on high for 5 minutes. Quick-release pressure.

2. Select saute setting, and adjust for medium heat. Stir in cheese and heavy cream. Cook and stir until mixture has thickened, 3-4 minutes. Transfer to serving dish. Sprinkle with onion and reserved bacon. Serve dip with soft pretzel bites.

¼ CUP DIP: 213 cal., 19g fat (10g sat. fat), 60mg chol., 378mg sod., 2g carb. (1g sugars, 0 fiber), 8g pro.

AIR-FRYER POTATO CHIPS

I received an air fryer for Christmas one year. I use this handy countertop appliance to make one of my favorite snacks—potato chips.
—Melissa Obernesser, Oriskany, NY

PREP: 20 MIN. + SOAKING
COOK: 15 MIN./BATCH • **MAKES:** 6 SERVINGS

- **2 large potatoes**
- **Olive oil-flavored cooking spray**
- **½ tsp. sea salt**
- **Minced fresh parsley, optional**

1. Preheat the air fryer to 360°. Using a mandoline or vegetable peeler, cut the potatoes into very thin slices. Transfer to a large bowl; add enough ice water to cover. Soak for 15 minutes; drain. Add more ice water and soak another 15 minutes.

2. Drain potatoes; place on towels and pat dry. Spritz potatoes with cooking spray; sprinkle with salt. In batches, place potato slices in a single layer on greased tray in air-fryer basket. Cook until crisp and golden brown, 15-17 minutes, stirring and turning every 5-7 minutes. If desired, sprinkle with parsley.

1 CUP: 148 cal., 1g fat (0 sat. fat), 0 chol., 252mg sod., 32g carb. (2g sugars, 4g fiber), 4g pro. **DIABETIC EXCHANGES:** 2 starch.

ORANGE-GLAZED CHICKEN & CHORIZO MEATBALLS

These tasty southwestern meatballs warm up a buffet. I add pomegranate seeds, jalapeno pepper jelly and cilantro to make everything pop with color.

—Jeanne Holt, St. Paul, MN

PREP: 25 MIN. + STANDING • **BAKE:** 15 MIN.
MAKES: ABOUT 3½ DOZEN

- **1 cup corn bread croutons**
- **1¼ cups mild picante sauce, divided**
- **5 Tbsp. thawed orange juice concentrate, divided**
- **6 Tbsp. chopped fresh cilantro leaves, divided**
- **1 large egg, lightly beaten**
- **1 tsp. salt**
- **1 lb. ground chicken**
- **6 oz. fresh chorizo**
- **1¼ cups orange marmalade**
- **½ cup jalapeno pepper jelly**
- **⅔ cup finely chopped peeled mango**
- **⅔ cup pomegranate seeds, divided, optional**

1. Preheat oven to 375°. Crush croutons into fine crumbs. Add ½ cup picante sauce and 1 Tbsp. orange juice concentrate; let stand 10 minutes.

2. Stir in 2 Tbsp. cilantro, egg and salt. Crumble chicken and chorizo into crouton mixture; mix lightly but thoroughly. With wet hands, shape into 1-in. balls. Place on a greased rack in a 15x10-in. baking pan. Bake until a thermometer reads 165°, 15-20 minutes.

3. Meanwhile, in a small saucepan over medium heat, stir together marmalade, pepper jelly, remaining picante sauce and remaining orange juice concentrate. Bring to a boil. Reduce heat; simmer 5 minutes. Stir in the mango, 1 Tbsp. cilantro and, if desired, ⅓ cup pomegranate seeds. Pour the sauce over meatballs. Serve with the remaining fresh cilantro and, if desired, pomegranate seeds.

1 MEATBALL: 71 cal., 2g fat (1g sat. fat), 14mg chol., 169mg sod., 11g carb. (9g sugars, 0 fiber), 3g pro.

BACON, CHEDDAR & SWISS CHEESE BALL

When it's time for a party, everyone requests this cheese ball. It works as a spreadable dip and also makes a fabulous hostess gift.
—Sue Franklin, Lake St. Louis, MO

PREP TIME: 20 MIN. + CHILLING
MAKES: 2 CHEESE BALLS (4 CUPS)

- **1 pkg. (8 oz.) cream cheese, softened**
- **½ cup sour cream**
- **2 cups shredded Swiss cheese**
- **2 cups shredded sharp cheddar cheese**
- **1 cup crumbled cooked bacon (about 12 strips), divided**
- **½ cup chopped pecans, toasted, divided**
- **½ cup finely chopped onion**
- **1 jar (2 oz.) diced pimientos, drained**
- **2 Tbsp. sweet pickle relish**
- **¼ tsp. salt**
- **¼ tsp. pepper**
- **¼ cup minced fresh parsley**
- **1 Tbsp. poppy seeds**
- **Assorted crackers**

1. In a large bowl, beat cream cheese and sour cream until smooth. Stir in shredded cheeses, ½ cup bacon, ¼ cup pecans, onion, pimientos, pickle relish, salt and pepper. Refrigerate, covered, for at least 1 hour.
2. In a small bowl, mix parsley, poppy seeds and remaining bacon and pecans. Spread half the parsley mixture on a large plate. Shape half the cheese mixture into a ball; roll in the parsley mixture to coat evenly. Cover. Repeat. Refrigerate at least 1 hour. Serve with crackers.
NOTE: To toast nuts, bake in a shallow pan in a 350° oven for 5-10 minutes or cook in a skillet over low heat until lightly browned, stirring occasionally.
2 TBSP.: 116 cal., 10g fat (5g sat. fat), 22mg chol., 194mg sod., 2g carb. (1g sugars, 0 fiber), 6g pro.

BELLA BASIL RASPBERRY TEA

Give iced tea a grown-up twist. Beautiful basil lends a bright flavor and the raspberries add a ruby-red color. You'll love the fun fizz and make-ahead convenience.
—Laurie Bock, Lynden, WA

PREP: 45 MIN. + CHILLING
MAKES: 6 SERVINGS

- **3 cups fresh raspberries**
- **1 cup sugar**
- **1 cup packed fresh basil leaves, coarsely chopped**
- **¼ cup lime juice**
- **2 black tea bags**
- **1 bottle (1 liter) carbonated water or 1 bottle (750 milliliters) sparkling rose wine**
- **Ice cubes**
- **Optional: Fresh raspberries and basil leaves**

1. In a large saucepan, combine the raspberries, sugar, basil and lime juice. Mash berries. Cook over medium heat until berries release juices, 7 minutes.
2. Remove from the heat; add tea bags. Cover and steep for 20 minutes. Strain, discarding tea bags and raspberry seeds. Transfer tea to a 2-qt. pitcher. Cover and refrigerate until serving.
3. Just before serving, slowly add the carbonated water or wine. Serve over ice. If desired, top with raspberries and basil.
1 CUP: 281 cal., 0 fat (0 sat. fat), 0 chol., 9mg sod., 44g carb. (37g sugars, 4g fiber), 1g pro.

CRANBERRY ORANGE MIMOSAS

Mimosas are an elegant addition to Sunday brunch. My recipe uses tart cranberry juice to balance the sweetness of champagne and orange juice.
—Shannon Stephens, Lake in the Hills, IL

PREP: 10 MIN. • **MAKES:** 12 SERVINGS

- 2 **cups fresh or frozen cranberries**
- 3 **cups orange juice, divided**
- 2 **Tbsp. lemon juice**
- 3 **bottles (750 ml each) champagne, chilled**
- **Fresh mint leaves, optional**

1. Place cranberries and 1 cup orange juice in a blender; cover and process until pureed, stopping to scrape down sides of jar with a rubber spatula as needed. Add lemon juice and remaining orange juice; cover and process until blended.
2. Pour ⅓ cup cranberry mixture into each champagne flute or wine glass. Top with ¾ cup champagne; serve with fresh mint if desired.

1 SERVING: 163 cal., 0 fat (0 sat. fat), 0 chol., 0 sod., 11g carb. (6g sugars, 1g fiber), 1g pro.

SLOW-COOKER CANDIED NUTS

I like giving spiced nuts as holiday gifts. This slow-cooker recipe with ginger and cinnamon is so good, you just might use it all year long.
—Yvonne Starlin, Westmoreland, TN

PREP: 10 MIN. • **COOK:** 2 HOURS + COOLING
MAKES: 4 CUPS

- ½ **cup butter, melted**
- ½ **cup confectioners' sugar**
- 1½ **tsp. ground cinnamon**
- ¼ **tsp. ground ginger**
- ¼ **tsp. ground allspice**
- 1½ **cups pecan halves**
- 1½ **cups walnut halves**
- 1 **cup unblanched almonds**

1. In a greased 3-qt. slow cooker, mix butter, confectioners' sugar and spices. Add nuts; toss to coat. Cook, covered, on low 2-3 hours or until nuts are crisp, stirring once.
2. Transfer nuts to waxed paper to cool completely. Store in an airtight container.

⅓ CUP: 327 cal., 31g fat (7g sat. fat), 20mg chol., 64mg sod., 11g carb. (6g sugars, 3g fiber), 6g pro.

CREAMY PUMPKIN HUMMUS

I love to serve this pumpkin hummus with sliced apples, pears and pita chips. Top it with toasted pumpkin seeds, a drizzle of pumpkin oil or even fried sage leaves.
—James Schend, Pleasant Prairie, WI

TAKES: 25 MIN. • **MAKES:** 3 CUPS

- 1 **can (15 oz.) garbanzo beans or chickpeas, rinsed and drained**
- 1 **cup canned pumpkin**
- ⅓ **cup tahini**
- ¼ **cup olive oil or pumpkin seed oil**
- 3 **Tbsp. orange juice**
- 1 **Tbsp. toasted sesame oil**
- 1 **tsp. ground cumin**
- 1 **tsp. minced garlic**
- ¼ **tsp. salt**
- 2 **Tbsp. pumpkin seed oil or olive oil, optional**
- ¼ **cup salted pumpkin seeds or pepitas**
- ¼ **cup pomegranate seeds**
- **Baked pita chips and sliced apples and pears**

In a food processor, combine the first 9 ingredients; cover and process until smooth. Transfer to a serving platter or bowl. Garnish with oil if desired; top with pumpkin seeds and pomegranate seeds. Serve with pita chips, apples and pears.

¼ CUP: 153 cal., 12g fat (2g sat. fat), 0 chol., 104mg sod., 9g carb. (2g sugars, 3g fiber), 4g pro. **DIABETIC EXCHANGES:** 2½ fat, ½ starch.

JAMES SCHEND
Pleasant Prairie, WI

CHAMPAGNE PARTY PUNCH

Because a New Year's party would not be complete without a little bubbly, this champagne-spiked cocktail is a perfect addition to the menu.
—*Taste of Home* Test Kitchen

PREP: 15 MIN. + CHILLING
MAKES: 18 SERVINGS (ABOUT 3¼ QT.)

- **1 cup sugar**
- **1 cup water**
- **2 cups unsweetened apple juice**
- **2 cups unsweetened pineapple juice**
- **½ cup lemon juice**
- **⅓ cup thawed orange juice concentrate**
- **¼ cup lime juice**
- **2 cups ice cubes**
- **1 qt. ginger ale, chilled**
- **1 bottle (750 ml) champagne, chilled**

1. In a large pitcher, combine sugar and water; stir until sugar is dissolved. Add apple juice, pineapple juice, lemon juice, orange juice concentrate and lime juice. Refrigerate until serving.

2. Just before serving, pour into a punch bowl and add ice cubes. Slowly add ginger ale and champagne.

¾ CUP: 129 cal., 0 fat (0 sat. fat), 0 chol., 8mg sod., 26g carb. (25g sugars, 0 fiber), 0 pro.

STICKY SESAME CAULIFLOWER

Sesame chicken is one of my favorite takeout dishes, but I'm trying to eliminate unnecessary calories and fat from my diet. This recipe gives me a healthier alternative that uses fresh veggies and never compromises on flavor.
—Anthony Ashmore, Bohemia, NY

PREP: 40 MIN. • **BAKE:** 25 MIN.
MAKES: 12 SERVINGS

- **1 cup dry bread crumbs**
- **½ cup cornmeal**
- **2 Tbsp. all-purpose flour**
- **½ tsp. salt**
- **½ tsp. garlic powder**
- **½ tsp. pepper**

BATTER

- **1 cup all-purpose flour**
- **1 Tbsp. adobo seasoning**
- **1 tsp. garlic powder**
- **½ tsp. salt**
- **½ tsp. pepper**
- **1 bottle (12 oz.) beer**
- **1 large head cauliflower, broken into florets (about 8 cups)**
- **1 Tbsp. peanut oil**

SAUCE

- **¼ cup orange juice**
- **¼ cup sweet chili sauce**
- **¼ cup island teriyaki sauce**
- **2 Tbsp. sesame oil**
- **1 tsp. soy sauce**
- **½ tsp. rice vinegar**
- **½ tsp. Sriracha chili sauce**
- **Optional: Thinly sliced green onions, grated orange zest and sesame seeds**

1. Preheat oven to 400°. In a shallow bowl, combine the first 6 ingredients. For the batter, in a large bowl, mix the flour, adobo seasoning, garlic powder, salt and pepper; whisk in beer until smooth. Dip cauliflower in batter, then in the bread crumb mixture. Place on a greased baking sheet. Drizzle with peanut oil; gently toss to coat. Bake until golden brown and cauliflower is just tender, 25-30 minutes.

2. Meanwhile, for sauce, in a small saucepan, combine orange juice, chili sauce, teriyaki sauce, sesame oil, soy sauce, vinegar and Sriracha chili sauce. Cook and stir over low heat just until warmed, about 5 minutes.

3. Transfer cauliflower to a large bowl. Drizzle with sauce; gently toss to coat. Serve with toppings of your choice.

⅔ CUP: 140 cal., 4g fat (1g sat. fat), 0 chol., 714mg sod., 23g carb. (8g sugars, 2g fiber), 4g pro.

CHEESY BEEF TACO DIP

This cheesy, warm dip is a hit with my family, and guests rave about it, too. It makes a big pot, so it's ideal for parties. The best part is you don't need a utensil for serving—just set out a big bowl brimming with tortilla chips!
—Carol Smith, Sanford, NC

TAKES: 20 MIN. • **MAKES:** 10 CUPS

- **2 lbs. ground beef**
- **1 large onion, finely chopped**
- **1 medium green pepper, finely chopped**
- **1 lb. Velveeta, cubed**
- **1 lb. pepper jack cheese, cubed**
- **1 jar (16 oz.) taco sauce**
- **1 can (10 oz.) diced tomatoes and green chiles, drained**
- **1 can (4 oz.) mushroom stems and pieces, drained and chopped**
- **1 can (2¼ oz.) sliced ripe olives, drained**
- **Tortilla chips**

In a large skillet, cook the beef, onion and green pepper over medium heat until the meat is no longer pink; drain. Stir in the cheeses, taco sauce, diced tomatoes, mushrooms and olives. Cook and stir over low heat until cheese is melted. Serve warm with tortilla chips.

¼ CUP: 127 cal., 9g fat (5g sat. fat), 30mg chol., 332mg sod., 3g carb. (2g sugars, 0 fiber), 9g pro.

TACO PUMPKIN SEEDS

Here's a hot idea—toast seeds from a freshly cut pumpkin in taco seasoning and a bit of garlic salt. The savory combination packs a tasty punch!
—*Taste of Home* Test Kitchen

PREP: 15 MIN. • **BAKE:** 15 MIN. + COOLING
MAKES: 1 CUP

- **1 cup seeds from freshly cut pumpkin, washed and dried**
- **2 Tbsp. vegetable oil**
- **1 to 2 Tbsp. taco seasoning**
- **¼ to ½ tsp. garlic salt**

In a large skillet, saute pumpkin seeds in oil for 5 minutes or until lightly browned. Using a slotted spoon, transfer seeds to an ungreased 15x10x1-in. baking pan. Sprinkle with taco seasoning and garlic salt; stir to coat. Spread into a single layer. Bake at 325° for 15-20 minutes or until crisp. Remove to paper towels to cool completely. Store in an airtight container for up to 3 weeks.

2 TBSP.: 70 cal., 5g fat (1g sat. fat), 0 chol., 161mg sod., 5g carb. (0 sugars, 0 fiber), 1g pro.

CRISPY OVEN-FRIED OYSTERS

These flavorful breaded and baked oysters, served with a zippy jalapeno mayonnaise, are guaranteed to impress. I entered the recipe in a seafood contest and took first place in the hors d'oeuvres category.
—Marie Rizzio, Interlochen, MI

TAKES: 30 MIN. • **MAKES:** ABOUT 2½ DOZEN (ABOUT ⅔ CUP JALAPENO MAYONNAISE)

- ¾ **cup all-purpose flour**
- ⅛ **tsp. salt**
- ⅛ **tsp. pepper**
- 2 **large eggs**
- 1 **cup dry bread crumbs**
- ⅔ **cup grated Romano cheese**
- ¼ **cup minced fresh parsley**
- ½ **tsp. garlic salt**
- 1 **pint shucked oysters or 2 cans (8 oz. each) whole oysters, drained**
- 2 **Tbsp. olive oil**

JALAPENO MAYONNAISE

- ¼ **cup mayonnaise**
- ¼ **cup sour cream**
- 2 **medium jalapeno peppers, seeded and finely chopped**
- 2 **Tbsp. whole milk**
- 1 **tsp. lemon juice**
- ¼ **tsp. grated lemon zest**
- ⅛ **tsp. salt**
- ⅛ **tsp. pepper**

1. Preheat oven to 400°. In a shallow bowl, combine flour, salt and pepper. In another shallow bowl, whisk eggs. In a third bowl, combine bread crumbs, cheese, parsley and garlic salt.

2. Coat oysters with flour mixture, then dip in eggs, and coat with the crumb mixture. Place in a greased 15x10x1-in. baking pan; drizzle with oil.

3. Bake until golden brown, 12-15 minutes. Meanwhile, in a bowl, whisk mayonnaise ingredients. Serve with oysters.

NOTE: Wear disposable gloves when cutting hot peppers; the oils can burn skin. Avoid touching your face.

1 OYSTER WITH ABOUT 1 TSP. JALAPENO MAYONNAISE: 75 cal., 4g fat (1g sat. fat), 25mg chol., 146mg sod., 6g carb. (0 sugars, 0 fiber), 3g pro.

CHAI TEA

Warm up a chilly December evening—or any day at all—with this inviting tea. The spices shine through, and it's even more delicious when stirred with a cinnamon stick.
—Kelly Pacowta, Danbury, CT

TAKES: 20 MIN. • **MAKES:** 4 SERVINGS

- 4 **whole cloves**
- 2 **whole peppercorns**
- 4 **tea bags**
- 4 **tsp. sugar**
- ¼ **tsp. ground ginger**
- 1 **cinnamon stick (3 in.)**
- 2½ **cups boiling water**
- 2 **cups 2% milk**

1. Place cloves and peppercorns in a large bowl; with the end of a wooden spoon handle, crush the spices until aromas are released.

2. Add tea bags, sugar, ginger, cinnamon stick and boiling water. Cover and steep for 6 minutes. Meanwhile, in a small saucepan, heat the milk.

3. Strain tea, discarding spices and tea bags. Stir in hot milk. Pour into mugs.

1 CUP: 92 cal., 4g fat (2g sat. fat), 12mg chol., 49mg sod., 10g carb. (10g sugars, 0 fiber), 4g pro.

GRILLED BRUSCHETTA

Here's my go-to appetizer in the summer when tomatoes and basil are fresh from the garden. The balsamic glaze takes this bruschetta recipe over the top. I use a Tuscan herb or basil-infused olive oil, but it works well with plain olive oil, too.

—Brittany Allyn, Mesa, AZ

PREP: 30 MIN. • **GRILL:** 5 MIN.
MAKES: 16 SERVINGS

- **½ cup balsamic vinegar**
- **1½ cups chopped and seeded plum tomatoes**
- **2 Tbsp. finely chopped shallot**
- **1 Tbsp. minced fresh basil**
- **2 tsp. plus 3 Tbsp. olive oil, divided**
- **1 garlic clove, minced**
- **16 slices French bread baguette (½ in. thick)**
- **Sea salt and grated Parmesan cheese**

1. In a small saucepan, bring vinegar to a boil; cook until liquid is reduced to 3 Tbsp., 8-10 minutes. Remove from the heat. Meanwhile, combine tomatoes, shallot, basil, 2 tsp. olive oil and garlic. Cover and refrigerate until serving.

2. Brush remaining oil over both sides of baguette slices. Grill, uncovered, over medium heat until bread is golden brown on both sides.

3. Top toasts with tomato mixture. Drizzle with balsamic syrup; sprinkle with sea salt and Parmesan. Serve immediately.

1 APPETIZER: 58 cal., 3g fat (0 sat. fat), 0 chol., 49mg sod., 7g carb. (3g sugars, 0 fiber), 1g pro. **DIABETIC EXCHANGES:** ½ starch, ½ fat.

READER REVIEW

"So easy and so good! I'll be making this often!"

XXCSKIER, TASTEOFHOME.COM

EDEN DRANGER
Los Angeles, CA

PULLED PORK DOUGHNUT HOLE SLIDERS

This slider recipe was created by accident when I had a surplus of root beer left over from a party. Now we can't have pulled pork any other way!
—Eden Dranger, Los Angeles, CA

PREP: 55 MIN. • **COOK:** 8 HOURS
MAKES: 5 DOZEN

1 bottle (2 liters) root beer
1½ cups barbecue sauce
1½ tsp. salt
1 tsp. minced fresh gingerroot
1 bone-in pork shoulder roast (about 3 lbs.)

SLAW
½ cup mayonnaise or Miracle Whip
2 Tbsp. white vinegar
1 Tbsp. maple syrup
1 pkg. (14 oz.) coleslaw mix

ASSEMBLY
60 plain doughnut holes
60 appetizer skewers
Additional barbecue sauce, optional

1. In a large saucepan, bring root beer to a boil. Reduce heat to medium-high; cook, uncovered, until liquid is reduced by half, 30-45 minutes. Transfer to a 5- or 6-qt. slow cooker. Stir in barbecue sauce, salt and ginger. Add roast, turning to coat.
2. Cook, covered, on low until pork is tender, 8-10 hours. For slaw, in a large bowl, mix mayonnaise, vinegar and syrup. Stir in coleslaw mix. Refrigerate, covered, until flavors are blended, at least 1 hour.
3. Remove the pork from slow cooker; skim fat from cooking juices. Remove meat from bones; shred with 2 forks. Return juices and pork to slow cooker; heat through.
4. To serve, cut doughnut holes in half; cut a thin slice off bottoms to level. Serve pork and slaw in doughnut holes; secure with skewers. If desired, serve sliders with additional barbecue sauce.
FREEZE OPTION: Freeze cooled pork mixture in freezer containers. To use, partially thaw in refrigerator overnight. Heat through in a covered saucepan, stirring gently.
1 SLIDER: 138 cal., 7g fat (2g sat. fat), 13mg chol., 218mg sod., 14g carb. (10g sugars, 0 fiber), 5g pro.

LEMONY SNACK MIX

I'm on a gluten-restricted diet. I came up with this snack mix one day when I wanted something fast and easy that tasted like lemon bars. It makes a great gift, and folks love the light and fresh citrus flavor.
—Patricia Sensenich, Olathe, KS

TAKES: 15 MIN. • **MAKES:** 2¾ QT.

5 cups Rice Chex
4 cups Corn Chex
1½ cups white baking chips
4 tsp. grated lemon zest
2 Tbsp. lemon juice
¼ cup butter, softened
1½ cups confectioners' sugar
¼ cup yellow coarse sugar, optional

1. Place cereals in a large bowl. In top of a double boiler or a metal bowl over hot water, melt baking chips with lemon zest and juice; stir until smooth. Stir in butter until blended.
2. Pour over cereal; toss to coat. Add confectioners' sugar and, if desired, coarse sugar; toss to coat. Spread onto waxed paper to cool. Store in an airtight container.
¾ CUP: 288 cal., 11g fat (7g sat. fat), 15mg chol., 215mg sod., 46g carb. (29g sugars, 1g fiber), 3g pro.

DRIED FRUIT ENERGY BARS

These bars are the perfect breakfast option for busy people. They're easy to make ahead and jam-packed with ingredients such as chia seeds, quinoa and oats, which will keep you fueled throughout the day.
—Andrea Potischman, Menlo Park, CA

PREP: 10 MIN. • **COOK:** 10 MIN. + CHILLING
MAKES: 9 SERVINGS

- ¼ cup quinoa, rinsed
- 10 Medjool dates, pitted
- 3 Tbsp. coconut oil
- ⅔ cup almond butter
- 3 Tbsp. whey protein powder
- ½ tsp. vanilla extract
- 2 Tbsp. unsweetened coconut flakes
- 1 Tbsp. chia seeds
- 2 cups old-fashioned oats

1. Line an 8-in. square baking pan with parchment, letting ends extend up sides. Prepare quinoa according to package directions. Transfer to a large bowl. Set aside and allow to cool completely.
2. In a food processor, combine dates, coconut oil, almond butter, protein powder and vanilla. Cover and pulse until blended. Add coconut and chia seeds. Pulse until combined. Add oats and cooked quinoa. Pulse until combined.
3. Press firmly into prepared pan. Cover and refrigerate for at least 1 hour or until set. Lifting with parchment, remove from pan. Using a serrated knife, cut into bars. Store in the refrigerator.
1 BAR: 239 cal., 13g fat (5g sat. fat), 1mg chol., 45mg sod., 26g carb. (8g sugars, 5g fiber), 7g pro.

EASY CITRUS SLUSH

Our church's hostess committee has relied on this refreshing drink for bridal and baby showers and other events. We often use different flavored gelatins to match the decor of the occasion.
—Joy Bruce, Welch, OK

PREP: 15 MIN. + FREEZING
MAKES: ABOUT 25 SERVINGS (ABOUT 6 QT.)

- 2½ cups sugar
- 1 pkg. (3 oz.) lemon gelatin
- 1 pkg. (3 oz.) pineapple gelatin
- 4 cups boiling water
- 1 can (12 oz.) frozen pineapple juice concentrate, thawed
- 1 cup lemon juice
- 1 envelope (0.23 oz.) unsweetened lemonade Kool-Aid mix
- 10 cups cold water
- 2 liters ginger ale, chilled
- Lime slices, optional

1. In a large container, dissolve the sugar and gelatins in boiling water. Stir in the pineapple juice concentrate, lemon juice, drink mix and cold water. If desired, divide among smaller containers. Cover and freeze, stirring several times.
2. Remove from freezer at least 1 hour before serving. Stir until the mixture becomes slushy. Just before serving, place 9 cups slush mixture in a punch bowl; stir in 1 liter ginger ale. Repeat with remaining slush and ginger ale. If desired, garnish with lime slices.
1 CUP: 157 cal., 0 fat (0 sat. fat), 0 chol., 25mg sod., 40g carb. (39g sugars, 0 fiber), 1g pro.

STUFFED ASIAGO-BASIL MUSHROOMS

Even if you don't like mushrooms, you will have to try them with these pretty appetizers, which taste divine. For a main dish, double the filling and use large portobellos.
—Lorraine Caland, Shuniah, ON

PREP: 25 MIN. • **BAKE:** 10 MIN.
MAKES: 2 DOZEN

- **24 baby portobello mushrooms (about 1 lb.), stems removed**
- **½ cup reduced-fat mayonnaise**
- **¾ cup shredded Asiago cheese**
- **½ cup loosely packed basil leaves, stems removed**
- **¼ tsp. white pepper**
- **12 cherry tomatoes, halved**
- **Thinly sliced or shaved Parmesan cheese, optional**

1. Preheat oven to 375°. Place mushroom caps in a greased 15x10x1-in. baking pan. Bake 10 minutes. Meanwhile, place the mayonnaise, Asiago cheese, basil leaves and pepper in a food processor; process until blended.

2. Drain juices from mushrooms. Fill each with 1 rounded tsp. mayonnaise mixture; top each with a tomato half.

3. Bake for 8-10 minutes or until lightly browned. If desired, top with thinly sliced or shaved Parmesan cheese.

1 APPETIZER: 35 cal., 3g fat (1g sat. fat), 5mg chol., 50mg sod., 2g carb. (1g sugars, 0 fiber), 2g pro.

GINGER PORK LETTUCE WRAPS

When I make these Asian-spiced lettuce wraps, I remind my family that they're meant to be an appetizer, not dinner. Either way, we enjoy filling up on the tasty bites.
—Mary Kisinger, Medicine Hat, AB

TAKES: 30 MIN. • **MAKES:** 2 DOZEN

- **1 lb. lean ground pork**
- **1 medium onion, chopped**
- **¼ cup hoisin sauce**
- **4 garlic cloves, minced**
- **1 Tbsp. minced fresh gingerroot**
- **1 Tbsp. red wine vinegar**
- **1 Tbsp. reduced-sodium soy sauce**
- **2 tsp. Thai chili sauce**
- **1 can (8 oz.) sliced water chestnuts, drained and finely chopped**
- **4 green onions, chopped**
- **1 Tbsp. sesame oil**
- **24 Bibb or Boston lettuce leaves**

1. In a large skillet, cook pork and onion over medium heat 6-8 minutes or until pork is no longer pink and onion is tender, breaking up pork into crumbles.

2. Stir in hoisin sauce, garlic, ginger, vinegar, soy sauce and chili sauce until blended. Add water chestnuts, green onions and oil; heat through. To serve, place pork mixture in lettuce leaves; fold lettuce over filling.

FREEZE OPTION: Freeze cooled meat mixture in freezer containers. To use, partially thaw in refrigerator overnight. Heat through in a saucepan, stirring occasionally; add water if necessary.

1 FILLED LETTUCE WRAP: 54 cal., 3g fat (1g sat. fat), 11mg chol., 87mg sod., 4g carb. (2g sugars, 1g fiber), 4g pro.

BUFFALO CHICKEN EGG ROLLS

This crunchy delight gets its start in the slow cooker. Tuck the chicken mixture in egg roll wrappers and bake, or use smaller wonton wrappers for a bite-sized version.
—Tara Odegaard, Omaha, NE

PREP: 35 MIN. • **COOK:** 3 HOURS
MAKES: 16 EGG ROLLS

- **1½ lbs. boneless skinless chicken breasts**
- **2 Tbsp. ranch salad dressing mix**
- **½ cup Buffalo wing sauce**
- **2 Tbsp. butter**
- **16 egg roll wrappers**
- **⅓ cup crumbled feta cheese**
- **⅓ cup shredded part-skim mozzarella cheese**
- **Ranch salad dressing, optional**

1. In a 3-qt. slow cooker, combine chicken, dressing mix and wing sauce. Cook, covered, on low until chicken is tender, 3-4 hours.
2. Preheat oven to 425°. Shred chicken with 2 forks; stir in butter.
3. With a corner of an egg roll wrapper facing you, place 3 Tbsp. chicken mixture just below center of wrapper; top with 1 tsp. each feta and mozzarella cheeses. (Cover remaining wrappers with a damp paper towel until ready to use.) Fold the bottom corner over filling; moisten the remaining wrapper edges with water. Fold side corners toward center over filling; roll up tightly, pressing at the tip to seal. Place on a parchment-lined baking sheet seam side down. Repeat, adding additional baking sheets as needed
4. Bake until golden brown, 15-20 minutes. Let stand 5 minutes before serving. Serve warm, with ranch dressing for dipping if desired.
HEALTH TIP: Lighten up this Buffalo chicken recipe by serving it in Bibb lettuce cups instead of egg roll wrappers.
1 EGG ROLL: 174 cal., 4g fat (2g sat. fat), 33mg chol., 716mg sod., 21g carb. (0 sugars, 1g fiber), 13g pro.

CREAMY CARAMEL MOCHA

Indulge in a coffeehouse-quality drink at Christmastime or any time at all. With whipped cream and a butterscotch drizzle, this mocha treat will perk up even the sleepiest person at the table.

—*Taste of Home* Test Kitchen

TAKES: 20 MIN. • **MAKES:** 6 SERVINGS

- **½ cup heavy whipping cream**
- **1 Tbsp. confectioners' sugar**
- **1 tsp. vanilla extract, divided**
- **¼ cup Dutch-processed cocoa**
- **1½ cups half-and-half cream**
- **4 cups hot strong brewed coffee**
- **½ cup caramel flavoring syrup**
- **Butterscotch-caramel ice cream topping**

1. In a bowl, beat whipping cream until it begins to thicken. Add the confectioners' sugar and ½ tsp. vanilla; beat until stiff peaks form.

2. In a large saucepan over medium heat, whisk cocoa and half-and-half cream until smooth. Heat until bubbles form around sides of pan. Whisk in coffee, caramel syrup and remaining ½ tsp. vanilla. Top servings with whipped cream; drizzle with the butterscotch topping.

NOTE: To prepare mocha in a slow cooker, prepare the whipped cream as directed. Whisk together the cocoa, half-and-half, coffee, caramel syrup and remaining vanilla in a 3-qt. slow cooker. Cook, covered, for 2-3 hours or until heated through. Serve as directed.

1 CUP COFFEE WITH 2 TBSP. WHIPPED CREAM: 220 cal., 14g fat (9g sat. fat), 57mg chol., 38mg sod., 19g carb. (16g sugars, 1g fiber), 3g pro.

READER REVIEW

"Loved this! I served it in Mason jars to my guests and everyone raved about it! Easy and delicious!"

BILLL MUCK, TASTEOFHOME.COM

AIR-FRYER ROSEMARY SAUSAGE MEATBALLS

These air-fryer meatballs were created as hors d'oeuvres for a friend's wedding and became an instant hit. Now we enjoy them often at our house.

—Steve Hansen, Redmond, WA

PREP: 20 MIN. • **COOK:** 10 MIN./BATCH
MAKES: ABOUT 2 DOZEN

- **2 Tbsp. olive oil**
- **4 garlic cloves, minced**
- **1 tsp. curry powder**
- **1 large egg, lightly beaten**
- **1 jar (4 oz.) diced pimientos, drained**
- **¼ cup dry bread crumbs**
- **¼ cup minced fresh parsley**
- **1 Tbsp. minced fresh rosemary**
- **2 lbs. bulk pork sausage**
- **Pretzel sticks, optional**

1. Preheat air fryer to 400°. In a small skillet, heat oil over medium heat; saute garlic with curry powder until tender, 1-2 minutes. Cool slightly.

2. In a bowl, combine egg, pimientos, bread crumbs, parsley, rosemary and garlic mixture. Add sausage; mix lightly but thoroughly.

3. Shape into 1¼-in. balls. Place in a single layer on tray in air-fryer basket; cook for 7-10 minutes or until lightly browned and cooked through. If desired, serve with pretzel sticks.

1 MEATBALL: 96 cal., 8g fat (2g sat. fat), 24mg chol., 208mg sod., 2g carb. (0 sugars, 0 fiber), 4g pro.

1 FAVORITE
5 WAYS
Margaritas
2
4
3
1
5

1) RASPBERRY-GINGER FROZEN MARGARITA

Ginger, raspberries and lime form a wonderful flavor combination, so I thought I'd try adding them to my margarita. This cocktail is perfect for warm-weather parties.
—James Schend, Pleasant Prairie, WI

TAKES: 10 MIN. • **MAKES:** 1 SERVING

1 lime wedge
Coarse sugar, optional
1½ oz. blanco tequila
1 oz. ginger liqueur
1 oz. raspberry liqueur
½ oz. freshly squeezed lime juice
1 cup frozen unsweetened raspberries
Optional: Sliced crystallized ginger and fresh raspberries

Moisten rim of 1 cocktail glass with lime wedge. If desired, sprinkle sugar on a plate; dip rim in sugar. In a blender, add tequila, ginger liqueur, raspberry liqueur, lime juice and raspberries. Puree until smooth; pour into prepared glass. Garnish with the lime wedge and, if desired, crystallized ginger and raspberries.

1 SERVING: 382 cal., 1g fat (0 sat. fat), 0 chol., 4mg sod., 42g carb. (29g sugars, 9g fiber), 2g pro.

2) BLUEBERRY-MINT FROZEN MARGARITA

Refreshing and fruity, a frozen blueberry margarita makes the perfect summer drink.
—James Schend, Pleasant Prairie, WI

TAKES: 10 MIN. • **MAKES:** 1 SERVING

1 lime wedge
Coarse sugar, optional
1½ oz. blanco tequila
1 oz. Triple Sec
½ oz. freshly squeezed lime juice
1 cup frozen unsweetened blueberries
4 fresh mint leaves
Fresh blueberries, optional

1. Moisten the rim of 1 cocktail glass with lime wedge. If desired, sprinkle sugar on a plate; dip rim in sugar.

2. In a blender, combine tequila, Triple Sec, lime juice, blueberries and mint. Puree until smooth. Pour into prepared glasses. Garnish with lime wedge and, if desired, blueberries and additional mint sprigs.

1 SERVING: 287 cal., 1g fat (0 sat. fat), 0 chol., 4mg sod., 34g carb. (25g sugars, 4g fiber), 1g pro.

3) FROZEN COCONUT MARGARITA

Take your margarita to the tropics with a touch of coconut.
—James Schend, Pleasant Prairie, WI

TAKES: 10 MIN. • **MAKES:** 1 SERVING

1 lime wedge
Chopped toasted shredded coconut, optional
2 oz. cream of coconut
1½ oz. blanco tequila
1 oz. Triple Sec
½ oz. freshly squeezed lime juice
1 cup crushed ice

Moisten rim of 1 cocktail glass with lime wedge. If desired, sprinkle coconut on a plate; dip rim in coconut. Place cream of coconut, tequila, Triple Sec and lime juice in a blender; add ice. Cover and process until smooth. Pour into prepared glass. Garnish with lime wedge and, if desired, additional coconut.

1 SERVING: 426 cal., 10g fat (8g sat. fat), 0 chol., 33mg sod., 49g carb. (46g sugars, 0 fiber), 0 pro.

4) STRAWBERRY-BASIL FROZEN MARGARITA

Add lush basil for an unexpected flavor upgrade to the classic strawberry marg.
—James Schend, Pleasant Prairie, WI

TAKES: 10 MIN. • **MAKES:** 1 SERVING

1 lime wedge
Coarse sugar, optional
1½ oz. blanco tequila
1 oz. Triple Sec
½ oz. freshly squeezed lime juice
1 cup frozen unsweetened sliced strawberries
4 fresh basil leaves
Fresh strawberries, optional

1. Moisten rim of 1 cocktail glass with lime wedge. If desired, sprinkle sugar on a plate; dip rim in sugar.

2. Place tequila, Triple Sec, lime juice, strawberries and basil in a blender; cover and process until smooth. Pour mixture into prepared glass. Garnish with lime wedge and, if desired, strawberries and additional basil leaves.

1 SERVING: 256 cal., 0 fat (0 sat. fat), 0 chol., 3mg sod., 28g carb. (18g sugars, 3g fiber), 0 pro.

5) SRIRACHA-MANGO FROZEN MARGARITA

The sweetness of the mango helps offset the spiciness of the Sriracha, giving this cocktail a unique and fun twist.
—James Schend, Pleasant Prairie, WI

TAKES: 10 MIN. • **MAKES:** 1 SERVING

1 lime wedge
Coarse sea salt, optional
1½ oz. blanco tequila
1 oz. mango nectar
½ oz. freshly squeezed lime juice
½ tsp. Sriracha chili sauce
1 cup frozen mango chunks
Sliced peeled mango, optional

1. Moisten rim of 1 cocktail glass with lime wedge. If desired, sprinkle salt on a plate; dip rim in salt.

2. Place tequila, mango nectar, lime juice, Sriracha and frozen mango in a blender; cover and process until smooth. Pour into prepared glass. Garnish with lime wedge and, if desired, sliced mango.

1 SERVING: 240 cal., 0 fat (0 sat. fat), 0 chol., 82mg sod., 38g carb. (32g sugars, 4g fiber), 1g pro.

DID YOU KNOW?

A margarita is a cocktail that's a combination of tequila, orange liqueur and fresh lime juice. A margarita can be enjoyed on the rocks or blended, with a salted, sugared or plain rim, and is usually served with a slice of lime.

Breakfast & Brunch

Great mornings start with great food. Whether you're looking for a comforting casserole to prepare ahead of brunch or a tasty on-the-go delight as you rush off to work, each of these sunny staples will jump-start the day!

PUFFY APPLE OMELET

With all the eggs our chickens produce, I could easily make this omelet every day! It's festive and pretty for a special occasion, but you could fix it anytime—including for a light supper.
—Melissa Davenport, Campbell, MN

TAKES: 30 MIN. • **MAKES:** 2 SERVINGS

- **3 Tbsp. all-purpose flour**
- **¼ tsp. baking powder**
- **⅛ tsp. salt, optional**
- **2 large eggs, separated, room temperature**
- **3 Tbsp. 2% milk**
- **1 Tbsp. lemon juice**
- **3 Tbsp. sugar**

TOPPING

- **1 large apple, peeled if desired, and thinly sliced**
- **1 tsp. sugar**
- **¼ tsp. ground cinnamon**

1. Preheat oven to 375°. Mix flour, baking powder and, if desired, salt. In a small bowl, whisk together egg yolks, milk and lemon juice; stir into flour mixture.
2. In another bowl, beat egg whites on medium speed until foamy. Gradually add sugar, 1 Tbsp. at a time, beating on high after each addition until stiff peaks form. Fold into flour mixture.
3. Pour into a 9-in. deep-dish pie plate coated with cooking spray. Arrange apple slices over top. Mix sugar and cinnamon; sprinkle over apple.
4. Bake, uncovered, 18-20 minutes or until a knife inserted in the center comes out clean. Serve immediately.

1 PIECE: 253 cal., 5g fat (2g sat. fat), 188mg chol., 142mg sod., 44g carb. (32g sugars, 2g fiber), 9g pro.

EGGNOG FRENCH TOAST

This recipe is a favorite of our family, not only at Christmas but any time of year. We especially like it when we go camping. It makes a hearty breakfast.
—Robert Northrup, Las Cruces, NM

PREP: 10 MIN. • **COOK:** 30 MIN.
MAKES: 8 SERVINGS

- **8 large eggs**
- **2 cups eggnog**
- **¼ cup sugar**
- **½ tsp. vanilla or rum extract**
- **24 slices English muffin bread**
- **Confectioners' sugar, optional**
- **Maple syrup**

In a bowl, beat eggs, eggnog, sugar and extract; soak bread for 2 minutes per side. Cook on a greased hot griddle until golden brown on both sides and cooked through. Dust with confectioners' sugar if desired. Serve with syrup.

3 SLICES: 541 cal., 10g fat (4g sat. fat), 223mg chol., 832mg sod., 87g carb. (18g sugars, 6g fiber), 24g pro.

TEST KITCHEN TIP

Butter extra French toast slices, sprinkle with confectioners' sugar, cut into fourths and freeze them. When you're in a hurry, microwave the thawed sticks for a quick and easy breakfast.

PEAR-BERRY BREAKFAST TARTS

It's tricky to get a full batch of pancakes or waffles on the table while they're all still hot. I love these breakfast tarts that bake in the oven all at once. They make busy mornings easy!
—Joan Elbourn, Gardner, MA

PREP: 45 MIN. + CHILLING • **BAKE:** 20 MIN.
MAKES: 10 SERVINGS

- **½ cup butter, softened**
- **1 cup sugar, divided**
- **2 large eggs, room temperature**
- **2½ cups all-purpose flour**
- **2 tsp. baking powder**
- **2 cups chopped peeled pears (about 2 large)**
- **2 Tbsp. cornstarch**
- **2 Tbsp. water**
- **½ cup fresh raspberries**
- **1 large egg white**
- **3 to 5 Tbsp. 2% milk, divided**
- **1⅓ cups confectioners' sugar**
- **Food coloring, optional**

1. Cream butter and ½ cup sugar until light and fluffy, 5-7 minutes. Add the eggs, 1 at a time, beating well after each addition. In another bowl, whisk the flour and baking powder; gradually beat into creamed mixture to form a dough. Divide dough in half; shape each into a rectangle. Wrap and refrigerate 1 hour.

2. Meanwhile, in a small saucepan over medium heat, combine the pears and remaining sugar. Cook and stir until the sugar is dissolved and pears are softened, 6-8 minutes. In a small bowl, mix the cornstarch and water until smooth; stir into pear mixture. Return to a boil, stirring constantly; cook and stir 1-2 minutes or until thickened. Remove from heat; cool. Stir in raspberries.

3. Preheat oven to 350°. On a lightly floured surface, roll half the dough into a 15x8-in. rectangle. Cut into ten 4x3-in. rectangles. Transfer to parchment-lined baking sheets; spoon about 2 Tbsp. filling over each pastry to within ½ in. of edges. Roll the remaining dough into a 15x8-in. rectangle; cut into ten 4x3-in. rectangles and place over filling. Press edges with a fork to seal. Whisk egg white and 1 Tbsp. milk; brush over the pastries. Bake until pastries are golden brown and filling is bubbly, 20-25 minutes.

4. Remove from baking sheets to wire racks to cool. For icing, mix confectioners' sugar and enough of remaining milk to reach desired consistency; tint with food coloring if desired. Spread or drizzle the icing on pastries.

1 TART: 379 cal., 11g fat (6g sat. fat), 62mg chol., 193mg sod., 67g carb. (39g sugars, 2g fiber), 5g pro.

SAUSAGE-VEGETABLE EGG BAKE

When we were kids, our mom tucked homegrown Swiss chard inside this comfy casserole. Now I grow the chard, make the dish and savor the memories.
—Cathy Banks, Encinitas, CA

PREP: 25 MIN. • **BAKE:** 55 MIN.
MAKES: 8 SERVINGS

- 1 pkg. (19½ oz.) Italian turkey sausage links, casings removed
- 1 Tbsp. butter
- ¾ lb. sliced fresh mushrooms
- 3 cups thinly sliced Swiss chard
- ¼ cup white wine
- 3 garlic cloves, minced
- 9 large eggs
- 1¼ cups 2% milk
- ¼ tsp. salt
- ¼ tsp. pepper
- 1 cup shredded part-skim mozzarella cheese
- ¼ cup grated Parmesan or shredded fontina cheese
- Minced fresh parsley

1. Preheat oven to 350°. In a large skillet, cook the sausage over medium heat for 5-7 minutes or until it is no longer pink, breaking into crumbles. Using a slotted spoon, transfer sausage to a greased 13x9-in. baking dish, spreading evenly. Remove drippings from pan.
2. In same skillet, heat the butter over medium-high heat. Add mushrooms; cook and stir until tender, 3-5 minutes. Add the Swiss chard, wine and garlic; cook and stir until the chard is tender and liquid is almost evaporated, 1-2 minutes longer. Add to baking dish.
3. In a large bowl, whisk the eggs, milk, salt and pepper until blended; pour over the vegetable mixture. Sprinkle with mozzarella cheese.
4. Bake, uncovered, 45 minutes. Sprinkle with Parmesan cheese. Bake until a knife inserted in the center comes out clean, 10-15 minutes longer. Let stand 5 minutes before serving. Sprinkle with parsley.

1 PIECE: 248 cal., 15g fat (6g sat. fat), 253mg chol., 640mg sod., 6g carb. (3g sugars, 1g fiber), 21g pro.

PEANUT BUTTER PANCAKES

Wondering how to make peanut butter pancakes? These morning treats are one of my husband's specialties. It's not unusual for him to wake me with those hot-from-the griddle cakes!
—Dorothy Pritchett, Wills Point, TX

TAKES: 15 MIN. • **MAKES:** 8 PANCAKES

- 1 cup pancake mix
- 2 Tbsp. sugar
- 1 large egg, room temperature
- ⅓ cup peanut butter
- 1 can (5 oz.) evaporated milk
- ⅓ cup water

HONEY BUTTER

- ¼ cup butter, softened
- 2 Tbsp. honey
- Optional: Chopped salted peanuts and maple syrup

1. In a large bowl, combine pancake mix and sugar. In a small bowl, beat egg and peanut butter; add milk and water. Stir into dry ingredients just until moistened.
2. Pour batter by ¼ cupfuls onto a lightly greased medium-hot griddle. Turn when bubbles form on top of pancakes; cook until second side is golden brown. In a small bowl, combine butter and honey until smooth. Serve with pancakes. If desired, top with chopped peanuts and maple syrup.

NOTE: Reduced-fat peanut butter is not recommended for this recipe.

2 PANCAKES: 595 cal., 35g fat (15g sat. fat), 127mg chol., 843mg sod., 58g carb. (32g sugars, 4g fiber), 16g pro.

COLORFUL BROCCOLI CHEDDAR CASSEROLE

When we host houseguests, we make this broccoli and cheese strata the night before so in the morning we can relax and visit while it bakes away in the oven.
—Gale Lalmond, Deering, NH

PREP: 25 MIN. + CHILLING • **BAKE:** 50 MIN.
MAKES: 8 SERVINGS

- **1 Tbsp. olive oil**
- **6 green onions, sliced**
- **2 cups fresh broccoli florets, chopped**
- **1 medium sweet red pepper, finely chopped**
- **2 garlic cloves, minced**
- **⅛ tsp. pepper**
- **5 whole wheat English muffins, split, toasted and quartered**
- **1½ cups shredded reduced-fat cheddar cheese, divided**
- **8 large eggs**
- **2½ cups fat-free milk**
- **2 Tbsp. Dijon mustard**
- **½ tsp. hot pepper sauce, optional**

1. In a large skillet, heat oil over medium-high heat. Add green onions; cook and stir until tender. Add broccoli, red pepper and garlic; cook and stir 4-5 minutes or until tender. Transfer to a large bowl; season with pepper.
2. Place English muffins in a greased 13x9-in. baking dish, cut sides up. Top muffins with vegetable mixture and sprinkle with 1 cup shredded cheese.
3. In a large bowl, whisk eggs, milk, mustard and, if desired, hot sauce. Pour over top. Refrigerate, covered, overnight.
4. Remove from refrigerator 30 minutes before baking. Preheat oven to 350°. Bake, covered, 30 minutes. Sprinkle with the remaining cheese. Bake, uncovered, until egg mixture is set, 20-30 minutes longer. Let stand 5 minutes before cutting.

1 PIECE: 273 cal., 12g fat (5g sat. fat), 228mg chol., 529mg sod., 25g carb. (9g sugars, 4g fiber), 19g pro. **DIABETIC EXCHANGES:** 2 medium-fat meat, 1½ starch, ½ fat.

CHOCOLATE PEANUT BUTTER OVERNIGHT OATS

Soon after I learned about overnight oats, I decided to create a recipe with my favorite sugary combination: chocolate peanut butter. Overnight oats are a perfect breakfast for busy mornings.
—Anna Bentley, Swanzey, NH

TAKES: 25 MIN• **MAKES:** 1 SERVING

- **½ cup old-fashioned oats**
- **⅓ cup chocolate or plain almond milk**
- **1 Tbsp. baking cocoa**
- **1 Tbsp. creamy peanut butter, warmed**
- **1 Tbsp. maple syrup**
- **Miniature dairy-free semisweet chocolate chips, optional**

In a small container or Mason jar, combine the oats, milk, cocoa, peanut butter and maple syrup. Seal; refrigerate overnight. If desired, top with additional peanut butter and mini chocolate chips.
½ CUP: 346 cal., 13g fat (2g sat. fat), 0 chol., 121mg sod., 53g carb. (21g sugars, 6g fiber), 10g pro.

BERRY BLAST SMOOTHIES

This is how I start every morning before a good workout. Just put everything in a blender and blend until smooth. That's it! Enjoy!
—Chris Michalowski, Dallas, TX

TAKES: 5 MIN. • **MAKES:** 2 SERVINGS

- **½ cup pomegranate-blueberry V8 juice blend**
- **1¼ cups frozen unsweetened mixed berries**
- **1 medium banana, sliced**
- **⅓ cup fat-free plain yogurt**

In a blender, combine all ingredients; cover and process until smooth. Pour into chilled glasses; serve immediately.
1 CUP: 144 cal., 0 fat (0 sat. fat), 1mg chol., 38mg sod., 35g carb. (24g sugars, 3g fiber), 2g pro.

GOAT CHEESE & HAM OMELET

As a busy working mom, my breakfast meals require minimal prep. I often combine the egg mixture beforehand and refrigerate overnight. Then all I have to do in the morning is heat up my skillet. My favorite part is the goat cheese filling, which gets nice and creamy from the heat of the omelet.
—Lynne Dieterle, Rochester, MI

TAKES: 20 MIN. • **MAKES:** 1 SERVING

- **4 large egg whites**
- **2 tsp. water**
- **⅛ tsp. pepper**
- **1 slice deli ham, finely chopped**
- **2 Tbsp. finely chopped green pepper**
- **2 Tbsp. finely chopped onion**
- **2 Tbsp. crumbled goat cheese**
- **Minced fresh parsley, optional**

1. In a small bowl, whisk egg whites, water and pepper until blended; stir in ham, green pepper and onion. Heat a large skillet coated with cooking spray over medium-high heat. Pour in egg white mixture. Mixture should set immediately at edges. As egg whites set, push cooked portions toward the center, letting uncooked egg flow underneath.
2. When no liquid egg remains, sprinkle goat cheese on 1 side. Fold omelet in half; slide onto a plate. If desired, sprinkle with minced fresh parsley.

1 OMELET: 143 cal., 4g fat (2g sat. fat), 27mg chol., 489mg sod., 5g carb. (3g sugars, 1g fiber), 21g pro. **DIABETIC EXCHANGES:** 3 lean meat, ½ fat.

HAWAIIAN HAM STRATA

I came up with this recipe because I love Hawaiian pizza and wanted a casserole I could make ahead and pop in the oven at the last minute. This dish is perfect for brunch or midday potlucks.

—Lisa Renshaw, Kansas City, MO

PREP: 20 MIN. + CHILLING
COOK: 30 MIN. + STANDING
MAKES: 8 SERVINGS

- **8 English muffins, cut into eighths and toasted**
- **3 cups cubed fully cooked ham**
- **1 can (20 oz.) pineapple tidbits, drained**
- **4 green onions, chopped**
- **1 jar (4 oz.) diced pimientos, drained**
- **1½ cups shredded cheddar cheese**
- **¼ cup grated Parmesan cheese**
- **1 jar (15 oz.) Alfredo sauce**
- **1½ cups evaporated milk**
- **4 large eggs, lightly beaten**
- **½ tsp. salt**
- **¼ tsp. cayenne pepper**

1. Combine first 5 ingredients. Transfer to a 13x9-in. baking dish; top with cheeses.
2. Whisk together remaining ingredients. Pour sauce over layers, pushing down, if necessary, with the back of a spoon to ensure muffins absorb liquid. Refrigerate, covered, 1 hour or overnight.
3. Preheat oven to 350°. Remove strata from refrigerator while oven heats. Bake, uncovered, until strata is golden and bubbly, 30-40 minutes. Let stand for 10 minutes before serving.

1 PIECE: 515 cal., 22g fat (12g sat. fat), 177mg chol., 1512mg sod., 48g carb. (16g sugars, 3g fiber), 31g pro.

READER REVIEW

"I loved this. It's a little messy to make but that's OK—and I recommend toasting all the muffins together in the oven to save time. I divided this into two 8x8 pans and froze one."

FEEN, TASTEOFHOME.COM

STRAWBERRY CHEESECAKE PANCAKES

More of a dessert than breakfast food, these luscious pancakes showcase the darlings of summer—strawberries! Both the sauce and creamy filling feature fresh ripe berries.

—Shirley Warren, Thiensville, WI

PREP: 40 MIN. • **COOK:** 5 MIN./BATCH
MAKES: 20 PANCAKES (¾ CUP SPREAD AND 3 CUPS SAUCE)

- **6 oz. cream cheese, softened**
- **1 Tbsp. sugar**
- **½ cup crushed strawberries**

PANCAKES

- **2 cups all-purpose flour**
- **¼ cup sugar**
- **4 tsp. baking powder**
- **½ tsp. salt**
- **2 large eggs, room temperature**
- **1½ cups 2% milk**
- **1 cup sour cream**
- **⅓ cup butter, melted**
- **1 cup chopped fresh strawberries**

SAUCE

- **3 cups crushed strawberries**
- **¼ cup seedless strawberry jam**
- **¼ cup water**

1. In a small bowl, beat cream cheese and sugar until smooth; stir in strawberries. Chill until serving.
2. In a large bowl, combine flour, sugar, baking powder and salt. Combine the eggs, milk, sour cream and butter. Stir into dry ingredients just until moistened. Fold in strawberries.
3. Pour the batter by ¼ cupfuls onto a greased hot griddle; turn when bubbles form on top. Cook until the second side is golden brown.
4. For the sauce, in a small saucepan, combine the strawberries, jam and water; heat through. Spread the cream cheese mixture over pancakes; top with sauce. (Refrigerate any remaining sauce for another use.)

2 PANCAKES WITH 1 TBSP. SPREAD AND 2 TBSP. SAUCE: 335 cal., 18g fat (11g sat. fat), 96mg chol., 413mg sod., 35g carb. (14g sugars, 2g fiber), 8g pro.

LISA RENSHAW
Kansas City, MO

EGG BASKETS BENEDICT

A little puff pastry turns Canadian bacon and eggs into a delicious take on eggs Benedict. We use a packaged hollandaise or cheese sauce for the finishing touch.
—Sally Jackson, Fort Worth, TX

TAKES: 30 MIN.
MAKES: 1 DOZEN (1 CUP SAUCE)

- **1 sheet frozen puff pastry, thawed**
- **12 large eggs**
- **6 slices Canadian bacon, finely chopped**
- **1 envelope hollandaise sauce mix**

1. Preheat oven to 400°. On a lightly floured surface, unfold puff pastry. Roll into a 16x12-in. rectangle; cut into twelve 4-in. squares. Place in greased muffin cups, pressing gently onto bottoms and up sides, allowing corners to point up.
2. Break and slip an egg into center of each pastry cup; sprinkle with Canadian bacon. Bake 10-12 minutes or until the pastry is golden brown, egg whites are completely set, and yolks begin to thicken but are not hard. Prepare hollandaise sauce according to package directions.
3. Remove pastry cups to wire racks. Serve warm with hollandaise sauce.

1 PASTRY CUP WITH ABOUT 1 TBSP. SAUCE: 237 cal., 15g fat (6g sat. fat), 201mg chol., 355mg sod., 14g carb. (1g sugars, 2g fiber), 10g pro.

GARDEN VEGETABLE QUICHE

Make your next brunch special with this fluffy deep-dish quiche. Fresh rosemary enhances this delightful egg dish that's chock-full of savory garden ingredients. It cuts nicely, too.
—Kristina Ledford, Indianapolis, IN

PREP: 30 MIN. + CHILLING
BAKE: 40 MIN. + STANDING
MAKES: 8 SERVINGS

- **Dough for single-crust pie**
- **1 Tbsp. butter**
- **1 small red onion, halved and thinly sliced**
- **½ cup sliced fresh mushrooms**
- **¼ cup finely chopped yellow summer squash**
- **½ cup fresh baby spinach**
- **3 garlic cloves, minced**
- **1 cup shredded Swiss cheese**
- **4 large eggs, lightly beaten**
- **1⅔ cups heavy whipping cream**
- **½ tsp. salt**
- **½ tsp. minced fresh rosemary**
- **¼ tsp. pepper**

1. On a lightly floured surface, roll dough to a ⅛-in.-thick circle; transfer to a 9-in. pie plate. Trim to ½ in. beyond rim of plate; flute edge. Refrigerate 30 minutes. Preheat oven to 425°. Line unpricked crust with a double thickness of foil. Fill with pie weights, dried beans or uncooked rice. Bake on a lower oven rack until edge is light golden brown, 15-20 minutes. Remove foil and weights; bake until bottom is golden brown, 3-6 minutes longer. Cool on a wire rack. Reduce oven setting to 350°.
2. In a skillet, melt the butter over medium heat. Add onion, mushrooms and squash; cook and stir until tender, 3-5 minutes. Add spinach and garlic; cook 1 minute longer. Spoon into crust; top with cheese.
3. In a large bowl, whisk eggs, cream, salt, rosemary and pepper until blended; pour over cheese. Cover edge of crust loosely with foil. Bake for 40-45 minutes or until a knife inserted in the center comes out clean. Let quiche stand for 10 minutes before cutting.

NOTE: To make dough, combine 1¼ cups all-purpose flour and ¼ tsp. salt; cut in ½ cup cold butter until crumbly. Gradually add 3-5 Tbsp. ice water, tossing with a fork until dough holds together when pressed. Shape into a disk; wrap. Refrigerate 1 hour.

1 PIECE: 451 cal., 38g fat (23g sat. fat), 196mg chol., 390mg sod., 18g carb. (2g sugars, 1g fiber), 11g pro.

OATMEAL BRULEE WITH GINGER CREAM

Here's a warm dish for a chilly morning. I love the crispy caramelized top and the raspberry surprise at the bottom.
—Yvonne Starlin, Westmoreland, TN

PREP: 30 MIN. • **BROIL:** 10 MIN.
MAKES: 4 SERVINGS

GINGER CREAM

- ½ cup heavy whipping cream
- 2 slices fresh gingerroot (about ¾-in. diameter)
- 1 cinnamon stick (3 in.)
- 1 Tbsp. grated orange zest
- 3 Tbsp. maple syrup
- ⅛ tsp. ground nutmeg

OATMEAL

- 4 cups water
- 2 cups old-fashioned oats
- ¼ cup chopped dried apricots
- ¼ cup dried cherries, chopped
- ½ tsp. salt
- 3 Tbsp. brown sugar
- 2 Tbsp. butter, softened
- 1 cup fresh or frozen unsweetened raspberries, thawed
- ¼ cup sugar

1. In a small saucepan, combine cream, ginger, cinnamon stick and orange zest; bring to a boil. Reduce the heat; simmer, covered, for 10 minutes. Remove from the heat; strain and discard solids. Stir in the syrup and nutmeg.
2. In a large saucepan, bring water to a boil; stir in the oats, apricots, cherries and salt. Reduce heat to medium; cook for 5 minutes, stirring occasionally. Remove from the heat; stir in the brown sugar and ¼ cup ginger cream. Let stand, covered, for 2 minutes.
3. Lightly grease four 10-oz. broiler-safe ramekins with butter; place the ramekins on a baking sheet. Divide the raspberries among ramekins. Spoon the oatmeal over raspberries; sprinkle evenly with sugar. Broil 4-6 in. from the heat for 7-9 minutes or until sugar is caramelized. Serve with remaining ginger cream.

1 SERVING WITH 1 TBSP. CREAM: 490 cal., 20g fat (11g sat. fat), 56mg chol., 359mg sod., 76g carb. (42g sugars, 7g fiber), 7g pro.

APPLES & CREAM PANCAKE

This pancake is delicious for breakfast or brunch. I usually make two because everyone wants more! With our own orchard, we have plenty of Delicious and Winesap apples—they make this a true midwestern meal.
—Ruth Schafer, Defiance, OH

TAKES: 25 MIN. • **MAKES:** 6 SERVINGS

- ½ cup 2% milk
- 2 large eggs, room temperature
- ½ cup all-purpose flour
- ¼ tsp. salt
- 1 to 2 Tbsp. butter
- ¼ cup packed brown sugar
- 3 oz. cream cheese, softened
- ½ cup sour cream
- ½ tsp. vanilla extract
- 1½ cups thinly sliced unpeeled apples
- ¼ cup chopped walnuts

1. In a small bowl, combine milk, eggs, flour and salt. Beat until smooth. Heat a cast-iron or ovenproof skillet in a 450° oven until hot. Add butter to the skillet; spread over entire bottom. Pour in batter; bake for 10 minutes or until golden brown.
2. Meanwhile, combine sugar and cream cheese. Blend in sour cream and vanilla. Fill pancake with ¾ cup cream cheese mixture and top with apples. Spread remaining cream cheese mixture over apples and sprinkle with nuts. Cut into wedges and serve immediately.

1 PIECE: 265 cal., 16g fat (8g sat. fat), 108mg chol., 204mg sod., 24g carb. (14g sugars, 1g fiber), 7g pro.

PUMPKIN SURPRISE MUFFINS

Filled with cream cheese and apricot preserves, these almond-topped pumpkin muffins are heavenly.

—Elizabeth Blondefield, San Jose, CA

PREP: 20 MIN. • **BAKE:** 20 MIN.
MAKES: 14 MUFFINS

- **2 cups all-purpose flour**
- **1 Tbsp. baking powder**
- **1 tsp. ground cinnamon**
- **¼ tsp. salt**
- **¼ tsp. ground ginger**
- **¼ tsp. ground nutmeg**
- **½ cup plus 3 Tbsp. sugar, divided**
- **2 large eggs, room temperature**
- **1 cup canned pumpkin**
- **½ cup sour cream**
- **6 Tbsp. butter, melted**
- **7 Tbsp. apricot preserves, divided**
- **4 oz. cream cheese, divided into 14 portions**
- **¼ cup sliced almonds**

1. Preheat oven to 400°. Whisk together the first 6 ingredients and ½ cup sugar. In another bowl, whisk the eggs, pumpkin, sour cream, melted butter and 3 Tbsp. preserves until blended. Add to the flour mixture; stir just until moistened.
2. Fill greased or paper-lined muffin cups half full with batter. Place a portion of cream cheese and about ¾ tsp. preserves in each muffin; cover with the remaining batter. Sprinkle with the almonds and remaining sugar.
3. Bake until the top springs back when touched, 20-25 minutes. Cool 5 minutes before removing from pans to a wire rack. Refrigerate leftovers.

1 MUFFIN: 243 cal., 11g fat (6g sat. fat), 50mg chol., 228mg sod., 33g carb. (16g sugars, 1g fiber), 4g pro.

PANCAKES FOR TWO

These light and fluffy pancakes are perfectly portioned for a little batch, so there's no need to worry about what to do with leftover batter.

—Annemarie Pietila, Farmington Hills, MI

TAKES: 15 MIN.
MAKES: ABOUT 8 PANCAKES

- **1¼ cups all-purpose flour**
- **1 Tbsp. sugar**
- **1 tsp. baking powder**
- **½ tsp. baking soda**
- **½ tsp. salt**
- **1 large egg, room temperature, lightly beaten**
- **1¼ cups buttermilk**
- **2 Tbsp. canola oil**
- **1 cup fresh or frozen blueberries, optional**

1. In a large bowl, combine flour, sugar, baking powder, baking soda and salt. Combine egg, buttermilk and oil; stir into dry ingredients just until blended. If desired, fold in blueberries.
2. Preheat griddle over medium heat. Lightly grease griddle. Pour the batter by ¼ cupfuls onto griddle; cook until bubbles on top begin to pop and the bottoms are golden brown. Turn; cook until the second side is golden brown.

NOTE: If using frozen blueberries, use without thawing to avoid discoloring the batter.

4 PANCAKES: 527 cal., 18g fat (3g sat. fat), 112mg chol., 1299mg sod., 74g carb. (15g sugars, 2g fiber), 16g pro.

READER REVIEW

"My family loved these. I added chocolate chips. It was the right amount for my husband and daughter."

QUEENLALISA, TASTEOFHOME.COM

NAYLET LaROCHELLE
Miami, FL

BACON & EGG CHILAQUILES

In Mexico and throughout the Southwest, chilaquiles are typically made for brunch using tortillas and any leftovers from the previous day's dinner. I love to bring this to family brunches as it gives the traditional eggs-and-bacon dish a unique twist. The empty pan proves that it's a favorite!
—Naylet LaRochelle, Miami, FL

PREP: 15 MIN. • **BAKE:** 25 MIN.
MAKES: 6 SERVINGS

- **3½ cups salsa**
- **½ cup sour cream**
- **1 pkg. (9 oz.) tortilla chips**
- **2 cups coarsely chopped fresh spinach**
- **2 cups shredded taco cheese blend or Mexican cheese blend**
- **12 bacon strips, cooked and crumbled**
- **6 large eggs**
- **⅓ cup crumbled Cotija or feta cheese**
- **¼ cup minced fresh cilantro**
- **Sliced avocado, optional**

1. Preheat oven to 350°. In a small bowl, combine salsa and sour cream. Arrange half the tortilla chips in a greased 13x9-in. baking pan. Layer with half the salsa mixture, all of the spinach, half the shredded cheese and half the bacon. Top with remaining tortilla chips, salsa mixture, shredded cheese and bacon.
2. Bake, until dish is heated through and the cheese is melted, 20-25 minutes. Meanwhile, heat a large nonstick skillet over medium-high heat. Break the eggs, 1 at a time, into pan; reduce heat to low. Cook until whites are set and yolks begin to thicken, turning once if desired.
3. Top chilaquiles with cooked eggs, Cotija cheese, cilantro and, if desired, avocado.

1 SERVING: 623 cal., 38g fat (15g sat. fat), 247mg chol., 1426mg sod., 41g carb. (6g sugars, 2g fiber), 25g pro.

CHEESY BACON BREAKFAST LASAGNA

I came up with this unique breakfast dish after looking for a way to use up a few extra no-boil lasagna noodles. Try switching up the different cheeses—Swiss, pepper jack and mozzarella taste delicious in this breakfast lasagna, too!
—Susan Kieboam, Amherstburg, ON

PREP: 30 MIN. + SOAKING
BAKE: 10 MIN. + COOLING
MAKES: 4 SERVINGS

- **3 no-cook lasagna noodles**
- **3 bacon strips, diced**
- **2 Tbsp. diced sweet or green onion**
- **2 Tbsp. diced sweet red pepper**
- **4 large eggs**

CHEESE SAUCE

- **2 Tbsp. butter**
- **2 Tbsp. all-purpose flour**
- **1 cup 2% milk**
- **1 tsp. grated Parmesan cheese**
- **¼ tsp. salt**
- **1 cup shredded sharp cheddar cheese**
- **3 Tbsp. whole-milk ricotta cheese**

1. Soak lasagna noodles in warm water for 20 minutes. In a small skillet, cook bacon, onion and red pepper over medium heat until bacon is crisp, 8-10 minutes. Remove 2 Tbsp. bacon mixture and drain on paper towels; reserve. Whisk eggs into skillet; cook and stir until cooked through.
2. Preheat oven to 350°. For cheese sauce, melt the butter in a small saucepan over medium heat; whisk in flour until smooth. Add the milk, Parmesan cheese and salt; cook and stir until thickened, 2-3 minutes. Remove from heat; stir cheddar cheese into hot mixture until smooth.
3. Drain the noodles on paper towels. To assemble lasagna, spread 3 Tbsp. cheese sauce over bottom of a greased 8x4-in. loaf pan. Layer with 1 lasagna noodle, 3 Tbsp. cheese sauce, half of the egg mixture and another lasagna noodle. Layer with 3 Tbsp. cheese sauce, ricotta cheese and remaining egg mixture. Top with the third noodle, remaining cheese sauce and reserved bacon mixture.
4. Bake until bubbly, 10-15 minutes. Cool 5 minutes before cutting.

1 SERVING: 443 cal., 31g fat (15g sat. fat), 253mg chol., 638mg sod., 19g carb. (5g sugars, 1g fiber), 21g pro.

MAKE-AHEAD BISCUITS & GRAVY BAKE

Biscuits and gravy are usually served together but prepared separately. I created a way to bake them all at once in this cozy casserole.
—Nancy McInnis, Olympia, WA

PREP: 20 MIN. + CHILLING. • **BAKE:** 25 MIN.
MAKES: 10 SERVINGS

- **1 lb. bulk pork sausage**
- **¼ cup all-purpose flour**
- **3 cups 2% milk**
- **1½ tsp. pepper**
- **1 tsp. paprika**
- **¼ tsp. chili powder**
- **2¼ cups biscuit/baking mix**
- **½ cup sour cream**
- **¼ cup butter, melted**

1. In a large skillet, cook sausage over medium heat 6-8 minutes or until no longer pink, breaking into crumbles. Remove with a slotted spoon; discard drippings, reserving ¼ cup in pan. Stir in flour until blended; cook and stir until golden brown (do not burn), 1-2 minutes. Gradually whisk in milk. Bring to a boil, stirring constantly; cook and stir until thickened, 2-3 minutes. Stir in sausage, pepper, paprika and chili powder. Pour mixture into a greased 13x9-in. baking dish. Cool completely.
2. Meanwhile, in a large bowl, mix baking mix, sour cream and melted butter until moistened. Turn onto a lightly floured surface; knead gently 8-10 times.
3. Pat or roll dough to ¾-in. thickness; cut with a floured 2½-in. biscuit cutter. Place the biscuits over gravy. Refrigerate, covered, overnight.
4. Preheat oven to 400°. Remove the casserole from refrigerator while oven heats. Bake, uncovered, until gravy is heated through and biscuits are golden brown, 22-25 minutes.

FREEZE OPTION: Cover and freeze unbaked biscuits and gravy. To use, partially thaw in refrigerator overnight. Remove from refrigerator 30 minutes before baking. Preheat oven to 400°. Bake as directed, increasing time as needed until gravy is heated through and biscuits are golden brown.

1 SERVING: 373 cal., 26g fat (11g sat. fat), 50mg chol., 640mg sod., 26g carb. (5g sugars, 1g fiber), 10g pro.

MAPLE APPLE BAKED OATMEAL

I've tried different types of fruit for this recipe, but apple seems to be my family's favorite. I mix the dry and wet ingredients in separate bowls the night before and combine them the next morning when it's ready to be baked.
—Megan Brooks, Saint Lazare, QC

PREP: 20 MIN. • **BAKE:** 25 MIN.
MAKES: 8 SERVINGS

- 3 **cups old-fashioned oats**
- 2 **tsp. baking powder**
- 1¼ **tsp. ground cinnamon**
- ½ **tsp. salt**
- ¼ **tsp. ground nutmeg**
- 2 **large eggs**
- 2 **cups fat-free milk**
- ½ **cup maple syrup**
- ¼ **cup canola oil**
- 1 **tsp. vanilla extract**
- 1 **large apple, chopped**
- ¼ **cup sunflower kernels or pepitas**

1. Preheat oven to 350°. In a large bowl, mix the first 5 ingredients. In a small bowl, whisk the eggs, milk, syrup, oil and vanilla until blended; stir into the dry ingredients. Let stand for 5 minutes. Stir in apple.
2. Transfer to an 11x7-in. baking dish coated with cooking spray. Sprinkle with sunflower kernels. Bake, uncovered, 25-30 minutes or until set and edges are lightly browned.

1 SERVING: 305 cal., 13g fat (2g sat. fat), 48mg chol., 325mg sod., 41g carb. (20g sugars, 4g fiber), 8g pro. **DIABETIC EXCHANGES:** 3 starch, 1½ fat.

BRUNCH BURRITOS

I use a second slow cooker to keep the tortillas warm and pliable when I serve these yummy breakfast burritos. Just place a clean wet cloth in the bottom, then cover it with foil and add the tortillas.
—Beth Osburn, Levelland, TX

PREP: 30 MIN. • **COOK:** 4 HOURS
MAKES: 10 SERVINGS

- 1 **lb. bulk pork sausage, cooked and drained**
- ½ **lb. bacon strips, cooked and crumbled**
- 18 **large eggs, lightly beaten**
- 2 **cups frozen shredded hash brown potatoes, thawed**
- 1 **large onion, chopped**
- 1 **can (10¾ oz.) condensed cheddar cheese soup, undiluted**
- 1 **can (4 oz.) chopped green chiles**
- 1 **tsp. garlic powder**
- ½ **tsp. pepper**
- 2 **cups shredded cheddar cheese**
- 10 **flour tortillas (10 in.), warmed**
- **Optional toppings: Jalapeno peppers, salsa and hot pepper sauce**

1. In a large mixing bowl, combine the first 9 ingredients. Pour half of the egg mixture into a 4- or 5-qt. slow cooker coated with cooking spray. Top with half of the cheese. Repeat layers.
2. Cook, covered, on low 4-5 hours or until center is set and a thermometer reads 160°.
3. Spoon ¾ cup egg mixture across the center of each tortilla. Fold bottom and sides of tortilla over filling and roll up. Add toppings of your choice.

1 BURRITO: 683 cal., 38g fat (15g sat. fat), 449mg chol., 1650mg sod., 41g carb. (3g sugars, 7g fiber), 35g pro.

BRIE & SAUSAGE BRUNCH BAKE

I've made this brunch bake for holidays as well as for a weekend at a friend's cabin, and I always get requests for the recipe. It's make-ahead convenient, reheats well and even tastes great the next day.
—Becky Hicks, Forest Lake, MN

PREP: 30 MIN. + CHILLING
BAKE: 50 MIN. + STANDING
MAKES: 12 SERVINGS

- 1 **lb. bulk Italian sausage**
- 1 **small onion, chopped**
- 8 **cups cubed day-old sourdough bread**
- ½ **cup chopped roasted sweet red peppers**
- ½ **lb. Brie cheese, rind removed, cubed**
- ⅔ **cup grated Parmesan cheese**
- 2 **Tbsp. minced fresh basil or 2 tsp. dried basil**
- 8 **large eggs**
- 2 **cups heavy whipping cream**
- 1 **Tbsp. Dijon mustard**
- 1 **tsp. pepper**
- ½ **tsp. salt**
- ¾ **cup shredded part-skim mozzarella cheese**
- 3 **green onions, sliced**

1. In a large skillet, cook sausage and onion over medium heat until meat is no longer pink; drain.
2. Place bread cubes in a greased 13x9-in. baking dish. Layer with sausage mixture, red peppers, Brie and Parmesan cheeses and basil. In a large bowl, whisk the eggs, cream, mustard, pepper and salt; pour over top. Cover and refrigerate overnight.
3. Remove from refrigerator 30 minutes before baking. Preheat oven to 350°. Bake, uncovered, 45-50 minutes or until a knife inserted in the center comes out clean.
4. Sprinkle with mozzarella cheese. Bake 4-6 minutes or until cheese is melted. Let stand 10 minutes before cutting. Sprinkle with green onions.

1 PIECE: 451 cal., 34g fat (18g sat. fat), 217mg chol., 843mg sod., 16g carb. (3g sugars, 1g fiber), 19g pro.

CREAMY EGGS & MUSHROOMS AU GRATIN

I turn to this dish when I want a brunch recipe that has the crowd appeal of scrambled eggs but is a little more special. The Parmesan sauce is simple but rich and delicious.
—Deborah Williams, Peoria, AZ

PREP: 15 MIN. • **COOK:** 25 MIN.
MAKES: 8 SERVINGS

- 2 **Tbsp. butter**
- 1 **lb. sliced fresh mushrooms**
- 1 **green onion, chopped**

SAUCE

- 2 **Tbsp. butter**
- 3 **Tbsp. all-purpose flour**
- ½ **tsp. salt**
- ⅛ **tsp. pepper**
- 1 **cup 2% milk**
- ½ **cup heavy whipping cream**
- 2 **Tbsp. grated Parmesan cheese**

EGGS

- 16 **large eggs**
- ¼ **tsp. salt**
- ⅛ **tsp. pepper**
- ¼ **cup butter, cubed**
- ½ **cup grated Parmesan cheese**
- 1 **green onion, finely chopped**

1. In a large broiler-safe skillet, heat butter over medium-high heat. Add the mushrooms; cook and stir until browned, 4-6 minutes. Add the green onion; cook 1 minute longer. Remove from pan with a slotted spoon. Wipe skillet clean.
2. For sauce, in a small saucepan, melt butter over medium heat. Stir in flour, salt and pepper until smooth; gradually whisk in milk and cream. Bring to a boil, stirring constantly; cook and stir until thickened, 2-4 minutes. Remove from the heat; stir in cheese.
3. Preheat broiler. For eggs, in a large bowl, whisk eggs, salt and pepper until blended. In same skillet, heat butter over medium heat. Pour in egg mixture; cook and stir just until eggs are thickened and no liquid egg remains. Remove from heat.
4. Spoon half the sauce over the eggs; top with mushrooms. Add remaining sauce; sprinkle with cheese. Broil 4-5 in. from heat 4-6 minutes or until top is lightly browned. Sprinkle with green onion.

1 SERVING: 363 cal., 29g fat (15g sat. fat), 431mg chol., 591mg sod., 8g carb. (3g sugars, 1g fiber), 18g pro.

CHEESY BACON & GRITS CASSEROLE

I was craving grits for breakfast, so I created this masterpiece with fresh corn and leftover bacon. Serve with avocado and hot sauce.
—Rebecca Yankovich, Springfield, VA

PREP: 30 MIN. • **BAKE:** 35 MIN. + STANDING
MAKES: 8 SERVINGS

- 6 bacon strips, chopped
- 3 cups water
- 1 cup 2% milk
- ¾ tsp. salt
- 1 cup uncooked old-fashioned grits
- 2 cups shredded Colby-Monterey Jack cheese, divided
- 2 large eggs, room temperature, lightly beaten
- 1 cup fresh or frozen corn, thawed
- ¼ tsp. pepper
- Sliced avocado, optional

1. Preheat oven to 350°. In a large skillet, cook bacon over medium heat until crisp, stirring occasionally. Remove with a slotted spoon; drain on paper towels.
2. Meanwhile, in a Dutch oven, bring water, milk and salt to a boil. Slowly stir in the grits. Reduce heat to low; cook, covered, until thickened, 15-20 minutes, stirring occasionally. Remove from heat. Stir in 1½ cups cheese until melted. Slowly stir in eggs until blended. Stir in bacon, corn and pepper. Transfer to a greased 2-qt. baking dish. Sprinkle with the remaining ½ cup cheese.
3. Bake, uncovered, 35-40 minutes or until edges are golden brown and cheese is melted. Let stand 10 minutes before serving. If desired, serve with avocado.

FREEZE OPTION: Cool unbaked casserole; cover and freeze. To use, partially thaw in refrigerator overnight. Remove casserole from the refrigerator 30 minutes before baking. Preheat oven to 350°. Bake grits as directed until heated through and a thermometer inserted in center reads 165°, increasing time to 45-55 minutes.

¾ CUP: 261 cal., 13g fat (8g sat. fat), 81mg chol., 534mg sod., 23g carb. (3g sugars, 1g fiber), 13g pro.

PROSCIUTTO-PESTO BREAKFAST STRATA

I'd never tried prosciutto before, but this recipe instantly made me a fan! The layers of flavor in this dish are brilliant, making it well worth the time and a must for your recipe box.
—Vicki Anderson, Farmington, MN

PREP: 25 MIN. + CHILLING • **COOK:** 50 MIN.
MAKES: 10 SERVINGS

- **2 cups 2% milk**
- **1 cup white wine or chicken broth**
- **1 loaf (1 lb.) French bread, cut into ½-in. slice**
- **¼ cup minced fresh basil**
- **¼ cup minced fresh parsley**
- **3 Tbsp. olive oil**
- **½ lb. thinly sliced smoked Gouda cheese**
- **½ lb. thinly sliced prosciutto**
- **3 medium tomatoes, thinly sliced**
- **½ cup prepared pesto**
- **4 large eggs**
- **½ cup heavy whipping cream**
- **½ tsp. salt**
- **¼ tsp. pepper**

1. In a shallow bowl, combine milk and wine. Dip both sides of the bread in milk mixture; squeeze gently to remove excess liquid. Layer the bread slices in a greased 13x9-in. baking dish.
2. Sprinkle with basil and parsley; drizzle with oil. Layer with half of the cheese, half of the prosciutto and all of the tomatoes; drizzle with half of the pesto. Top with remaining cheese, prosciutto and pesto.
3. In a small bowl, whisk eggs, cream, salt and pepper until blended; pour over top. Refrigerate strata, covered, several hours or overnight.
4. Preheat oven to 350°. Remove strata from refrigerator while oven heats. Bake, uncovered, until top is golden brown and a knife inserted in the center comes out clean, 50-60 minutes. Let strata stand for 5-10 minutes before serving.

1 PIECE: 440 cal., 26g fat (10g sat. fat), 138mg chol., 1215mg sod., 30g carb. (7g sugars, 2g fiber), 22g pro.

YANKEE RANCHEROS

After my in-laws began to affectionately refer to me as a Yankee, I decided I needed to learn to make a few Tex-Mex-style dishes. These breakfast rancheros are super easy and make my family happy.
—Darla Andrews, Boerne, TX

TAKES: 25 MIN. • **MAKES:** 4 SERVINGS

- **5 cups frozen shredded hash brown potatoes (about 15 oz.)**
- **1 cup refried beans**
- **¼ cup salsa**
- **2 naan flatbreads, halved**
- **4 large eggs**
- **½ cup shredded cheddar cheese or Mexican cheese blend**
- **Additional salsa, optional**

1. Cook potatoes according to package directions for stovetop.
2. Meanwhile, in a microwave-safe bowl, mix beans and salsa. Microwave, covered, on high until heated through, 1-2 minutes, stirring once. In a large skillet, heat the naan over medium-high heat until lightly browned, 2-3 minutes per side; remove from pan. Keep warm.
3. Coat same skillet with cooking spray; place over medium-high heat. Break eggs, 1 at a time, into pan; reduce heat to low. Cook until whites are set and yolks begin to thicken, turning once if desired.
4. To serve, spread bean mixture over naan. Top with potatoes, eggs and cheese. If desired, serve with additional salsa.

1 SERVING: 430 cal., 23g fat (6g sat. fat), 202mg chol., 703mg sod., 40g carb. (4g sugars, 4g fiber), 16g pro.

CREPE QUICHE CUPS

When it comes to new recipes, I'm always up for a challenge. These crepe cups have turned out to be one of my favorite things to serve while entertaining. They're a nice change for brunch on holiday mornings when my family is gathered around.
—Sheryl Riley, Unionville, MO

PREP: 40 MIN. + CHILLING • **BAKE:** 25 MIN.
MAKES: 16 CREPE CUPS

- **2 large eggs, room temperature**
- **1 cup plus 2 Tbsp. 2% milk**
- **2 Tbsp. butter, melted**
- **1 cup all-purpose flour**
- **⅛ tsp. salt**

FILLING

- **½ lb. bulk pork sausage**
- **¼ cup chopped onion**
- **3 large eggs**
- **½ cup 2% milk**
- **½ cup mayonnaise**
- **2 cups shredded cheddar cheese**

1. For crepe batter, in a small bowl, beat the eggs, milk and butter. Combine flour and salt; add to egg mixture and mix well. Cover and refrigerate for 1 hour.
2. In a small skillet, cook sausage and onion over medium heat until meat is no longer pink; drain. In a large bowl, whisk the eggs, milk and mayonnaise. Stir in sausage mixture and cheese; set aside.
3. Heat a lightly greased 8-in. nonstick skillet. Stir crepe batter; pour 2 Tbsp. into center of skillet. Lift and tilt pan to coat bottom evenly. Cook until the top appears dry; turn and cook 15-20 seconds longer.
4. Remove to a wire rack. Repeat with remaining batter, greasing skillet as needed. When cool, stack crepes with waxed paper or paper towels in between.
5. Line greased muffin cups with crepes; fill two-thirds full with sausage mixture. Bake at 350° for 15 minutes. Cover loosely with foil; bake 10-15 minutes longer or until a knife inserted in the center comes out clean.

1 SERVING: 209 cal., 16g fat (7g sat. fat), 96mg chol., 246mg sod., 8g carb. (2g sugars, 0 fiber), 8g pro.

APPLE PANCAKES WITH CIDER SYRUP

Tender pancakes are filled with raisins and minced apple, then drizzled with apple cider syrup. These are wonderful anytime.
—April Harmon, Greeneville, TN

TAKES: 30 MIN.
MAKES: 6 PANCAKES (⅔ CUP SYRUP)

- **½ cup all-purpose flour**
- **¼ cup whole wheat flour**
- **2 tsp. sugar**
- **¼ tsp. baking soda**
- **¼ tsp. salt**
- **¼ tsp. ground cinnamon**
- **⅔ cup finely chopped peeled apple**
- **¼ cup raisins**
- **⅔ cup buttermilk**
- **1 large egg, separated, room temperature**
- **2 tsp. butter, melted**
- **¼ tsp. vanilla extract**

SYRUP

- **¼ cup sugar**
- **2 tsp. cornstarch**
- **⅔ cup apple cider or juice**
- **1 cinnamon stick (1½ in.)**
- **Dash ground nutmeg**
- **Additional butter, optional**

1. In a small bowl, combine the first 6 ingredients; stir in the apple and raisins. Combine the buttermilk, egg yolk, butter and vanilla; stir into dry ingredients. In a small bowl, beat the egg white until soft peaks form; fold into batter.
2. Pour batter by heaping ¼ cupfuls onto a hot greased griddle; turn when bubbles form on top. Cook until the second side is lightly browned.
3. Meanwhile, in a saucepan, combine the sugar, cornstarch and cider until smooth; add cinnamon stick. Bring to a boil over medium heat; cook and stir for 2 minutes or until thickened. Discard the cinnamon stick. Stir nutmeg into the syrup. Serve pancakes with warm syrup and, if desired, additional butter.

3 PANCAKES WITH ⅓ CUP SYRUP: 492 cal., 6g fat (3g sat. fat), 116mg chol., 605mg sod., 101g carb. (58g sugars, 4g fiber), 12g pro.

Soups & Sandwiches

Soup's on! And grab a plate for a sandwich, too. The deliciously fun, creative flavors in these recipes take the ultimate lunch combo to brand-new heights!

SAUSAGE POTATO SOUP

After a full day of teaching and coaching, I'm often too tired to spend a lot of time preparing dinner. So I rely on this thick, chunky blend that I can have on the table in 30 minutes. The whole family enjoys the wonderful flavor of the smoked sausage.

—Jennifer LeFevre, Hesston, KS

TAKES: 30 MIN. • **MAKES:** 6 SERVINGS

½ lb. smoked kielbasa, diced
6 medium potatoes, peeled and cubed
2 cups frozen corn
1½ cups chicken broth
1 celery rib, sliced
¼ cup sliced carrot
½ tsp. garlic powder
½ tsp. onion powder
½ tsp. salt
¼ tsp. pepper
1½ cups whole milk
⅔ cup shredded cheddar cheese
1 tsp. minced fresh parsley

1. In a large saucepan, cook the kielbasa over medium heat until lightly browned, about 5 minutes; drain and set aside. In the same pan, combine potatoes, corn, broth, celery, carrot and seasonings. Bring to a boil.

2. Reduce heat; cover and simmer until vegetables are tender, about 15 minutes. Add milk, cheese, parsley and sausage. Cook and stir over low heat until cheese is melted and soup is heated through, about 5 minutes.

1 CUP: 377 cal., 17g fat (7g sat. fat), 45mg chol., 817mg sod., 44g carb. (8g sugars, 3g fiber), 14g pro.

READER REVIEW

"This soup recipe is amazing! My family gets all-a-flutter when they find out Sausage Potato Soup is on the menu. It's become our favorite go-to comfort food."

JUDIEANNE, TASTEOFHOME.COM

EGG-TOPPED AVOCADO TOAST

We always have avocados on hand, so it's easy to make this quick toast for my husband and me. It's great for breakfast, lunch or a snack.
—Kallee Krong-McCreery, Escondido, CA

TAKES: 20 MIN. • **MAKES:** 2 SERVINGS

- **2 slices multigrain bread, toasted**
- **2 tsp. butter**
- **½ medium ripe avocado, peeled and thinly sliced**
- **4 thin slices tomato**
- **2 thin slices red onion**
- **2 large eggs**
- **⅛ tsp. seasoned salt**
- **2 Tbsp. shredded cheddar cheese**
- **2 bacon strips, cooked and crumbled**

1. Spread each slice of toast with butter; place on a plate. Top with avocado; mash gently with a fork. Top with the tomato and onion.
2. To poach each egg, place ½ cup water in a small microwave-safe bowl or glass measuring cup; carefully break an egg into the water. Microwave, covered, on high 1 minute. Microwave in 10-second intervals until white is set and yolk begins to thicken; let stand 1 minute. Using a slotted spoon, place egg over sandwich.
3. Sprinkle eggs with seasoned salt. Top with cheese and bacon.

HEALTH TIP: Skip the cheese and bacon to reduce the saturated fat.

1 OPEN-FACED SANDWICH: 313 cal., 21g fat (7g sat. fat), 211mg chol., 492mg sod., 18g carb. (4g sugars, 5g fiber), 15g pro.

SALMON SALAD SANDWICHES

These are perfect to pack in your kids' lunch boxes when they can't face another boring sandwich. We love the salmon, cream cheese and dill tucked inside a crusty roll. The carrots and celery add a nice crunch.
—Yvonne Shust, Shoal Lake, MB

TAKES: 10 MIN. • **MAKES:** 2 SERVINGS

- **3 oz. cream cheese, softened**
- **1 Tbsp. mayonnaise**
- **1 Tbsp. lemon juice**
- **1 tsp. dill weed**
- **¼ to ½ tsp. salt**
- **⅛ tsp. pepper**
- **1 can (6 oz.) pink salmon, drained, bones and skin removed**
- **½ cup shredded carrot**
- **½ cup chopped celery**
- **Lettuce leaves**
- **2 whole wheat buns, split**
- **Sliced tomatoes**

In a large bowl, beat the cream cheese, mayonnaise, lemon juice, dill, salt and pepper until smooth. Add the salmon, carrot and celery and mix well. Place a lettuce leaf and about ½ cup salmon salad on each bun and top with tomato.

1 SANDWICH: 463 cal., 29g fat (12g sat. fat), 87mg chol., 1158mg sod., 28g carb. (5g sugars, 5g fiber), 25g pro.

TIFFANY IHLE
Bronx, NY

SAUSAGE & KALE LENTIL STEW

I made a pot of this soup while visiting my sister and her family. Now I bring it along when I stop by, or I pack up a few containers for my nephew, who appreciates a home-cooked meal while he's away at college.
—Tiffany Ihle, Bronx, NY

PREP: 20 MIN. • **COOK:** 45 MIN.
MAKES: 6 SERVINGS (2 QT.)

- **1 lb. bulk pork sausage**
- **10 baby carrots, chopped (about ¾ cup)**
- **1 small onion, finely chopped**
- **4 garlic cloves, minced**
- **4 plum tomatoes, halved**
- **¾ cup roasted sweet red peppers**
- **1 cup dried lentils, rinsed**
- **2 cans (14½ oz. each) vegetable broth**
- **1 bay leaf**
- **½ tsp. ground cumin**
- **¼ tsp. pepper**
- **2 cups coarsely chopped fresh kale**

1. In a Dutch oven, cook sausage, carrots and onion over medium-high heat until sausage is no longer pink, breaking up sausage into crumbles, 8-10 minutes. Stir in garlic; cook 2 minutes longer. Drain.
2. Place tomatoes and red peppers in a food processor; process until finely chopped. Add to sausage mixture; stir in lentils, broth and seasonings. Bring to a boil. Reduce the heat; simmer, covered, 20 minutes, stirring occasionally.
3. Stir in kale; cook until lentils and kale are tender, 10-15 minutes. Remove the bay leaf.

FREEZE OPTION: Freeze cooled stew in freezer containers. To use, partially thaw in refrigerator overnight. Heat through in a saucepan, stirring occasionally.

1⅓ CUPS: 339 cal., 17g fat (5g sat. fat), 41mg chol., 1007mg sod., 29g carb. (5g sugars, 5g fiber), 17g pro.

CLUB ROLL-UPS

Packed with deli meat, cheese and olives, these roll-ups are always a hit at parties. Experiment with different meat and salad dressing flavors.
—Linda Searl, Pampa, TX

TAKES: 25 MIN. • **MAKES:** 8 SERVINGS

- **3 oz. cream cheese, softened**
- **½ cup ranch salad dressing**
- **2 Tbsp. ranch salad dressing mix**
- **8 bacon strips, cooked and crumbled**
- **½ cup finely chopped onion**
- **1 can (2¼ oz.) sliced ripe olives, drained**
- **1 jar (2 oz.) diced pimientos, drained**
- **¼ cup diced canned jalapeno peppers**
- **8 flour tortillas (10 in.), room temperature**
- **8 thin slices deli ham**
- **8 thin slices deli turkey**
- **8 thin slices deli roast beef**
- **2 cups shredded cheddar cheese**

1. In a small bowl, beat the cream cheese, ranch dressing and dressing mix until well blended. In another bowl, combine the bacon, onion, olives, pimientos and jalapenos.
2. Spread cream cheese mixture over tortillas; layer with ham, turkey and roast beef. Sprinkle with bacon mixture and cheddar cheese; roll up.

1 ROLL-UP: 554 cal., 29g fat (12g sat. fat), 80mg chol., 1802mg sod., 39g carb. (2g sugars, 7g fiber), 27g pro.

THE ULTIMATE CHICKEN NOODLE SOUP

My first Colorado winter was so cold, all I wanted to eat was soup. This recipe is in heavy rotation at our house from November to April.
—Gina Nistico, Denver, CO

PREP: 15 MIN. • **COOK:** 45 MIN. + STANDING
MAKES: 10 SERVINGS (ABOUT 3½ QT.)

- 2½ lbs. bone-in chicken thighs
- ½ tsp. salt
- ½ tsp. pepper
- 1 Tbsp. canola oil
- 1 large onion, chopped
- 1 garlic clove, minced
- 10 cups chicken broth
- 4 celery ribs, chopped
- 4 medium carrots, chopped
- 2 bay leaves
- 1 tsp. minced fresh thyme or ¼ tsp. dried thyme
- 3 cups uncooked kluski or other egg noodles (about 8 oz.)
- 1 Tbsp. chopped fresh parsley
- 1 Tbsp. lemon juice
- Optional: Additional salt and pepper

1. Pat chicken dry with paper towels; sprinkle with salt and pepper. In a 6-qt. stockpot, heat oil over medium-high heat. Add chicken in batches, skin side down; cook 3-4 minutes or until dark golden brown. Remove chicken from pan; remove and discard skin. Discard the drippings, reserving 2 Tbsp.
2. Add onion to drippings; cook and stir over medium-high heat 4-5 minutes or until tender. Add garlic; cook 1 minute longer. Add broth, stirring to loosen browned bits from pan. Bring to a boil. Return chicken to pan. Add celery, carrots, bay leaves and thyme. Reduce the heat; simmer, covered, until chicken is tender, 25-30 minutes.
3. Transfer chicken to a plate. Remove soup from heat. Add noodles; let stand, covered, until tender, 20-22 minutes.
4. Meanwhile, when the chicken is cool enough to handle, remove the meat from bones; discard bones. Shred meat into bite-sized pieces. Return the meat to the stockpot. Stir in parsley and lemon juice. If desired, adjust seasoning with additional salt and pepper. Discard bay leaves.

1⅓ CUPS: 239 cal., 12g fat (3g sat. fat), 68mg chol., 1176mg sod., 14g carb. (3g sugars, 2g fiber), 18g pro.

HAM & POTATO SALAD SANDWICHES

These little sandwiches with zingy toppings are super simple to pull together. This classic version originated in a deli in Prague, where they're a popular winter party food.
—Cara McDonald, Winter Park, CO

TAKES: 15 MIN. • **MAKES:** 6 SERVINGS

- **1½ cups deli potato salad**
- **6 diagonally cut French bread baguette slices (½ in. thick)**
- **6 oz. fully cooked ham, thinly sliced**
- **6 slices tomato**
- **12 dill pickle slices**
- **2 hard-boiled large eggs, sliced**
- **2 slices red onion, separated into rings**

Spread ¼ cup potato salad on each baguette slice. Layer with ham, tomato, pickle, eggs and onion.
1 OPEN-FACED SANDWICH: 229 cal., 10g fat (2g sat. fat), 96mg chol., 821mg sod., 25g carb. (3g sugars, 2g fiber), 12g pro.

EGG SALAD POCKETS

Here's a delectable and satisfying sandwich that's perfect for packing. It doesn't get soggy because you line the pita pockets with lettuce before adding the egg salad.
—Karen Ann Bland, Gove, KS

TAKES: 20 MIN. • **MAKES:** 3 SERVINGS

- **3 oz. cream cheese, softened**
- **¼ cup Miracle Whip**
- **1 celery rib, finely chopped**
- **2 Tbsp. finely chopped onion**
- **1 Tbsp. sweet pickle relish**
- **¾ tsp. dill weed**
- **½ tsp. salt**
- **½ tsp. ground mustard**
- **6 hard-boiled large eggs, chopped**
- **3 pita breads (6 in.), halved**
- **6 lettuce leaves**

In a small bowl, combine cream cheese and Miracle Whip. Add the celery, onion, relish, dill weed, salt and mustard. Gently stir in eggs. Line pita halves with lettuce; fill each with ½ cup egg salad.
2 POCKETS: 497 cal., 27g fat (10g sat. fat), 462mg chol., 1148mg sod., 42g carb. (6g sugars, 2g fiber), 21g pro.

APPLE & PROSCIUTTO SANDWICHES

Prepared on an indoor grill, these Italian-style sandwiches are spread with homemade rosemary pesto. They're wonderful on a cool day with a bowl of butternut squash soup.
—Elizabeth Bennett, Mill Creek, WA

TAKES: 20 MIN. • **MAKES:** 8 SERVINGS

- **¼ cup olive oil**
- **½ cup chopped walnuts**
- **2 Tbsp. grated Parmesan cheese**
- **2 Tbsp. minced fresh rosemary**
- **1 loaf (12 oz.) focaccia bread**
- **8 thin slices prosciutto**
- **1 medium apple, sliced**
- **6 oz. Brie cheese, rind removed and sliced**

1. In a blender, combine the oil, walnuts, cheese and rosemary; cover and process until blended and nuts are finely chopped. With a bread knife, split the focaccia into 2 horizontal layers. Spread the rosemary mixture over cut sides of bread.
2. On the bottom half of bread, layer the prosciutto, apple and Brie; replace bread top. Cut into quarters.
3. Cook on an indoor grill for 2-3 minutes or until bread is browned and cheese is melted. To serve, cut each wedge in half.

1 SANDWICH: 336 cal., 21g fat (6g sat. fat), 35mg chol., 668mg sod., 27g carb. (4g sugars, 2g fiber), 13g pro.

CHICKEN & BROCCOLI RABE SOUP WITH TORTELLINI

With chicken, pasta and a bold tomato broth, this hearty and inviting soup is like a big comforting hug in a bowl!
—Cyndy Gerken, Naples, FL

PREP: 15 MIN. • **COOK:** 45 MIN.
MAKES: 10 SERVINGS (3½ QT.)

- 1 lb. broccoli rabe
- ½ tsp. ground nutmeg
- ¼ tsp. pepper, divided
- 2 Tbsp. olive oil
- ¼ lb. diced pancetta or 4 bacon strips, chopped
- 1 large onion, chopped
- 4 garlic cloves, minced
- 2 cartons (32 oz. each) chicken stock
- 1 can (15 oz.) tomato sauce
- 3 fresh thyme sprigs
- 3 Tbsp. minced fresh parsley
- 1 bay leaf
- ¼ cup grated Parmesan cheese
- 1 pkg. (19 oz.) frozen cheese tortellini
- 1 rotisserie chicken, skin removed, shredded
- Additional grated Parmesan cheese

1. Fill a Dutch oven two-thirds full with water; bring to a boil. Cut ½ in. off ends of broccoli rabe; trim woody stems. Coarsely chop stems and leaves; add to the boiling water. Cook, uncovered, just until broccoli rabe is crisp-tender, 1-2 minutes. Drain and remove from pan; sprinkle with the nutmeg and ⅛ tsp. pepper.
2. In same Dutch oven, heat olive oil over medium heat. Add pancetta; cook until brown and crisp, 4-5 minutes. Add onion and remaining pepper; cook until tender, 3-4 minutes. Stir in garlic; cook 1 minute longer. Add the next 6 ingredients and broccoli rabe; bring to a boil. Reduce heat; simmer, covered, 30 minutes. Meanwhile, cook tortellini according to the package directions; drain.
3. Discard bay leaf and thyme sprigs from soup. Add chicken to soup; heat through. To serve, spoon tortellini into individual bowls; pour soup into bowls. Sprinkle with additional Parmesan.

1⅓ CUPS: 328 cal., 13g fat (4g sat. fat), 72mg chol., 1058mg sod., 24g carb. (3g sugars, 3g fiber), 28g pro.

ASIAN CHICKEN CRUNCH WRAPS

My kids love all kinds of wraps and Asian foods. This is an easy go-to in our house that works for everyone.
—Mary Lou Timpson, Colorado City, AZ

TAKES: 25 MIN. • **MAKES:** 4 SERVINGS

- 8 frozen breaded chicken tenders (about 10 oz.)
- 2 cups coleslaw mix
- ½ cup sweet chili sauce
- 2 green onions, chopped
- 2 Tbsp. chopped fresh cilantro
- 1 tsp. soy sauce
- 4 flour tortillas (8 in.), warmed
- ½ cup dry roasted peanuts, chopped

1. Bake chicken tenders according to package directions. Meanwhile, in a large bowl, toss coleslaw mix with chili sauce, green onions, cilantro and soy sauce.
2. Arrange chicken down center of each tortilla; top with coleslaw mixture and peanuts. Fold sides of tortillas over filling and roll up. Cut each diagonally in half.

1 WRAP: 519 cal., 21g fat (3g sat. fat), 13mg chol., 1250mg sod., 66g carb. (19g sugars, 7g fiber), 19g pro.

SWEET & SPICY PEANUT BUTTER-BACON SANDWICHES

I craved peanut butter and bacon toast while pregnant. Then I sampled a friend's peanut butter with chile pepper in it and loved it. The little zip made the sandwich better.
—Carolyn Eskew, Dayton, OH

TAKES: 10 MIN. • **MAKES:** 2 SERVINGS

- ¼ cup peanut butter
- 4 slices cinnamon-raisin bread
- ⅛ tsp. cayenne pepper
- 4 crisp cooked bacon strips
- 2 tsp. honey

Spread peanut butter on 2 bread slices; sprinkle with cayenne. Top with bacon strips and drizzle with honey. Top with remaining bread.

1 SANDWICH: 461 cal., 26g fat (6g sat. fat), 23mg chol., 664mg sod., 43g carb. (15g sugars, 6g fiber), 21g pro.

FAMILY-PLEASING SLOPPY JOE SANDWICHES

My grandchildren love these sandwiches. I like this recipe because it can be made ahead of time and can also be put in the slow cooker. The sandwich meat freezes well, too.
—Patricia Ringle, Edgar, WI

PREP: 10 MIN. • **COOK:** 45 MIN.
MAKES: 8 SERVINGS

- **2 lbs. ground beef**
- **1 large onion, chopped**
- **1¼ cups ketchup**
- **½ cup water**
- **1 Tbsp. brown sugar**
- **1 Tbsp. white vinegar**
- **½ tsp. salt**
- **½ tsp. ground mustard**
- **½ tsp. chili powder**
- **¼ tsp. ground allspice**
- **8 sandwich buns, split**

1. In a Dutch oven, cook beef and onion over medium heat until meat is no longer pink; drain. Stir in the ketchup, water, brown sugar, vinegar, salt, mustard, chili powder and allspice. Bring mixture to a boil. Reduce heat; simmer, uncovered, until heated through, 35-40 minutes.
2. Spoon about ½ cup meat mixture onto each bun.

1 SANDWICH: 441 cal., 15g fat (7g sat. fat), 56mg chol., 1016mg sod., 49g carb. (12g sugars, 3g fiber), 28g pro.

READER REVIEW

"I tried these for something different than my go-to sloppy joe recipe, and they were a hit. The spices are nicely balanced, and there is a slight sweetness from the brown sugar that we all enjoyed."

AMSM, TASTEOFHOME.COM

WHITE BEAN SOUP WITH ESCAROLE

Pantry staples make this healthy soup so simple to prepare. When I can't find escarole, I substitute fresh spinach. Just add to the soup pot moments before serving.
—Gina Samokar, North Haven, CT

PREP: 15 MIN. • **COOK:** 35 MIN.
MAKES: 8 SERVINGS (2 QT.)

- **1 Tbsp. olive oil**
- **1 small onion, chopped**
- **5 garlic cloves, minced**
- **3 cans (14½ oz. each) reduced-sodium chicken broth**
- **1 can (14½ oz.) diced tomatoes, undrained**
- **½ tsp. Italian seasoning**
- **¼ tsp. crushed red pepper flakes**
- **1 cup uncooked whole wheat orzo pasta**
- **1 bunch escarole or spinach, coarsely chopped (about 8 cups)**
- **1 can (15 oz.) cannellini beans, rinsed and drained**
- **¼ cup grated Parmesan cheese**

1. In a Dutch oven, heat oil over medium heat. Add onion and garlic; cook and stir until tender. Add broth, tomatoes, Italian seasoning and pepper flakes; bring to a boil. Reduce heat; simmer, uncovered, 15 minutes.
2. Stir in orzo and escarole. Return to a boil; cook 12-14 minutes or until orzo is tender. Add beans; heat through, stirring occasionally. Sprinkle servings with cheese.

FREEZE OPTION: Freeze cooled soup in freezer containers. To use, partially thaw in refrigerator overnight. Heat through in a saucepan, stirring occasionally; add broth if necessary.

1 CUP SOUP WITH 1½ TSP. CHEESE: 174 cal., 3g fat (1g sat. fat), 2mg chol., 572mg sod., 28g carb. (3g sugars, 8g fiber), 9g pro.
DIABETIC EXCHANGES: 1 starch, 1 vegetable, 1 lean meat, ½ fat.

FIG, CARAMELIZED ONION & GOAT CHEESE PANINI

A taste of this sandwich whisks you to the Italian countryside. It combines sweet honey, dried figs, tangy goat cheese, nutty Asiago and salty prosciutto. We often pack it in our picnic basket for summer or fall outings.
—Maria Brennan, Middlebury, CT

PREP: 1 HOUR • **GRILL:** 5 MIN./BATCH
MAKES: 6 SERVINGS

- **6 Tbsp. butter, divided**
- **3 large onions, halved and thinly sliced**
- **1 Tbsp. sugar**
- **¼ tsp. salt**
- **12 dried figs, sliced**
- **1 cup water**
- **3 Tbsp. honey**
- **12 slices slices Italian bread (½ in. thick)**
- **8 oz. Asiago cheese, sliced**
- **12 thin slices prosciutto**
- **¾ cup crumbled goat cheese**
- **Balsamic glaze, optional**

1. In a large skillet, heat 2 Tbsp. butter over medium heat. Add onions, sugar and salt; cook and stir until softened, about 15 minutes. Reduce heat to medium-low; cook 30-40 minutes or until deep golden brown, stirring occasionally.
2. Meanwhile, place the figs, water and honey in a small saucepan. Bring to a boil; reduce the heat. Simmer, uncovered, for 20 minutes or until the liquid is almost evaporated.
3. Preheat panini maker or indoor electric grill. Layer 6 slices of bread with Asiago cheese, prosciutto, crumbled goat cheese, caramelized onions and figs; top with the remaining bread. Spread the outsides of sandwiches with remaining butter.
4. Cook sandwiches, covered, until the bread is browned and the cheese is melted, 4-5 minutes. If desired, drizzle with balsamic glaze.

1 SANDWICH: 572 cal., 31g fat (18g sat. fat), 108mg chol., 1144mg sod., 52g carb. (25g sugars, 5g fiber), 26g pro.

BERNIE'S PORK CHOP SANDWICHES

My aunt worked in Butte, Montana, and whenever we visited we had pork chop sandwiches. This recipe is a take on that old favorite.
—Jeanette Kotecki, Billings, MT

TAKES: 25 MIN. • **MAKES:** 4 SERVINGS

- **¾ cup cornmeal**
- **1 cup all-purpose flour**
- **½ tsp. onion powder**
- **½ tsp. garlic powder**
- **½ tsp. dry mustard**
- **½ tsp. paprika**
- **1 cup fat-free milk**
- **4 boneless pork loin chops (3 oz. each)**
- **½ tsp. salt**
- **¼ tsp. pepper**
- **2 Tbsp. canola oil**
- **4 whole wheat hamburger buns, split and warmed**
- **Optional: Thinly sliced onion, pickle slices and prepared mustard**

1. Place cornmeal in a shallow bowl. In another bowl, mix flour and spices; add milk, stirring just until dry ingredients are moistened. Pound chops with a meat mallet to ¼-in. thickness; season with salt and pepper.
2. In two batches, heat oil in a large cast-iron or other heavy skillet over medium heat. Lightly coat chops with cornmeal. Dip in batter, allowing excess to drip off; place in skillet. Cook until golden brown, 2-4 minutes per side. Drain on paper towels. Serve in buns, topping with remaining ingredients as desired.

1 SANDWICH: 476 cal., 15g fat (3g sat. fat), 42mg chol., 564mg sod., 60g carb. (6g sugars, 5g fiber), 26g pro.

GARLIC BREAD TUNA MELTS

There's something extra comforting about a tuna melt on a chilly day. Take it up a few notches with garlic, cheese and tomatoes.
—Aimee Bachmann, North Bend, WA

TAKES: 20 MIN. • **MAKES:** 4 SERVINGS

- **¼ cup butter, cubed**
- **3 garlic cloves, minced**
- **4 French rolls or hoagie buns, split**
- **2 cans (one 12 oz., one 5 oz.) albacore white tuna in water, drained and flaked**
- **¼ cup reduced-fat mayonnaise**
- **1¼ tsp. dill weed, divided**
- **8 slices cheddar cheese**
- **8 slices tomato**

1. Preheat broiler. In a microwave, melt butter with garlic. Place rolls on a baking sheet, cut side up; brush with the butter mixture. Broil 2-3 in. from heat until lightly browned, 2-3 minutes.
2. In a small bowl, mix tuna, mayonnaise and 1 tsp. dill. Layer roll bottoms with tuna mixture and cheese. Broil until the cheese is melted, 1-2 minutes longer. Top with tomato; sprinkle with remaining dill. Replace tops; serve immediately.

1 SANDWICH: 704 cal., 41g fat (19g sat. fat), 146mg chol., 1314mg sod., 36g carb. (3g sugars, 2g fiber), 49g pro.

GARLICKY CHEDDAR CHEESE BISQUE

I came up with a cheddar cheese soup some time ago and decided to give it a boost with a variety of root vegetables. Crushed pita chips and fresh parsley make fun garnishes.
—Patricia Harmon, Baden, PA

PREP: 30 MIN. • **COOK:** 40 MIN.
MAKES: 6 SERVINGS

- **1 Tbsp. butter**
- **1 Tbsp. canola oil**
- **1 medium leek (white portion only), sliced**
- **½ cup chopped carrot**
- **½ cup chopped celery**
- **½ cup chopped peeled parsnip**
- **1 tsp. salt**
- **½ tsp. pepper**
- **6 garlic cloves, minced**
- **2 cans (14½ oz. each) chicken broth**
- **⅔ cup dry white wine**
- **2 Tbsp. cornstarch**
- **¼ cup cold water**
- **1 can (12 oz.) evaporated milk**
- **2 cups shredded sharp white cheddar cheese**
- **Crushed baked pita chips**
- **Minced fresh parsley**

1. In a large saucepan, heat butter and oil over medium heat. Add vegetables, salt and pepper; cook and stir 7-8 minutes or until vegetables are crisp-tender. Add garlic; cook 1-2 minutes longer.
2. Stir in broth and wine; bring to a boil. Reduce heat; simmer, uncovered, for 15-20 minutes or until vegetables are tender. Remove from heat; cool slightly. Meanwhile, in a small bowl, mix the cornstarch and water until smooth.
3. Process soup in batches in a food processor until smooth. Return all to pan. Stir in evaporated milk and cornstarch mixture; bring to a boil. Reduce the heat; simmer, uncovered, until thickened and bubbly, stirring frequently. Add cheese; cook and stir until the cheese is blended. Top servings with crushed pita chips and minced fresh parsley.

1 CUP : 320 cal., 19g fat (12g sat. fat), 68mg chol., 1307mg sod., 18g carb. (9g sugars, 1g fiber), 13g pro.

NORTHWEST SALMON CHOWDER

I've lived on a farm in the Yakima Valley all my life. I have a big garden, and by the end of fall, my cellar shelves are full of canned fruits and vegetables. This recipe uses some of the root vegetables I grow—along with the delicious salmon that is so plentiful here.
—Josephine Parton, Granger, WA

PREP: 10 MIN. • **COOK:** 1 HOUR
MAKES: 8 SERVINGS (2 QT.)

- **½ cup each chopped celery, onion and green pepper**
- **1 garlic clove, minced**
- **3 Tbsp. butter**
- **1 can (14½ oz.) chicken broth**
- **1 cup uncooked diced peeled potatoes**
- **1 cup shredded carrots**
- **1½ tsp. salt**
- **½ tsp. pepper**
- **¼ to ¾ tsp. dill weed**
- **1 can (14¾ oz.) cream-style corn**
- **2 cups half-and-half cream**
- **1¾ to 2 cups fully cooked salmon chunks or 1 can (14¾ oz.) salmon, drained, flaked, bones and skin removed**
- **Optional: Crumbled cooked bacon, chives and cracked black pepper**

1. In a large saucepan, saute celery, onion, green pepper and garlic in butter until the vegetables are tender. Add chicken broth, potatoes, carrots, salt, pepper and dill; bring to a boil.
2. Reduce heat; cover and simmer for 40 minutes or until the vegetables are nearly tender. Stir in the corn, cream and salmon. Simmer for 15 minutes or until heated through. If desired, garnish with bacon, chives and cracked black pepper.

1 CUP: 274 cal., 15g fat (8g sat. fat), 84mg chol., 1095mg sod., 18g carb. (5g sugars, 2g fiber), 16g pro.

TEST KITCHEN TIP

Cooked salmon can last in the fridge for 2 to 3 days, but it may expire sooner depending on the freshness of the fish when it was first cooked. Always check for signs of spoilage before serving. If it has a slimy texture, unpleasant odor or milky discoloration it should be tossed.

QUICK SAUSAGE TORTELLINI SOUP

I love that this soup is easy to make and uses common pantry ingredients. You can use other types of sausage or pasta if desired.
—Annalise Lau, Newberg, OR

PREP: 20 MIN. COOK 15 MIN.
MAKES: 8 SERVINGS (3 QT.)

- **3 Italian turkey sausage links, casings removed**
- **1 medium onion, chopped**
- **4 garlic cloves, minced**
- **¼ tsp. crushed red pepper flakes**
- **6 cups reduced-sodium chicken broth**
- **1 jar (24 oz.) pasta sauce**
- **1 can (15 oz.) crushed tomatoes**
- **2 Tbsp. tomato paste**
- **2 tsp. dried basil**
- **2 tsp. balsamic vinegar**
- **1 tsp. dried parsley flakes**
- **1½ tsp. sugar**
- **½ tsp. dried oregano**
- **¼ tsp. salt**
- **½ tsp. pepper**
- **2 cups frozen cheese tortellini**
- **Shredded Parmesan cheese, optional**

1. In a Dutch oven, cook the sausage and onion over medium heat 5-7 minutes or until the sausage is no longer pink and onion is tender, breaking up sausage into crumbles; drain. Add garlic and pepper flakes; cook 1 minute longer. Stir in the broth, pasta sauce, crushed tomatoes, tomato paste, basil, vinegar, parsley flakes, sugar, oregano, salt and pepper; bring to a boil.
2. Add tortellini; cook, uncovered, until tortellini are tender, 3-5 minutes, stirring occasionally. Serve soup immediately. If desired, top with cheese.

1½ CUPS: 192 cal., 5g fat (1g sat. fat), 24mg chol., 1167mg sod., 26g carb. (12g sugars, 4g fiber), 12g pro.

BLAIR LONERGAN
Rochelle, VA

GREEK GRILLED CHICKEN PITAS

I switched up my mom's recipe to create this tasty pita pocket variation. It's delicious and perfect for warm days. The creamy cucumber sauce goes great with fresh, crunchy veggies.
—Blair Lonergan, Rochelle, VA

PREP: 20 MIN. + MARINATING
GRILL: 10 MIN.
MAKES: 4 SERVINGS

- **1 lb. boneless skinless chicken breast halves**
- **½ cup balsamic vinaigrette**

CUCUMBER SAUCE

- **1 cup plain Greek yogurt**
- **½ cup finely chopped cucumber**
- **¼ cup finely chopped red onion**
- **1 Tbsp. minced fresh parsley**
- **1 Tbsp. lime juice**
- **1 garlic clove, minced**
- **¼ tsp. salt**
- **⅛ tsp. pepper**

PITAS

- **8 pita pocket halves**
- **½ cup sliced cucumber**
- **½ cup grape tomatoes, chopped**
- **½ cup sliced red onion**
- **½ cup crumbled feta cheese**

1. Marinate the chicken in the balsamic vinaigrette, covered, in refrigerator for at least 4 hours or overnight. In a small bowl, combine the sauce ingredients; chill the sauce until serving.
2. Drain and discard the marinade. On a lightly oiled grill rack, grill the chicken, covered, over medium heat or broil 4 in. from the heat until a thermometer reads 165°, 4-7 minutes on each side.
3. Cut chicken into strips. Fill each pita half with chicken, cucumber, tomatoes, onion and cheese; drizzle with sauce.

2 FILLED PITA HALVES: 428 cal., 14g fat (6g sat. fat), 85mg chol., 801mg sod., 41g carb. (7g sugars, 3g fiber), 33g pro.

GRILLED HUMMUS TURKEY SANDWICH

I created this toasted sandwich last summer using homemade hummus and veggies from our garden. We can't get enough!
—Gunjan Gilbert, Franklin, ME

TAKES: 15 MIN. • **MAKES:** 2 SERVINGS

- ½ cup hummus
- 4 slices whole wheat bread
- 4 oz. thinly sliced deli turkey
- 4 slices tomato
- 2 slices pepper jack cheese
- 4 tsp. butter, softened

1. Spread hummus on 2 bread slices; top with turkey, tomato, cheese and remaining bread. Spread outsides of the sandwiches with butter.
2. In a large skillet, toast sandwiches over medium heat until golden brown and the cheese is melted, 2-3 minutes per side.

HEALTH TIP: Cut saturated fat in half by omitting the butter and browning the sandwiches in nonstick cooking spray instead.

1 SANDWICH: 458 cal., 23g fat (10g sat. fat), 63mg chol., 1183mg sod., 36g carb. (3g sugars, 7g fiber), 28g pro.

BEST EVER POTATO SOUP

You'll be surprised at the taste of this rich, cheesy concoction—it's not a typical potato soup. I came up with the recipe after enjoying baked potato soup at one of our favorite restaurants. I added bacon, and we think that makes it even better.
—Coleen Morrissey, Sweet Valley, PA

TAKES: 30 MIN. • **MAKES:** 8 SERVINGS (2 QT.)

- 6 bacon strips, diced
- 3 cups cubed peeled potatoes
- 1 small carrot, grated
- ½ cup chopped onion
- 1 Tbsp. dried parsley flakes
- ½ tsp. salt
- ½ tsp. pepper
- ½ tsp. celery seed
- 1 can (14½ oz.) chicken broth
- 3 Tbsp. all-purpose flour
- 3 cups 2% milk
- 8 oz. Velveeta, cubed
- 2 green onions, thinly sliced, optional

1. In a large saucepan, cook the bacon over medium heat until crisp, stirring occasionally; drain the drippings. Add vegetables, seasonings and broth; bring to a boil. Reduce heat; simmer, covered, until potatoes are tender, 10-15 minutes.
2. Mix flour and milk until smooth; stir into soup. Bring to a boil, stirring constantly; cook and stir until thickened, about 2 minutes. Stir in cheese until melted. If desired, serve with green onions.

1 CUP: 250 cal., 13g fat (7g sat. fat), 35mg chol., 823mg sod., 22g carb. (8g sugars, 2g fiber), 12g pro.

TEST KITCHEN TIP

If you prefer a thicker soup, you can add an another tablespoon of flour, or substitute some of the 2% milk for whole or heavy cream.

COBB SALAD WRAPS

A homemade dressing lightens up these refreshing tortilla wraps. The avocado, bacon, blue cheese and tomato deliver the flavors I enjoy most while keeping me on track with my healthy eating plan.
—Lynne Van Wagenen, Salt Lake City, UT

TAKES: 15 MIN. • **MAKES:** 4 SERVINGS

- 2 **cups cubed cooked chicken breast**
- ½ **cup chopped avocado**
- 4 **bacon strips, cooked and crumbled**
- 1 **celery rib, thinly sliced**
- 1 **green onion, sliced**
- 2 **Tbsp. chopped ripe olives**
- 2 **Tbsp. crumbled blue cheese**
- 2 **Tbsp. lemon juice**
- 1 **Tbsp. honey**
- 1½ **tsp. Dijon mustard**
- 1 **garlic clove, minced**
- ¼ **tsp. dill weed**
- ¼ **tsp. salt**
- ⅛ **tsp. pepper**
- 1 **Tbsp. olive oil**
- 4 **romaine leaves, torn**
- 4 **whole wheat tortillas (8 in.), warmed**
- 1 **medium tomato, chopped**

1. In a small bowl, combine chicken, avocado, bacon, celery, onion, olives and cheese. In another small bowl, combine lemon juice, honey, mustard, garlic, dill weed, salt and pepper. Whisk in oil. Pour over the chicken mixture; toss to coat.
2. Place romaine on each tortilla; top with ⅔ cup chicken mixture. Sprinkle with tomato; roll up.

1 WRAP: 372 cal., 14g fat (3g sat. fat), 65mg chol., 607mg sod., 32g carb. (6g sugars, 6g fiber), 29g pro. **DIABETIC EXCHANGES:** 3 lean meat, 2 starch, 1 fat.

LIMA BEAN SOUP

A yearly Lima Bean Festival in nearby West Cape May honors the many growers in the region and showcases different recipes using their crops. This comforting chowder was a contest winner several years ago.
—Kathleen Olsack, North Cape May, NJ

PREP: 10 MIN. • **COOK:** 30 MIN.
MAKES: 12 SERVINGS (3 QT.)

- 3 **cans (14½ oz. each) chicken broth**
- 2 **cans (15¼ oz. each) lima beans, rinsed and drained**
- 3 **medium carrots, thinly sliced**
- 2 **medium potatoes, peeled and diced**
- 2 **small sweet red peppers, chopped**
- 2 **small onions, chopped**
- 2 **celery ribs, thinly sliced**
- ¼ **cup butter**
- 1½ **tsp. dried marjoram**
- ½ **tsp. salt**
- ½ **tsp. pepper**
- ½ **tsp. dried oregano**
- 1 **cup half-and-half cream**
- 3 **bacon strips, cooked and crumbled**

1. In a Dutch oven or soup kettle, combine the first 12 ingredients; bring to a boil over medium heat. Reduce the heat; cover and simmer for 25-35 minutes or until the vegetables are tender.
2. Add cream; heat through but do not boil. Sprinkle with bacon just before serving.

1 CUP: 110 cal., 7g fat (4g sat. fat), 22mg chol., 431mg sod., 9g carb. (3g sugars, 2g fiber), 3g pro.

AIR-FRYER CHICKEN TACO POCKETS

We love these easy taco-flavored sandwiches made with crescent dough. They make a quick and easy lunch or supper with a bowl of soup or a crisp salad. I also like to cut them into smaller servings for parties.
—Donna Gribbins, Shelbyville, KY

TAKES: 25 MIN. • **MAKES:** 8 SERVINGS

- **2 tubes (8 oz. each) refrigerated crescent rolls**
- **½ cup salsa, plus more for serving**
- **½ cup sour cream**
- **2 Tbsp. taco seasoning**
- **1 cup shredded rotisserie chicken**
- **1 cup shredded cheddar cheese**
- **Optional: Shredded lettuce, guacamole and additional sour cream**

1. Preheat air fryer to 375°. Unroll 1 tube of crescent dough and separate into 2 rectangles; press perforations to seal. Repeat with second tube. In a bowl, combine salsa, sour cream and taco seasoning. Spoon chicken onto the left side of each rectangle; top with salsa mixture. Sprinkle with cheese. Fold dough over filling; pinch edges to seal.
2. In batches if necessary, place pockets on tray in air-fryer basket. Cook until golden brown, 13-15 minutes. Cut in half. Serve with salsa and desired toppings.

½ POCKET: 393 cal., 24g fat (7g sat. fat), 47mg chol., 896mg sod., 29g carb. (7g sugars, 0 fiber), 16g pro.

TEST KITCHEN TIP

Take extra care when pressing the crescent dough to seal the perforations. Patch any thin spots to prevent the filling from leaking while they bake in the air fryer.

CAJUN CHICKEN & RICE SOUP

We enjoy this comforting and spicy soup frequently in our household. It's good served with hot cornbread.
—Lisa Hammond, Higginsville, MO

PREP: 20 MIN. • **COOK:** 2 HOURS
MAKES: 8 SERVINGS (3 QT.)

- **1 stewing chicken (about 6 lbs.)**
- **2 bay leaves**
- **1 tsp. salt**
- **1 tsp. poultry seasoning**
- **1 tsp. pepper**
- **1 medium onion, chopped**
- **2 celery ribs, chopped**
- **1 Tbsp. butter**
- **12 garlic cloves, minced**
- **1 can (10 oz.) diced tomatoes and green chiles, drained**
- **¾ cup orange juice**
- **2 Tbsp. minced fresh cilantro**
- **2 tsp. Cajun seasoning**
- **1 tsp. dried oregano**
- **½ tsp. dried thyme**
- **½ tsp. ground cumin**
- **½ tsp. paprika**
- **2 cups cooked rice**
- **1 can (15 oz.) pinto beans, rinsed and drained**

1. Place chicken in a large stockpot; cover with water. Add bay leaves, salt, poultry seasoning and pepper. Bring to a boil. Reduce the heat; cover and simmer for 1½ hours or until chicken is tender.
2. Remove chicken from broth; set aside to cool. Strain broth, discarding seasonings. Set aside 6 cups broth for the soup; save remaining broth for another use. Skim fat from the soup broth. When cool enough to handle, remove the chicken from bones; discard bones. Shred and set aside 3 cups chicken (save the remaining chicken for another use).
3. In a large stockpot, saute the onion and celery in butter until onion is crisp-tender. Add the garlic; cook 1 minute longer. Stir in the tomatoes, orange juice, cilantro, seasonings and reserved broth. Bring to a boil. Reduce heat; cover and simmer for 15 minutes or until vegetables are tender. Stir in the rice, beans and reserved chicken; heat through.

1½ CUPS: 245 cal., 6g fat (2g sat. fat), 50mg chol., 709mg sod., 27g carb. (4g sugars, 4g fiber), 20g pro. **DIABETIC EXCHANGES:** 2 lean meat, 1½ starch, 1 vegetable.

CHEESY CREAM OF ASPARAGUS SOUP

Kids may not want to try a vegetable soup, but once they spoon up a mouthful of this cheesy variety, the flavor will keep them coming back for more.
—Muriel Lerdal, Humboldt, IA

TAKES: 25 MIN. • **MAKES:** 6 SERVINGS

- **2 pkg. (12 oz. each) frozen cut asparagus**
- **¼ cup butter**
- **2 Tbsp. all-purpose flour**
- **4 cups whole milk**
- **1 cup shredded Monterey Jack cheese**
- **4 to 5 drops hot pepper sauce**
- **1½ tsp. salt**
- **¾ to 1 tsp. pepper**
- **Roasted asparagus tips, optional**

1. Prepare the asparagus according to the package directions; drain and set aside. In a large saucepan, melt butter. Stir in flour until smooth; gradually add milk. Bring to a boil; cook and stir until thickened, about 2 minutes. Cool slightly.
2. Pour half of the milk mixture into a blender; add half the asparagus. Cover and process until very smooth; return soup to the saucepan. Repeat with the remaining milk mixture and asparagus. Stir in the cheese, hot pepper sauce, salt and pepper; heat through (do not boil). If desired, top with roasted asparagus tips.

¾ CUP: 261 cal., 19g fat (12g sat. fat), 59mg chol., 852mg sod., 12g carb. (9g sugars, 1g fiber), 12g pro.

1. In a large saucepan, combine the first 6 ingredients. Bring to a boil. Reduce heat; cover and simmer for 12-14 minutes or until vegetables are tender.
2. Meanwhile, in another saucepan, melt butter. Stir in flour and nutmeg until smooth. Gradually add milk. Bring to a boil; cook and stir for 2 minutes or until thickened. Stir into vegetable mixture; heat through. Sprinkle with cheese.

1 CUP: 200 cal., 11g fat (7g sat. fat), 36mg chol., 561mg sod., 19g carb. (5g sugars, 2g fiber), 7g pro.

SPICY FAJITA CHILI

Serve this with rolls or cornbread to soak up every delicious drop. Like more heat? Just use spicier versions of V8 juice and chili beans.

—Cathy Bell, Joplin, MO

PREP: 15 MIN. • **COOK:** 30 MIN.
MAKES: 8 SERVINGS (2 QT.)

- **1½ lbs. ground pork**
- **1 medium onion, chopped**
- **1 medium green pepper, chopped**
- **1 medium sweet red pepper, chopped**
- **1 garlic clove, minced**
- **2 cans (11½ oz. each) V8 juice**
- **1 can (16 oz.) chili beans, undrained**
- **1 can (10 oz.) diced tomatoes and green chiles**
- **2 Tbsp. chili powder**
- **1 tsp. seasoned salt**
- **½ tsp. seasoned pepper**
- **Shredded cheddar cheese**

1. In a Dutch oven, cook the pork, onion and peppers over medium heat until the meat is no longer pink. Add the garlic; cook 1 minute longer. Drain.
2. Stir in the V8 juice, beans, tomatoes, chili powder, seasoned salt and seasoned pepper. Bring to a boil. Reduce the heat; simmer, uncovered, for 20 minutes or until slightly thickened. Top with cheese.

FREEZE OPTION: Freeze cooled chili in freezer containers. To use, partially thaw in refrigerator overnight. Heat through in a saucepan, stirring occasionally; add broth if necessary.

1 CUP: 273 cal., 13g fat (5g sat. fat), 57mg chol., 782mg sod., 20g carb. (6g sugars, 6g fiber), 20g pro.

DILLY CHICKEN SANDWICHES

A creamy lemon-dill spread adds summery flavor to tender chicken and tomato layered between slices of grilled French bread. Serve it for lunch, or for a light and breezy dinner on the patio.

—Orien Major, Hinton, AB

TAKES: 30 MIN. • **MAKES:** 4 SERVINGS

- **4 boneless skinless chicken breast halves (4 oz. each)**
- **6 Tbsp. butter, divided**
- **1 garlic clove, minced**
- **¾ tsp. dill weed, divided**
- **8 slices French bread (½ in. thick)**
- **¼ cup cream cheese, softened**
- **2 tsp. lemon juice**
- **4 lettuce leaves**
- **8 slices tomato**

1. Flatten chicken to ¼-in. thickness; set aside. In a large skillet, saute garlic and ¼ tsp. dill in 3 Tbsp. butter for 1 minute. Add chicken; cook over medium heat until juices run clear, 3-4 minutes on each side. Remove and keep warm.
2. Spread both sides of bread with remaining butter. In a large skillet or griddle, grill bread on both sides until golden brown.
3. Meanwhile in a small bowl, combine the cream cheese, lemon juice and remaining ½ tsp. dill; spread on 1 side of the grilled bread. Place lettuce leaves, chicken and tomato on 4 slices of bread; top with the remaining bread.

1 SANDWICH: 490 cal., 27g fat (15g sat. fat), 123mg chol., 591mg sod., 32g carb. (2g sugars, 2g fiber), 30g pro.

BROCCOLI CHOWDER

I serve this comforting soup on cold evenings. Nutmeg seasons the light, creamy broth that's full of tender broccoli and diced potatoes.

—Sue Call, Beech Grove, IN

TAKES: 30 MIN.
MAKES: 6 SERVINGS

- **3 cups fresh broccoli florets**
- **2 cups diced peeled potatoes**
- **2 cups water**
- **⅓ cup sliced green onions**
- **1 tsp. salt**
- **½ tsp. pepper**
- **3 Tbsp. butter**
- **3 Tbsp. all-purpose flour**
- **⅛ tsp. ground nutmeg**
- **2 cups whole milk**
- **½ cup shredded cheddar cheese**

ITALIAN BEEF ON ROLLS

Here's one of my favorite slow-cooker recipes. With 29 grams of protein per serving, it's sure to keep you full and satisfied!
—Jami Hilker, Harrison, AR

PREP: 15 MIN. • **COOK:** 8 HOURS
MAKES: 8 SERVINGS

- **1 beef sirloin tip roast (2 lbs.)**
- **1 can (14½ oz.) diced tomatoes, undrained**
- **1 medium green pepper, chopped**
- **½ cup water**
- **1 Tbsp. sesame seeds**
- **1½ tsp. garlic powder**
- **1 tsp. fennel seed, crushed**
- **½ tsp. salt**
- **½ tsp. pepper**
- **8 kaiser rolls, split**

1. Place the roast in a 3-qt. slow cooker. In a small bowl, combine the tomatoes, green pepper, water and seasonings; pour over roast. Cover and cook on low for 8-9 hours or until meat is tender.
2. Remove roast; cool slightly. Skim fat from cooking juices; shred the beef and return to the slow cooker. Serve on rolls.

1 SANDWICH: 333 cal., 8g fat (2g sat. fat), 72mg chol., 573mg sod., 34g carb. (3g sugars, 3g fiber), 29g pro. **DIABETIC EXCHANGES:** 3 lean meat, 2 starch.

BRIE MUSHROOM SOUP

Simmer up the earthy flavor of mushrooms and the richness of Brie cheese in one creamy, delicious soup. I serve my family big bowlfuls on chilly days.
—Maria Emmerich, River Falls, WI

PREP: 15 MIN. • **COOK:** 20 MIN.
MAKES: 4 SERVINGS

- **¼ cup butter, cubed**
- **1 lb. sliced fresh mushrooms**
- **2 large onions, chopped**
- **1 can (14½ oz.) chicken broth**
- **1 Tbsp. paprika**
- **1 Tbsp. reduced-sodium soy sauce**
- **2 tsp. dill weed**
- **3 Tbsp. all-purpose flour**
- **1 cup 2% milk**
- **4 oz. Brie cheese, rind removed, cubed**
- **¼ cup minced fresh parsley**
- **2 tsp. lemon juice**
- **½ tsp. salt**
- **¼ tsp. pepper**

1. In a Dutch oven, heat the butter over medium-high heat. Add mushrooms and onions; cook and stir until tender. Stir in broth, paprika, soy sauce and dill. Bring to a boil. Reduce heat; simmer, covered, 5 minutes.
2. In a small bowl, whisk flour and milk until smooth. Stir into mushroom mixture. Bring to a boil; cook and stir until soup is thickened, 1-2 minutes. Reduce heat; add remaining ingredients. Cook and stir until cheese is melted (do not boil).

1¼ CUPS: 328 cal., 22g fat (14g sat. fat), 67mg chol., 1192mg sod., 21g carb. (9g sugars, 3g fiber), 14g pro.

CHEDDAR HAM SOUP

I knew this recipe was a keeper when my mother-in-law asked for it! The filling soup—chock-full of leftover ham, veggies and cheese—is creamy and comforting. Although the recipe makes enough to feed a crowd, don't expect leftovers!
—Marty Matthews, Clarksville, TN

TAKES: 30 MIN.
MAKES: 7 SERVINGS

- **2 cups diced peeled potatoes**
- **2 cups water**
- **½ cup sliced carrot**
- **¼ cup chopped onion**
- **¼ cup butter, cubed**
- **¼ cup all-purpose flour**
- **2 cups 2% milk**
- **¼ to ½ tsp. salt**
- **¼ tsp. pepper**
- **2 cups shredded cheddar cheese**
- **1½ cups cubed fully cooked ham**
- **1 cup frozen peas**

1. In a large saucepan, combine potatoes, water, carrot and onion. Bring to a boil. Reduce heat; cover and cook until tender, 10-15 minutes.
2. Meanwhile, in another saucepan, melt butter. Stir in flour until smooth. Gradually add the milk, salt and pepper. Bring to a boil; cook and stir until thickened, about 2 minutes. Stir in cheese until melted. Stir into undrained potato mixture. Add ham and peas; heat through.

1 CUP: 331 cal., 20g fat (12g sat. fat), 73mg chol., 772mg sod., 19g carb. (5g sugars, 2g fiber), 19g pro.

GOUDA TURKEY CLUB

With this recipe, two can enjoy the taste of something new and elegant in minutes. All you need to add is the ambiance for a bistro meal at home.
—Karen Harris, Littleton, CO

TAKES: 15 MIN. • **MAKES:** 2 SERVINGS

- **½ cup shredded smoked Gouda cheese**
- **4 tsp. mayonnaise**
- **1 Tbsp. thinly sliced green onion**
- **¼ tsp. garlic powder**
- **¼ tsp. coarsely ground pepper**
- **4 slices whole wheat bread, toasted**
- **2 tsp. butter, softened**
- **Romaine leaves**
- **4 slices tomato**
- **4 oz. sliced deli smoked turkey**
- **½ medium ripe avocado**

1. Mix the first 5 ingredients. Spread 2 slices of toast with butter, then with cheese mixture. Layer with lettuce, tomato and turkey.
2. Peel and mash avocado. Spread over the remaining slices of toast and place over turkey.

1 SANDWICH: 464 cal., 27g fat (10g sat. fat), 63mg chol., 995mg sod., 30g carb. (4g sugars, 6g fiber), 27g pro.

CRANBERRY-WALNUT CHICKEN SALAD SANDWICHES

I made these simple, yet special, sandwiches for a birthday party. Tangy cranberries and crunchy celery pep up the chicken. Leftover turkey works well, too.
—Shannon Tucker, Land O' Lakes, FL

TAKES: 15 MIN. • **MAKES:** 8 SERVINGS

- **½ cup mayonnaise**
- **2 Tbsp. honey Dijon mustard**
- **¼ tsp. pepper**
- **2 cups cubed rotisserie chicken**
- **1 cup shredded Swiss cheese**
- **½ cup chopped celery**
- **½ cup dried cranberries**
- **¼ cup chopped walnuts**
- **½ tsp. dried parsley flakes**
- **8 lettuce leaves**
- **16 slices pumpernickel bread**

1. In a large bowl, combine mayonnaise, mustard and pepper. Stir in the chicken, cheese, celery, dried cranberries, walnuts and parsley.
2. Place lettuce on 8 slices of bread; top each with ½ cup chicken salad. Top with remaining bread.

1 SANDWICH: 411 cal., 22g fat (5g sat. fat), 49mg chol., 469mg sod., 35g carb. (7g sugars, 5g fiber), 20g pro.

CREAMY CHICKEN RICE SOUP

I came up with this flavorful soup while making some adjustments to a favorite stovetop chicken casserole. We like this dish for lunch with a crisp roll and fresh fruit.
—Janice Mitchell, Aurora, CO

TAKES: 30 MIN.
MAKES: 4 SERVINGS

- **1 Tbsp. canola oil**
- **1 medium carrot, chopped**
- **1 celery rib, chopped**
- **½ cup chopped onion**
- **½ tsp. minced garlic**
- **⅓ cup uncooked long grain rice**
- **¾ tsp. dried basil**
- **¼ tsp. pepper**
- **2 cans (14½ oz. each) reduced-sodium chicken broth**
- **3 Tbsp. all-purpose flour**
- **1 can (5 oz.) evaporated milk**
- **2 cups cubed cooked chicken breast**

1. In a large saucepan, heat the oil over medium-high heat; saute carrot, celery and onion until tender. Add garlic; cook and stir 1 minute. Stir in rice, seasonings and broth; bring to a boil. Reduce heat; simmer, covered, until rice is tender, about 15 minutes.
2. Mix flour and milk until smooth; stir into soup. Bring to a boil; cook and stir until thickened, about 2 minutes. Stir in the chicken; heat through.

1¼ CUPS: 312 cal., 9g fat (3g sat. fat), 71mg chol., 699mg sod., 26g carb. (6g sugars, 1g fiber), 29g pro. **DIABETIC EXCHANGES:** 3 lean meat, 2 starch, 1 fat.

CURRIED BEEF PITA POCKETS

Anyone unsure about curry will be a curry lover forever after trying one of these!
—Mary Ann Kosmas, Minneapolis, MN

PREP: 5 MIN. • **COOK:** 30 MIN.
MAKES: 4 SERVINGS

- **1 lb. ground beef**
- **1 medium onion, chopped**
- **1 garlic clove, halved**
- **1 Tbsp. curry powder**
- **½ cup water**
- **½ tsp. salt**
- **½ tsp. sugar**
- **¼ tsp. pepper**
- **1 medium tomato, seeded and diced**
- **1 medium zucchini, diced**
- **8 pita pocket halves**
- **Refrigerated tzatziki sauce, optional**

1. In a large cast-iron or other heavy skillet, brown ground beef with the onion, garlic and curry; drain, discarding garlic. Stir in water, salt, sugar and pepper. Cover and simmer 15 minutes.
2. Add tomato and zucchini; cook just until heated through. Spoon meat mixture into pita breads. If desired, serve pita pockets with tzatziki sauce.

HEALTH TIP: A simple switch to 90% lean ground beef would save 4 grams of fat per serving; use 95% lean to save 8 grams of fat per serving.

2 FILLED PITA HALVES: 393 cal., 14g fat (5g sat. fat), 70mg chol., 665mg sod., 38g carb. (4g sugars, 3g fiber), 27g pro.

DID YOU KNOW?

Curry powder is typically a blend with a base of turmeric (a yellow spice from the ginger family) that includes a mix of spices such as cloves, cardamom, ginger, chili powder, nutmeg, fennel, caraway, ajowan seeds, dried basil, mustard seeds, mace, poppy seeds, sesame seeds, saffron and cinnamon.

1) AIR-FRIED BACON CHEESEBURGERS

This juicy burger only takes minutes to cook in your air fryer. I top it with crispy bacon and my special fry sauce.
—Elisabeth Larsen, Pleasant Grove, UT

PREP: 25 MIN. • **COOK:** 10 MIN.
MAKES: 4 SERVINGS

1 tsp. Worcestershire sauce
1 garlic clove, minced
½ tsp. seasoned salt
¼ tsp. pepper
1 lb. ground beef
4 slices sharp cheddar cheese
¼ cup mayonnaise
2 Tbsp. ketchup
1 Tbsp. cider vinegar
1 Tbsp. honey
4 hamburger buns, split and toasted
8 cooked bacon strips
½ cup french-fried onions
Optional: Lettuce leaves and sliced tomato

1. Preheat air fryer to 350°. In a large bowl, combine Worcestershire sauce, garlic, seasoned salt and pepper. Add beef; mix lightly but thoroughly. Shape into four ½-in.-thick patties.
2. In batches, place burgers in a single layer on tray in air-fryer basket. Cook until a thermometer reads 160°, 8-10 minutes, turning halfway through cooking. Remove burgers from basket. Top with cheese; cover until cheese is melted, 1-2 minutes.
3. Meanwhile, in a small bowl, combine mayonnaise, ketchup, vinegar and honey; spread over cut sides of buns. Top bun bottoms with bacon, burgers, french-fried onions and, if desired, lettuce and tomato. Replace tops.

1 BURGER: 708 cal., 46g fat (16g sat. fat), 124mg chol., 1277mg sod., 33g carb. (10g sugars, 1g fiber), 39g pro.

2) EASY GRILLED HAMBURGERS

These easy hamburgers come together in a snap. Grill and then add your favorite toppings.
—James Schend, Pleasant Prairie, WI

TAKES: 30 MIN. • **MAKES:** 4 SERVINGS

1⅓ lbs. ground beef
¾ tsp. salt
¼ tsp. pepper
4 hamburger buns, split and toasted
Optional toppings: Lettuce leaves, sliced tomato, sliced onion, bacon and mayonnaise

1. Shape ground beef into four ¾-in.-thick patties. Just before grilling, sprinkle with salt and pepper. Grill burgers, covered, over medium heat until a thermometer reads 160°, 5-7 minutes on each side. Top bun bottoms with burgers. If desired, serve with lettuce, tomato, onion, bacon and mayonnaise.

1 BURGER: 265 cal., 13g fat (5g sat. fat), 62mg chol., 495mg sod., 15g carb. (2g sugars, 1g fiber), 21g pro.

3) PAN-FRIED PESTO HAMBURGERS

Give basic burgers an Italian twist by topping them with pesto, roasted red peppers strips and mozzarella cheese.
—*Taste of Home* Test Kitchen

TAKES: 20 MIN. • **MAKES:** 4 SERVINGS

- **1½ lbs. ground beef**
- **⅛ tsp. salt**
- **⅛ tsp. pepper**
- **4 slices part-skim mozzarella cheese**
- **½ cup prepared pesto**
- **⅓ cup roasted sweet red pepper strips**
- **4 hamburger buns, split and toasted**

1. Shape beef into four ¾-in.-thick patties. Season with salt and pepper. In a large skillet, cook patties over medium heat until the meat is no longer pink, about 5 minutes on each side.
2. Top each burger with a slice of cheese, 2 Tbsp. pesto and pepper strips. Reduce heat; cover and simmer until cheese is melted, about 2 minutes. Serve on buns.

1 BURGER: 716 cal., 45g fat (17g sat. fat), 161mg chol., 779mg sod., 25g carb. (3g sugars, 2g fiber), 51g pro.

4) BAKED HAMBURGERS

Baking hamburgers in the oven makes them different from typical grilled versions. These are hearty and moist, and the onion gives them a special flavor. The sweet sauce further enhances their taste. Serve them on buns with your favorite toppings or as a breadless patty with veggies on the side.
—Marg Bisgrove, Widewater, AB

PREP: 10 MIN. • **BAKE:** 35 MIN.
MAKES: 2 SERVINGS

- **1 small onion, chopped**
- **¼ cup dry bread crumbs**
- **2 Tbsp. 2% milk**
- **¾ tsp. salt, divided**
- **¼ tsp. pepper**
- **½ lb. ground beef**
- **⅓ cup water**
- **2 Tbsp. brown sugar**
- **2 Tbsp. ketchup**
- **½ tsp. ground mustard**
- **½ tsp. white vinegar**
- **2 hamburger buns, optional**
- **Sliced red onion, optional**

1. In a small bowl, combine the onion, bread crumbs, milk, ½ tsp. salt and pepper. Crumble beef over mixture and mix lightly but thoroughly. Shape into 2 patties. Place in a greased 11x7-in. baking dish.
2. Combine water, brown sugar, ketchup, mustard, vinegar and remaining salt; pour over patties.
3. Bake, uncovered, at 350° until a thermometer reads 160°, 35-40 minutes. If desired, serve on buns with red onion.

1 BURGER: 363 cal., 15g fat (6g sat. fat), 77mg chol., 1240mg sod., 30g carb. (20g sugars, 1g fiber), 25g pro.

Sides, Salads & More

The perfect menu isn't complete without fresh and delicious side dishes to complement the main course. From picnic pleasers to speedy weeknight favorites, find the best sides, salads, condiments and more.

NOREEN McCORMICK DANEK
Cromwell, CT

BACON AVOCADO SALAD

Everyone in my family loves this bacon and avocado salad—even the younger kids! I serve it at every get-together I've hosted, and at this point, the recipe's been shared too many times to count.

—Noreen McCormick Danek, Cromwell, CT

TAKES: 25 MIN. • **MAKES:** 10 SERVINGS

¾ cup extra virgin olive oil
¼ cup red wine vinegar
4 tsp. sugar
2 garlic cloves, minced
1 tsp. salt
1 tsp. Dijon mustard

SALAD

1 bunch romaine, chopped (about 12 cups)
¾ lb. bacon strips, cooked and crumbled
3 medium tomatoes, chopped
1 medium red onion, halved and thinly sliced
3 medium ripe avocados, peeled and cubed
2 Tbsp. lemon juice
1 cup crumbled Gorgonzola or feta cheese

1. Place first 6 ingredients in a jar with a tight-fitting lid; shake well until blended. Refrigerate until serving.

2. In a large bowl, combine romaine, bacon, tomatoes and onion. Toss the avocados with lemon juice and add to salad. Sprinkle with cheese. Serve with dressing, shaking the jar to blend again if needed.

1⅓ CUPS: 339 cal., 31g fat (7g sat. fat), 22mg chol., 626mg sod., 10g carb. (4g sugars, 5g fiber), 9g pro.

READER REVIEW

"This is such a great salad. It's quick and easy to make, and definitely isn't lacking on flavor. My boyfriend, who doesn't usually like salads, took a second helping. We'll be making this again."

REBECCA719, TASTEOFHOME.COM

CASHEW-PEAR TOSSED SALAD

A friend who does a lot of catering fixed this salad for our staff Christmas party several years ago, and we all asked for the recipe. The unexpected sweet-salty mix and lovely dressing make it a standout.
—Arlene Muller, Kingwood, TX

TAKES: 15 MIN. • **MAKES:** 15 SERVINGS

- **1 bunch romaine, torn**
- **1 cup shredded Swiss cheese**
- **1 cup salted cashews**
- **1 medium pear, thinly sliced**
- **½ cup dried cranberries**

POPPY SEED VINAIGRETTE

- **⅔ cup olive oil**
- **½ cup sugar**
- **⅓ cup lemon juice**
- **2 to 3 tsp. poppy seeds**
- **2 tsp. finely chopped red onion**
- **1 tsp. prepared mustard**
- **½ tsp. salt**

In a large salad bowl, combine the romaine, cheese, cashews, pear and cranberries. In a small bowl, whisk the vinaigrette ingredients. Drizzle over salad and toss to coat.

1 CUP: 228 cal., 17g fat (4g sat. fat), 7mg chol., 171mg sod., 16g carb. (12g sugars, 1g fiber), 4g pro.

JALAPENO POPPER CORN SALAD

I created this recipe for a wedding I was catering, and it's a good thing I made buckets of it, because I couldn't stop eating it! This chilled creamy salad combines all the best flavors of jalapeno poppers with the delicate sweetness of fresh corn.
—Amanda Miller, Hutchinson, KS

PREP: 25 MIN. • **COOK:** 15 MIN. + COOLING
MAKES: 8 SERVINGS

- **1 medium onion, quartered**
- **2 jalapeno peppers**
- **1 cup sour cream**
- **1 cup mayonnaise**
- **2 oz. cream cheese, softened**
- **2 tsp. ground cumin**
- **1 tsp. garlic powder**
- **1 tsp. chili powder**
- **1 tsp. smoked paprika**
- **¼ tsp. salt**
- **¼ tsp. pepper**
- **4 cups fresh corn (about 8 ears), cooked and cooled**
- **1 cup shredded sharp cheddar cheese**
- **1 cup shredded pepper jack cheese**
- **½ cup crumbled cooked bacon, divided**

1. Grill the onion and jalapenos, covered, over medium-high heat or broil 4 in. from heat 3-5 minutes on each side or until lightly charred. Cool completely; chop into ½-in. pieces.
2. Combine the next 9 ingredients. Stir in corn, cheeses, half the bacon, and the grilled vegetables. Top with remaining bacon to serve.

¾ CUP: 476 cal., 40g fat (14g sat. fat), 47mg chol., 616mg sod., 18g carb. (7g sugars, 2g fiber), 14g pro.

GARLIC CREAM SAUCE

This creamy, rich, easy Alfredo sauce is a family favorite and a top request at all our gatherings. My brother-in-law even ate it for breakfast when I visited his family last year. You may like your sauce with more or less garlic; don't be afraid to alter the recipe to suit your taste.
—Joy McQuaid, Darlington, WI

TAKES: 20 MIN. • **MAKES:** 6 SERVINGS

¼ cup butter, cubed
4 garlic cloves, minced
4 oz. cream cheese, cubed
1 cup heavy whipping cream
1 cup shredded Parmesan cheese
¼ tsp. pepper
Hot cooked fettuccine
Minced fresh parsley, optional

In a large skillet, melt butter over medium heat. Add garlic; cook and stir 1 minute. Stir in the cream cheese until melted. Gradually add the cream. Bring to a boil. Reduce heat; simmer, uncovered, until slightly thickened, 3-5 minutes. Stir in Parmesan cheese and pepper. Serve over pasta. If desired, garnish with parsley and additional Parmesan cheese.
⅓ CUP: 329 cal., 32g fat (20g sat. fat), 94mg chol., 358mg sod., 3g carb. (2g sugars, 0 fiber), 8g pro.

FLAVORFUL PIZZA SAUCE

I could never find the perfect pizza sauce recipe. So I experimented with my own version until I got it just right. I think you'll enjoy it, too!
—Cheryl Williams, Evington, VA

TAKES: 15 MIN. • **MAKES:** ABOUT 2½ CUPS

2 cans (8 oz. each) tomato sauce
1 can (12 oz.) tomato paste
4 tsp. Worcestershire sauce
1 Tbsp. dried parsley flakes
1 Tbsp. Italian seasoning
1½ tsp. garlic powder
1 tsp. sugar
1 tsp. dried basil
1 tsp. dried oregano
¾ tsp. salt
¼ tsp. pepper

In a large bowl, combine all ingredients. Spread desired amount over a pizza crust or transfer to a storage container for later use. Refrigerate, covered, up to 1 week or freeze for up to 6 months.
2 TBSP.: 24 cal., 0 fat (0 sat. fat), 0 chol., 217mg sod., 5g carb. (3g sugars, 1g fiber), 1g pro.

HONEY-MUSTARD BRUSSELS SPROUTS SALAD

Even if you dislike Brussels sprouts salad, you will love this dish. The dressing is truly tasty, and it pairs so nicely with the apples, grapes and walnuts. You can also add whatever cheese, nuts or fruit you prefer.
—Sheila Sturrock, Coldwater, ON

TAKES: 25 MIN. • **MAKES:** 10 SERVINGS

1 lb. fresh Brussels sprouts, trimmed and shredded
2 medium tart apples, chopped
1 medium red onion, chopped
1 small sweet orange pepper, chopped
½ cup chopped walnuts
½ cup green grapes, sliced
½ cup shredded cheddar cheese
3 bacon strips, cooked and crumbled
¼ cup olive oil
2 Tbsp. red wine vinegar
2 Tbsp. honey mustard
1 garlic clove, minced
¼ tsp. salt
¼ tsp. pepper

In a large bowl, combine the first 8 ingredients. In a small bowl, whisk remaining ingredients; pour over salad. Toss to coat.
1 CUP: 170 cal., 12g fat (3g sat. fat), 8mg chol., 177mg sod., 13g carb. (7g sugars, 3g fiber), 5g pro. **DIABETIC EXCHANGES:** 2 fat, 1 starch.

5i

AIR-FRYER FRENCH FRIES

These low-calorie french fries are perfect because I can whip them up at a moment's notice with ingredients I have on hand. They are so crispy, you won't miss the deep fryer!
—Dawn Parker, Surrey, BC

PREP: 10 MIN. + SOAKING • **COOK:** 30 MIN.
MAKES: 4 SERVINGS

- **3 medium potatoes, cut into ½-in. strips**
- **2 Tbsp. coconut or avocado oil**
- **½ tsp. garlic powder**
- **¼ tsp. salt**
- **¼ tsp. pepper**
- **Chopped fresh parsley, optional**

1. Preheat air fryer to 400°. Add potatoes to a large bowl; add enough ice water to cover. Soak potatoes for 15 minutes. Drain potatoes; place on towels and pat dry.
2. Combine potatoes, oil, garlic powder, salt and pepper in second large bowl; toss to coat. In batches, place potatoes in a single layer on tray in greased air-fryer basket. Cook until crisp and golden brown, 15-17 minutes, stirring and turning every 5-7 minutes. If desired, sprinkle with chopped fresh parsley.

¾ CUP: 185 cal., 7g fat (6g sat. fat), 0 chol., 157mg sod., 28g carb. (1g sugars, 3g fiber), 3g pro. **DIABETIC EXCHANGES:** 2 starch, 1½ fat.

DID YOU KNOW?

The main difference between using an air fryer versus a deep fryer is the amount of oil you need. Air fryers use little to no oil because the unit heats up hot enough to crisp the food. So in that sense, air-fryer recipes are a bit healthier than deep-fried ones.

GARLIC-CHIVE WHIPPED BUTTER

Dress up ordinary bread or dinner rolls with this creamy garlic butter.
—Susan Stetzel, Gainesville, NY

TAKES: 10 MIN. • **MAKES:** ½ CUP

- **½ cup butter, softened**
- **¼ cup grated Parmesan cheese**
- **1 Tbsp. minced fresh chives**
- **1 to 2 garlic cloves, minced**

Beat all ingredients until blended. Store, tightly covered, in the refrigerator.

1 TBSP.: 113 cal., 12g fat (8g sat. fat), 33mg chol., 136mg sod., 1g carb. (0 sugars, 0 fiber), 1g pro.

BASIC WHITE SAUCE

For years, I've used this smooth sauce to make many dishes. The recipe can easily be doubled or tripled.
—Lois Gelzer, Standish, ME

TAKES: 10 MIN. • **MAKES:** 1 CUP

- **2 Tbsp. butter**
- **2 Tbsp. all-purpose flour**
- **⅛ tsp. salt**
- **Dash white pepper**
- **1 cup 2% milk**

In a small saucepan, melt butter over medium heat. Whisk in flour, salt and pepper until smooth. Gradually whisk in milk. Bring to a boil; cook and stir until thickened, 1-2 minutes.

2 TBSP.: 51 cal., 4g fat (2g sat. fat), 12mg chol., 81mg sod., 3g carb. (1g sugars, 0 fiber), 1g pro.

SAUCY BAKED BEANS

My family enjoys these baked beans with cornbread, but they also round out any cookout menu. Canned pork and beans make preparation easy.
—Phyllis Schmalz, Kansas City, KS

PREP: 15 MIN. • **BAKE:** 1¼ HOURS
MAKES: 12 SERVINGS

- **2 cans (28 oz. each) pork and beans**
- **1½ cups packed brown sugar**
- **½ lb. sliced bacon, cooked and crumbled**
- **1 cup finely chopped onion**
- **1 cup cola**
- **1 cup ketchup**
- **2 Tbsp. ground mustard**

Preheat oven to 325°. In a large bowl, mix all ingredients. Transfer to a greased 3-qt. baking dish. Bake, uncovered, until bubbly, 1¼-1½ hours.

¾ CUP: 293 cal., 5g fat (1g sat. fat), 5mg chol., 793mg sod., 59g carb. (42g sugars, 7g fiber), 9g pro.

BRUSSELS SPROUTS SALAD

My husband and I like Brussels sprouts, so I'm always looking for new ways to use them. I most often serve this colorful salad with roast pork or duck.
—Nancy Korondan, Yorkville, IL

TAKES: 20 MIN. • **MAKES:** 8 SERVINGS

- **1½ lbs. fresh Brussels sprouts, trimmed and halved**
- **2 green onions, chopped**
- **½ cup olive oil**
- **2 Tbsp. lemon juice**
- **1 to 1½ tsp. Dijon mustard**
- **½ tsp. salt**
- **½ tsp. dried thyme**
- **¼ tsp. pepper**
- **1 bunch red leaf lettuce or radicchio, torn**
- **2 Tbsp. slivered almonds, toasted**

1. Place Brussels sprouts in a large saucepan; add 1 in. of water. Bring to a boil. Reduce heat; simmer, covered, until tender, 8-10 minutes. Drain; rinse with cold water and pat dry. Combine with green onions.
2. Meanwhile, whisk together the next 6 ingredients. Toss 2 Tbsp. of dressing with lettuce; transfer to a serving bowl. Pour remaining dressing over Brussels sprouts and onions; toss to coat. Mound on lettuce. Sprinkle with almonds.

NOTE: To toast nuts, bake in a shallow pan in a 350° oven for 5-10 minutes or cook in a skillet over low heat until lightly browned, stirring occasionally.

1 CUP: 171 cal., 15g fat (2g sat. fat), 0 chol., 192mg sod., 9g carb. (2g sugars, 4g fiber), 4g pro. **DIABETIC EXCHANGES:** 3 fat, 2 vegetable.

MUSHROOM-GRUYERE SCALLOPED POTATOES

When I started cooking, the only mushrooms I used were the button variety. Now I love experimenting with different types. This is wonderful as a side dish to accompany a grilled steak, or even as a main dish with a salad of mixed greens.
—Nadine Mesch, Mount Healthy, OH

PREP: 30 MIN. • **BAKE:** 1 HOUR + STANDING
MAKES: 10 SERVINGS

- **6 Tbsp. butter, divided**
- **½ lb. each sliced fresh shiitake, baby portobello and button mushrooms**
- **1 Tbsp. sherry, optional**
- **5 Tbsp. all-purpose flour**
- **3 cups half-and-half cream**
- **3 Tbsp. minced fresh rosemary**
- **1½ tsp. salt**
- **1 tsp. pepper**
- **2 cups shredded Gruyere cheese**
- **2 lbs. red potatoes, thinly sliced**
- **½ tsp. paprika**

1. Preheat oven to 350°. In a large skillet, heat 1 Tbsp. butter over medium-high heat. Add mushrooms; cook and stir until tender. If desired, stir in sherry and cook until evaporated, 1-2 minutes longer. Remove from pan.
2. In same pan, melt remaining butter over medium heat. Stir in flour until smooth; gradually whisk in cream. Bring to a boil, stirring constantly; cook and stir until thickened, about 2 minutes. Reduce heat to medium-low. Stir in rosemary, salt and pepper. Gradually add cheese, stirring until melted. Remove from heat.
3. Arrange potatoes in an even layer in a greased 13x9-in. baking dish. Top with mushrooms and sauce mixture; sprinkle with paprika.
4. Bake casserole, covered, 40 minutes. Bake, uncovered, until golden brown and bubbly, 20-25 minutes longer. Let stand 15 minutes before serving.

¾ CUP: 442 cal., 29g fat (18g sat. fat), 104mg chol., 599mg sod., 23g carb. (4g sugars, 3g fiber), 20g pro.

RADISH ASPARAGUS SALAD

Lemon zest and mustard in the dressing add the perfect punch to crisp asparagus and spicy radishes in this fun spring salad. My family loves it!
—Nancy Latulippe, Simcoe, ON

TAKES: 25 MIN. • **MAKES:** 6 SERVINGS

- **1 lb. fresh asparagus, trimmed and cut into 2-in. pieces**
- **7 radishes, thinly sliced**
- **2 Tbsp. sesame seeds**

DRESSING

- **2 Tbsp. olive oil**
- **2 Tbsp. thinly sliced green onion**
- **1 Tbsp. white wine vinegar**
- **1 Tbsp. lemon juice**
- **2 tsp. honey**
- **1 tsp. Dijon mustard**
- **¼ tsp. garlic powder**
- **¼ tsp. grated lemon zest**
- **¼ tsp. pepper**

1. In a large saucepan, bring 6 cups water to a boil. Add asparagus; cover and boil for 3 minutes. Drain and immediately place asparagus in ice water. Drain and pat dry.
2. Transfer to a large bowl; add radishes and sesame seeds. Place the dressing ingredients in a jar with a tight-fitting lid; shake well. Pour over salad; toss to coat.

⅔ CUP: 73 cal., 6g fat (1g sat. fat), 0 chol., 28mg sod., 5g carb. (3g sugars, 1g fiber), 2g pro. **DIABETIC EXCHANGES:** 1 vegetable, 1 fat.

SWEET POTATO & CHIPOTLE CASSEROLE

Classic sweet potato casserole topped with marshmallows is good, but my version with a streusel topping is a blockbuster. Everyone who tries it gives it double thumbs up!
—Diana Malach, Vancouver, WA

PREP: 45 MIN. • **BAKE:** 35 MIN.
MAKES: 18 SERVINGS

- **6 lbs. sweet potatoes, peeled and cubed (about 20 cups)**
- **1 to 2 chipotle peppers in adobo sauce, finely chopped**
- **1 cup heavy whipping cream**
- **4 large eggs, beaten**
- **1 tsp. salt**

TOPPING

- **1 cup packed brown sugar**
- **¾ cup all-purpose flour**
- **¾ tsp. ground ginger**
- **¾ tsp. ground cumin**
- **½ tsp. ground cloves**
- **¼ tsp. cayenne pepper**
- **⅓ cup cold butter**
- **1½ cups chopped pecans**

1. Preheat oven to 350°. Place the sweet potatoes in a large stockpot; cover with water. Bring to a boil. Reduce heat; cook, uncovered, 15-20 minutes or until sweet potatoes are tender.
2. Drain; return potatoes to pot. Mash potatoes with chipotle pepper to reach desired consistency. Cool slightly. Stir in the cream, eggs and salt. Transfer to a greased 13x9-in. baking dish (dish will be full).
3. For topping, in a large bowl, mix brown sugar, flour and spices; cut in butter until crumbly. Stir in chopped pecans. Sprinkle over casserole. Bake, uncovered, until a thermometer reads 160°, 35-40 minutes.

¾ CUP: 377 cal., 16g fat (6g sat. fat), 69mg chol., 204mg sod., 55g carb. (28g sugars, 6g fiber), 6g pro.

LEMON COUSCOUS WITH BROCCOLI

I combined two recipes to create this side with broccoli and pasta. The splash of lemon adds nice flavor. Instead of toasted almonds, you could also sprinkle servings with grated Parmesan cheese.
—Beth Dauenhauer, Pueblo, CO

TAKES: 25 MIN. • **MAKES:** 6 SERVINGS

- **1 Tbsp. olive oil**
- **4 cups fresh broccoli florets, cut into small pieces**
- **1 cup uncooked whole wheat couscous**
- **2 garlic cloves, minced**
- **1¼ cups reduced-sodium chicken broth**
- **1 tsp. grated lemon zest**
- **1 tsp. lemon juice**
- **½ tsp. salt**
- **½ tsp. dried basil**
- **¼ tsp. coarsely ground pepper**
- **1 Tbsp. slivered almonds, toasted**

1. In a large cast-iron or other heavy skillet, heat oil over medium-high heat. Add the broccoli; cook and stir until crisp-tender.
2. Add couscous and garlic; cook and stir 1-2 minutes longer. Stir in broth, lemon zest, lemon juice and seasonings; bring to a boil. Remove from heat; let stand, covered, 5-10 minutes or until broth is absorbed. Fluff with a fork. Sprinkle with slivered almonds.

NOTE: With origins in the Middle East and North Africa, couscous is a commercially produced grain product usually made from semolina and shaped into tiny beads. It can be found in the rice or pasta section of the grocery store. It is available in regular or quick-cooking forms. Use as a side dish and in salads like rice or pasta.

⅔ CUP: 115 cal., 3g fat (0 sat. fat), 0 chol., 328mg sod., 18g carb. (1g sugars, 4g fiber), 5g pro. **DIABETIC EXCHANGES:** 1 starch, ½ fat.

SPECIAL SESAME CHICKEN SALAD

With its delicious mix of crunchy peanuts, tangy dried cranberries and mandarin oranges, this colorful pasta salad is a definite crowd-pleaser. Water chestnuts and a teriyaki dressing give this main dish its Asian flare.
—Carolee Ewell, Santaquin, UT

PREP: 30 MIN. + CHILLING
MAKES: 22 SERVINGS

- **1 pkg. (16 oz.) bow tie pasta**
- **1 cup canola oil**
- **⅔ cup white wine vinegar**
- **⅔ cup teriyaki sauce**
- **⅓ cup sugar**
- **½ tsp. pepper**
- **3 cans (11 oz. each) mandarin oranges, drained**
- **2 cans (8 oz. each) sliced water chestnuts, drained**
- **2 cups cubed cooked chicken**
- **1⅓ cups honey-roasted peanuts**
- **1 pkg. (9 oz.) fresh spinach, torn**
- **1 pkg. (5 oz.) dried cranberries**
- **6 green onions, chopped**
- **½ cup minced fresh parsley**
- **¼ cup sesame seeds, toasted**

1. Cook pasta according to the package directions; drain and place in a very large bowl.
2. In a small bowl, combine oil, vinegar, teriyaki sauce, sugar and pepper. Pour over pasta and toss to coat. Cover and refrigerate for 2 hours.
3. Just before serving, add the remaining ingredients; gently toss to coat.

1 CUP: 302 cal., 16g fat (2g sat. fat), 11mg chol., 358mg sod., 32g carb. (13g sugars, 3g fiber), 10g pro.

SO-SWEET SQUASH PICKLES

These crunchy pickles, seasoned with celery seed and mustard seed, have a sweet-sour taste. The colorful blend of yellow squash, sweet red pepper and chopped onion makes a beautiful presentation.
—Eleanor Sundman, Farmington, CT

PREP: 20 MIN. + STANDING
COOK: 10 MIN. + CHILLING
MAKES: 4 CUPS

- **3 small yellow summer squash, thinly sliced**
- **1 large sweet red pepper, cut into ¼-in. strips**
- **1 medium onion, chopped**
- **1 Tbsp. salt**
- **1 cup sugar**
- **¾ cup white vinegar**
- **¾ tsp. mustard seed**
- **¾ tsp. celery seed**
- **¼ tsp. ground mustard**

1. Place squash, pepper and onion in a colander over a plate; sprinkle with salt and toss. Let stand 1 hour to drain.
2. In a large saucepan, combine the remaining ingredients; bring to a boil, stirring to dissolve sugar. Add vegetables; return to a boil. Remove from the heat; cool completely.
3. Transfer mixture to a storage container; refrigerate, covered, at least 4 days before serving. May be stored in refrigerator up to 3 weeks.

½ CUP: 123 cal., 0 fat (0 sat. fat), 0 chol., 225mg sod., 30g carb. (28g sugars, 2g fiber), 1g pro.

STEAKHOUSE MUSHROOM CASSEROLE

This meatless casserole is one of my all-time favorites. Loaded with fresh mushrooms and draped in a rich cream sauce, it's a home-style side dish that will have everyone scooping up seconds! Pair it with your favorite beef entree.
—Rosemary Janz, Concord, NC

PREP: 25 MIN. + CHILLING • **BAKE:** 30 MIN.
MAKES: 8 SERVINGS

- **2 lbs. sliced fresh mushrooms**
- **¾ cup butter, divided**
- **1 cup heavy whipping cream**
- **1 large egg yolk**
- **1 Tbsp. minced fresh parsley**
- **1 Tbsp. lemon juice**
- **1 tsp. salt**
- **½ tsp. paprika**
- **2 cups crushed butter-flavored crackers**

1. In a large skillet, saute mushrooms in batches in ¼ cup butter until mushrooms are tender and liquid is evaporated. In a large bowl, whisk the cream, egg yolk, parsley, lemon juice, salt and paprika. Add mushrooms and stir until blended.
2. Transfer to a greased 8-in. square baking dish. Melt remaining butter; stir in cracker crumbs until blended. Sprinkle over the mushroom mixture. Cover and refrigerate overnight.
3. Remove from refrigerator 30 minutes before baking. Preheat the oven to 350°. Bake, uncovered, 30-35 minutes or until a thermometer reads 160° and topping is golden brown.

¾ CUP: 406 cal., 35g fat (19g sat. fat), 103mg chol., 634mg sod., 20g carb. (5g sugars, 2g fiber), 7g pro.

READER REVIEW

"Wow! This dish was excellent! My son-in-law who 'hates' mushrooms loved it!"

POOKIE136, TASTEOFHOME.COM

TOMATO, AVOCADO & GRILLED CORN SALAD

With ripe tomatoes, fresh basil and grilled corn, this salad tastes just like summer!
—Angela Spengler, Niceville, FL

PREP: 20 MIN. • **GRILL:** 10 MIN. + COOLING
MAKES: 8 SERVINGS

- **1 medium ear sweet corn, husks removed**
- **3 large red tomatoes, sliced**
- **3 large yellow tomatoes, sliced**
- **¾ tsp. kosher salt, divided**
- **½ tsp. pepper, divided**
- **2 medium ripe avocados, peeled and sliced**
- **¼ cup olive oil**
- **2 Tbsp. red wine vinegar**
- **1 Tbsp. minced fresh basil, plus more for garnish**
- **⅓ cup crumbled feta cheese**

1. Grill corn, covered, over medium heat 10-12 minutes or until lightly browned and tender, turning occasionally. Cool slightly. Cut corn from cob.
2. Arrange tomato slices on a large serving platter. Sprinkle with ½ tsp. salt and ¼ tsp. pepper. Top with the avocado slices. Whisk together oil, vinegar, basil and remaining salt and pepper; drizzle half over the tomatoes and avocado. Top with grilled corn and feta; drizzle remaining dressing over top. Garnish with additional chopped basil.

1 SERVING: 164 cal., 13g fat (2g sat. fat), 3mg chol., 237mg sod., 11g carb. (4g sugars, 4g fiber), 3g pro. **DIABETIC EXCHANGES:** 2 fat, 1 vegetable, ½ starch.

ULTIMATE SCALLOPED POTATOES

This tasty variation on traditional scalloped potatoes is dressed up with garlic, Swiss cheese and Parmesan cheese.
—Glenda Malan, Lake Forest, CA

PREP: 20 MIN. + COOLING • **BAKE:** 1 HOUR
MAKES: 6 SERVINGS

- **1 tsp. butter, softened**
- **1 cup heavy whipping cream**
- **⅓ cup whole milk**
- **1 tsp. salt**
- **½ tsp. pepper**
- **2 garlic cloves, crushed**
- **6 medium potatoes**
- **1 cup shredded Swiss cheese**
- **¼ cup shredded Parmesan cheese**

1. Grease a shallow 13x9-in. baking dish with the butter; set aside. In a small saucepan, combine the cream, milk, salt, pepper and garlic. Cook just until bubbles begin to form around the sides of the pan. Remove from the heat; cool mixture for 10 minutes.
2. Peel and thinly slice the potatoes; pat dry with paper towels. Layer half of the potatoes in prepared baking dish; top with half the cream mixture and half the cheeses. Repeat layers.
3. Bake, covered, at 350° for 40 minutes. Uncover and continue baking until the potatoes are tender, 20-25 minutes longer. Let stand for 5-10 minutes before serving.

1 SERVING: 402 cal., 22g fat (14g sat. fat), 77mg chol., 538mg sod., 41g carb. (6g sugars, 3g fiber), 12g pro.

TEST KITCHEN TIP
To keep your sliced potatoes from going brown, place them in cold water until you're ready to assemble the dish.

HAWAIIAN MACARONI SALAD

This recipe tastes just like the mac salad from a Hawaiian restaurant we love in our town. I had to figure out how to make it at home because my husband was getting tired of going to the restaurant and ordering enough for our whole family. Sometimes I use green onions and serve the salad with a drizzle of teriyaki sauce and a sprinkle of sesame seeds.
—Blaine Kahle, Florence, OR

TAKES: 30 MIN. • **MAKES:** 10 SERVINGS

- **1 pkg. (16 oz.) uncooked elbow macaroni**
- **2 cups mayonnaise**
- **¼ cup 2% milk**
- **2 Tbsp. cider vinegar**
- **1 large carrot, grated**
- **1 celery rib, finely chopped, optional**
- **2 Tbsp. grated onion**
- **1 Tbsp. brown sugar**
- **½ tsp. salt**
- **½ tsp. pepper**
- **Chopped green onions, optional**

1. Cook macaroni according to package directions; drain and rinse with cold water. Cool completely.
2. For dressing, in a small bowl, whisk next 9 ingredients. Add pasta to a large serving bowl. Add dressing; gently toss to coat. Refrigerate until serving. If desired, garnish with green onions.

¾ CUP: 464 cal., 33g fat (5g sat. fat), 4mg chol., 353mg sod., 36g carb. (4g sugars, 2g fiber), 6g pro.

GREEN BEANS AMANDINE

It's hard to improve on the taste Mother Nature gives to fresh green beans, but my mom has done just that for years using this recipe. The almonds are a crunchy addition.
—Brenda DuFresne, Midland, MI

TAKES: 20 MIN. • **MAKES:** 4 SERVINGS

- **1 lb. fresh or frozen green beans, cut into 2-in. pieces**
- **½ cup water**
- **¼ cup slivered almonds**
- **2 Tbsp. butter**
- **1 tsp. lemon juice**
- **¼ tsp. seasoned salt, optional**

1. Place beans and water in a large skillet or saucepan and bring to a boil. Cover and cook until crisp-tender, 10-15 minutes; drain and set aside.
2. In a large skillet, cook almonds in butter over low heat. Stir in lemon juice and, if desired, seasoned salt. Add beans and heat through.

¾ CUP: 125 cal., 9g fat (4g sat. fat), 15mg chol., 53mg sod., 10g carb. (3g sugars, 5g fiber), 4g pro. **DIABETIC EXCHANGES:** 2 fat, 1 vegetable.

TEST KITCHEN TIP

To choose green beans that are perfectly fresh, make sure the pods are firm and not too lumpy. If the beans inside are too big, the texture will be tough when cooked. You can also use frozen green beans in this recipe with good results.

EVERYTHING MASHED POTATO CASSEROLE

Here is a great dish for the holidays or to take to a covered dish event. If I need to keep it warm for a long time, I sometimes place the mixture into a slow cooker and then add the sour cream, bacon, cheese and chives.
—Pamela Shank, Parkersburg, WV

PREP: 30 MIN. • **BAKE:** 15 MIN.
MAKES: 12 SERVINGS

- **3 lbs. potatoes (about 9 medium), peeled and quartered**
- **1 pkg. (8 oz.) cream cheese, cubed**
- **½ cup butter, cubed**
- **½ cup whole milk**
- **¼ tsp. salt**
- **¼ tsp. pepper**
- **2 cups sour cream**
- **2 cups shredded cheddar cheese**
- **3 bacon strips, cooked and crumbled**
- **1 Tbsp. minced chives**

1. Place potatoes in a large saucepan and cover with water. Bring to a boil. Reduce heat; cover and simmer for 15-20 minutes or until tender. Drain.
2. In a large bowl, mash potatoes. Beat in the cream cheese, butter, milk, salt and pepper until fluffy. Transfer to a greased 3-qt. baking dish. Spread sour cream over the top.
3. Bake casserole, uncovered, at 350° for 10 minutes. Sprinkle with cheddar cheese, bacon and minced chives. Bake 5 minutes longer or until heated through and the cheese is melted.

¾ CUP: 433 cal., 33g fat (22g sat. fat), 114mg chol., 340mg sod., 20g carb. (4g sugars, 1g fiber), 10g pro.

HEAVENLY APPLESAUCE

Every year my husband and I take our two daughters to an orchard to pick apples so we can make this luscious applesauce for family and neighbors. Serve it as a side dish with your favorite meal or scoop it over vanilla ice cream for a luscious dessert!
—Jennifer Purcell, Vermilion, OH

PREP: 25 MIN. • **COOK:** 6 HOURS
MAKES: ABOUT 8 SERVINGS

- **5 lbs. apples, peeled and sliced (about 13 cups)**
- **¾ cup packed light brown sugar**
- **⅔ cup unsweetened apple juice**
- **2 tsp. ground cinnamon**
- **1 tsp. pumpkin pie spice**
- **1 Tbsp. vanilla extract**

1. In a 5- or 6-qt. slow cooker, combine the first 5 ingredients. Cook, covered, on low 6-8 hours or until apples are soft.
2. Add vanilla; stir to break up apples. Serve applesauce warm or refrigerate and serve cold.

FREEZE OPTION: Freeze cooled applesauce in freezer containers. To use, thaw in the refrigerator overnight.

⅔ CUP: 211 cal., 1g fat (0 sat. fat), 0 chol., 7mg sod., 54g carb. (48g sugars, 4g fiber), 0 pro.

FOUR-CHEESE MACARONI

I adapted this recipe from one a friend gave to me. It has a distinctive blue cheese taste and is a filling side dish.
—Darlene Marturano, West Suffield, CT

TAKES: 20 MIN. • **MAKES:** 8 SERVINGS

- **1 pkg. (16 oz.) elbow macaroni**
- **¼ cup butter, cubed**
- **¼ cup all-purpose flour**
- **½ tsp. salt**
- **⅛ tsp. pepper**
- **3 cups 2% milk**
- **2 cups shredded cheddar cheese**
- **1½ cups shredded Swiss cheese**
- **½ cup crumbled blue cheese**
- **½ cup grated Parmesan cheese**

1. Cook macaroni according to package directions. Meanwhile, in a Dutch oven, melt butter over medium heat. Stir in flour, salt and pepper until smooth; gradually whisk in milk. Bring to a boil, stirring constantly; cook and stir until thickened, about 2 minutes.
2. Reduce heat to low; stir in cheeses until melted. Drain macaroni; add to the cheese sauce and stir until coated.

1 CUP: 508 cal., 23g fat (13g sat. fat), 65mg chol., 603mg sod., 51g carb. (6g sugars, 2g fiber), 26g pro.

GRILLED SOUTHWESTERN POTATO SALAD

This salad is perfect with a grilled steak for a Tex-Mex meal, and most of it can even be prepared out in the backyard. Poblanos and cayenne make it pop.

—Johnna Johnson, Scottsdale, AZ

PREP: 30 MIN. • **GRILL:** 20 MIN. + STANDING
MAKES: 6 SERVINGS

- **1½ lbs. large red potatoes, quartered lengthwise**
- **3 Tbsp. olive oil**
- **2 poblano peppers**
- **2 medium ears sweet corn, husks removed**
- **½ cup buttermilk**
- **½ cup sour cream**
- **1 Tbsp. lime juice**
- **1 jalapeno pepper, seeded and minced**
- **1 Tbsp. minced fresh cilantro**
- **1½ tsp. garlic salt**
- **1 tsp. ground cumin**
- **¼ to ½ tsp. cayenne pepper**
- **Lime wedges**

1. Place potatoes in a large saucepan; add water to cover. Bring to a boil. Reduce the heat; cook, uncovered, 5 minutes. Drain potatoes and toss with oil.
2. Grill poblanos, covered, over high heat 8-10 minutes or until skins are blistered and blackened on all sides, turning occasionally. Immediately place peppers in a small bowl; let stand, covered, for 20 minutes. Reduce grill temperature to medium heat.
3. Grill corn and potatoes, covered, over medium heat 12-15 minutes or until tender and lightly browned, turning occasionally. Cool slightly.
4. Peel off and discard charred skin from poblanos; remove stems and seeds. Cut peppers into ½-in. pieces and place in a large bowl. Cut corn from cobs and cut potatoes into ¾-in. pieces; add to peppers.
5. In a small bowl, whisk buttermilk, sour cream and lime juice until blended; stir in the jalapeno, cilantro and seasonings. Add to the potato mixture, stirring in as much dressing as desired to coat. Serve with lime wedges. Refrigerate leftovers.

¾ CUP: 229 cal., 11g fat (4g sat. fat), 14mg chol., 301mg sod., 28g carb. (6g sugars, 3g fiber), 5g pro.

JOHNNA JOHNSON
Scottsdale, AZ

RHUBARB JELLY

To be honest, I don't especially like cooking. My husband, however, loves it! Now that he's retired, Bob's taken up making jelly. I help him with the pouring and skimming for this one—my own personal favorite. It's nice as both a breakfast spread and a topping for pork or other meat.

—Jean Coleman, Ottawa, ON

PREP: 20 MIN. + STANDING
PROCESS: 10 MIN.
MAKES: 8 HALF-PINTS

- **4½ to 5 lbs. rhubarb (4½ to 5 qt.), cut into 1-in. pieces**
- **7 cups sugar**
- **1 to 2 drops red food coloring, optional**
- **2 pouches (3 oz. each) liquid fruit pectin**

1. Grind the rhubarb in a food processor or grinder. Line a strainer with 4 layers of cheesecloth and place over a bowl. Place rhubarb in strainer; cover with edges of cheesecloth. Let stand for 30 minutes or until liquid measures 3½ cups. Pour juice into a Dutch oven; add the sugar and, if desired, food coloring.
2. Bring to a boil over high heat, stirring constantly. Add pectin; bring to a full rolling boil. Boil for 1 minute, stirring constantly. Remove from the heat; let stand a few minutes. Skim off foam. Carefully ladle hot mixture into hot half-pint jars, leaving ¼-in. headspace. Remove air bubbles; wipe rims. Center lids on jars; screw on bands until fingertip tight. Place the jars into canner with hot water, ensuring that they are completely covered with water. Bring water to a boil; process for 10 minutes. Remove jars and let cool.

NOTE: The processing time listed is for altitudes of 1,000 feet or less. Add 1 minute to the processing time for each 1,000 feet of additional altitude.

2 TBSP.: 92 cal., 0 fat (0 sat. fat), 0 chol., 2mg sod., 24g carb. (22g sugars, 1g fiber), 0 pro.

PECAN-STUFFED BUTTERNUT SQUASH

I love autumn, when butternut squash is at its peak. This is one of my favorite ways to prepare it. The squash is tender, and the creamy pecan filling is fabulous.

—Sherry Little, Cabot, AR

PREP: 10 MIN. • **BAKE:** 1¼ HOURS
MAKES: 8 SERVINGS

- **2 medium butternut squash (about 3 lbs. each)**
- **¾ tsp. salt**
- **Pepper, optional**
- **4 oz. cream cheese, softened**
- **¼ cup butter, softened**
- **3 Tbsp. brown sugar**
- **½ cup chopped pecans**

1. Cut each squash in half lengthwise; discard seeds. Place squash cut side down in two 13x9-in. baking dishes; add ½-in. water. Bake, uncovered, at 350° for 1 hour.
2. Turn squash over; sprinkle with salt and pepper if desired. In a small bowl, beat the cream cheese, butter and brown sugar until light and fluffy; stir in pecans. Spoon into squash cavities.
3. Bake 15-20 minutes longer or until the filling is lightly browned and squash is tender.

¼ STUFFED SQUASH: 299 cal., 16g fat (7g sat. fat), 31mg chol., 317mg sod., 40g carb. (13g sugars, 10g fiber), 5g pro.

1 FAVORITE 4 WAYS *Corn on the Cob*

1) BAKED BUTTERY-ONION CORN ON THE COB

My mother has been making this recipe for years. Every time I make it for company they rave and can't believe how easy it is!
—Lisa Denson, Decatur, AL

TAKES: 20 MIN. • **MAKES:** 4 SERVINGS

- **½ cup butter, melted**
- **1 envelope onion soup mix**
- **4 medium ears sweet corn, husked**

1. In a small bowl, combine butter and soup mix; rub over corn. Place each ear of corn on a 12x10-in. piece of heavy-duty foil. Fold foil over corn and seal tightly.
2. Bake at 450° for 15-20 minutes or until corn is tender, turning packet once.

1 EAR OF CORN: 297 cal., 24g fat (15g sat. fat), 60mg chol., 792mg sod., 21g carb. (3g sugars, 3g fiber), 4g pro.

2) SLOW-COOKER SRIRACHA CORN

A restaurant here advertised Sriracha corn on the cob, but I knew I could make my own. The golden ears cooked up a little sweet, a little smoky and a little hot—perfect, if you ask my three teenage boys!
—Julie Peterson, Crofton, MD

PREP: 15 MIN. • **COOK:** 3 HOURS
MAKES: 8 SERVINGS

- **½ cup butter, softened**
- **2 Tbsp. honey**
- **1 Tbsp. Sriracha chili sauce**
- **1 tsp. smoked paprika**
- **½ tsp. kosher salt**
- **8 small ears sweet corn, husked**
- **¼ cup water**
- **Additional smoked paprika, optional**

1. Mix first 5 ingredients. Place each ear of corn on a 12x12-in. piece of heavy-duty foil and spread with 1 Tbsp. of the butter mixture. Wrap foil around corn, sealing tightly. Place in a 6-qt. slow cooker.
2. Add water; cook, covered, on low for 3-4 hours or until the corn is tender. If desired, sprinkle corn with additional paprika before serving.

1 EAR OF CORN: 209 cal., 13g fat (8g sat. fat), 31mg chol., 287mg sod., 24g carb. (11g sugars, 2g fiber), 4g pro.

3) EASY GRILLED CORN WITH CHIPOTLE-LIME BUTTER

Grilling corn in the husks is so easy. There's no need to remove the silk and tie the husk closed before grilling. Just soak, grill and add your favorite flavored butter.
—*Taste of Home* Test Kitchen

PREP: 5 MIN. + SOAKING • **GRILL:** 25 MIN.
MAKES: 8 SERVINGS

- **8 large ears sweet corn in husks**
- **½ cup butter, softened**
- **1½ tsp. grated lime zest**
- **1 tsp. minced fresh cilantro**
- **½ tsp. salt**
- **½ tsp. ground chipotle pepper**
- **Coarse sea salt, optional**

1. In a large stockpot, cover corn with cold water. Soak 30 minutes; drain. Grill corn, covered, over medium heat until tender, turning occasionally, 25-30 minutes.
2. Meanwhile, combine next 5 ingredients. Carefully peel back husks; discard silk. Spread the butter mixture over corn. If desired, sprinkle with coarse sea salt.

1 EAR OF CORN WITH 2 TBSP. BUTTER: 225 cal., 13g fat (8g sat. fat), 31mg chol., 265mg sod., 27g carb. (9g sugars, 3g fiber), 5g pro.

4) SWEET PAN-FRIED CORN WITH PARMESAN & CILANTRO

A little tart and a touch sassy, this fun way to fix corn will be a hit. Just a few minutes of pan frying gives it a delightful golden color.
—Faye Sloan, Las Vegas, NV

TAKES: 25 MIN. • **MAKES:** 4 SERVINGS

- **4 large ears sweet corn, husked**
- **⅓ cup grated Parmesan cheese**
- **6 Tbsp. olive oil, divided**
- **1 Tbsp. lime juice**
- **1 garlic clove, minced**
- **1 tsp. ground cumin**
- **½ tsp. hot pepper sauce**
- **¼ tsp. salt**
- **¼ tsp. pepper**
- **¼ cup minced fresh cilantro**

1. Place corn in a stockpot; cover with water. Bring to a boil; cover and cook for 3-5 minutes or until tender. Drain.
2. In a bowl, combine the cheese, 5 Tbsp. oil, lime juice, garlic, cumin, pepper sauce, salt and pepper. Brush 1 Tbsp. over each ear of corn.
3. In a large skillet, cook corn in remaining oil over medium heat for 4-6 minutes or until lightly browned, turning occasionally. Stir the cilantro into the remaining cheese mixture; brush over corn.

1 EAR OF CORN: 336 cal., 24g fat (4g sat. fat), 6mg chol., 277mg sod., 28g carb. (5g sugars, 4g fiber), 7g pro.

Hearty Main Dishes

Make a hectic day a little easier and whip up one of these most-requested weeknight dinners. Here you will find easy and delicious ideas for chicken, beef, pork, fish, pasta—even enticing vegetarian dishes.

PAN-ROASTED CHICKEN & VEGETABLES

This one-dish meal tastes as if it took hours of hands-on time, but the simple ingredients can be prepped in minutes. The rosemary gives it a rich flavor, and the meat juices cook the veggies to perfection. So easy!
—Sherri Melotik, Oak Creek, WI

PREP: 15 MIN. • **BAKE:** 45 MIN.
MAKES: 6 SERVINGS

- **2 lbs. red potatoes (about 6 medium), cut into ¾-in. pieces**
- **1 large onion, coarsely chopped**
- **2 Tbsp. olive oil**
- **3 garlic cloves, minced**
- **1¼ tsp. salt, divided**
- **1 tsp. dried rosemary, crushed, divided**
- **¾ tsp. pepper, divided**
- **½ tsp. paprika**
- **6 bone-in chicken thighs (about 2¼ lbs.), skin removed**
- **6 cups fresh baby spinach (about 6 oz.)**

1. Preheat oven to 425°. In a large bowl, combine potatoes, onion, oil, garlic, ¾ tsp. salt, ½ tsp. rosemary and ½ tsp. pepper; toss to coat. Transfer to a 15x10x1-in. baking pan coated with cooking spray.

2. In a small bowl, mix paprika and the remaining salt, rosemary and pepper. Sprinkle chicken with paprika mixture; arrange over vegetables. Roast until a thermometer inserted in chicken reads 170°-175° and vegetables are just tender, 35-40 minutes.

3. Remove chicken to a serving platter; keep warm. Top vegetables with spinach. Roast until vegetables are tender and spinach is wilted, 8-10 minutes longer. Stir vegetables to combine; serve with the chicken.

1 CHICKEN THIGH WITH 1 CUP VEGETABLES: 357 cal., 14g fat (3g sat. fat), 87mg chol., 597mg sod., 28g carb. (3g sugars, 4g fiber), 28g pro. **DIABETIC EXCHANGES:** 4 lean meat, 1½ starch, 1 vegetable, 1 fat.

AIR-FRYER CHICKEN TENDERS

I added all of the components of a loaded baked potato—cheddar, potato, bacon, sour cream and chives—to my latest quick and easy dish. Every kid will love these chicken tenders!
—Cyndy Gerken, Naples, FL

PREP: 25 MIN. • **COOK:** 15 MIN./BATCH
MAKES: 4 SERVINGS

- **½ cup panko bread crumbs**
- **½ cup potato sticks, crushed**
- **½ cup crushed cheese crackers**
- **¼ cup grated Parmesan cheese**
- **2 bacon strips, cooked and crumbled**
- **2 tsp. minced fresh chives**
- **¼ cup butter, melted**
- **1 Tbsp. sour cream**
- **1 lb. chicken tenderloins**
- **Additional sour cream and chives**

1. Preheat air fryer to 400°. In a shallow bowl, combine the first 6 ingredients. In another shallow bowl, whisk butter and sour cream. Dip chicken in butter mixture, then in the crumb mixture, patting to help coating adhere.
2. In batches, arrange chicken in a single layer on greased tray in air-fryer basket; spritz with cooking spray. Cook until the coating is golden brown and chicken is no longer pink, 7-8 minutes on each side. Serve chicken tenders with additional sour cream and chives.
1 SERVING: 256 cal., 14g fat (7g sat. fat), 84mg chol., 267mg sod., 6g carb. (0 sugars, 0 fiber), 29g pro.

BEEF & BLUE CHEESE PENNE WITH PESTO

Unique and simple to prepare, this delicious pasta dish is filled with fresh flavors—and it's as healthy as it is hearty. Best of all, it takes just 30 minutes to set this meal on the table.
—Frances Pietsch, Flower Mound, TX

TAKES: 30 MIN. • **MAKES:** 4 SERVINGS

- **2 cups uncooked whole wheat penne pasta**
- **2 beef tenderloin steaks (6 oz. each)**
- **¼ tsp. salt**
- **¼ tsp. pepper**
- **5 oz. fresh baby spinach (about 6 cups), coarsely chopped**
- **2 cups grape tomatoes, halved**
- **⅓ cup prepared pesto**
- **¼ cup chopped walnuts**
- **¼ cup crumbled Gorgonzola cheese**

1. Cook the pasta according to the package directions.
2. Meanwhile, sprinkle steaks with salt and pepper. Grill steaks, covered, over medium heat or broil 4 in. from heat 5-7 minutes on each side or until meat reaches desired doneness (for medium-rare, a thermometer should read 135°; medium, 140°; medium-well, 145°).
3. Drain pasta; transfer to a large bowl. Add the spinach, tomatoes, pesto and walnuts; toss to coat. Cut steak into thin slices. Serve pasta mixture with beef; sprinkle with cheese.
NOTE: Gorgonzola is an Italian cheese from the blue cheese family. It is cream-yellow in color with characteristic blue veins. Like blue cheese, it has a bold flavor and crumbles easily, making it a tasty addition to salads and sauces.
1 SERVING: 532 cal., 22g fat (6g sat. fat), 50mg chol., 434mg sod., 49g carb. (3g sugars, 9g fiber), 35g pro.

COLLEEN DELAWDER
Herndon, VA

SHREDDED GREEN CHILE BEEF

This Tex-Mex pulled beef roast is tender, slightly spicy, juicy and so delicious served over mashed potatoes or rice. The beef also makes the best soft tacos you've ever had. Save any leftover pulled beef in the liquid to prevent it from drying out.
—Colleen Delawder, Herndon, VA

PREP: 25 MIN. • **COOK:** 7 HOURS
MAKES: 12 SERVINGS

- 2 **large sweet onions, halved and thinly sliced**
- 4 **Tbsp. packed brown sugar, divided**
- 1 **Tbsp. paprika**
- 1½ **tsp. salt**
- 1 **tsp. cayenne pepper**
- 1 **tsp. chili powder**
- 1 **tsp. garlic powder**
- ½ **tsp. pepper**
- 1 **boneless beef chuck roast (about 3 lbs.)**
- 2 **Tbsp. canola oil**
- 1 **can (28 oz.) green enchilada sauce**
- **Mashed potatoes, optional**

1. Place onions and 3 Tbsp. brown sugar in a 5- or 6-qt. slow cooker. Combine the remaining brown sugar and the next 6 ingredients; coat beef with the mixture.
2. In a large skillet, heat oil over medium-high heat; brown the beef, 1-2 minutes on each side. Transfer to slow cooker; pour enchilada sauce over beef. Cook, covered, on low until the beef is tender, 7-9 hours. Remove beef; shred meat with 2 forks. Return to slow cooker; heat through. If desired, serve over potatoes.
1 CUP BEEF MIXTURE: 278 cal., 15g fat (4g sat. fat), 74mg chol., 658mg sod., 14g carb. (8g sugars, 1g fiber), 23g pro. **DIABETIC EXCHANGES:** 3 lean meat, 1 starch, ½ fat.

DID YOU KNOW?
Chuck roast comes mainly from the shoulder section of the steer, as well as parts of the neck, ribs and the upper arm. It's a large part of the animal and is typically an affordable cut of meat.

PAN-SEARED SALMON WITH DILL SAUCE

This is one of my husband's favorite recipes. Salmon is a go-to for busy nights because it cooks so quickly and goes with so many different flavors. The creamy dill sauce with cucumber tastes light and fresh.
—Angela Spengler, Niceville, FL

TAKES: 25 MIN. • **MAKES:** 4 SERVINGS

- 1 **Tbsp. canola oil**
- 4 **salmon fillets (6 oz. each)**
- 1 **tsp. Italian seasoning**
- ¼ **tsp. salt**
- ½ **cup reduced-fat plain yogurt**
- ¼ **cup reduced-fat mayonnaise**
- ¼ **cup finely chopped cucumber**
- 1 **tsp. snipped fresh dill**

1. In a large skillet, heat oil over medium-high heat. Sprinkle salmon with Italian seasoning and salt. Place in skillet, skin side down. Reduce heat to medium. Cook until fish just begins to flake easily with a fork, about 5 minutes on each side.
2. Meanwhile, in a small bowl, combine yogurt, mayonnaise, cucumber and dill. Serve with salmon.
HEALTH TIP: This nutritious salmon dish provides about 2 grams of omega-3 fatty acids. Salmon is one of the best sources for this healthy fat.
1 SALMON FILLET WITH ¼ CUP SAUCE: 366 cal., 25g fat (4g sat. fat), 92mg chol., 349mg sod., 4g carb. (3g sugars, 0 fiber), 31g pro.
DIABETIC EXCHANGES: 4 lean meat, 2½ fat.

CABBAGE SAUSAGE SUPPER

Everyone is surprised at how this flavorful combination is created with just a few easy ingredients. I complete the meal with a fruity no-bake dessert.
—Ruby Williams, Bogalusa, LA

PREP: 10 MIN. • **COOK:** 40 MIN.
MAKES: 12 SERVINGS

- 2 lbs. smoked sausage, halved and cut into ¾-in. slices
- 1 large onion, cut into eighths
- 1 medium head cabbage, chopped
- ½ cup water
- 1 lb. carrots, cut into ½-in. slices
- 5 medium potatoes, peeled and cut into ¾-in. cubes

In a Dutch oven or soup kettle, cook the sausage and onion over medium heat until the sausage is lightly browned and onion is tender; drain. Add cabbage and water. Cover and cook on low for 10 minutes. Stir in carrots and potatoes. Cover and cook for 25-30 minutes or until the vegetables are tender.

1¼ CUPS: 190 cal., 4g fat (1g sat. fat), 34mg chol., 675mg sod., 28g carb. (0 sugars, 4g fiber), 13g pro.

ZESTY GRILLED HAM

If it's ham, my kids will eat it, and they like this kicked-up recipe best of all. Even the small ones eat adult-sized portions, so be sure to make plenty.
—Mary Ann Lien, Tyler, TX

TAKES: 15 MIN. • **MAKES:** 4 SERVINGS

- ⅓ cup packed brown sugar
- 2 Tbsp. prepared horseradish
- 4 tsp. lemon juice
- 1 fully cooked bone-in ham steak (1 lb.)

1. Place brown sugar, horseradish and lemon juice in a small saucepan; bring to a boil, stirring constantly. Brush over both sides of ham.
2. Place ham on an oiled grill rack over medium heat. Grill, covered, until glazed and heated through, 7-10 minutes, turning steak occasionally.

1 SERVING: 180 cal., 5g fat (2g sat. fat), 44mg chol., 845mg sod., 20g carb. (19g sugars, 0 fiber), 14g pro.

BUCATINI WITH SAUSAGE & KALE

I was short on time, but wanted to make an elegant dinner for my husband and me. That night, we ate this simple pasta starring spicy sausage and our homegrown kale.
—Angela Lemoine, Howell, NJ

TAKES: 30 MIN. • **MAKES:** 6 SERVINGS

- **1 pkg. (12 oz.) bucatini pasta or fettuccine**
- **2 tsp. plus 3 Tbsp. olive oil, divided**
- **1 lb. regular or spicy bulk Italian sausage**
- **5 garlic cloves, thinly sliced**
- **8 cups chopped fresh kale (about 5 oz.)**
- **¾ tsp. salt**
- **¼ tsp. pepper**
- **Shredded Romano cheese**

1. Cook pasta according to the package directions, decreasing time by 3 minutes. Drain, reserving 2 cups pasta water. Toss pasta with 2 tsp. oil.
2. In a 6-qt. stockpot, cook the sausage over medium heat until no longer pink, 5-7 minutes, breaking sausage into large crumbles. Add garlic and remaining oil; cook and stir 2 minutes. Stir in kale, salt and pepper; cook, covered, over medium-low heat until the kale is tender, about 10 minutes, stirring occasionally.
3. Add pasta and reserved pasta water; bring to a boil. Reduce heat; simmer, uncovered, until pasta is al dente and liquid is absorbed, about 3 minutes, tossing to combine. Sprinkle with cheese.
1⅓ CUPS: 512 cal., 30g fat (8g sat. fat), 51mg chol., 898mg sod., 43g carb. (2g sugars, 3g fiber), 19g pro.

READER REVIEW

"This recipe is absolutely delicious. Even our kids who typically wouldn't like kale love it in this recipe! I don't change anything unless I add even more garlic."

KODYUNSTAD, TASTEOFHOME.COM

CORNMEAL CATFISH WITH AVOCADO SAUCE

When I was growing up in California, my mother often made catfish. Now I cook it with my own twist. When only frozen catfish fillets are available, I thaw them in the refrigerator overnight and they work just as well as fresh.
—Mary Lou Cook, Welches, OR

TAKES: 25 MIN.
MAKES: 4 SERVINGS (¾ CUP SAUCE)

- **1 medium ripe avocado, peeled and cubed**
- **⅓ cup reduced-fat mayonnaise**
- **¼ cup fresh cilantro leaves**
- **2 Tbsp. lime juice**
- **½ tsp. garlic salt**
- **¼ cup cornmeal**
- **1 tsp. seafood seasoning**
- **4 catfish fillets (6 oz. each)**
- **3 Tbsp. canola oil**
- **1 medium tomato, chopped**

1. Place first 5 ingredients in a food processor; process until blended.
2. In a shallow bowl, mix the cornmeal and seafood seasoning. Dip the catfish in cornmeal mixture to coat both sides; shake off excess.
3. In a large skillet, heat oil over medium heat. Add the catfish in batches; cook for 4-5 minutes on each side or until the fish flakes easily with a fork. Top with avocado sauce and chopped tomato.
1 FILLET WITH 3 TBSP. SAUCE: 505 cal., 37g fat (6g sat. fat), 87mg chol., 649mg sod., 15g carb. (2g sugars, 4g fiber), 29g pro.

4. Spread the sauce over crusts; top with pepperoni and cheeses. Bake until cheese is melted, 8-10 minutes. Cut into squares.

FREEZE OPTION: Bake the crusts and assemble pizzas as directed. Securely wrap and freeze unbaked pizzas. To use, unwrap the pizzas; bake as directed, increasing time as necessary.

2 PIECES: 460 cal., 23g fat (10g sat. fat), 56mg chol., 1096mg sod., 39g carb. (4g sugars, 3g fiber), 25g pro.

TERIYAKI GLAZED CHICKEN

I love to experiment with food. We're able to buy sweet onions grown on Maui, so I stir-fry them with chicken and carrots for a tasty teriyaki meal.

—Kel Brenneman, Riverdale, CA

TAKES: 30 MIN. • **MAKES:** 4 SERVINGS

- **1 lb. boneless skinless chicken breast halves, cut into strips**
- **3 Tbsp. canola oil, divided**
- **4 medium carrots, julienned**
- **1 medium sweet onion, julienned**
- **½ cup soy sauce**
- **¼ cup packed brown sugar**
- **Hot cooked rice**
- **Optional: Sesame seeds, toasted, and sliced green onions**

1. In a large skillet or wok, stir-fry the chicken in 2 Tbsp. oil until no longer pink, 6-8 minutes. Remove the chicken and set aside.

2. In the same skillet, stir-fry carrots in remaining oil for 2 minutes. Add onion; stir-fry until the vegetables are tender, 2-4 minutes longer.

3. Combine soy sauce and brown sugar; add to skillet. Bring to a boil. Return chicken to skillet. Boil until sauce is slightly thickened, about 5 minutes. Serve with rice. Sprinkle with sesame seeds and green onions if desired.

HEALTH TIP: Using reduced-sodium soy sauce will decrease sodium content to about 1,200 milligrams for each serving, but that's still high. To cut even more, replace some of the soy sauce with reduced-sodium broth or water.

1 SERVING: 324 cal., 13g fat (2g sat. fat), 63mg chol., 1922mg sod., 23g carb. (20g sugars, 3g fiber), 28g pro.

PEPPERONI PAN PIZZA

I've spent years trying to come up with the perfect homemade crust and sauce, and I use both in this classic pepperoni pizza. I fix this for my husband and sons often, and it always satisfies our hearty appetites.

—Susan Lindahl, Alford, FL

PREP: 30 MIN. • **BAKE:** 10 MIN.
MAKES: 2 PIZZAS (9 PIECES EACH)

- **2¾ to 3 cups all-purpose flour**
- **1 pkg. (¼ oz.) active dry yeast**
- **¼ tsp. salt**
- **1 cup warm water (120° to 130°)**
- **1 Tbsp. canola oil**

SAUCE

- **1 can (14½ oz.) diced tomatoes, undrained**
- **1 can (6 oz.) tomato paste**
- **1 Tbsp. canola oil**
- **1 tsp. salt**
- **½ tsp. each dried basil, oregano, marjoram and thyme**
- **¼ tsp. garlic powder**
- **¼ tsp. pepper**

PIZZAS

- **1 pkg. (3½ oz.) sliced pepperoni**
- **5 cups shredded part-skim mozzarella cheese**
- **¼ cup grated Parmesan cheese**
- **¼ cup grated Romano cheese**

1. In a large bowl, combine 2 cups flour, yeast and salt. Add the water and oil; beat until smooth. Add enough remaining flour to form a soft dough.

2. Turn onto a floured surface; knead until smooth and elastic, 5-7 minutes. Cover and let stand for 10 minutes. Meanwhile, in a small bowl, combine the tomatoes, tomato paste, oil and seasonings.

3. Divide dough in half; press into two 15x10x1-in. baking pans coated with cooking spray. Prick dough generously with a fork. Bake at 425° until lightly browned, 12-16 minutes.

PORK WITH MUSTARD SAUCE

Back when I was a girl, I couldn't wait until I was grown up and could start cooking for my own family. Now that I am, I enjoy using pork. The tender meat and the rich mustard sauce in this recipe are delectable together.
—Irma Pomeroy, Enfield, CT

TAKES: 30 MIN. • **MAKES:** 4 SERVINGS

- 1 lb. pork tenderloin
- 2 Tbsp. butter
- ½ cup beef broth
- ¾ tsp. dried tarragon
- ½ cup heavy whipping cream
- 1 Tbsp. Dijon mustard
- Salt and pepper to taste
- Hot cooked noodles, optional

1. Cut tenderloin into 8 pieces. Slice each piece again, but do not cut all the way through; open and flatten each piece, pounding lightly with meat mallet.
2. In a large skillet over medium-high heat, cook the pork in butter until no longer pink, 5-6 minutes on each side. Remove to a serving dish and keep warm; discard drippings.
3. In the same skillet, cook broth and tarragon over high heat until reduced by half. Reduce heat; stir in cream and mustard. Season with salt and pepper. Spoon over pork. Serve with noodles if desired.

2 PIECES PORK WITH 3 TBSP. SAUCE: 292 cal., 21g fat (12g sat. fat), 119mg chol., 311mg sod., 2g carb. (1g sugars, 0 fiber), 24g pro.

FETTUCCINE WITH BLACK BEAN SAUCE

When my husband went on a heart-smart diet, I had to come up with new ways to get more vegetables into our daily menus. This recipe for meatless spaghetti sauce is a winner. It's especially delicious with spinach fettuccine.
—Marianne Neuman, East Troy, WI

TAKES: 30 MIN. • **MAKES:** 5 SERVINGS

- 6 oz. uncooked fettuccine
- 1 small green pepper, chopped
- 1 small onion, chopped
- 1 Tbsp. olive oil
- 2 cups garden-style pasta sauce
- 1 can (15 oz.) black beans, rinsed and drained
- 2 Tbsp. minced fresh basil or 2 tsp. dried basil
- 1 tsp. dried oregano
- ½ tsp. fennel seed
- ¼ tsp. garlic salt
- 1 cup shredded part-skim mozzarella cheese
- Additional chopped fresh basil, optional

1. Cook the fettuccine according to the package directions. Meanwhile, in a large saucepan, saute green pepper and onion in oil until tender. Stir in the pasta sauce, black beans and seasonings.
2. Bring to a boil. Reduce heat; simmer, uncovered, for 5 minutes. Drain the fettuccine. Top with sauce and sprinkle with cheese. If desired, top with chopped fresh basil.

HEALTH TIP: Since you're eating a healthy dinner, switch up your noodle game, too. Try this dish with whole wheat, buckwheat, quinoa, chickpea or multigrain pasta.

¾ CUP PASTA WITH ¾ CUP SAUCE: 350 cal., 10g fat (3g sat. fat), 17mg chol., 761mg sod., 51g carb. (12g sugars, 8g fiber), 16g pro.
DIABETIC EXCHANGES: 2½ starch, 2 vegetable, 1 lean meat, 1 fat.

READER REVIEW

"Instead of pasta, I used spaghetti squash. It was excellent. I have made this recipe more than once."

PBARSTAD, TASTEOFHOME.COM

AIR-FRYER FAJITA-STUFFED CHICKEN

I had all the ingredients for fajitas, but wanted to try an air-fried version. Since my air fryer is a small one, I was afraid it would be difficult to get as much filling as I could in each stuffed chicken breast. I achieved this by cutting slits in the breasts and then filling them.
—Joan Hallford, North Richland Hills, TX

PREP: 20 MIN. • **COOK:** 15 MIN./BATCH
MAKES: 4 SERVINGS

- 4 **boneless skinless chicken breast halves (6 oz. each)**
- 1 **small onion, halved and thinly sliced**
- ½ **medium green pepper, thinly sliced**
- 1 **Tbsp. olive oil**
- 1 **Tbsp. chili powder**
- 1 **tsp. ground cumin**
- ½ **tsp. salt**
- ¼ **tsp. garlic powder**
- 4 **oz. cheddar cheese, cut into 4 slices**
- **Optional: Salsa, sour cream, minced fresh cilantro, jalapeno slices and guacamole**

1. Preheat air fryer to 375°. Cut a pocket horizontally in the thickest part of each chicken breast half. Fill with onion and green pepper. In a small bowl, combine olive oil and seasonings; rub over chicken.
2. In batches, place chicken on greased tray in air-fryer basket. Cook 6 minutes. Top chicken with cheese slices; secure with toothpicks. Cook until a thermometer inserted in chicken reads at least 165°, 6-8 minutes longer. Discard toothpicks. If desired, serve with toppings of your choice.
1 CHICKEN BREAST HALF: 347 cal., 17g fat (7g sat. fat), 126mg chol., 628mg sod., 5g carb. (1g sugars, 1g fiber), 42g pro.

MANGO CHUTNEY CHICKEN CURRY

My father invented this recipe while we were traveling together. Adjust the amount of curry according to your taste and desired heat level.
—Dina Moreno, Seattle, WA

TAKES: 25 MIN. • **MAKES:** 4 SERVINGS

- 1 **Tbsp. canola oil**
- 1 **lb. boneless skinless chicken breasts, cubed**
- 1 **Tbsp. curry powder**
- 2 **garlic cloves, minced**
- ¼ **tsp. salt**
- ¼ **tsp. pepper**
- ½ **cup mango chutney**
- ½ **cup half-and-half cream**

1. In a large skillet, heat oil over medium-high heat; brown chicken. Stir in the curry powder, garlic, salt and pepper; cook until aromatic, 1-2 minutes longer.
2. Stir in chutney and cream. Bring to boil. Reduce the heat; simmer, uncovered, until the chicken is no longer pink, 4-6 minutes, stirring occasionally.
½ CUP: 320 cal., 9g fat (3g sat. fat), 78mg chol., 558mg sod., 30g carb. (19g sugars, 1g fiber), 24g pro.

NACHO PIE

In place of the ground beef and mozzarella cheese, consider topping this zesty pie with lean ground sausage and cheddar cheese. It tastes just as good.
—LaVerna Mjones, Moorhead, MN

TAKES: 30 MIN. • **MAKES:** 6 SERVINGS

- **4 cups nacho tortilla chips, coarsely crushed**
- **1 lb. ground beef**
- **½ cup chopped onion**
- **1 can (16 oz.) chili beans, undrained, warmed**
- **1 can (8 oz.) tomato sauce**
- **1 cup shredded part-skim mozzarella cheese**

1. Place the chips in a lightly greased 9-in. pie plate and set aside.
2. In a large skillet, cook beef and onion over medium heat until meat is no longer pink; drain. Spoon over chips. Top with beans, tomato sauce and cheese.
3. Bake, uncovered, at 375° until heated through and the mozzarella is melted, 7-8 minutes.

1 SERVING: 462 cal., 24g fat (7g sat. fat), 59mg chol., 841mg sod., 40g carb. (3g sugars, 6g fiber), 26g pro.

LEMONY VEGETABLES & PASTA

My refreshing pasta dish comes together in less than an hour. Its simplicity and flavor combinations are reminiscent of authentic Italian cuisine.
—Erin Mylroie, Santa Clara, UT

PREP: 25 MIN. • **COOK:** 15 MIN.
MAKES: 7 SERVINGS

- **1 lb. fresh asparagus, trimmed and cut into 1-in. pieces**
- **1 medium sweet red pepper, cut into 1-in. pieces**
- **1 medium red onion, sliced**
- **1 Tbsp. olive oil**
- **½ tsp. salt**
- **¼ tsp. pepper**
- **4½ cups uncooked bow tie pasta**
- **1 Tbsp. butter**
- **1 Tbsp. all-purpose flour**
- **3 garlic cloves, minced**
- **¼ tsp. crushed red pepper flakes**
- **1 cup vegetable broth**
- **1 cup shredded Parmesan cheese**
- **½ cup sour cream**
- **2 Tbsp. lemon juice**
- **1 Tbsp. grated lemon zest**
- **½ cup chopped pistachios**
- **¼ cup fresh basil leaves, thinly sliced**
- **Additional shredded Parmesan cheese**

1. In a large bowl, combine asparagus, red pepper, onion, oil, salt and pepper. Transfer to a greased 15x10x1-in. baking pan. Bake at 450° for 10-15 minutes or until golden brown, stirring once.
2. Meanwhile, cook pasta according to package directions. In a large saucepan, melt butter over medium heat. Stir in the flour, garlic and pepper flakes until blended. Whisk in broth until blended. Bring to a boil over medium-high heat; cook and stir 2 minutes or until liquid is thickened and bubbly.
3. Reduce heat. Stir in the cheese, sour cream, lemon juice and zest; heat through. Drain pasta and place in a large bowl. Add the cheese sauce and asparagus mixture; toss to coat. Sprinkle with pistachios, basil and additional cheese.

1½ CUPS: 366 cal., 15g fat (6g sat. fat), 24mg chol., 559mg sod., 45g carb. (5g sugars, 4g fiber), 15g pro.

FILIPINO CHICKEN ADOBO

My mom always makes her saucy chicken adobo recipe when I come home to visit. I think it's even better the next day as leftovers—she says it's because of the vinegar.
—Michael Moya, New York, NY

PREP: 10 MIN. + MARINATING
COOK: 30 MIN.
MAKES: 6 SERVINGS

- **1 cup white vinegar**
- **¼ cup soy sauce**
- **1 whole garlic bulb, smashed and peeled**
- **2 tsp. kosher salt**
- **1 tsp. coarsely ground pepper**
- **1 bay leaf**
- **2 lbs. bone-in chicken thighs or drumsticks**
- **1 Tbsp. canola oil**
- **1 cup water**

1. In a shallow dish, combine the first 6 ingredients. Add chicken; refrigerate, covered, 20-30 minutes. Drain, reserving marinade. Pat chicken dry.
2. In a large skillet, heat oil over medium-high heat; brown chicken. Stir in water and reserved marinade. Bring to a boil. Reduce heat; simmer, uncovered, until chicken is no longer pink and sauce is slightly reduced, 20-25 minutes. Discard bay leaf. If desired, serve chicken with cooking sauce.

NOTE: Chicken adobo is a very flavorful dish with a mildly sweet, tangy garlic and soy flavor. The acid in the vinegar breaks down the fibers in the chicken, making it very tender.

1 SERVING: 234 cal., 15g fat (4g sat. fat), 71mg chol., 1315mg sod., 2g carb. (0 sugars, 0 fiber), 22g pro.

READER REVIEW

"This is one of my favorite recipes. I was given the recipe by my neighbor, who got it from her Filipino grandmother. We serve it with sticky rice, and yes, it is even better the next day!"

NOPALITO, TASTEOFHOME.COM

CHINESE CASHEW CHICKEN PIZZA

I make this quick weeknight dinner recipe when I'm craving takeout pizza and Chinese food. I take advantage of shortcuts such as premade pizza crust and rotisserie chicken to cut down on my time in the kitchen.
—Joseph Sciascia, San Mateo, CA

TAKES: 30 MIN. • **MAKES:** 8 SERVINGS

- **1 prebaked 12-in. pizza crust or flatbread**
- **1 Tbsp. sesame oil**
- **¾ cup hoisin sauce**
- **2 tsp. chili garlic sauce**
- **1½ cups shredded cooked chicken**
- **4 green onions, chopped, divided**
- **½ cup chopped sweet red pepper**
- **⅓ cup shredded carrots**
- **½ cup chopped cashews**
- **3 Tbsp. chopped fresh cilantro**
- **1¼ cups shredded mozzarella cheese**

1. Preheat oven to 425°. Place pizza crust on a pizza pan; brush with sesame oil. In small bowl, combine the hoisin sauce and chili garlic sauce; brush ⅓ cup over crust. Toss the remaining mixture with chicken; sprinkle over the crust. Top with 2 green onions, red pepper, carrots, cashews and cilantro. Sprinkle mozzarella over top.
2. Bake until cheese is lightly browned, 12-15 minutes. Let stand 5 minutes; sprinkle with remaining 2 green onions.
1 PIECE: 357 cal., 15g fat (5g sat. fat), 38mg chol., 876mg sod., 37g carb. (9g sugars, 2g fiber), 19g pro.

TEST KITCHEN TIP

Pizza night is the perfect time to enjoy full-flavored, fatty cheeses. Full-fat cheeses provide better melting coverage compared to low-moisture cheeses, which also end up having a rubbery texture. We recommend a combo of mozzarella for meltability and provolone for flavor. Experiment and have fun!

ROXANNE CHAN
Albany, CA

SPAGHETTI & MEATBALL SKILLET SUPPER

I developed this one-skillet spaghetti dish to cut down on cooking time on busy nights. The beans, artichokes and tomatoes bump up the nutrition factor, while the lemon and parsley make it pop with brightness. Try it for a new twist on a classic meal.
—Roxanne Chan, Albany, CA

TAKES: 30 MIN. • **MAKES:** 6 SERVINGS

- **1 Tbsp. olive oil**
- **12 oz. frozen fully cooked Italian turkey meatballs**
- **1 can (28 oz.) whole tomatoes, undrained, broken up**
- **1 can (15 oz.) cannellini beans, rinsed and drained**
- **1 can (14 oz.) water-packed quartered artichoke hearts, drained**
- **½ tsp. Italian seasoning**
- **1 can (14½ oz.) reduced-sodium chicken broth**
- **4 oz. uncooked spaghetti, broken into 2-in. pieces (about 1⅓ cups)**
- **¼ cup chopped fresh parsley**
- **1 Tbsp. lemon juice**
- **Grated Parmesan cheese**

1. In a large skillet, heat oil over medium heat; add the meatballs and cook until browned slightly, turning occasionally.
2. Add tomatoes, beans, artichoke hearts, Italian seasoning and broth; bring to a boil. Stir in spaghetti; return to a boil. Reduce the heat; simmer, covered, until spaghetti is tender, 10-12 minutes. Stir occasionally.
3. Stir in parsley and lemon juice. Serve with cheese.
1⅓ CUPS: 330 cal., 10g fat (2g sat. fat), 43mg chol., 1051mg sod., 38g carb. (5g sugars, 6g fiber), 20g pro.

GOLDEN APRICOT-GLAZED TURKEY BREAST

Basted with a simple glaze, this tender turkey bakes to a lovely golden brown. Make it the centerpiece of a holiday spread or enjoy it for a special Sunday dinner.
—Greg Fontenot, The Woodlands, TX

PREP: 10 MIN.
BAKE: 1½ HOURS + STANDING
MAKES: 15 SERVINGS

- ½ **cup apricot preserves**
- ¼ **cup balsamic vinegar**
- ¼ **tsp. pepper**
- **Dash salt**
- 1 **bone-in turkey breast (5 lbs.)**

1. Preheat the oven to 325°. Combine the preserves, vinegar, pepper and salt. Place turkey breast on a rack in a large shallow roasting pan.
2. Bake, uncovered, 1½-2 hours or until a thermometer reads 170°, basting every 30 minutes with apricot mixture. (Cover loosely with foil if turkey browns too quickly.) Cover and let stand 15 minutes before slicing.
4 OZ. COOKED TURKEY: 236 cal., 8g fat (2g sat. fat), 81mg chol., 84mg sod., 8g carb. (5g sugars, 0 fiber), 32g pro. **DIABETIC EXCHANGES:** 4 lean meat, ½ starch.

SPICY SWEET SHRIMP WITH PINEAPPLE SALSA

I wanted to find a way to use pineapple salsa in a recipe. I came up with this simple, quick and delicious dish!
—Erin Schillo, Northfield, OH

TAKES: 30 MIN. • **MAKES:** 8 SERVINGS

- 1½ **cups uncooked basmati rice**
- ¾ **cup canned black beans, rinsed and drained**
- 2 **tsp. canola oil**
- ½ **cup finely chopped onion**
- 1½ **cups unsweetened pineapple juice**
- ¼ **cup packed brown sugar**
- 1 **Tbsp. Sriracha chili sauce**
- 3 **cups cubed fresh pineapple**
- 1 **medium sweet red pepper, diced**
- 1 **cup chopped fresh cilantro**
- 1 **small red onion, finely chopped**
- 2 **Tbsp. lime juice**
- ¼ **tsp. salt**
- ¼ **tsp. pepper**
- 1½ **lbs. peeled and deveined shrimp (31-40 per lb.)**

1. Cook the rice according to package the directions. Stir in the beans; cover and keep warm.
2. While rice cooks, heat oil in a large skillet over medium-high heat. Saute onion until tender, 3-4 minutes. Stir in pineapple juice, brown sugar and chili sauce; bring to a boil. Cook, uncovered, on high until liquid is reduced to ½ cup, 10-12 minutes.
3. For the salsa, toss pineapple with red pepper, cilantro, red onion, lime juice, salt and pepper.
4. Once sauce has reduced, stir in shrimp and return just to a boil. Reduce the heat; simmer, uncovered, until the shrimp turn pink, 2-3 minutes. Serve with rice mixture and salsa.
1 SERVING: 356 cal., 3g fat (0 sat. fat), 129mg chol., 312mg sod., 59g carb. (20g sugars, 3g fiber), 22g pro.

SOUR CREAM & DILL CHICKEN

This recipe is an updated version of the Sunday dinner my mother would prepare.
—Rebekah Brown, Three Hills, AB

PREP: 10 MIN. • **BAKE:** 1 HOUR
MAKES: 4 SERVINGS

- **8 chicken drumsticks, skin removed**
- **Pepper to taste**
- **1 can (10½ oz.) condensed cream of mushroom soup, undiluted**
- **1 envelope onion soup mix**
- **1 cup sour cream**
- **1 Tbsp. lemon juice**
- **1 Tbsp. fresh dill, chopped or 1 tsp. dill weed**
- **1 can (4 oz.) mushroom stems and pieces, drained**
- **Paprika**
- **Cooked wide egg noodles, optional**

1. Place the chicken in a single layer in a 13x9-in. baking dish. Sprinkle with pepper. Combine the soup, soup mix, sour cream, lemon juice, dill and mushrooms; pour over chicken. Sprinkle with paprika.
2. Bake, uncovered, at 350° until chicken is tender, about 1 hour. If desired, serve over egg noodles and sprinkle with additional dill.
2 DRUMSTICKS: 359 cal., 21g fat (9g sat. fat), 98mg chol., 1346mg sod., 13g carb. (3g sugars, 2g fiber), 29g pro.

TORTELLINI WITH SAUSAGE & MASCARPONE

When I crave Italian comfort food on a busy night, this fast and yummy dish is my top pick. It's table-ready in less time than it takes to order takeout.
—Gerry Vance, Millbrae, CA

TAKES: 20 MIN. • **MAKES:** 6 SERVINGS

- **1 pkg. (20 oz.) refrigerated cheese tortellini**
- **8 oz. bulk Italian sausage**
- **1 jar (24 oz.) pasta sauce with mushrooms**
- **½ cup shredded Parmesan cheese**
- **1 carton (8 oz.) mascarpone cheese**
- **Crushed red pepper flakes, optional**

1. Prepare tortellini according to package directions. Meanwhile, in a large cast-iron or other heavy skillet, cook the sausage over medium heat until no longer pink, 6-8 minutes, breaking into crumbles; drain. Stir in pasta sauce; heat through.
2. Drain tortellini, reserving 1 cup cooking water. Add tortellini to sauce with enough reserved cooking water to reach desired consistency; toss to coat. Stir in Parmesan cheese; dollop with mascarpone cheese. If desired, sprinkle with red pepper flakes.
1 CUP: 637 cal., 37g fat (17g sat. fat), 113mg chol., 1040mg sod., 57g carb. (11g sugars, 4g fiber), 24g pro.

MEXICAN TURKEY MEAT LOAF

Here's a zesty, flavorful meat loaf you can sink your teeth into! Pair it with black beans, rice, green salad with lime vinaigrette or any of your favorite Tex-Mex side dishes.
—Kristen Miller, Glendale, WI

PREP: 25 MIN. • **COOK:** 3 HOURS + STANDING
MAKES: 1 LOAF (6 SERVINGS)

- 2 slices white bread, torn into small pieces
- ⅓ cup 2% milk
- 1 lb. lean ground turkey
- ½ lb. fresh chorizo
- 1 medium sweet red pepper, finely chopped
- 1 small onion, finely chopped
- 1 jalapeno pepper, seeded and finely chopped
- 2 large eggs, lightly beaten
- 2 Tbsp. minced fresh cilantro
- 2 garlic cloves, minced
- 2 tsp. chili powder
- 1 tsp. salt
- 1 tsp. ground cumin
- ½ tsp. dried oregano
- ½ tsp. pepper
- ¼ tsp. cayenne pepper
- ⅔ cup salsa, divided
- Additional minced fresh cilantro
- Hot cooked Spanish rice

1. Combine bread and milk in a large bowl; let stand until liquid is absorbed. Add next 14 ingredients and ⅓ cup salsa; mix lightly but thoroughly.

2. On an 18x7-in. piece of heavy-duty foil, shape meat mixture into a 10x6-in. oval loaf. Lifting with foil, transfer to a 6-qt. oval slow cooker. Press ends of foil up sides of slow cooker.

3. Cook, covered, on low 3-4 hours or until a thermometer reads 165°. Lifting with foil, drain the fat into slow cooker before removing meat loaf to a platter; top with the remaining salsa and sprinkle with cilantro. Let stand 10 minutes before slicing. Serve with rice.

1 PIECE: 335 cal., 20g fat (6g sat. fat), 149mg chol., 1109mg sod., 11g carb. (4g sugars, 1g fiber), 27g pro.

GLAZED PINEAPPLE HAM

This was the first time that I have ever done our holiday ham, and I was thrilled with how crispy and succulent it turned out. It's going to be a new tradition.
—Chrissy Clark, Boise, ID

PREP: 15 MIN.
BAKE: 2¼ HOURS + STANDING
MAKES: 20 SERVINGS

1 fully cooked bone-in ham (7 to 9 lbs.)
Whole cloves

GLAZE/SAUCE

2 Tbsp. cornstarch
¼ cup cold water
2½ cups packed dark brown sugar, divided
1 can (20 oz.) unsweetened crushed pineapple, undrained
¼ cup lemon juice
2 Tbsp. Dijon mustard
¼ tsp. salt
1 cup packed light brown sugar

1. Preheat oven to 325°. Place ham on a rack in a shallow roasting pan. Using a sharp knife, score surface of ham with ¼-in.-deep cuts in a diamond pattern; insert a clove in each diamond. Cover ham and bake 2-2½ hours or until a thermometer reaches 130°.

2. Meanwhile, in a large saucepan, dissolve cornstarch in water; stir in 2 cups dark brown sugar, pineapple, lemon juice, Dijon mustard and salt. Bring to a boil over medium-high heat; cook and stir for 1-2 minutes or until slightly thickened. Reserve 2 cups for sauce; keep warm.

3. Remove ham from oven. Increase the oven setting to 425°. Pour the remaining pineapple mixture over ham. In a small bowl, mix light brown sugar and the remaining dark brown sugar; spread over ham.

4. Bake ham, uncovered, 10-15 minutes longer or until a thermometer reads 140°. Serve with reserved sauce.

5 OZ. COOKED HAM WITH ABOUT 1 TBSP. SAUCE: 300 cal., 4g fat (1g sat. fat), 70mg chol., 912mg sod., 44g carb. (41g sugars, 0 fiber), 23g pro.

TROPICAL SWEET & SPICY PORK TENDERLOIN

When we're craving something sweet and spicy, pork tenderloin cooked with chipotle, barbecue sauce and pineapple delivers!
—Cyndy Gerken, Naples, FL

TAKES: 30 MIN. • **MAKES:** 4 SERVINGS

1 pork tenderloin (1 lb.), cut into 1-in. cubes
¼ tsp. salt
¼ tsp. pepper
2 Tbsp. olive oil
1 medium onion, chopped
1 medium green pepper, chopped
3 garlic cloves, minced
1 cup chicken stock
1 can (20 oz.) pineapple tidbits, drained
1 cup honey barbecue sauce
½ cup packed brown sugar
2 finely chopped canned chipotle peppers plus 2 tsp. adobo sauce
2 Tbsp. reduced-sodium soy sauce
Hot cooked rice

1. Sprinkle pork with salt and pepper. In a large skillet, heat oil over medium-high heat. Add the pork; cook until browned, 4-6 minutes. Remove.

2. In same skillet, cook onion and pepper until softened, 2-4 minutes. Add garlic; cook 1 minute. Return pork to pan; stir in chicken stock. Cook, covered, until pork is tender, about 5 minutes.

3. Stir in the next 5 ingredients; simmer, uncovered, until sauce is thickened, about 5 minutes. Serve with rice.

1½ CUPS: 539 cal., 11g fat (2g sat. fat), 64mg chol., 1374mg sod., 82g carb. (72g sugars, 2g fiber), 25g pro.

SPICY ISLAND SHRIMP

My husband got this recipe while he was living on St. Croix. We've served the zippy shrimp dish on several holiday occasions. I'm amazed at how even those who claim not to care for shrimp come out of their shells and devour them when they're prepared this way!
—Teresa Methe, Minden, NE

PREP: 20 MIN. • **COOK:** 20 MIN.
MAKES: 6 SERVINGS

- 1 large green pepper, chopped
- 1 large onion, chopped
- ½ cup butter cubed
- 2¼ lbs. uncooked large shrimp, peeled and deveined
- 2 cans (8 oz. each) tomato sauce
- 3 Tbsp. chopped green onions
- 1 Tbsp. minced fresh parsley
- 1 tsp. salt
- 1 tsp. pepper
- 1 tsp. paprika
- ½ tsp. garlic powder
- ½ tsp. dried oregano
- ½ tsp. dried thyme
- ¼ to ½ tsp. white pepper
- ¼ to ½ tsp. cayenne pepper
- Optional: Hot cooked rice and thinly sliced green onions

1. In a large skillet, saute green pepper and onion in butter until tender. Reduce heat; add shrimp. Cook for 5 minutes or until shrimp turn pink.

2. Stir in the tomato sauce, green onions, parsley and seasonings. Bring to a boil. Reduce the heat; simmer, uncovered, for 20 minutes or until slightly thickened. If desired, serve with rice and additional green onions.

1 SERVING: 293 cal., 17g fat (10g sat. fat), 293mg chol., 1013mg sod., 7g carb. (3g sugars, 2g fiber), 29g pro.

TASTY LENTIL TACOS

My husband has to watch his cholesterol. Finding dishes that are healthy for him and yummy for our five children is a challenge sometimes, but this fun taco recipe is a huge hit with everyone.
—Michelle Thomas, Bangor, ME

PREP: 15 MIN. • **COOK:** 40 MIN.
MAKES: 6 SERVINGS

- 1 tsp. canola oil
- 1 medium onion, finely chopped
- 1 garlic clove, minced
- 1 cup dried lentils, rinsed
- 1 Tbsp. chili powder
- 2 tsp. ground cumin
- 1 tsp. dried oregano
- 2½ cups vegetable or reduced-sodium chicken broth
- 1 cup salsa
- 12 taco shells
- 1½ cups shredded lettuce
- 1 cup chopped fresh tomatoes
- 1½ cups shredded reduced-fat cheddar cheese
- 6 Tbsp. fat-free sour cream

1. In a large nonstick skillet, heat oil over medium heat; saute onion and garlic until tender. Add lentils and seasonings; cook and stir 1 minute. Stir in broth; bring to a boil. Reduce heat; simmer, covered, until lentils are tender, 25-30 minutes.

2. Cook, uncovered, until the mixture is thickened, 6-8 minutes; stir occasionally. Mash lentils slightly; stir in salsa and heat through. Serve in taco shells. Top with remaining ingredients.

2 TACOS: 365 cal., 12g fat (5g sat. fat), 21mg chol., 777mg sod., 44g carb. (5g sugars, 6g fiber), 19g pro. **DIABETIC EXCHANGES:** 2½ starch, 2 lean meat, 1 vegetable, 1 fat.

READER REVIEW

"I love this recipe. It's easy, inexpensive and a great meat substitute. You can make tacos, burritos or a taco salad with the lentil mixture. Also, it freezes well!"

KSKONBERG, TASTEOFHOME.COM

Casserole Entrees

Creamy, cheesy, noodle-y and baked to bubbly, melty perfection, these wow-worthy casseroles are perfect for busy weeknights and special occasions alike. Grab your baking dish—it's time for comfort food!

SPANISH RICE & CHICKEN

My mother has always been an avid cook, and my sister, two brothers and I were raised on this casserole. When I polled our family to see which recipe I should share, this fresh-tasting, well-seasoned chicken bake came out on top. I know you'll enjoy it as much as we do.
—Cindy Clark, Mechanicsburg, PA

PREP: 20 MIN. • **COOK:** 1 HOUR
MAKES: 6 SERVINGS

- **1 broiler/fryer chicken (3 lbs.), cut up**
- **1 tsp. garlic salt**
- **1 tsp. celery salt**
- **1 tsp. paprika**
- **1 cup uncooked rice**
- **¾ cup chopped onion**
- **¾ cup chopped green pepper**
- **¼ cup minced fresh parsley**
- **1½ cups chicken broth**
- **1 cup chopped tomatoes**
- **1½ tsp. chili powder**
- **1 tsp. salt**

1. Preheat oven to 425°. Place chicken in a greased 13x9-in. baking dish. Combine the garlic salt, celery salt and paprika; sprinkle over chicken. Bake, uncovered, for 20 minutes.
2. Remove chicken from dish. Combine rice, onion, green pepper and parsley; spoon into pan. In a saucepan, bring broth, tomatoes, chili powder and salt to a boil. Pour over rice mixture; mix well. Place chicken pieces on top. Cover and bake until chicken registers at least 165° and rice is tender, 40-45 minutes.

1 SERVING: 345 cal., 12 g fat (3 g sat. fat), 73 mg chol., 1,448 mg sod., 30g carb., 2g fiber, 27 g pro.

READER REVIEW

"This is a great recipe. The seasoning for the chicken is simple, but very tasty! The rice turned out well too. It looks as if you really fussed for dinner when you didn't."

PEYTONFAN18, TASTEOFHOME.COM

MONTEREY SPAGHETTI

Our family leads an active life, so I make a lot of casseroles. It's so nice to have a hearty, nutritious dish my kids will eat. Topped with cheese and french-fried onions, this tasty bake is a hit at our house.
—Janet Hibler, Cameron, MO

PREP: 15 MIN. • **BAKE:** 35 MIN.
MAKES: 8 SERVINGS

- **4 oz. spaghetti, broken into 2-in. pieces**
- **1 large egg**
- **1 cup sour cream**
- **¼ cup grated Parmesan cheese**
- **¼ tsp. garlic powder**
- **2 cups shredded Monterey Jack cheese**
- **1 pkg. (10 oz.) frozen chopped spinach, thawed and drained**
- **1 can (2.8 oz.) french-fried onions, divided**

Cook spaghetti according to package directions. Meanwhile, in a large bowl, beat the egg. Add sour cream, Parmesan cheese and garlic powder. Drain the spaghetti; add to egg mixture with Monterey Jack cheese, spinach and half of the onions. Pour into a greased 2-qt. baking dish. Cover and bake at 350° for 30 minutes or until heated though. Top with remaining onions; return to the oven for 5 minutes or until onions are golden brown.

1 SERVING: 311 cal., 20g fat (11g sat. fat), 74mg chol., 333mg sod., 18g carb. (2g sugars, 1g fiber), 13g pro.

SOUTHWESTERN TACO CASSEROLE

Try this fun riff on traditional tacos when you're looking for something different. This recipe puts the same signature Southwestern flavors into a comforting casserole.
—Bonnie King, Lansing, MI

PREP: 20 MIN. • **BAKE:** 20 MIN.
MAKES: 8 SERVINGS

- **2½ lbs. ground beef**
- **2 envelopes taco seasoning**
- **⅔ cup water**
- **1 can (16 oz.) kidney beans, rinsed and drained**
- **1 cup shredded Monterey Jack or pepper jack cheese**
- **2 large eggs, lightly beaten**
- **1 cup 2% milk**
- **1½ cups biscuit/baking mix**
- **1 cup sour cream**
- **1 cup shredded cheddar cheese**
- **2 cups shredded lettuce**
- **1 medium tomato, diced**
- **1 can (2¼ oz.) sliced ripe olives, drained**

1. Preheat oven to 400°. In a large skillet, cook beef over medium heat until the meat is no longer pink, 8-10 minutes, breaking into crumbles; drain. Stir in the taco seasoning and water. Bring to a boil. Reduce the heat; simmer, uncovered, for 5 minutes. Stir in beans.
2. Spoon meat mixture into a greased 8-in. square baking dish. Sprinkle with Monterey Jack cheese. In a large bowl, combine eggs, milk and biscuit mix until moistened. Pour over cheese.
3. Bake, uncovered, until lightly browned and a knife inserted in the center comes out clean, 20-25 minutes. Spread with sour cream. Top with cheddar cheese, lettuce, tomato and olives.

1 SERVING: 633 cal., 36g fat (16g sat. fat), 170mg chol., 1485mg sod., 36g carb. (5g sugars, 4g fiber), 41g pro.

CHICKEN CHEDDAR STUFFING CASSEROLE

Chock-full of homey, comforting flavor, this tasty chicken casserole is a great way to use up leftover cooked chicken. Plus it's quick to assemble because it calls for pantry items.
—Cathy Smith, Wyoming, MI

PREP: 15 MIN. • **BAKE:** 30 MIN.
MAKES: 2 CASSEROLES (6 SERVINGS EACH)

- **2 pkg. (6 oz. each) chicken stuffing mix**
- **2 cans (10½ oz. each) condensed cream of mushroom soup, undiluted**
- **1 cup 2% milk**
- **4 cups cubed cooked chicken**
- **2 cups frozen corn**
- **2 cans (8 oz. each) mushroom stems and pieces, drained**
- **4 cups shredded cheddar cheese**

1. Preheat oven to 350°. Prepare stuffing mixes according to package directions. Meanwhile, in a large bowl, combine soup and milk. Spread stuffing into 2 greased 8-in. square baking dishes. Layer with chicken, corn, mushrooms, soup mixture and cheese.
2. Cover and bake until cheese is melted, 30-35 minutes.

FREEZE OPTION: Cover and freeze unbaked casseroles for up to 3 months. Remove from freezer 30 minutes before baking (do not thaw). Preheat oven to 350°. Bake, covered, 1½ hours. Uncover; bake until heated through, 10-15 minutes longer.

1 SERVING: 373 cal., 21g fat (12g sat. fat), 96mg chol., 822mg sod., 21g carb. (3g sugars, 1g fiber), 26g pro.

SPINACH & SQUASH PIEROGI CASSEROLE

Here's a tasty casserole made with pierogies, buttery Polish dumplings stuffed with tasty fillings such as potatoes and cheese, cabbage, pork, even fruit. This recipe contains no meat, making it a top pick for vegetarians. Feel free to use pre-packaged ingredients to save time. Choose any kind of savory pirogies or if you're feeling adventurous, make your own!
—Susan Skrtich, Hamilton, ON

PREP: 35 MIN. • **BAKE:** 55 MIN. + STANDING
MAKES: 6 SERVINGS

- **1 tsp. olive oil**
- **1 medium onion, chopped**
- **1 Tbsp. minced garlic**
- **1 Tbsp. minced fresh basil**
- **½ tsp. salt**
- **½ tsp. pepper**
- **1 cup meatless pasta sauce**
- **1 pkg. (14 oz.) frozen potato and cheese pierogi, thawed**
- **1½ cups frozen chopped spinach, thawed and squeezed dry**
- **1 large egg, room temperature, lightly beaten**
- **1 cup frozen cubed butternut squash (about 5 oz.)**
- **1½ cups shredded part-skim mozzarella cheese**
- **½ cup sour cream, optional**

1. Preheat oven to 350°. Line a 9x5-in. loaf pan with foil, letting ends extend up sides; grease foil.
2. In a small skillet, heat oil over medium-high heat. Add onion; cook and stir until tender, 6-8 minutes. Add the garlic, basil, salt and pepper; cook 1 minute longer. Remove from heat.
3. Spread ½ cup pasta sauce into prepared pan. Top with pierogi; press firmly. Top with onion mixture. Mix spinach and egg; spoon over onion mixture. Spread squash evenly over spinach; spoon remaining ½ cup pasta sauce over top. Sprinkle with cheese. Bake until bubbly and cheese is golden brown, 55-65 minutes.
4. Let stand 10 minutes. Lifting with foil, remove from pan. Cut into slices. Serve with sour cream if desired.

1 SERVING: 269 cal., 9g fat (4g sat. fat), 54mg chol., 855mg sod., 33g carb. (10g sugars, 4g fiber), 14g pro.

ZUCCHINI RICOTTA BAKE

I have made this lasagna-like zucchini casserole frequently over the years and shared the recipe with many people. Best of all, it's a little bit lighter than other layered casseroles, making it an ideal choice for anyone trying to eat right.
—Eleanor Hauserman, Huntsville, AL

PREP: 15 MIN. • **BAKE:** 1 HOUR + STANDING
MAKES: 12 SERVINGS

- **2 lbs. zucchini**
- **1 carton (15 oz.) reduced-fat ricotta cheese**
- **½ cup egg substitute**
- **½ cup dry bread crumbs, divided**
- **5 Tbsp. grated Parmesan cheese, divided**
- **1 Tbsp. minced fresh parsley**
- **¼ tsp. dried oregano**
- **¼ tsp. dried basil**
- **⅛ tsp. pepper**
- **1 jar (28 oz.) meatless pasta sauce**
- **1½ cups shredded reduced-fat mozzarella cheese**

1. Preheat oven to 350°. Cut zucchini lengthwise into ¼-in. slices. Place in a basket over 1 in. of boiling water. Cover and steam until just tender, 5-6 minutes. Drain; pat dry.
2. In a large bowl, combine ricotta, egg substitute, 3 Tbsp. bread crumbs, 3 Tbsp. Parmesan, parsley, oregano, basil and pepper; set aside.
3. Spread a third of the spaghetti sauce in a 13x9-in. baking dish coated with cooking spray. Sprinkle with 2 Tbsp. dry bread crumbs. Cover with half of the zucchini, ricotta mixture and mozzarella. Repeat layers of sauce, zucchini, ricotta mixture and mozzarella. Cover with remaining spaghetti sauce.
4. Combine remaining 3 Tbsp. crumbs and 2 Tbsp. Parmesan; sprinkle over top. Cover and bake 45 minutes. Uncover; bake until golden brown, 15 minutes longer. Let stand 15 minutes before cutting.

1 PIECE: 150 cal., 5g fat (3g sat. fat), 20mg chol., 513mg sod., 14g carb. (8g sugars, 2g fiber), 11g pro. **DIABETIC EXCHANGES:** 1 lean meat, 1 vegetable, 1 fat, ½ starch.

FAVORITE CREAMY CHICKEN CASSEROLE

I created this noodle casserole when my husband was craving a dish his aunt used to make. It tastes and smells great and is now a staple at our house.
—Mari Warnke, Fremont, WI

PREP: 20 MIN. • **BAKE:** 40 MIN.
MAKES: 2 CASSEROLES (5 SERVINGS EACH)

4 cups uncooked egg noodles
4 cups cubed cooked chicken
1 pkg. (16 oz.) frozen peas and carrots
2 cups 2% milk
2 cans (10½ oz. each) condensed cream of celery soup, undiluted
2 cans (10½ oz. each) condensed cream of chicken soup, undiluted
1 cup chopped onion
2 Tbsp. butter, melted
½ tsp. salt
½ tsp. pepper

1. Preheat oven to 350°. Cook noodles according to the package directions. Meanwhile, in a large bowl, combine remaining ingredients. Drain noodles; add to chicken mixture.
2. Transfer the mixture to 2 greased 8-in. square baking dishes. Cover and bake for 30 minutes. Uncover; bake until heated through, 10-15 minutes.

FREEZE OPTION: Cover and freeze unbaked casseroles for up to 3 months. To use, partially thaw in refrigerator overnight. Remove from refrigerator 30 minutes before baking. Cover and microwave on high 10-12 minutes or until heated through and a thermometer inserted in center reads 165°, stirring twice.

1⅓ CUPS: 344 cal., 15g fat (5g sat. fat), 80mg chol., 996mg sod., 29g carb. (4g sugars, 5g fiber), 23g pro.

TEST KITCHEN TIP

If there are only one or two people in your household, or you want to save the leftovers for grab-and-go work or school lunches, cut the casserole into smaller portions instead of freezing the whole dish. Be sure to affix a label on the container with the recipe name, instructions for baking or reheating and the use-by date.

GREEN PEPPER CASSEROLE

I always prepare this family favorite when peppers and onions are in season.
—Ellen Lloyd, Greenfield, WI

PREP: 10 MIN. • **COOK:** 1 HOUR 25 MIN.
MAKES: 12 SERVINGS

3 lbs. ground beef
5 small onions, chopped
3 cans (10½ oz. each) condensed tomato soup, undiluted
1 Tbsp. paprika
3 medium green peppers, chopped
1 can (16 oz.) peas, drained
1 can (8 oz.) mushroom stems and pieces, drained
1 jar (4 oz.) pimientos, drained
Salt and pepper to taste
1 pkg. (16 oz.) medium pasta shells
Grated Parmesan cheese

1. In a Dutch oven, cook the beef and onions over medium heat until no longer pink, 5-7 minutes, breaking up beef into crumbles; drain. Add soup and paprika. Cover and simmer 1 hour.
2. Stir in green peppers, peas, mushroom stems, pimientos, salt and pepper. Cover and simmer until the peppers are tender, 15 minutes.
3. Meanwhile, cook macaroni according to package directions; drain. Place in a large serving bowl; top with the meat mixture. Sprinkle with Parmesan cheese.

1 SERVING: 440 cal., 15g fat (5g sat. fat), 70mg chol., 471mg sod., 48g carb. (11g sugars, 5g fiber), 28g pro.

BACON POT PIE

I love the combination of bacon and cheese. Add some veggies and a homemade flaky pie crust and you have a comforting Sunday night meal or a cozy, filling breakfast.
—Ashley Hudd, Holton, MI

PREP: 30 MIN. • **COOK:** 50 MIN
MAKES: 8 SERVINGS

- 2 cups all-purpose flour
- ⅓ cup shortening
- ¼ cup cold butter
- 5 to 7 Tbsp. ice water

FILLING
- 2 medium red potatoes, chopped
- 1 Tbsp. water
- 2 Tbsp. butter
- 3 Tbsp. all-purpose flour
- 2 cups 2% milk
- ¼ tsp. garlic powder
- ¼ tsp. pepper
- 1 lb. bacon strips, cooked and crumbled
- 1 medium onion, chopped
- 1 cup chopped fresh or frozen broccoli, thawed
- 1 cup shredded cheddar cheese

1. Place flour in a large bowl; cut in the shortening and butter until crumbly. Gradually add ice water 1 tablespoonful at a time, tossing with a fork until dough holds together when pressed. Divide the dough in half. Shape each into a disk; wrap and refrigerate 1 hour or overnight.
2. Preheat oven to 375°. In a microwave-safe bowl, combine potatoes and water; microwave, covered, on high until tender, 4-5 minutes. Cool; drain. In a small saucepan, melt butter over medium heat. Stir in flour until smooth; gradually whisk in milk, garlic powder and pepper. Bring to a boil, stirring constantly; cook and stir 2-3 minutes or until thickened. Cool.
3. On a lightly floured surface, roll half of the dough to a ⅛-in.-thick circle; transfer to a 9-in. deep-dish pie plate. Trim even with rim. Place potatoes in crust. Top with the bacon, onion, broccoli and cheese. Pour sauce over top. Roll remaining dough to a ⅛-in.-thick circle. Place over filling. Trim, seal and flute edge. Cut slits in top. Place on a baking sheet.
4. Bake until crust is golden brown and filling is bubbly, 50-60 minutes. Let stand 10 minutes before serving.

1 SERVING: 493 cal., 31g fat (14g sat. fat), 62mg chol., 558mg sod., 36g carb. (4g sugars, 2g fiber), 17g pro.

2-FOR-1 CHICKEN TETRAZZINI

A good friend shared a version of this recipe with me 35 years ago. I pay it forward by bringing the second casserole to friends when they are unable to cook.
—Helen McPhee, Savoy, IL

PREP: 30 MIN. • **BAKE:** 20 MIN.
MAKES: 2 CASSEROLES (4 SERVINGS EACH)

- 1 pkg. (12 oz.) spaghetti
- ⅓ cup butter, cubed
- ⅓ cup all-purpose flour
- ¾ tsp. salt
- ¼ tsp. white pepper
- 1 can (14½ oz.) chicken broth
- 1½ cups half-and-half cream
- 1 cup heavy whipping cream
- 4 cups cubed cooked chicken
- 3 cans (4 oz. each) mushroom stems and pieces, drained
- 1 jar (4 oz.) sliced pimientos, drained
- ½ cup grated Parmesan cheese

1. Cook spaghetti according to package directions. Meanwhile, in a Dutch oven, melt butter. Stir in the flour, salt and pepper until smooth. Gradually add the broth, half-and-half and whipping cream. Bring to a boil; cook and stir until mixture is thickened, about 2 minutes.
2. Remove from the heat. Stir in chicken, mushrooms and pimientos. Drain spaghetti; add to chicken mixture and toss to coat.
3. Transfer to 2 greased 11x7-in. baking dishes. Sprinkle with cheese. Cover and freeze 1 casserole for up to 2 months. Bake the second casserole, uncovered, at 350° until heated through, 20-25 minutes.
4. To use frozen casserole, thaw in the refrigerator overnight. Cover and bake at 350° for 30 minutes. Uncover; bake until heated through, 15-20 minutes more. Stir before serving.

1 CUP: 576 cal., 30g fat (17g sat. fat), 144mg chol., 814mg sod., 41g carb. (4g sugars, 2g fiber), 31g pro.

CONTEST-WINNING TACO CASSEROLE

My preschooler doesn't eat ground beef unless it's taco flavored, so I came up with this casserole we all like. To make assembly easy, I prepare the taco meat and freeze several bags at a time. I also cook the noodles over the weekend for a timely supper later in the week.
—Kathy Wilson, Romeoville, IL

PREP: 15 MIN. • **BAKE:** 30 MIN.
MAKES: 6 SERVINGS

- **3 cups uncooked bow tie pasta**
- **1 lb. ground beef**
- **¼ cup chopped onion**
- **2 cups shredded cheddar cheese**
- **1 jar (16 oz.) salsa**
- **1 can (14½ oz.) diced tomatoes, undrained**
- **1 envelope taco seasoning**
- **2 cups nacho tortilla chips, crushed**

1. Preheat oven to 350°. Cook pasta according to the package directions. Meanwhile, in a large skillet, cook beef and onion over medium heat until meat is no longer pink; drain. Add cheese, salsa, tomatoes and taco seasoning. Drain pasta; stir into beef mixture.
2. Transfer to a greased 11x7-in. baking dish. Cover and bake 20 minutes. Uncover; sprinkle with tortilla chips. Bake until heated through, about 10 minutes longer.

1 CUP: 578 cal., 28g fat (11g sat. fat), 84mg chol., 1377mg sod., 53g carb. (6g sugars, 3g fiber), 29g pro.

ABERDEEN BEEF PIE

Set in the middle of the table, this hearty beef pie will be the center of attention. With chunks of tender beef and tasty vegetables under a flaky pastry crust, this is pure comfort food.
—Peggy Goodrich, Enid, OK

PREP: 1½ HOURS
BAKE: 35 MIN. + STANDING
MAKES: 12 SERVINGS

- **¼ lb. sliced bacon, diced**
- **3 lbs. beef stew meat, cut into 1-in. cubes**
- **1 cup chopped onion**
- **1½ cups halved fresh baby carrots**
- **6 Tbsp. all-purpose flour**
- **1 cup beef broth**
- **1 Tbsp. Worcestershire sauce**
- **1 pkg. (10 oz.) frozen peas**
- **½ tsp. salt**
- **½ tsp. pepper**
- **1 sheet refrigerated pie crust**
- **1 large egg, lightly beaten, optional**

1. Preheat oven to 375°. In a Dutch oven, cook bacon over medium heat until crisp. Remove to paper towels to drain. Brown the beef in drippings in batches; drain and set beef aside. Add onion to pan; saute until crisp-tender. Add the carrots, bacon and beef.
2. Meanwhile, in a small bowl, combine flour, broth and Worcestershire sauce until smooth; add to beef mixture. Bring to a boil. Reduce heat; cover and simmer until meat is tender, 1 to 1½ hours. Stir in peas, salt and pepper. Transfer to an ungreased 11x7-in. baking dish.
3. On a lightly floured surface, roll out crust into a 12x8-in. rectangle. Cut slits in crust. Place over the filling; trim and seal edges. If desired, brush with beaten egg. Bake until crust is golden and filling is bubbly, 35-40 minutes. Let stand for 15 minutes before serving. Refrigerate the leftovers.

1 SERVING: 308 cal., 14g fat (6g sat. fat), 76mg chol., 389mg sod., 18g carb. (3g sugars, 2g fiber), 25g pro.

FIVE-CHEESE ZITI AL FORNO

After having the five-cheese ziti at Olive Garden, I tried to make my own homemade version—and I think I got pretty close. I always double this and freeze the second one for another meal.
—Keri Whitney, Castro Valley, CA

PREP: 20 MIN.
BAKE: 30 MIN. + STANDING
MAKES: 12 SERVINGS

- **1½ lbs. (about 7½ cups) uncooked ziti or small tube pasta**
- **2 jars (24 oz. each) marinara sauce**
- **1 jar (15 oz.) Alfredo sauce**
- **2 cups shredded part-skim mozzarella cheese, divided**
- **½ cup reduced-fat ricotta cheese**
- **½ cup shredded provolone cheese**
- **½ cup grated Romano cheese**

TOPPING
- **½ cup grated Parmesan cheese**
- **½ cup panko bread crumbs**
- **3 garlic cloves, minced**
- **2 Tbsp. olive oil**
- **Optional: Minced fresh parsley or basil, optional**

1. Preheat oven to 350°. Cook the pasta according to package directions for al dente; drain.
2. Meanwhile, in a large saucepan, combine the marinara sauce, Alfredo sauce, 1 cup mozzarella and the ricotta, provolone and Romano. Cook over medium heat until the sauce begins to simmer and cheeses are melted. Stir in cooked pasta; pour mixture into a greased 13x9-in. baking dish. Top with remaining mozzarella cheese.
3. In a small bowl, stir together the Parmesan, bread crumbs, garlic and olive oil; sprinkle over pasta.
4. Bake, uncovered, until the mixture is bubbly and topping is golden brown, 30-40 minutes. Let stand 10 minutes before serving. If desired, garnish with fresh parsley or basil.

FREEZE OPTION: Cool the unbaked casserole; cover and freeze. To use, partially thaw in refrigerator overnight. Remove from refrigerator 30 minutes before baking. Preheat oven to 350°. Cover casserole with foil; bake 50 minutes. Uncover; bake until heated through and a thermometer inserted in center reads 165°, 15-20 minutes longer.

1 CUP: 449 cal., 15g fat (8g sat. fat), 32mg chol., 960mg sod., 59g carb. (11g sugars, 4g fiber), 21g pro.

TURKEY SHEPHERD'S PIE

We live way out in the country, and the nearest grocery store is 25 miles away. So I've become quite skilled at turning leftovers into second-time-around successes like this.
—Linda Howe, Jackman, ME

PREP: 10 MIN. • **BAKE:** 45 MIN.
MAKES: 5 SERVINGS

- **2 cups cubed cooked turkey**
- **¾ cup turkey gravy**
- **1 cup shredded carrots**
- **2 cups prepared stuffing**
- **1 can (15¼ oz.) whole kernel corn, drained**
- **2 cups warm mashed potatoes**
- **Minced fresh parsley, optional**

Preheat the oven to 325°. In a greased 2-qt. baking dish, layer the turkey, gravy, carrots, stuffing and corn. Top with the potatoes. Bake, uncovered, until edges of potatoes are browned, 45-50 minutes. If desired, sprinkle with parsley.

1 SERVING: 407 cal., 12g fat (3g sat. fat), 47mg chol., 1133mg sod., 47g carb. (7g sugars, 4g fiber), 23g pro.

TEST KITCHEN TIP

If you plan to repurpose leftovers in a new recipe, like this Shepherd's Pie, first divvy up the leftover hot food into small portions, then place it in shallow dishes to cool quickly. Wait until any steam has stopped rising before chilling. Aways store leftovers in airtight covered containers.

OLD-FASHIONED CHICKEN POTPIE

This potpie is a good way to use up leftover chicken. It's not fancy, but it's so delicious I sometimes serve it as a special company dinner. My husband enjoys it more than the original roasted bird with all the fixings!
—Marilyn Hockey, Lisle, ON

PREP: 30 MIN. • **BAKE:** 30 MIN.
MAKES: 6 SERVINGS

- ⅓ **cup butter**
- ⅓ **cup all-purpose flour**
- 1 **garlic clove, minced**
- ½ **tsp. salt**
- ¼ **tsp. pepper**
- 1½ **cups water**
- ⅔ **cup 2% milk**
- 2 **tsp. chicken bouillon granules**
- 2 **cups cubed cooked chicken**
- 1 **cup frozen mixed vegetables**

PASTRY

- 1⅔ **cups all-purpose flour**
- 2 **tsp. celery seed**
- 1 **pkg. (8 oz.) cream cheese, cubed**
- ⅓ **cup cold butter**

1. Preheat oven to 425°. In a saucepan, melt butter over medium heat. Stir in flour, garlic, salt and pepper until blended. Gradually stir in water, milk and bouillon. Bring to a boil; cook and stir until thickened, 1-2 minutes. Remove from the heat. Stir in chicken and vegetables; set aside.
2. For pastry, in a large bowl, combine flour and celery seed. Cut in cream cheese and butter until crumbly. Work mixture by hand until dough forms a ball. On a lightly floured surface, roll two-thirds of dough into a 12-in. square. Transfer to an 8-in. square baking dish. Pour filling into crust. Roll remaining dough into 9-in. square; place over the filling. Trim, seal and flute edges. Cut slits in pastry.
3. Bake until crust is golden brown and filling is bubbly, 30-35 minutes.

1 SERVING: 592 cal., 38g fat (22g sat. fat), 136mg chol., 823mg sod., 40g carb. (4g sugars, 3g fiber), 22g pro.

PIZZA MACARONI BAKE

What do you get when you combine macaroni and cheese with pizza fixings? This hearty, family-pleasing casserole! It's so easy and so tasty.
—Nancy Porterfield, Gap Mills, WV

PREP: 30 MIN. • **BAKE:** 20 MIN.
MAKES: 8 SERVINGS

- 1 **pkg. (7¼ oz.) macaroni and cheese dinner mix**
- 6 **cups water**
- 1 **lb. ground beef**
- 1 **medium onion, chopped**
- 1 **small green pepper, chopped**
- 1 **cup shredded cheddar cheese**
- 1 **jar (14 oz.) pizza sauce**
- 1 **pkg. (3½ oz.) sliced pepperoni**
- 1 **cup shredded part-skim mozzarella cheese**

1. Set the cheese packet from dinner mix aside. In a saucepan, bring water to a boil. Add macaroni; cook for 8-10 minutes or until tender.
2. Meanwhile, in a large skillet, cook the beef, onion and green pepper over medium heat until meat is no longer pink; drain. Drain macaroni; stir in the contents of cheese packet.
3. Transfer to a greased 13x9-in. baking dish. Sprinkle with cheddar cheese. Top with the beef mixture, pizza sauce, pepperoni and mozzarella cheese.
4. Bake, uncovered, at 350° until heated through, 20-25 minutes.

1 SERVING: 376 cal., 20g fat (9g sat. fat), 64mg chol., 827mg sod., 13g carb. (6g sugars, 2g fiber), 23g pro.

SHORTCUT SAUSAGE LASAGNA

My family and friends love this great-tasting lasagna. The recipe is almost foolproof. Best of all, there's no need to precook the noodles.
—Cindy Moore, Rhinelander, WI

PREP: 15 MIN. • **COOK:** 30 MIN.
MAKES: 6 SERVINGS

- **1 lb. bulk Italian sausage**
- **1 jar (14 oz.) meatless spaghetti sauce**
- **½ cup chopped onion**
- **½ cup chopped green pepper**
- **½ cup water**
- **1 can (2¼ oz.) sliced ripe olives, drained**
- **¼ tsp. salt**
- **6 uncooked lasagna noodles**
- **1 cup ricotta cheese**
- **2 cups shredded part-skim mozzarella cheese**
- **¼ to ½ cup grated Parmesan cheese**

1. Crumble Italian sausage into a large microwave-safe bowl. Cover; microwave on high for 3-5 minutes or until meat is no longer pink, stirring once; drain. Stir in spaghetti sauce, onion, green pepper, water, olives and salt.
2. In a greased 11x7-in. microwave-safe dish, layer 1⅓ cups meat sauce, then 3 noodles, ½ cup ricotta cheese and ½ cup mozzarella cheese. Repeat layers. Top with remaining meat sauce. Sprinkle with Parmesan cheese.
3. Cover and microwave at 70% power for 21-24 minutes or until noodles are tender. Sprinkle with the remaining 1 cup mozzarella cheese. Microwave, uncovered, on high for 45-60 seconds or until cheese is melted. Let stand 5 minutes before cutting.

1 SERVING: 443 cal., 25g fat (12g sat. fat), 78mg chol., 1091mg sod., 31g carb. (10g sugars, 3g fiber), 26g pro.

SPINACH & CHEESE LASAGNA ROLLS

These Italian-inspired roll-ups are fast to make and fun to eat. They look elegant but are also family-friendly.
—Cindy Romberg, Mississauga, ON

PREP: 25 MIN. + CHILLING • **BAKE:** 35 MIN.
MAKES: 6 SERVINGS

- **1 pkg. (10 oz.) frozen chopped spinach, thawed and squeezed dry**
- **1 cup shredded part-skim mozzarella cheese**
- **1 cup 2% cottage cheese**
- **¾ cup grated Parmesan cheese, divided**
- **1 large egg, lightly beaten**
- **6 lasagna noodles, cooked and drained**
- **1 jar (24 oz.) marinara sauce**

1. In a small bowl, combine the spinach, mozzarella, cottage cheese, ½ cup Parmesan cheese and egg. Spread a heaping ⅓ cupful over each noodle. Roll up; place seam side down in a 9-in. square baking dish coated with cooking spray. Cover and refrigerate overnight.
2. Remove from refrigerator 30 minutes before baking. Pour marinara sauce over the roll-ups.
3. Cover and bake at 350° until bubbly, 33-38 minutes. Sprinkle with remaining ¼ cup Parmesan cheese.

1 LASAGNA ROLL: 301 cal., 11g fat (5g sat. fat), 56mg chol., 963mg sod., 33g carb. (9g sugars, 4g fiber), 18g pro.

EASY CHICKEN CASSEROLE

This may be a basic chicken casserole, but I never bring home leftovers whenever I take it to a potluck. The hearty dish has lots of appeal, and I especially like that the crumb topping adds a bit of crunch to each serving.
—Faye Hintz, Springfield, MO

PREP: 15 MIN. • **BAKE:** 30 MIN.
MAKES: 10 SERVINGS

- **8 cups cubed cooked chicken**
- **2 cans (10½ oz. each) condensed cream of chicken soup, undiluted**
- **1 cup sour cream**
- **1 cup crushed Ritz crackers (about 25 crackers)**
- **2 Tbsp. butter, melted**
- **1 tsp. celery seed**
- **Optional: Fresh parsley and sweet red pepper rings**

1. Preheat oven to 350°. Combine chicken, soup and sour cream; spread into a greased 13x9-in. baking dish. Combine crumbs, butter and celery seed; sprinkle over chicken mixture.
2. Bake, uncovered, until casserole is bubbly, 30-35 minutes. If desired, garnish with parsley and red pepper.

1 CUP: 386 cal., 21g fat (8g sat. fat), 116mg chol., 629mg sod., 12g carb. (2g sugars, 1g fiber), 35g pro.

READER REVIEW

"This is a go-to recipe for our family. It's frequently requested for dinner, and it hits the spot when you need some good old-fashioned comfort food!"

MOMNERIN, TASTEOFHOME.COM

SAVORY WINTER SQUASH PIE

Instead of using frozen winter squash, you can roast butternut or acorn squash until tender then mash it before getting started on this recipe. The bacon roses are a fun garnish, but this dish can easily be made without them.
—Erica Sinclair, Hamilton, ON

PREP: 50 MIN. + CHILLING
BAKE: 35 MIN. + COOLING
MAKES: 8 SERVINGS

- ¾ cup all-purpose flour
- ½ tsp. salt
- 3 Tbsp. shortening
- 3 Tbsp. cold butter
- 2 to 3 Tbsp. ice water

BACON ROSES (OPTIONAL)

- 8 bacon strips
- 3 Tbsp. maple syrup
- 3 Tbsp. packed brown sugar

TOPPING

- 1 Tbsp. maple syrup
- 1 Tbsp. brown sugar

FILLING

- 4 large eggs, room temperature
- 1 cup frozen cooked winter squash
- ½ cup 2% milk
- ½ cup shredded Swiss cheese or part-skim mozzarella cheese
- ½ cup 2% cottage cheese
- ¼ cup all-purpose flour
- 1½ tsp. minced fresh rosemary or ½ tsp. dried rosemary, crushed
- ½ tsp. salt
- ½ tsp. ground nutmeg
- ½ tsp. minced fresh thyme or ¼ tsp. dried thyme
- ¼ tsp. pepper
- ¼ tsp. cayenne pepper
- Optional: fresh rosemary and fresh thyme leaves

1. In a large bowl, mix flour and salt; cut in shortening and butter until crumbly. Gradually add ice water, tossing with a fork until dough holds together when pressed. Shape into a disk; wrap and refrigerate 1 hour or overnight.
2. Preheat oven to 375°. For optional bacon roses, brush bacon with 3 Tbsp. syrup. Roll bacon strip up; for larger roses use 2 strips. Secure bottoms with toothpicks. Dip top of each bacon rose in the 3 Tbsp. brown sugar. Arrange on a foil-lined rimmed baking sheet. Bake until bacon is cooked through, 25-30 minutes.
3. On a lightly floured cutting board, roll dough to a ⅛-in.-thick circle; cut into 1-in.-wide strips. Brush with syrup and sprinkle with brown sugar. Chill until ready to use.
4. Meanwhile, in a large bowl, whisk eggs, squash and milk until smooth. Stir in cheeses, flour, rosemary, salt, nutmeg, thyme, pepper and cayenne. Pour into a greased 9-in. pie plate. Bake 20 minutes.
5. Working quickly, arrange chilled dough strips over hot filling in a lattice pattern. Trim at edge of pie plate. Bake until crust is golden brown and the center is set, 15-20 minutes. Cool 10 minutes on a wire rack before serving. If desired, garnish pie with bacon roses and rosemary and thyme leaves.

1 PIECE: 245 cal., 14g fat (6g sat. fat), 113mg chol., 428mg sod., 20g carb. (5g sugars, 1g fiber), 9g pro.

WEAVING THE LATTICE CRUST: Working with pie dough over the warm pie can be tricky. Avoid this by tracing the rim of the pie plate on a sheet of parchment before you start preparing the recipe. Flip the parchment over and place on a baking sheet; arrange the dough into a lattice over the tracing, using the marked circle to know how big to make it. Place in freezer until firm; when ready, transfer lattice to the top of custard and bake as directed. Because the pie dough is frozen, you may need to increase the bake time a little to get the crust golden brown.

HAM & SWISS CASSEROLE

When I prepare this noodle casserole for church gatherings, it's always a hit. It can easily be doubled or tripled for a crowd.
—Doris Barb, El Dorado, KS

PREP: 15 MIN. • **BAKE:** 40 MIN.
MAKES: 8 SERVINGS

- **1 pkg. (8 oz.) egg noodles, cooked and drained**
- **2 cups cubed fully cooked ham**
- **2 cups shredded Swiss cheese**
- **1 can (10¾ oz.) condensed cream of celery soup, undiluted**
- **1 cup sour cream**
- **½ cup chopped green pepper**
- **½ cup chopped onion**

1. In a greased 13x9-in. baking dish, layer half the noodles, ham and cheese.
2. In a large bowl, combine the soup, sour cream, green pepper and onion; spread half over the top. Repeat layers. Bake, uncovered, at 350° until heated through, 40-45 minutes.

1 SERVING: 360 cal., 18g fat (10g sat. fat), 92mg chol., 815mg sod., 27g carb. (4g sugars, 1g fiber), 20g pro.

BLACK BEAN & CHICKEN ENCHILADA LASAGNA

Twice a month I make chicken enchiladas, lasagna-style. It's a regular with us because assembly is easy and my whole family gives it a thumbs-up.
—Cheryl Snavely, Hagerstown, MD

PREP: 30 MIN. • **BAKE:** 25 MIN. + STANDING
MAKES: 8 SERVINGS

- **2 cans (10 oz. each) enchilada sauce**
- **12 corn tortillas (6 in.)**
- **2 cups coarsely shredded rotisserie chicken**
- **1 small onion, chopped**
- **1 can (15 oz.) black beans, rinsed and drained**
- **3 cans (4 oz. each) whole green chiles, drained and coarsely chopped**
- **3 cups crumbled queso fresco or shredded Mexican cheese blend**
- **2 medium ripe avocados**
- **2 Tbsp. sour cream**
- **2 Tbsp. lime juice**
- **½ tsp. salt**
- **Chopped fresh tomatoes and cilantro**

1. Preheat oven to 350°. Spread ½ cup enchilada sauce into a greased 13x9-in. baking dish; top with 4 tortillas, 1 cup chicken, ¼ cup onion, ¼ cup beans, ⅓ cup green chiles and 1 cup cheese. Repeat layers. Drizzle with ½ cup enchilada sauce; top with the remaining tortillas, onion, beans, chiles, sauce and cheese.
2. Bake, uncovered, until lasagna is bubbly and cheese is melted, 25-30 minutes. Let stand 10 minutes before serving.
3. Meanwhile, pit and peel 1 avocado; place in a food processor. Add the sour cream, lime juice and salt; process until smooth. Pit, peel and cut the remaining avocado into small cubes.
4. Top lasagna with tomatoes, cilantro and cubed avocado. Serve with the avocado sauce.

1 PIECE WITH 1 TBSP. SAUCE: 407 cal., 18g fat (7g sat. fat), 64mg chol., 857mg sod., 39g carb. (4g sugars, 8g fiber), 28g pro.

MOM'S WHITE LASAGNA

My mom made this lasagna for special occasions, such as birthdays. I inherited her cookbooks after she passed. Tucked inside one of them, I found this recipe folded into a letter she penned to me while I was stationed overseas. It's a rich, hearty dish that reminds me of home.
—Janet Wing, Minot, ND

PREP: 30 MIN.
BAKE: 40 MIN. + STANDING
MAKES: 12 SERVINGS

- **9 lasagna noodles**
- **1 lb. bulk Italian sausage**
- **2 celery ribs, chopped**
- **1 medium onion, chopped**
- **3 garlic cloves, minced**
- **½ cup white wine**
- **1 cup half-and-half cream**
- **3 oz. cream cheese, cubed**
- **¼ cup minced fresh basil**
- **2 tsp. minced fresh oregano or ½ tsp. dried oregano**
- **1 tsp. pepper**
- **¾ tsp. salt**
- **1 large egg, lightly beaten**
- **2 cups shredded white cheddar cheese**
- **1½ cups 2% cottage cheese**
- **¾ lb. fresh mozzarella cheese, sliced**
- **1½ cups shredded Gouda cheese**
- **Optional: Additional minced fresh basil and oregano**

1. Preheat oven to 375°. Cook noodles according to package directions for al dente. Meanwhile, in a large skillet, cook sausage, celery, onion and garlic over medium heat 6-8 minutes or until sausage is no longer pink, breaking up sausage into crumbles; drain off grease.
2. Stir in wine. Bring to a boil; cook for 3-4 minutes or until liquid is reduced by half. Add cream, cream cheese, herbs, pepper and salt; stir until cream cheese is melted. Drain noodles.
3. In a small bowl, combine egg, cheddar and cottage cheese.
4. In a greased 13x9-in. baking dish, layer 3 lasagna noodles, half of the sausage mixture, half of the cheddar mixture and half of the mozzarella slices. Repeat the layers. Top with the remaining noodles; sprinkle with Gouda cheese.
5. Bake, covered, 40-50 minutes or until bubbly and cheese is melted. Let stand 15 minutes before serving. If desired, sprinkle with additional basil and oregano.

1 PIECE: 462 cal., 30g fat (16g sat. fat), 111mg chol., 787mg sod., 20g carb. (5g sugars, 1g fiber), 24g pro.

SEAFOOD CASSEROLE

A family favorite, this rice casserole is filled with plenty of seafood and veggies. It's hearty, homey and easy to make!
—Nancy Billups, Princeton, IA

PREP: 20 MIN. • **BAKE:** 40 MIN.
MAKES: 6 SERVINGS

- **1 pkg. (6 oz.) long grain and wild rice**
- **1 lb. frozen crabmeat, thawed, or 2½ cups canned lump crabmeat, drained**
- **1 lb. cooked shrimp, peeled, deveined and cut into ½-in. pieces**
- **2 celery ribs, chopped**
- **1 medium onion, finely chopped**
- **½ cup finely chopped green pepper**
- **1 can (4 oz.) mushroom stems and pieces, drained**
- **1 jar (2 oz.) diced pimientos, drained**
- **1 cup mayonnaise**
- **1 cup 2% milk**
- **½ tsp. pepper**
- **Dash Worcestershire sauce**
- **¼ cup dry bread crumbs**

1. Cook rice according to the package directions. Meanwhile, preheat the oven to 375°.
2. In a large bowl, combine the crab, shrimp, celery, onion, green pepper, mushrooms and pimientos. In a small bowl, whisk mayonnaise, milk, pepper and Worcestershire sauce; stir into the seafood mixture. Stir in rice.
3. Transfer to a greased 13x9-in. baking dish. Sprinkle with the dry bread crumbs. Bake, uncovered, until bubbly, roughly 40-50 minutes.

1½ CUPS: 585 cal., 34g fat (5g sat. fat), 209mg chol., 1045mg sod., 31g carb. (5g sugars, 2g fiber), 37g pro.

Slow-Cooker & Instant Pot® Dinners

Pulling together fantastic meals is a breeze when you take advantage of your favorite countertop kitchen appliances. Whether dinner slowly simmers away in the slow cooker or is cooked fast and easy in the pressure cooker, you'll find the ideal dish to fit your schedule.

KOREAN PULLED PORK TACOS

I created this unique pulled pork recipe so we could replicate our favorite food truck tacos at home. They're a little sweet, a little spicy and totally delicious any time of year.
—Julie Orr, Fullerton, CA

PREP: 25 MIN. • **COOK:** 8 HOURS
MAKES: 10 SERVINGS

- **½ cup reduced-sodium soy sauce**
- **½ cup water**
- **3 Tbsp. brown sugar**
- **2 Tbsp. sesame oil**
- **1 Tbsp. baking cocoa**
- **3 tsp. chili powder**
- **1 garlic clove, minced**
- **¼ tsp. ground ginger**
- **1 boneless pork shoulder butt roast (4-5 lbs.)**

SLAW

- **3 Tbsp. sugar**
- **2 Tbsp. reduced-sodium soy sauce**
- **1 Tbsp. Sriracha chili sauce**
- **2 tsp. sesame oil**
- **1 tsp. rice vinegar**
- **1 pkg. (14 oz.) coleslaw mix**
- **1 Tbsp. toasted sesame seeds, optional**

ASSEMBLY

- **20 flour tortillas (6 in.), warmed**
- **Optional: Thinly sliced green onions and additional Sriracha chili sauce**

1. Whisk together first 8 ingredients. Place roast in a 6-qt. slow cooker. Pour the soy sauce mixture over the top. Cook, covered, on low until the pork is tender, 8-10 hours.
2. About 1 hour before serving, mix first 5 slaw ingredients until blended. Place coleslaw mix in a large bowl; toss with dressing and, if desired, sesame seeds. Refrigerate, covered, until serving.
3. Remove roast; skim fat from cooking juices. Shred pork with 2 forks; return to slow cooker and heat through. Serve in tortillas with slaw. If desired, serve with green onions and additional chili sauce.

FREEZE OPTION: Freeze cooled pork mixture in freezer containers. To use, partially thaw in refrigerator overnight. Heat through in a saucepan, stirring occasionally; add water or broth if necessary.

2 TACOS: 603 cal., 29g fat (10g sat. fat), 108mg chol., 1177mg sod., 46g carb. (11g sugars, 4g fiber), 37g pro.

FARM-STYLE BBQ RIBS

Inspiration struck when I saw a recipe similar to this one in a newspaper. My version was an instant hit with my husband and our friends. It got even better when I discovered how easy it is to make in the slow cooker.
—Bette Jo Welton, Eugene, OR

PREP: 20 MIN. • **COOK:** 6 HOURS
MAKES: 4 SERVINGS

- **4 lbs. bone-in beef short ribs**
- **1 can (15 oz.) thick and zesty tomato sauce**
- **1½ cups water**
- **1 medium onion, chopped**
- **1 can (6 oz.) tomato paste**
- **⅓ cup packed brown sugar**
- **3 Tbsp. cider vinegar**
- **3 Tbsp. Worcestershire sauce**
- **2 Tbsp. chili powder**
- **4 garlic cloves, minced**
- **2 tsp. ground mustard**
- **1½ tsp. salt**

Place ribs in a 5- or 6-qt. slow cooker. In a large saucepan, combine the remaining ingredients. Bring to a boil. Reduce heat; simmer, uncovered, 5 minutes or until slightly thickened. Pour over ribs; cook, covered, on low 6-8 hours or until tender.
1 SERVING: 578 cal., 24g fat (9g sat. fat), 110mg chol., 2503mg sod., 46g carb. (32g sugars, 7g fiber), 44g pro.

BRISKET & BEAN BURRITOS

This easy recipe is stuffed with not one, but two kinds of meat: smoky bacon and tender beef brisket.
—Ruth Weatherford, Huntington Beach, CA

PREP: 20 MIN. • **COOK:** 4½ HOURS
MAKES: 10 SERVINGS

- **2 lbs. fresh beef brisket**
- **1 cup chopped onion**
- **3 bacon strips, diced**
- **1 can (8 oz.) tomato sauce**
- **¾ tsp. pepper**
- **¼ tsp. salt**
- **1 can (16 oz.) refried beans**
- **½ cup salsa**
- **1 can (4 oz.) chopped green chiles**
- **1½ cups shredded Monterey Jack cheese**
- **10 flour tortillas (10 in.), warmed**

1. Place brisket in a 5-qt. slow cooker; top with onion and bacon. Combine tomato sauce, pepper and salt; pour over meat. Cook, covered, on low until meat is tender, 4½-5 hours.
2. In a microwave-safe bowl, combine the refried beans, salsa and chiles. Microwave, covered, on high until heated through, 2-3 minutes.
3. Remove meat from slow cooker; when cool enough to handle, shred with 2 forks. Layer bean mixture, meat and cheese on each tortilla. Fold bottom and sides of tortilla over filling and roll up. Serve immediately.

FREEZE OPTION: Individually wrap the burritos in foil and freeze in a freezer container. To use, partially thaw overnight in the refrigerator. Preheat oven to 350°. Bake foil-wrapped burritos on a baking sheet until heated through. To reheat just 1 burrito, remove foil and rewrap in damp paper towel; microwave on high until heated through, turning once. Let stand for 15 seconds. May be frozen up to 2 months.
1 BURRITO: 483 cal., 17g fat (7g sat. fat), 62mg chol., 963mg sod., 42g carb. (2g sugars, 9g fiber), 33g pro.

PRESSURE-COOKER TEQUILA SALSA CHICKEN

I tasted this dish at a local Mexican restaurant when celebrating a friend's birthday. I fell in love with the spicy, smoky flavor from the tequila and decided to try it at home in my pressure cooker. Boy, was it a success! It's also fabulous stuffed into flour tortillas or for making nachos. This can be made with frozen chicken breasts; just increase the cooking time to 15 minutes.

—Trisha Kruse, Eagle, ID

TAKES: 15 MIN. • **MAKES:** 3 CUPS

- **1 envelope taco seasoning**
- **1 lb. boneless skinless chicken breasts**
- **1 cup chunky salsa**
- **¼ cup tequila**
- **Hot cooked rice**
- **Optional: Avocado slices, chopped fresh cilantro and lime wedges**

1. Sprinkle taco seasoning over chicken breasts; place in a 6-qt. electric pressure cooker. Combine salsa and tequila; pour over chicken. Lock lid; close pressure-release valve. Adjust to pressure-cook on high for 6 minutes. Quick-release pressure. A thermometer inserted in chicken should read at least 165°.
2. Remove chicken. When cool enough to handle, shred meat with 2 forks; return to pressure cooker. Serve with rice and desired toppings.

¾ CUP: 187 cal., 3g fat (1g sat. fat), 63mg chol., 1107mg sod., 11g carb. (2g sugars, 0 fiber), 23g pro.

PRESSURE-COOKER CHICKEN CHOP SUEY

If you're going to have a busy evening, here's a wonderful way to ensure you can still have a healthy and satisfying supper. It's tasty, traditional and easy, too.

—Melody Littlewood, Royal City, WA

PREP: 20 MIN. • **COOK:** 5 MIN.
MAKES: 9 SERVINGS

- **1½ lbs. boneless skinless chicken thighs, cut into 2-in. pieces**
- **½ lb. sliced fresh mushrooms**
- **2 celery ribs, sliced**
- **1 medium onion, chopped**
- **1 can (14 oz.) bean sprouts, rinsed and drained**
- **1 can (8 oz.) bamboo shoots, drained**
- **1 can (8 oz.) sliced water chestnuts, drained**
- **½ cup frozen shelled edamame**
- **1 can (14½ oz.) reduced-sodium chicken broth**
- **½ cup reduced-sodium soy sauce**
- **1 Tbsp. minced fresh gingerroot**
- **¼ tsp. crushed red pepper flakes**
- **¼ cup cornstarch**
- **¼ cup cold water**
- **Hot cooked rice**

1. Place the chicken in a 6-qt. electric pressure cooker. Top with mushrooms, celery, onion, bean sprouts, bamboo shoots, water chestnuts and edamame. In a small bowl, combine the broth, soy sauce, ginger and pepper flakes. Pour over chicken and vegetables.
2. Lock lid; close the pressure-release valve. Adjust to pressure-cook on high for 3 minutes. Quick-release pressure. A thermometer inserted in chicken should read at least 170°.
3. Select saute setting and adjust for low heat. In a small bowl, mix cornstarch and water until smooth; stir into meat mixture. Simmer, stirring mixture constantly, until thickened, 1-2 minutes. Serve with rice.

1 CUP: 182 cal., 6g fat (2g sat. fat), 50mg chol., 709mg sod., 13g carb. (3g sugars, 2g fiber), 19g pro. **DIABETIC EXCHANGES:** 2 lean meat, 1 vegetable, ½ starch.

SLOW-COOKED BBQ PORK RIBS

You probably already have all the ingredients required for this recipe. These ribs turn out so sweet, tangy and fork-tender.
—Annette Thompson, Woodbury, VT

PREP: 20 MIN. • **COOK:** 7 HOURS
MAKES: 8 SERVINGS

- **4 lbs. boneless country-style pork ribs**
- **2 cups ketchup**
- **¼ cup packed brown sugar**
- **¼ cup maple syrup**
- **¼ cup prepared mustard**
- **¼ cup reduced-sodium soy sauce**
- **2 Tbsp. lemon juice**
- **2 tsp. dried minced garlic**
- **⅛ tsp. pepper**

1. Place ribs in a 5- or 6-qt. slow cooker. Combine the remaining ingredients; pour over the ribs. Cover and cook on low for 7-9 hours or until the meat is tender.
2. Remove ribs and keep warm. Skim fat from sauce; serve sauce with ribs.

5 OZ. COOKED PORK: 480 cal., 21g fat (8g sat. fat), 130mg chol., 1247mg sod., 31g carb. (29g sugars, 0 fiber), 40g pro.

PRESSURE-COOKER CHICKEN MARBELLA

This dish is sweet, briny, savory, herbal and packs a big punch of garlic flavor. The Mediterranean flavors make me think of dinner on the patio with family or friends.
—Beth Jacobson, Milwaukee, WI

PREP: 30 MIN. • **COOK:** 10 MIN. + RELEASING
MAKES: 6 SERVINGS

- **1 cup reduced-sodium chicken broth**
- **1 cup pitted green olives, divided**
- **1 cup pitted dried plums, divided**
- **2 Tbsp. dried oregano**
- **2 Tbsp. packed brown sugar**
- **2 Tbsp. capers, drained**
- **2 Tbsp. olive oil**
- **4 garlic cloves, minced**
- **½ tsp. salt**
- **½ tsp. pepper**
- **6 bone-in chicken thighs, skin removed (about 2 lbs.)**
- **1 Tbsp. minced fresh parsley**
- **1 Tbsp. white wine**
- **1 Tbsp. lemon juice**
- **Hot cooked couscous**

1. Place the chicken broth, ½ cup olives, ½ cup dried plums, oregano, brown sugar, capers, oil, garlic, salt and pepper in a food processor; process until smooth. Transfer the mixture to a 6-qt. electric pressure cooker. Place the chicken in pressure cooker. Lock lid; close pressure-release valve. Adjust to pressure-cook on high for 10 minutes. Allow the pressure to naturally release for 10 minutes, then quick-release any remaining pressure.
2. Chop remaining olives and dried plums. Remove chicken; keep warm. Stir parsley, wine, lemon juice and remaining olives and plums into olive mixture. Serve with chicken and couscous.

1 CHICKEN THIGH: 352 cal., 17g fat (3g sat. fat), 77mg chol., 908mg sod., 26g carb. (13g sugars, 2g fiber), 23g pro.

TERESA DEVONO
Red Lion, PA

SLOW-COOKER BEEF TOSTADAS

I dedicate these slow-simmered tostadas to my husband, the only Italian man I know who can't get enough of Mexican flavors. Be sure to pile on your favorite toppings.

—Teresa DeVono, Red Lion, PA

PREP: 20 MIN. • **COOK:** 6 HOURS
MAKES: 6 SERVINGS

- **1 large onion, chopped**
- **¼ cup lime juice**
- **1 jalapeno pepper, seeded and minced**
- **1 serrano pepper, seeded and minced**
- **1 Tbsp. chili powder**
- **3 garlic cloves, minced**
- **½ tsp. ground cumin**
- **1 beef top round steak (about 1½ lbs.)**
- **1 tsp. salt**
- **½ tsp. pepper**
- **¼ cup chopped fresh cilantro**
- **12 corn tortillas (6 in.)**
- **Cooking spray**

TOPPINGS

- **1½ cups shredded lettuce**
- **1 medium tomato, finely chopped**
- **¾ cup shredded sharp cheddar cheese**
- **¾ cup reduced-fat sour cream, optional**

1. Place the first 7 ingredients in a 3- or 4-qt. slow cooker. Cut steak in half and sprinkle with salt and pepper; add to slow cooker. Cook, covered, on low until meat is tender, 6-8 hours.
2. Remove meat; cool slightly. Shred meat with 2 forks. Return beef to slow cooker and stir in cilantro; heat through. Spritz both sides of tortillas with cooking spray. Place in a single layer on baking sheets; broil 1-2 minutes on each side or until crisp. Spoon beef mixture over tortillas; top with lettuce, tomato, cheese and, if desired, sour cream.

NOTE: Wear disposable gloves when cutting hot peppers; the oils can burn skin. Avoid touching your face.

2 TOSTADAS: 372 cal., 13g fat (6g sat. fat), 88mg chol., 602mg sod., 30g carb. (5g sugars, 5g fiber), 35g pro. **DIABETIC EXCHANGES:** 4 lean meat, 2 starch, ½ fat.

5i

PRESSURE-COOKED MESQUITE RIBS

When we're missing the taste of grilled food during winter, these tangy ribs give us that same smoky barbecue flavor we love. They're so simple, and fall-off-the-bone delicious, too!
—Sue Evans, Marquette, MI

PREP: 15 MIN.
COOK: 35 MIN. + RELEASING
MAKES: 8 SERVINGS

- **1 cup water**
- **2 Tbsp. cider vinegar**
- **1 Tbsp. soy sauce**
- **4 lbs. pork baby back ribs, cut into serving-size portions**
- **2 Tbsp. mesquite seasoning**
- **¾ cup barbecue sauce, divided**

1. Combine water, vinegar and soy sauce in a 6-qt. electric pressure cooker. Rub the ribs with mesquite seasoning; add to the pressure cooker. Lock lid; close pressure-release valve. Adjust to pressure-cook on high for 35 minutes. Let the pressure naturally release for 10 minutes, then quick-release any remaining pressure.
2. Remove ribs to a foil-lined baking sheet. Preheat broiler. Brush ribs with half the barbecue sauce. Broil 4-6 in. from heat until glazed. Brush with the remaining barbecue sauce.

1 SERVING: 329 cal., 21g fat (8g sat. fat), 81mg chol., 678mg sod., 10g carb. (8g sugars, 0 fiber), 23g pro.

BEEF OSSO BUCCO

Our beef osso bucco boasts a thick, savory sauce complemented by the addition of gremolata, a chopped herb condiment made of lemon zest, garlic and parsley.
—*Taste of Home* Test Kitchen

PREP: 30 MIN. • **COOK:** 7 HOURS
MAKES: 6 SERVINGS

- **½ cup all-purpose flour**
- **¾ tsp. salt, divided**
- **½ tsp. pepper**
- **6 beef shanks (14 oz. each)**
- **2 Tbsp. butter**
- **1 Tbsp. olive oil**
- **½ cup white wine or beef broth**
- **1 can (14½ oz.) diced tomatoes, undrained**
- **1½ cups beef broth**
- **2 medium carrots, chopped**
- **1 medium onion, chopped**
- **1 celery rib, sliced**
- **1 Tbsp. dried thyme**
- **1 Tbsp. dried oregano**
- **2 bay leaves**
- **3 Tbsp. cornstarch**
- **¼ cup cold water**

GREMOLATA

- **⅓ cup minced fresh parsley**
- **1 Tbsp. grated lemon zest**
- **1 Tbsp. grated orange zest**
- **2 garlic cloves, minced**
- **Polenta, optional**

1. In a large resealable container, combine the flour, ½ tsp. salt and pepper. Add beef, a few pieces at a time, and shake to coat.
2. In a large skillet, brown beef in butter and oil. Transfer meat and drippings to a 6-qt. slow cooker. Add wine to the skillet, stirring to loosen browned bits from pan; pour over meat. Add the tomatoes, broth, carrots, onion, celery, thyme, oregano, bay leaves and remaining salt.
3. Cover and cook on low for 7-9 hours or until meat is tender. Discard bay leaves.
4. Skim fat from cooking juices; transfer juices to a large saucepan. Bring to a boil. Combine the cornstarch and water until smooth; gradually stir into the pan. Bring to a boil; cook and stir for 2 minutes or until thickened.
5. In a small bowl, combine the gremolata ingredients. Serve beef with gremolata and sauce. If desired, serve over polenta.

1 SHANK WITH 1 CUP SAUCE AND 4 TSP. GREMOLATA: 398 cal., 15g fat (6g sat. fat), 112mg chol., 640mg sod., 17g carb. (5g sugars, 4g fiber), 47g pro.

SHREDDED BEEF BURRITO FILLING

Make your next party a taco bar or burrito bar! Set out the beef in the slow cooker set on warm along with tortillas, shredded cheese, salsa, sour cream and chopped lettuce, jalapenos, onions and tomatoes. For a variation, I mix a can of refried beans into 3 or 4 cups of the cooked beef filling.
—Hope Wasylenki, Gahanna, OH

PREP: 20 MIN. • **COOK:** 7 HOURS
MAKES: 12 SERVINGS

- **5 lbs. boneless beef chuck roast, cut into 4 pieces**
- **½ cup beef broth**
- **2 Tbsp. canola oil**
- **1 medium onion, finely chopped**
- **2 jalapeno peppers, seeded and finely chopped**
- **2 garlic cloves, minced**
- **2 Tbsp. chili powder**
- **1 Tbsp. ground cumin**
- **⅛ tsp. salt**
- **1 can (28 oz.) crushed tomatoes in puree**
- **1 jar (16 oz.) salsa verde**

Optional: Tortillas, shredded cheddar cheese, sour cream, guacamole, salsa and fresh cilantro leaves

1. In a 6-qt. slow cooker, combine beef and broth. Cook, covered, on low until meat is tender, 6-8 hours. Remove meat; discard juices. When cool enough to handle, shred with 2 forks. Return to slow cooker.
2. In a large skillet, heat oil over medium heat. Add onion and jalapenos; cook and stir until softened, 3-4 minutes. Add garlic and seasonings; cook 1 minute longer. Stir in crushed tomatoes and salsa; bring to a boil. Pour mixture over shredded beef; stir to combine. Cook, covered, on high until heated through, about 1 hour.
3. If desired, serve filling (using tongs) on tortillas for burritos or tacos and add toppings.

FREEZE OPTION: Freeze cooled meat mixture in freezer containers. To use, partially thaw in refrigerator overnight. Heat through in a saucepan, stirring occasionally.

1 SERVING: 379 cal., 21g fat (7g sat. fat), 123mg chol., 509mg sod., 9g carb. (5g sugars, 2g fiber), 39g pro.

TASTY PORK RIBS

I like to serve these tender country-style ribs over rice. A tantalizing aroma and zippy Cajun barbecue sauce are sure to make these ribs a favorite at your house.
—Michelle Rominger, Albia, IA

PREP: 10 MIN. • **COOK:** 6 HOURS
MAKES: 8 SERVINGS

- **4 lbs. bone-in country-style pork ribs**
- **1 cup ketchup**
- **1 cup barbecue sauce**
- **¼ cup packed brown sugar**
- **¼ cup Worcestershire sauce**
- **1 Tbsp. balsamic vinegar**
- **1 Tbsp. molasses**
- **1 garlic clove, minced**
- **2 Tbsp. dried minced onion**
- **1 tsp. Cajun seasoning**
- **1 tsp. ground mustard**
- **½ tsp. salt**
- **¼ tsp. pepper**

1. Place the ribs in a 5-qt. slow cooker. Combine the remaining ingredients; pour over ribs.
2. Cover and cook on low until meat is tender, 6-7 hours.

1 SERVING: 371 cal., 14g fat (5g sat. fat), 86mg chol., 1076mg sod., 34g carb. (30g sugars, 1g fiber), 27g pro.

PRESSURE-COOKER SESAME CHICKEN

Your family will love the flavorful sauce that coats this chicken, and you'll love how quick and easy it is to make. If you serve gluten-free meals, use tamari instead of soy sauce.
—Karen Kelly, Germantown, MD

TAKES: 20 MIN. • **MAKES:** 4 SERVINGS

- 1½ lbs. boneless skinless chicken breasts, cut into 1-in. pieces
- 1 Tbsp. sesame oil
- ¼ cup honey
- ¼ cup soy sauce or gluten-free tamari soy sauce
- ¼ cup water
- 3 garlic cloves, minced
- ¼ tsp. crushed red pepper flakes
- 3 tsp. cornstarch
- 2 Tbsp. cold water
- 1 Tbsp. sesame seeds
- Hot cooked rice
- Thinly sliced green onions, optional

1. Select saute or browning setting on a 6-qt. electric pressure cooker. Adjust for medium heat; add sesame oil. When oil is hot, brown the chicken in batches. Press cancel. Return all to the pressure cooker. In a small bowl, whisk honey, soy sauce, water, garlic and pepper flakes; stir into pressure cooker. Lock lid; close pressure-release valve. Adjust to pressure-cook on high for 4 minutes.
2. Quick-release pressure. In a bowl, mix cornstarch and water until smooth; stir into pressure cooker. Select saute setting and adjust for low heat. Simmer, stirring constantly, until thickened, 1-2 minutes. Serve with rice. Sprinkle with sesame seeds and, if desired, green onions.

1 SERVING: 311 cal., 9g fat (2g sat. fat), 94mg chol., 1004mg sod., 20g carb. (17g sugars, 0 fiber), 37g pro.

READER REVIEW

"My picky son loved this recipe. Mild but yummy flavor, good texture, and fast and easy because it's in the Instant Pot®."

SHANNON HUDGENS SOEHL, TASTEOFHOME.COM

PRESSURE-COOKER HERBED TURKEY BREASTS

Tender turkey breast is enhanced with an array of flavorful herbs in this juicy, comforting dish.
—Laurie Mace, Los Osos, CA

PREP: 25 MIN. + MARINATING
COOK: 20 MIN. + RELEASING
MAKES: 12 SERVINGS

- **1 can (14½ oz.) chicken broth**
- **½ cup lemon juice**
- **¼ cup packed brown sugar**
- **¼ cup fresh sage**
- **¼ cup fresh thyme leaves**
- **¼ cup lime juice**
- **¼ cup cider vinegar**
- **¼ cup olive oil**
- **1 envelope onion soup mix**
- **2 Tbsp. Dijon mustard**
- **1 Tbsp. minced fresh marjoram**
- **1½ tsp. paprika**
- **1 tsp. garlic powder**
- **1 tsp. pepper**
- **½ tsp. salt**
- **2 boneless skinless turkey breast halves (2 lbs. each)**
- **Optional: Additional fresh thyme and marjoram, and lemon wedges**

1. In a blender, process first 15 ingredients until blended. Place the turkey in a bowl or shallow dish; pour marinade over turkey and turn to coat. Refrigerate, covered, for 8 hours or overnight, turning occasionally.
2. Transfer the turkey and marinade to a 6-qt. electric pressure cooker. Lock lid; close the pressure-release valve. Adjust to pressure-cook on high for 20 minutes.
3. Let the pressure release naturally for 10 minutes; quick-release any remaining pressure. A thermometer inserted in the turkey breasts should read at least 165°. Remove the turkey from pressure cooker; tent with foil. Let stand 10 minutes before slicing. If desired, top turkey breasts with additional fresh thyme and marjoram and serve with lemon wedges.

5 OZ. COOKED TURKEY: 219 cal., 5g fat (1g sat. fat), 87mg chol., 484mg sod., 5g carb. (3g sugars, 0 fiber), 36g pro. **DIABETIC EXCHANGES:** 5 lean meat.

BEEF IN MUSHROOM GRAVY

This is one of the best and easiest meals I've ever made. It has only four ingredients, and they all go into the pot at once. The meat is nicely seasoned and makes its own gravy. It tastes wonderful over mashed potatoes.
—Margery Bryan, Moses Lake, WA

PREP: 10 MIN. • **COOK:** 7 HOURS
MAKES: 6 SERVINGS

- **2½ lbs. beef top round steak**
- **1 to 2 envelopes onion soup mix**
- **1 can (10¾ oz.) condensed cream of mushroom soup, undiluted**
- **½ cup water**
- **Mashed potatoes, optional**

Cut the steak into 6 serving pieces; place in a 3-qt. slow cooker. Combine the soup mix, soup and water; pour over the beef. Cover and cook on low for 7-8 hours or until meat is tender. If desired, serve with mashed potatoes.

FREEZE OPTION: Place the beef in freezer containers; top with gravy. Cool and freeze. To use, partially thaw beef mixture in the refrigerator overnight. Heat through in a covered saucepan, stirring occasionally; add water if necessary.

1 SERVING: 241 cal., 7g fat (2g sat. fat), 87mg chol., 810mg sod., 7g carb. (1g sugars, 1g fiber), 35g pro.

PRESSURE-COOKER SWEET & SOUR BRISKET

Here's one dish that never gets old in our house. The brisket is tender and juicy with a great sweet and sour twist.
—Jolie Albertazzie, Moreno Valley, CA

PREP: 15 MIN.
COOK: 1¼ HOURS + RELEASING
MAKES: 10 SERVINGS

- **1 can (28 oz.) crushed tomatoes**
- **1 medium onion, halved and thinly sliced**
- **½ cup raisins**
- **¼ cup packed brown sugar**
- **2 Tbsp. lemon juice**
- **3 garlic cloves, minced**
- **1 fresh beef brisket (3 lbs.)**
- **½ tsp. salt**
- **¼ tsp. pepper**

1. In a small bowl, combine the tomatoes, onion, raisins, brown sugar, lemon juice and garlic. Pour half the mixture into a 6-qt. pressure cooker.
2. Sprinkle the meat with salt and pepper. Transfer to the pressure cooker. Top with remaining tomato mixture. Lock the lid in place; adjust to pressure-cook on high for 1¼ hours. Allow pressure to naturally release for 10 minutes, then quick-release any remaining pressure.
3. Remove brisket to a serving platter and keep warm. Skim fat from cooking juices. Thinly slice meat across the grain. Serve with tomato mixture.

NOTE: This is a fresh beef brisket, not corned beef.

4 OZ. COOKED BEEF WITH ⅓ CUP SAUCE: 247 cal., 6g fat (2g sat. fat), 58mg chol., 314mg sod., 19g carb. (14g sugars, 2g fiber), 30g pro.

TEST KITCHEN TIP

Cooked brisket will last up to 4 days in the fridge, and 2 months in the freezer. Store in an airtight container, or wrap the meat tightly in freezer wrap or foil.

SLOW-COOKER TURKEY BREAST WITH CRANBERRY GRAVY

I created this recipe when I was craving Thanksgiving dinner, and it was still more than a month away. You get all the flavors of a holiday feast in no time. Add a vegetable and some mashed potatoes and you're done!
—Cyndy Gerken, Naples, FL

PREP: 25 MIN. • **COOK:** 3 HOURS
MAKES: 12 SERVINGS

- **2 boneless skinless turkey breast halves (2 to 3 lbs. each)**
- **½ tsp. salt**
- **½ tsp. pepper**
- **3 fresh thyme sprigs**
- **2 Tbsp. butter**
- **1 cup whole-berry cranberry sauce**
- **1 cup apple cider or juice**
- **½ cup chicken stock**
- **1 envelope onion soup mix**
- **2 Tbsp. maple syrup**
- **1 Tbsp. Worcestershire sauce**
- **¼ cup all-purpose flour**
- **¼ cup water**

1. Place turkey in a 5- or 6-qt. slow cooker; sprinkle with salt and pepper. Add thyme and dot with butter. Combine cranberry sauce, cider, stock, soup mix, syrup and Worcestershire; pour over the turkey. Cook, covered, on low 3-4 hours or until a thermometer inserted in turkey reads at least 165°. Remove turkey and keep warm.
2. Transfer the remaining cranberry mixture to a large saucepan; discard thyme sprigs. Combine the flour and water until smooth. Bring cranberry mixture to a boil; gradually stir in flour mixture until smooth. Cook and stir until thickened, about 2 minutes. Slice turkey; serve with cranberry gravy.

5 OZ. COOKED TURKEY WITH ⅓ CUP SAUCE: 259 cal., 4g fat (2g sat. fat), 91mg chol., 537mg sod., 17g carb. (10g sugars, 1g fiber), 36g pro.

SWEET & SPICY PEANUT CHICKEN

Chicken thighs and a slow cooker—that's a marriage made in culinary heaven! Juicy and flavorful, this simple dish will make you swoon when you return home and find it ready. The filling is also excellent in lettuce wraps.
—Janice Elder, Charlotte, NC

PREP: 25 MIN. • **COOK:** 6 HOURS
MAKES: 6 SERVINGS

- **1½ lbs. boneless skinless chicken thighs**
- **1 cup chicken broth**
- **1 cup pepper jelly**
- **½ cup creamy peanut butter**
- **¼ cup reduced-sodium soy sauce**
- **2 garlic cloves, minced**
- **¼ tsp. salt**
- **¼ tsp. pepper**
- **½ cup chopped dry roasted peanuts**
- **½ cup chopped sweet red pepper**
- **Optional: Hot cooked rice and lime wedges**

1. Place the chicken in a 3- or 4-qt. slow cooker. Combine the broth, jelly, peanut butter, soy sauce and garlic in small bowl; pour over chicken. Cook, covered, on low until chicken is tender, 6-8 hours.
2. Remove chicken from slow cooker and cool slightly. Shred with 2 forks. Skim fat from cooking juices. Return meat to slow cooker. Stir in salt and pepper.
3. Sprinkle each serving with peanuts and red pepper. If desired, serve with rice and lime wedges.

1 SERVING: 525 cal., 25g fat (5g sat. fat), 76mg chol., 914mg sod., 48g carb. (32g sugars, 3g fiber), 30g pro.

JANICE ELDER
Charlotte, NC

MARINATED POT ROAST

I've long used whole or ground cloves as my secret ingredient in cooking and baking. Added to an overnight marinade, they provide the gravy in this meaty main dish with great flavor.
—Marijane Rea, Portland, OR

PREP: 10 MIN. + MARINATING
COOK: 8 HOURS
MAKES: 12 SERVINGS

- **1 cup dry white wine or beef broth**
- **⅓ cup reduced-sodium soy sauce**
- **1 Tbsp. olive oil**
- **4 garlic cloves, minced**
- **2 green onions, thinly sliced**
- **1½ tsp. ground ginger**
- **¼ tsp. pepper**
- **4 whole cloves**
- **1 beef top round roast (4 lbs.)**
- **5 tsp. cornstarch**
- **5 tsp. cold water**

1. In a large resealable container, combine the first 8 ingredients. Cut roast in half; add to marinade. Seal container and turn to coat; refrigerate overnight.
2. Place roast and marinade in a 5-qt. slow cooker. Cover and cook on low for 8-10 hours or until the meat is tender. Remove the roast to a serving platter and keep warm. Pour cooking juices into a 2-cup measuring cup; discard whole cloves.
3. In a saucepan, combine cornstarch and cold water until smooth; stir in 1½ cups cooking juices. Bring to a boil; cook and stir for 2 minutes or until thickened. Serve with the roast.

3 OZ. COOKED BEEF: 225 cal., 6g fat (2g sat. fat), 84mg chol., 299mg sod., 3g carb. (0 sugars, 0 fiber), 34g pro.

FREEZE OPTION: Place beef and vegetables in freezer containers; top with the cooking juices. Cool and freeze. To use, partially thaw in the refrigerator overnight. Heat through in a covered saucepan, stirring gently; add broth if necessary.

1 CUP BEEF MIXTURE: 248 cal., 12g fat (4g sat. fat), 74mg chol., 652mg sod., 10g carb. (5g sugars, 2g fiber), 24g pro. **DIABETIC EXCHANGES:** 3 lean meat, 1 vegetable.

PRESSURE-COOKER BEEF DAUBE PROVENCAL

My dish is perfect on chilly nights, especially after we have been out chopping wood. It's melt-in-your-mouth delicious.
—Brenda Ryan, Marshall, MO

PREP: 30 MIN. • **COOK:** 30 MIN. + RELEASING
MAKES: 8 SERVINGS

- **1 boneless beef chuck roast or venison roast (about 2 lbs.), cut into 1-in. cubes**
- **1½ tsp. salt, divided**
- **½ tsp. coarsely ground pepper, divided**
- **2 tsp. olive oil**
- **2 cups chopped carrots**
- **1½ cups chopped onion**
- **12 garlic cloves, crushed**
- **1 Tbsp. tomato paste**
- **1 cup dry red wine**
- **1 can (14½ oz.) diced tomatoes, undrained**
- **½ cup beef broth**
- **1 tsp. chopped fresh rosemary**
- **1 tsp. chopped fresh thyme**
- **1 bay leaf**
- **Dash ground cloves**
- **Hot cooked pasta or mashed potatoes**

1. Sprinkle beef with ½ tsp. salt and ¼ tsp. pepper. Select saute setting on a 6-qt. electric pressure cooker. Adjust for medium heat; add oil. When oil is hot, brown beef in batches. Set aside.
2. Add the carrots, onion and garlic to the pressure cooker; cook and stir until the vegetables are golden brown, 4-6 minutes. Add the tomato paste; cook and stir until fragrant, about 1 minute. Add the wine, stirring to loosen browned bits. Return the beef to pressure cooker. Add tomatoes, broth, rosemary, thyme, bay leaf, cloves and the remaining 1 tsp. salt and ¼ tsp. pepper. Press cancel.
3. Lock lid; close pressure-release valve. Adjust to pressure-cook on high for 30 minutes. Let pressure release naturally for 10 minutes, then quick-release any remaining pressure. A thermometer inserted in beef should read at least 160°. Discard bay leaf. Serve with hot cooked pasta. If desired, sprinkle with additional thyme.

SLOW-COOKED PEACHY SPARERIBS

Canned peaches make a delightful addition to my flavorful sparerib sauce. Served over rice, the sweet-tangy ribs make a sensational meal any time of year.
—Jeanne Brino, Woodbury, MN

PREP: 10 MIN. • **COOK:** 5½ HOURS
MAKES: 8 SERVINGS

- **4 lbs. pork spareribs**
- **1 can (15¼ oz.) sliced peaches, undrained**
- **½ cup packed brown sugar**
- **¼ cup ketchup**
- **¼ cup white vinegar**
- **2 Tbsp. soy sauce**
- **1 garlic clove, minced**
- **1 tsp. salt**
- **1 tsp. pepper**
- **2 Tbsp. cornstarch**
- **2 Tbsp. cold water**
- **Hot cooked rice**

1. Cut ribs into serving-sized pieces. In a large skillet, brown ribs on all sides; drain.
2. Transfer meat to a 5-qt. slow cooker. Combine the peaches, brown sugar, ketchup, vinegar, soy sauce, garlic, salt and pepper; pour over ribs. Cover and cook on low for 5½-6 hours or until meat is tender.
3. Remove pork and peaches to a serving platter; keep warm. Skim fat from cooking juices; transfer to a small saucepan. Bring liquid to a boil. Combine the cornstarch and water until smooth. Gradually stir into the pan. Bring to a boil; cook and stir for 2 minutes or until thickened. Serve with pork and rice.

6 OZ. COOKED PORK: 518 cal., 32g fat (12g sat. fat), 128mg chol., 727mg sod., 24g carb. (22g sugars, 0 fiber), 31g pro.

SLOW-COOKER FLANK STEAK FAJITAS

As a busy teacher, it's so nice to come home to a warm meal after a day in the classroom. I'm not the only one who thinks so—these beefy fajitas go fast at faculty potlucks, too.
—Mary Holmgren, Mackinaw, IL

PREP: 10 MIN. • **COOK:** 6 HOURS
MAKES: 8 SERVINGS

- **1 beef flank steak (2 lbs.), halved crosswise**
- **1 medium green pepper, cut into strips**
- **1 medium sweet red pepper, cut into strips**
- **1 medium onion, halved and sliced**
- **1 envelope fajita seasoning mix**
- **½ cup beer or reduced-sodium beef broth**
- **8 flour tortillas (8 in.), warmed**
- **1 cup pico de gallo**
- **Chopped fresh cilantro**

1. Place the first 5 ingredients in a 5-qt. slow cooker. Pour beer over top. Cook, covered, on low until the meat is tender, 6-8 hours.
2. Remove beef from slow cooker. Strain vegetable mixture; return vegetables to slow cooker. (Discard cooking juices or save for another use.) Shred the beef with 2 forks; add to the vegetables and heat through. Serve in tortillas with pico de gallo and cilantro.

1 SERVING: 361 cal., 12g fat (4g sat. fat), 54mg chol., 668mg sod., 34g carb. (2g sugars, 3g fiber), 27g pro. **DIABETIC EXCHANGES:** 3 lean meat, 2 starch.

SWEDISH MEATBALLS ALFREDO

I'm a big fan of this potluck-perfect dish. It takes much less time than many other slow-cooker recipes. Plus, it's easy—and I'm all for the easy!
—Carole Bess White, Portland, OR

PREP: 10 MIN. • **COOK:** 2 HOURS
MAKES: 10 SERVINGS

- **2 jars (15 oz. each) roasted garlic Alfredo sauce**
- **2 cups heavy whipping cream**
- **2 cups sour cream**
- **¾ tsp. hot pepper sauce**
- **½ tsp. garlic powder**
- **½ tsp. dill weed**
- **⅛ tsp. pepper**
- **1 pkg. (32 oz.) frozen fully cooked Swedish meatballs, thawed**
- **Paprika**
- **Hot cooked egg noodles**

1. In a 5-qt. slow cooker, combine the first 7 ingredients. Stir in the meatballs. Cook, covered, on low until meatballs are heated through, 2-3 hours.
2. Sprinkle meatballs with paprika. Serve with noodles.

1 CUP: 766 cal., 67g fat (38g sat. fat), 238mg chol., 1357mg sod., 16g carb. (7g sugars, 2g fiber), 21g pro.

SPRING HERB ROAST

This marvelous beef roast lets you forget about it while it's slow cooking (but the aroma will remind you). We serve it with brown rice or mashed potatoes.

—Donna Roberts, Manhattan, KS

PREP: 20 MIN. • **COOK:** 4 HOURS + STANDING
MAKES: 8 SERVINGS

- **2 large onions, halved and sliced (about 3 cups)**
- **½ lb. sliced fresh mushrooms**
- **1 beef rump roast or bottom round roast (3 to 4 lbs.)**
- **2 tsp. salt**
- **½ tsp. pepper**
- **1 Tbsp. canola oil**
- **1½ cups water**
- **2 Tbsp. tomato paste**
- **3 garlic cloves, minced**
- **½ tsp. each dried basil, marjoram and thyme**
- **Minced fresh parsley**

1. Place onions and mushrooms in a 5- or 6-qt. slow cooker. Sprinkle roast with salt and pepper. In a large skillet, heat oil over medium-high heat; brown roast on all sides. Transfer to slow cooker.
2. In a small bowl, mix the water, tomato paste, garlic, basil, marjoram and thyme; pour over roast. Cook, covered, on low for 4-5 hours or until the meat is tender (a thermometer should read at least 145°).
3. Remove roast from slow cooker; tent with foil. Let stand 15 minutes before slicing. Serve with onion mixture; sprinkle with parsley.

5 OZ. COOKED BEEF WITH ¼ CUP VEGETABLE MIXTURE: 257 cal., 10g fat (3g sat. fat), 101mg chol., 650mg sod., 6g carb. (3g sugars, 1g fiber), 35g pro. **DIABETIC EXCHANGES:** 5 lean meat, 1 vegetable, ½ fat.

TEST KITCHEN TIP

To sear a roast before slow cooking, heat oil in a skillet or Dutch oven on the stove, then brown the roast for about one minute per side before transferring it to the slow cooker. This step will add even more flavor to your final dish.

TURKEY LEG POT ROAST

Well-seasoned turkey legs and tender veggies make an ideal dinner for a crisp fall day. The recipe couldn't be easier!

—Rick and Vegas Pearson, Cadillac, MI

PREP: 15 MIN. • **COOK:** 5 HOURS
MAKES: 3 SERVINGS

- **3 medium potatoes, quartered**
- **2 cups fresh baby carrots**
- **2 celery ribs, cut into 2½-in. pieces**
- **1 medium onion, peeled and quartered**
- **3 garlic cloves, peeled and quartered**
- **½ cup chicken broth**
- **3 turkey drumsticks (12 oz. each), skin removed**
- **2 tsp. seasoned salt**
- **1 tsp. dried thyme**
- **1 tsp. dried parsley flakes**
- **¼ tsp. pepper**
- **Chopped fresh parsley, optional**

In a greased 5-qt. slow cooker, combine the first 6 ingredients. Place drumsticks over vegetables. Sprinkle with seasoned salt, thyme, parsley and pepper. Cover and cook on low for 5-5½ hours or until the turkey is tender. If desired, top with chopped fresh parsley just before serving.

1 SERVING: 460 cal., 7g fat (2g sat. fat), 202mg chol., 1416mg sod., 44g carb. (10g sugars, 6g fiber), 54g pro.

Breads, Rolls & Muffins

Every day deserves a slice of buttery goodness. Bring the joy of homemade bread to your kitchen with these baked beauties, including cheesy biscuits, crumb-topped muffins, quick breads, breakfast pastries, cast-iron classics and other oven-fresh favorites.

CHOCOLATE PINWHEEL BREAD

This swirled yeast bread is chock-full of chocolate chips. The sweet slices don't need any butter. Keep one loaf and share the other with a neighbor.
—Dawn Onuffer, Crestview, FL

PREP: 30 MIN. + RISING
BAKE: 40 MIN. + COOLING
MAKES: 2 LOAVES (16 PIECES EACH)

- **1 pkg. (¼ oz.) active dry yeast**
- **1 cup warm 2% milk (110° to 115°)**
- **¼ cup sugar**
- **1 tsp. salt**
- **2 large eggs, room temperature**
- **4 oz. cream cheese, softened**
- **4 to 4½ cups bread flour**

FILLING

- **4 oz. cream cheese, softened**
- **½ cup confectioners' sugar**
- **2 Tbsp. baking cocoa**
- **1 cup semisweet chocolate chips**
- **1 large egg, beaten**

1. In a large bowl, dissolve the yeast in warm milk. Add the sugar, salt, eggs, cream cheese and 2 cups flour; beat until smooth. Stir in enough remaining flour to form a soft dough.
2. Turn onto a floured surface; knead until smooth and elastic, 6-8 minutes. Place in a greased bowl, turning once to grease top. Cover and let rise in a warm place until doubled, about 1 hour.
3. Punch dough down. Turn onto a floured surface; divide in half. Roll each portion into a 12x8-in. rectangle. For the filling, in a small bowl, beat the cream cheese, confectioners' sugar and cocoa until smooth. Spread over each rectangle to within ½ in. of edges. Sprinkle with chocolate chips. Roll up jelly-roll style, starting with a short side; pinch seam to seal. Place seam side down in 2 greased 9x5-in. loaf pans. Cover and let rise until doubled, about 45 minutes.
4. Brush tops of loaves with egg. Bake at 350° for 25 minutes. Cover loosely with foil. Bake 15-20 minutes longer or until loaves sound hollow when tapped. Remove from pans to wire racks to cool.

1 PIECE: 127 cal., 5g fat (3g sat. fat), 29mg chol., 105mg sod., 19g carb. (7g sugars, 1g fiber), 4g pro.

PARMESAN HERB LOAF

This savory round loaf is one of my best quick bread recipes. I serve slices accompanied by individual ramekins filled with olive oil infused with herbs for dipping. This loaf is on the small side, so you may decide to make two.
—Dianne Culley, Olive Branch, MS

PREP: 15 MIN. • **BAKE:** 30 MIN.
MAKES: 1 LOAF (8 SERVINGS)

- **1¼ cups all-purpose flour**
- **3 Tbsp. plus 1 tsp. grated Parmesan cheese, divided**
- **1½ tsp. sugar**
- **1½ tsp. dried minced onion**
- **1¼ tsp. Italian seasoning, divided**
- **½ tsp. baking powder**
- **¼ tsp. baking soda**
- **¼ tsp. salt**
- **½ cup sour cream**
- **2 Tbsp. plus 2 tsp. 2% milk**
- **4½ tsp. butter, melted**
- **1 large egg white, lightly beaten**

1. In a small bowl, combine the flour, 3 Tbsp. Parmesan cheese, sugar, onion, 1 tsp. Italian seasoning, baking powder, baking soda and salt. In another bowl, whisk the sour cream, milk and butter. Stir mixture into dry ingredients just until moistened.
2. Turn onto a floured surface; knead for 1 minute. Shape into a round loaf; place on a baking sheet coated with cooking spray. With kitchen scissors, cut a ¼-in.-deep cross in top of loaf. Brush with egg white. Sprinkle with the remaining 1 tsp. cheese and ¼ tsp. Italian seasoning.
3. Bake at 350° for 30-35 minutes or until golden brown. Serve warm.

1 PIECE: 123 cal., 4g fat (2g sat. fat), 9mg chol., 217mg sod., 17g carb. (2g sugars, 1g fiber), 4g pro.

READER REVIEW

"I love this bread, it is so simple and absolutely delicious! My boyfriend requests it every time we have pasta."

RHILER, TASTEOFHOME.COM

BUTTERNUT SQUASH DINNER ROLLS

These wholesome rolls are a pleasant addition to any entree. I get many requests for them around the holidays. I have a big family—16 grandchildren—so I make about 100 dozen in December for relatives and friends.
—Ula Kessler, Liberty Center, OH

PREP: 30 MIN. + RISING • **BAKE:** 15 MIN.
MAKES: 5 DOZEN

- **2 Tbsp. plus 1 tsp. active dry yeast**
- **¾ tsp. plus 1 cup sugar, divided**
- **½ cup warm water (110° to 115°)**
- **2 cups warm milk (110° to 115°)**
- **¼ cup butter, softened**
- **2 cups mashed cooked butternut squash**
- **2 tsp. salt**
- **¼ cup toasted wheat germ**
- **10 to 11½ cups all-purpose flour**
- **Additional butter**

1. In a large bowl, dissolve the yeast and ¾ tsp. sugar in warm water; let stand for 5 minutes. Add the milk, butter, squash, salt and the remaining 1 cup sugar; mix until smooth. Add the wheat germ and 4 cups flour; beat until smooth. Stir in enough remaining flour to form a soft dough. Turn onto a floured surface; knead dough until smooth and elastic, about 6-8 minutes.
2. Place in a greased bowl, turning once to grease the top. Cover and let rise in a warm place until doubled, about 1 hour. Punch dough down and divide into thirds; divide each portion into 20 pieces. Shape into balls.
3. Place on greased baking sheets. Cover rolls and let rise until doubled, about 30 minutes. Bake at 350° 15-17 minutes or until golden brown. Brush with butter. Remove to wire racks.

1 ROLL: 107 cal., 1g fat (1g sat. fat), 3mg chol., 88mg sod., 21g carb. (4g sugars, 1g fiber), 3g pro.

CHEDDAR BUTTERMILK BISCUITS

Every bite of these flaky biscuits gets a little kick from cayenne pepper and sharp cheddar cheese. They're a nice accompaniment to soup and stew.
—Kimberly Nuttall, San Marcos, CA

PREP: 20 MIN. • **BAKE:** 15 MIN.
MAKES: 7 BISCUITS

- **2 cups all-purpose flour**
- **2 Tbsp. sugar**
- **4 tsp. baking powder**
- **½ tsp. salt**
- **¼ to ½ tsp. cayenne pepper**
- **½ cup cold butter, cubed**
- **½ cup shredded sharp cheddar cheese**
- **¾ cup buttermilk**

1. In a large bowl, combine the flour, sugar, baking powder, salt and cayenne. Cut in butter until mixture resembles coarse crumbs. Add the cheese and toss. Stir in buttermilk just until moistened.
2. Turn onto a lightly floured surface; knead 8-10 times. Pat or roll dough to 1 in. thickness; cut with a floured 2½-in. biscuit cutter. Place biscuits 1 in. apart in a large ungreased cast-iron or other ovenproof skillet. Bake at 425° until golden brown, 15-18 minutes. Serve warm.

1 BISCUIT: 304 cal., 16g fat (10g sat. fat), 44mg chol., 651mg sod., 32g carb. (5g sugars, 1g fiber), 7g pro.

APPLE PEAR COFFEE CAKE

A friend gave me this recipe to make for a breakfast I was hosting. The pan was empty before the breakfast was over! It's one of my most-requested recipes, probably because it's a bit different.
—Joanne Hoschette, Paxton, MA

PREP: 15 MIN. • **BAKE:** 35 MIN.
MAKES: 15 SERVINGS

- **½ cup butter, softened**
- **1 cup sugar**
- **2 large eggs, room temperature**
- **1 tsp. vanilla extract**
- **2 cups all-purpose flour**
- **3 tsp. baking powder**
- **1 tsp. baking soda**
- **½ tsp. salt**
- **1 cup sour cream**
- **1¼ cups chopped peeled apples**
- **½ cup chopped peeled pear**

TOPPING
- **1 cup packed brown sugar**
- **1 tsp. ground cinnamon**
- **2 Tbsp. cold butter**
- **½ cup chopped pecans**

1. Preheat oven to 350°. In a large bowl, cream butter and sugar until light and fluffy, 5-7 minutes. Beat in eggs and vanilla. Combine the flour, baking powder, baking soda and salt; add to creamed mixture alternately with sour cream. Fold in apples and pear. Pour into a greased 13x9-in. baking dish.
2. In a small bowl, combine brown sugar and cinnamon. Cut in butter until the mixture resembles coarse crumbs. Stir in pecans. Sprinkle over batter.
3. Bake until a toothpick inserted in the center comes out clean, 35-40 minutes. Cool on a wire rack.

1 PIECE: 313 cal., 14g fat (7g sat. fat), 59mg chol., 342mg sod., 44g carb. (30g sugars, 1g fiber), 4g pro.

BASIL PARMESAN BREAD

The combination of basil, Parmesan cheese and sun-dried tomatoes gives this hearty bread a flavor that will take you right to Tuscany! Serve with your favorite pasta dish.
—Sherry Hulsman, Louisville, KY

PREP: 25 MIN. + RISING
BAKE: 25 MIN. + COOLING
MAKES: 2 LOAVES (16 PIECES EACH)

- **1 pkg. (¼ oz.) active dry yeast**
- **1½ cups warm water (110° to 115°)**
- **½ cup warm 2% milk (110° to 115°)**
- **3 Tbsp. sugar**
- **3 Tbsp. olive oil**
- **2 tsp. salt**
- **5 to 6 cups bread flour**
- **1 cup shredded Parmesan cheese**
- **¼ cup chopped oil-packed sun-dried tomatoes**
- **3 tsp. dried basil**
- **1 tsp. hot pepper sauce**

1. In a large bowl, dissolve yeast in warm water. Add milk, sugar, oil, salt and 4 cups flour. Beat on medium speed until smooth. Stir in the cheese, tomatoes, basil, pepper sauce and enough remaining flour to form a soft dough (dough will be sticky).
2. Turn dough onto a floured surface; knead until smooth and elastic, roughly 6-8 minutes. Place in a greased bowl, turning once to grease the top. Cover and let rise in a warm place until doubled, about 1½ hours.
3. Punch down dough. Divide in half and shape into loaves. Place in 2 greased 9x5-in. loaf pans. Cover with kitchen towels; let rise in a warm place until doubled, about 1 hour. Preheat the oven to 375°.
4. Bake bread until golden brown, roughly 25-30 minutes. Remove from pans to wire racks to cool.

1 PIECE: 94 cal., 2g fat (1g sat. fat), 2mg chol., 195mg sod., 16g carb. (1g sugars, 1g fiber), 4g pro.

DID YOU KNOW?

Unlike quick bread, yeast bread requires some kneading to help the dough come together and develop gluten. Gluten gives bread the right texture and helps it hold its shape.

TENDER WHOLE WHEAT ROLLS

Even though these are whole wheat rolls they have a light texture and are soft and tender. This recipe reminds me of lots of happy meals with my family.
—Wilma Orlano, Carroll, IA

PREP: 40 MIN. + RISING • **BAKE:** 10 MIN.
MAKES: 2 DOZEN

- **1½ cups boiling water**
- **⅓ cup wheat bran**
- **3 Tbsp. ground flaxseed**
- **1½ tsp. salt**
- **1 tsp. ground cinnamon**
- **⅓ cup honey**
- **¼ cup canola oil**
- **2 pkg. (¼ oz. each) active dry yeast**
- **¼ cup warm water (110° to 115°)**
- **2 tsp. sugar**
- **1½ cups whole wheat flour**
- **2½ to 3 cups bread flour**

1. In a small bowl, pour boiling water over the wheat bran, flaxseed, salt and cinnamon. Add the honey and oil. Let stand until mixture cools to 110°-115°, stirring occasionally.
2. In a large bowl, dissolve yeast in warm water. Add the sugar, whole wheat flour and wheat bran mixture. Beat on medium speed for 3 minutes. Stir in enough bread flour to form a firm dough.
3. Turn onto a floured surface; knead until smooth and elastic, 6-8 minutes. Place in a greased bowl, turning once to grease the top. Cover and let rise in a warm place until doubled, about 1 hour. Punch the dough down.
4. Turn onto a lightly floured surface; divide into 24 pieces. Shape each into a roll. Place 2 in. apart on greased baking sheets. Cover and let rise until doubled, about 30 minutes.
5. Bake at 375° for 10-15 minutes or until golden brown. Remove rolls from pans to wire racks.

1 ROLL: 120 cal., 3g fat (0 sat. fat), 0 chol., 149mg sod., 22g carb. (4g sugars, 2g fiber), 4g pro. **DIABETIC EXCHANGES:** 1½ starch, ½ fat.

CHAPATI BREADS

My daughter and I make this Indian flatbread frequently. It's so fun and goes well with any spiced dish. We use the extras to make sandwich wraps.
—Joyce McCarthy, Sussex, WI

PREP: 20 MIN. • **COOK:** 5 MIN./BATCH
MAKES: 10 SERVINGS

- **1½ cups all-purpose flour**
- **½ cup whole wheat flour**
- **1 tsp. salt**
- **¼ tsp. garlic powder, optional**
- **¾ cup hot water (140°)**
- **2 Tbsp. olive oil**

In a large bowl, combine the flours, salt and, if desired, garlic powder. Stir in water and oil. Turn onto a floured surface; knead until smooth and elastic, 8-10 minutes. Cover and let rest for 30 minutes. Divide dough into 10 portions. On a lightly floured surface, roll each dough portion into a 6-in. circle. In a large cast-iron or other heavy skillet, cook breads over medium heat until lightly browned, 1 minute on each side. Keep warm.

1 FLATBREAD: 113 cal., 3g fat (0 sat. fat), 0 chol., 237mg sod., 19g carb. (0 sugars, 1g fiber), 3g pro. **DIABETIC EXCHANGES:** 1 starch, ½ fat.

CARAMEL-PECAN PUMPKIN PULL-APARTS

We love sticky buns made with my husband's angel biscuit dough, caramel and pecans. For a twist, try apple butter or applesauce instead of the pumpkin.
—Carolyn Kumpe, El Dorado, CA

PREP: 40 MIN. + CHILLING • **BAKE:** 25 MIN.
MAKES: 16 SERVINGS

- ¼ cup butter, cubed
- 1 cup chopped pecans
- ¾ cup packed brown sugar
- ½ cup heavy whipping cream
- ¼ cup honey

DOUGH

- 1 pkg. (¼ oz.) active dry yeast
- ¼ cup warm water (110° to 115°)
- 2¼ to 2½ cups all-purpose flour
- ¼ cup sugar
- 1 tsp. pumpkin pie spice
- ¾ tsp. salt
- ½ tsp. baking soda
- ½ tsp. baking powder
- ½ tsp. ground cinnamon
- ¼ cup cold butter, cubed
- ½ cup solid-pack pumpkin
- ½ cup buttermilk
- 1 tsp. vanilla extract

1. In a small saucepan, melt butter over medium heat. Add pecans; cook and stir 2-3 minutes or until pecans are fragrant. Stir in brown sugar, cream and honey; cook and stir until sugar is dissolved and mixture begins to darken. Pour into a greased 9-in. square baking pan.
2. In a bowl, dissolve yeast in warm water. In a large bowl, whisk 2¼ cups flour, sugar, pie spice, salt, baking soda, baking powder and cinnamon. Cut in butter until crumbly. Add pumpkin, buttermilk, vanilla and yeast mixture; mix well.
3. Turn the dough onto a floured surface; knead gently 8-10 times, adding additional flour if needed. Roll the dough into a 9-in. square. Cut the dough into 16 squares; arrange over pecan mixture. Cover and refrigerate overnight.
4. Remove pan from the refrigerator 30 minutes before baking. Preheat oven to 400°. Uncover; bake 24-28 minutes or until golden brown. Carefully invert onto a platter; serve warm.

1 PIECE: 266 cal., 14g fat (6g sat. fat), 26mg chol., 219mg sod., 33g carb. (19g sugars, 2g fiber), 3g pro.

HOMEMADE BAGELS

Instead of going to a baker, head to the kitchen and surprise your family with homemade bagels. For variation and flavor, sprinkle the tops with cinnamon sugar instead of sesame and poppy seeds.
—Rebecca Phillips, Burlington, CT

PREP: 30 MIN. + RISING
BAKE: 20 MIN. + COOLING
MAKES: 1 DOZEN

- 1 tsp. active dry yeast
- 1¼ cups warm 2% milk (110° to 115°)
- ½ cup butter, softened
- 2 Tbsp. sugar
- 1 tsp. salt
- 1 large egg yolk room temperature
- 3¾ to 4¼ cups all-purpose flour
- Sesame or poppy seeds, optional

1. In a large bowl, dissolve yeast in warm milk. Add the butter, sugar, salt and egg yolk; mix well. Stir in enough flour to form a soft dough.
2. Turn onto a floured surface; knead until smooth and elastic, 6-8 minutes. Place in a greased bowl, turning once to grease top. Cover and let rise in a warm place until doubled, about 1 hour.
3. Punch dough down. Shape into 12 balls. Push thumb through centers to form a 1½-in. hole. Stretch and shape the dough to form an even ring. Place on a floured surface. Cover and let rest for 10 minutes; flatten bagels slightly.
4. Fill a Dutch oven two-thirds full with water; bring to a boil. Drop bagels, 2 at a time, into the boiling water. Cook for 45 seconds; turn and cook 45 seconds longer. Remove with a slotted spoon; drain well on paper towels.
5. Sprinkle with sesame or poppy seeds if desired. Place 2 in. apart on greased baking sheets. Bake at 400° until golden brown, 20-25 minutes. Remove from pans to wire racks to cool.

1 BAGEL: 237 cal., 9g fat (5g sat. fat), 38mg chol., 271mg sod., 33g carb. (3g sugars, 1g fiber), 5g pro.

CAROLYN KUMPE
El Dorado, CA

AIR-FRYER BACON CRESCENT ROLLS

The mouthwatering aroma of warm bacon from these three-ingredient rolls will draw folks to the table once you throw the crescent rolls in. Air-fryer recipes, like this one, are fun for children to prepare and such a cinch to assemble with precooked bacon.
—Jane Nearing, Indianapolis, IN

PREP: 10 MIN. • **COOK:** 10 MIN./BATCH
MAKES: 8 SERVINGS

- **1 tube (8 oz.) refrigerated crescent rolls**
- **6 bacon strips, cooked and crumbled**
- **1 tsp. onion powder**

1. Preheat air fryer to 300°. Unroll crescent dough and separate into 8 triangles. Set aside 1 Tbsp. bacon. Sprinkle onion powder and remaining bacon over triangles. Roll up and sprinkle with remaining bacon, pressing lightly to adhere.
2. In batches, arrange the rolls, point side down, in a single layer on ungreased tray in air-fryer basket. Cook until golden brown, 8-10 minutes. Serve warm.

FREEZE OPTION: Freeze cooled rolls in freezer containers. To use, thaw at room temperature or, if desired, microwave each roll on high until heated through, 10-15 seconds.

1 ROLL: 133 cal., 7g fat (1g sat. fat), 6mg chol., 322mg sod., 12g carb. (3g sugars, 0 fiber), 4g pro.

CINNAMON ROLL CREAM CHEESE COFFEE CAKE

Cheesecake, coffee cake and cinnamon rolls all rolled into one!
—Deanna Smith, Meridian, ID

PREP: 35 MIN. • **BAKE:** 70 MIN. + COOLING
MAKES: 16 SERVINGS

- **½ cup butter, softened**
- **1 cup sugar**
- **1 large egg**
- **2 tsp. vanilla extract**
- **2¼ cups all-purpose flour**
- **2 tsp. baking powder**
- **1 tsp. ground cinnamon**
- **½ tsp. salt**
- **¾ cup 2% milk**

CHEESECAKE FILLING

- **2 pkg. (8 oz. each) cream cheese, softened**
- **½ cup sugar**
- **2 Tbsp. all-purpose flour**
- **3 tsp. vanilla extract**
- **2 large eggs, lightly beaten**

CINNAMON FILLING

- **1 cup packed brown sugar**
- **⅓ cup butter, melted**
- **2 Tbsp. ground cinnamon**

1. Preheat oven to 350°. Cream butter and sugar until light and fluffy. Beat in egg and vanilla. In another bowl, whisk flour, baking powder, cinnamon and salt; add to creamed mixture alternately with milk, beating well after each addition. Spread three-fourths of the batter into a greased 9-in. springform pan (batter will be thick). Set remaining batter aside.
2. In another bowl, beat cream cheese, sugar and flour until smooth. Beat in vanilla. Add eggs; beat on low speed just until combined. Pour over batter.
3. Mix cinnamon filling ingredients. Drop by tablespoonfuls over cream cheese mixture. Cut through cream cheese filling with a knife to swirl the cinnamon filling. Drop reserved batter by tablespoonfuls over filling. Place pan on a baking sheet.
4. Bake coffee cake until center is almost set, 70-80 minutes. Cover top loosely with foil during the last 30 minutes if needed to prevent overbrowning. Cool on a wire rack 10 minutes. Carefully run a knife around edge of pan to loosen. Cool for 1 hour; remove sides of pan. Serve warm. Refrigerate leftovers.

1 PIECE: 405 cal., 21g fat (12g sat. fat), 90mg chol., 322mg sod., 51g carb. (34g sugars, 2g fiber), 5g pro.

FOCACCIA BARESE

This focaccia has been in my mom's family for several generations. It is one of my most requested recipes whenever I am invited to a party—I am not allowed to attend unless I bring it!

—Dora Travaglio, Mount Prospect, IL

PREP: 30 MIN. + RISING • **BAKE:** 30 MIN.
MAKES: 8 SERVINGS

- **1⅛ tsp. active dry yeast**
- **¾ cup warm water (110° to 115°), divided**
- **½ tsp. sugar**
- **⅓ cup mashed potato flakes**
- **1½ tsp. plus 2 Tbsp. olive oil, divided**
- **¼ tsp. salt**
- **1¾ cups bread flour**

TOPPING

- **2 medium tomatoes, thinly sliced**
- **¼ cup pitted Greek olives, halved**
- **1½ tsp. minced fresh or dried oregano**
- **½ tsp. coarse salt**

1. In a large bowl, dissolve yeast in ½ cup warm water. Add sugar; let stand for 5 minutes. Add the potato flakes, 1½ tsp. oil, salt, 1 cup flour and remaining ¼ cup water. Beat until smooth. Stir in enough remaining flour to form a soft dough.
2. Turn onto a floured surface; knead until smooth and elastic, 6-8 minutes. Place in a greased bowl, turning once to grease the top. Cover and let rise in a warm place until doubled, about 1 hour. Punch dough down. Cover and let rest for 10 minutes.
3. Place 1 Tbsp. olive oil in a 10-in. cast-iron or other ovenproof skillet; tilt pan to evenly coat. Add dough; shape to fit pan. Cover and let rise until doubled, about 30 minutes.
4. With fingertips, make several dimples over top of dough. Brush with remaining 1 Tbsp. oil. Blot the tomato slices with paper towels. Arrange tomato slices and olives over dough; sprinkle with oregano and salt.
5. Bake at 375° for 30-35 minutes or until golden brown.

NOTE: Also known as kalamata olives, Greek olives are almond-shaped and range in size from ½ to 1 in. long. Dark eggplant in color, the kalamata olive is rich and fruity in flavor and can be found packed in either a vinegar brine or olive oil.

1 PIECE: 142 cal., 4g fat (1g sat. fat), 0 chol., 269mg sod., 24g carb. (1g sugars, 1g fiber), 4g pro.

ALMOND FLOUR BREAD

My almond flour bread recipe is keto-friendly. It's low in carbs with a fluffy, crumbly texture similar to a traditional loaf of bread.

—Caroline Baines, Spokane, WA

PREP: 10 MIN. • **BAKE:** 25 MIN.
MAKES: 10 SERVINGS

- **2 cups almond flour**
- **¼ cup chia seeds**
- **2 tsp. baking powder**
- **½ tsp. salt**
- **4 large eggs, room temperature**
- **¼ cup unsweetened almond milk or water**
- **¼ cup butter, melted or coconut oil, melted**

1. Preheat oven to 350°. In a large bowl, whisk almond flour, chia seeds, baking powder and salt. In another bowl, whisk eggs, almond milk and melted butter; stir into the dry ingredients just until moistened. Pour into a parchment-lined 8x4-in. loaf pan.
2. Bake until a toothpick inserted in center comes out clean and top is golden brown, 25-30 minutes. Cool in pan 10 minutes before removing to a wire rack to cool completely.

1 PIECE: 219 cal., 19g fat (4g sat. fat), 87mg chol., 292mg sod., 7g carb. (1g sugars, 4g fiber), 8g pro.

CONFETTI CORNBREAD

My grandmother Virginia always served Southwest cornbread. To honor her, I created a recipe that cuts down on the chopping but doesn't skimp on flavor.
—Angie Price, Bradford, TN

PREP: 20 MIN. • **BAKE:** 50 MIN.
MAKES: 12 SERVINGS

- **2 pkg. (8½ oz. each) cornbread/muffin mix**
- **¼ tsp. cayenne pepper**
- **2 large eggs, room temperature**
- **1 can (14¾ oz.) cream-style corn**
- **½ cup buttermilk**
- **¼ cup plus 1½ tsp. canola oil, divided**
- **1 cup shredded cheddar cheese**
- **1 small onion, chopped**
- **1 can (4 oz.) chopped green chiles**
- **1 jar (2 oz.) pimiento strips, drained**
- **1 jalapeno pepper, seeded and chopped**

1. Preheat oven to 350°. In a large bowl, combine muffin mixes and cayenne pepper. In another bowl, mix eggs, corn, buttermilk and ¼ cup oil until blended. Add to dry ingredients; stir just until moistened. Fold in cheese, onion, chiles, pimiento strips and jalapeno.
2. Brush remaining 1½ tsp. oil onto bottom of a 13x9-in. baking pan; place in oven until hot, 4-5 minutes. Pour batter into hot pan. Bake until edges are golden brown and a toothpick inserted in center comes out clean, 50-60 minutes. Cool in pan on a wire rack. Serve warm.

NOTE: Wear disposable gloves when cutting hot peppers; the oils can burn skin. Avoid touching your face.
1 PIECE: 299 cal., 14g fat (4g sat. fat), 42mg chol., 547mg sod., 36g carb. (10g sugars, 3g fiber), 7g pro.

CHIVE GARLIC BREAD

Start with a French bread loaf and dress it up with garlic and chives to make it irresistible. We like to serve this with lasagna or pasta, and we don't stop eating until the last crumbs have vanished from the bread platter.
—Kim Orr, West Grove, PA

TAKES: 20 MIN. • **MAKES:** 12 SERVINGS

- **¼ cup butter, softened**
- **¼ cup grated Parmesan cheese**
- **2 Tbsp. minced chives**
- **1 garlic clove, minced**
- **1 loaf (1 lb.) French bread, cut into 1-in. slices**

In a bowl, combine the butter, cheese, chives and garlic; spread on 1 side of each slice of bread. Wrap in a large piece of heavy-duty foil; seal tightly. Place on a baking sheet. Bake bread at 350° for 15-20 minutes or until heated through.
1 PIECE: 145 cal., 5g fat (3g sat. fat), 12mg chol., 300mg sod., 20g carb. (1g sugars, 1g fiber), 4g pro.

READER REVIEW

"Awesome recipe! It's utterly delicious and easy to make. So much more healthy than frozen garlic bread, too."

PINSTRIPES, TASTEOFHOME.COM

CRUMB-TOPPED PUMPKIN MUFFINS

These muffins just scream autumn to me. I love a rich, moist muffin that's topped with plenty of crumb topping. Honestly, the topping may be my favorite part!
—Andrea Potischman, Menlo Park, CA

PREP: 25 MIN. • **BAKE:** 25 MIN.
MAKES: 8 SERVINGS

- 1 cup all-purpose flour
- ¼ cup sugar
- ¼ cup packed brown sugar
- ½ tsp. baking soda
- ½ tsp. ground cinnamon
- ⅛ tsp. ground cloves
- Dash salt
- 1 large egg, room temperature
- ¾ cup canned pumpkin
- ½ cup coconut oil, melted
- ¼ cup sour cream

TOPPING
- ¼ cup all-purpose flour
- 2 Tbsp. sugar
- 1 Tbsp. brown sugar
- ⅛ tsp. ground cinnamon
- 4½ tsp. butter or coconut oil, metled

GLAZE
- ½ cup confectioners' sugar
- 1 Tbsp. 2% milk

1. Preheat oven to 350°. In a large bowl, whisk the first 7 ingredients. In another bowl, whisk egg, pumpkin, melted oil and sour cream until blended. Add to flour mixture; stir just until moistened. Fill 8 greased or paper-lined muffin cups.
2. For topping, in a small bowl, mix flour, sugars and cinnamon; stir in melted butter until crumbly. Sprinkle over batter; press lightly into the batter. Bake until a toothpick inserted in center comes out clean, 22-25 minutes. Cool 5 minutes before removing from pan to a wire rack.
3. Combine glaze ingredients; drizzle over muffins. Serve warm.

1 MUFFIN: 342 cal., 19g fat (15g sat. fat), 31mg chol., 131mg sod., 43g carb. (26g sugars, 1g fiber), 3g pro.

APPLE RAISIN QUICK BREAD

Cloves are a subtle but effective complement to the abundant apple pieces in this apple raisin quick bread.
—Gail Buss, New Bern, NC

PREP: 10 MIN. • **BAKE:** 1 HOUR + COOLING
MAKES: 2 LOAVES (16 PIECES EACH)

- **1¼ cups vegetable oil**
- **4 large eggs, room temperature**
- **4 tsp. vanilla extract**
- **3 cups all-purpose flour**
- **2½ cups sugar**
- **2 tsp. ground cinnamon**
- **1½ tsp. salt**
- **1½ tsp. baking soda**
- **1 tsp. ground cloves**
- **½ tsp. baking powder**
- **3 cups diced peeled tart apples**
- **⅔ cup raisins**
- **½ cup chopped nuts**

Preheat oven to 325°. In a bowl, beat oil, eggs and vanilla. Combine flour, sugar, cinnamon, salt, baking soda, cloves and baking powder; beat into the egg mixture. Stir in apples, raisins and nuts. Pour into 2 greased 9x5-in. loaf pans. Bake until a toothpick inserted in the center comes out clean, 60-70 minutes. Cool 10 minutes before removing from pans to wire racks.

1 PIECE: 217 cal., 10g fat (1g sat. fat), 23mg chol., 187mg sod., 29g carb. (19g sugars, 1g fiber), 3g pro.

HOLIDAY HERB-CHEESE ROLLS

These low-fat rolls are flavored with garlic, dill and cheese, and they're yummy even without butter! You can also fill them with your favorite savory sandwich filling to make tasty sliders.
—Nancy Boyd, Midlothian, VA

PREP: 45 MIN. + RISING • **BAKE:** 20 MIN.
MAKES: 2 DOZEN

- **4 to 4½ cups all-purpose flour**
- **¼ cup sugar**
- **2 Tbsp. mashed potato flakes**
- **1 pkg. (¼ oz.) active dry yeast**
- **2 tsp. salt**
- **½ tsp. dill weed**
- **¼ tsp. garlic powder**
- **2 cups water**
- **4½ tsp. butter**
- **1 cup old-fashioned oats**
- **1 large egg, room temperature**
- **¾ cup shredded part-skim mozzarella cheese**

TOPPING

- **2 Tbsp. fat-free milk**
- **4½ tsp. grated Parmesan cheese**
- **½ tsp. garlic powder**
- **½ tsp. dill weed**
- **½ tsp. dried basil**

1. In a large bowl, combine 1½ cups flour, sugar, potato flakes, yeast, salt, dill and garlic powder. In a small saucepan, bring water and butter just to a boil.
2. In a small bowl, pour boiling liquid over oats. Let stand until mixture cools to 120°-130°, stirring occasionally. Add to dry ingredients; beat just until moistened. Add egg; beat until smooth. Stir in enough remaining flour to form a firm dough (dough will be sticky).
3. Turn onto a floured surface; knead until smooth and elastic, 6-8 minutes. Knead in mozzarella cheese. Place in a large bowl coated with cooking spray, turning once to coat the top. Cover and let rise in a warm place until doubled, about 1¼ hours.
4. Punch dough down. Turn onto a lightly floured surface; divide into 24 pieces. Shape each into a ball. Place in a 13x9-in. baking pan coated with cooking spray; brush milk over rolls.
5. In a small bowl, combine the remaining ingredients; sprinkle over tops. Cover and let rise until nearly doubled, 45 minutes.
6. Preheat oven to 375°. Bake rolls for 20-25 minutes or until golden brown. Remove from pan to a wire rack. Refrigerate leftovers.

1 ROLL: 119 cal., 2g fat (1g sat. fat), 13mg chol., 228mg sod., 21g carb. (3g sugars, 1g fiber), 4g pro.

RHUBARB NUT MUFFINS

Muffins are my weakness. And when I make these to take to a gathering, I always come home with an empty plate.
—Mary Kay Morris, Cokato, MN

PREP: 15 MIN. • **BAKE:** 20 MIN. + COOLING
MAKES: ABOUT 10 MUFFINS

- 1½ cups all-purpose flour
- ¾ cup packed brown sugar
- ½ tsp. baking soda
- ½ tsp. salt
- 1 large egg, room temperature
- ⅓ cup canola oil
- ½ cup buttermilk
- 1 tsp. vanilla extract
- 1 cup diced fresh or frozen rhubarb
- ½ cup chopped walnuts

TOPPING

- ¼ cup packed brown sugar
- ½ cup chopped walnuts
- ½ tsp. ground cinnamon

1. In a large bowl, combine flour, brown sugar, baking soda and salt. In a small bowl, whisk the egg, oil, buttermilk and vanilla. Stir into the dry ingredients just until moistened. Fold in the rhubarb and walnuts.
2. Fill greased or paper-lined muffin cups about two-thirds full. Combine the topping ingredients; sprinkle over muffins. Bake at 375° for 20-25 minutes or until a toothpick inserted in the center of a muffin comes out clean. Cool the muffins for 5 minutes before removing from pan to a wire rack.

NOTE: If using frozen rhubarb, measure the rhubarb while still frozen, then let it thaw completely. Drain in a colander, but do not press liquid out.

1 MUFFIN: 307 cal., 15g fat (2g sat. fat), 22mg chol., 210mg sod., 39g carb. (23g sugars, 1g fiber), 6g pro.

CHEDDAR LOAVES

Swirls of cheddar cheese give these loaves a rich flavor. Try a slice or two for sandwiches, toasted for breakfast or served with a salad.
—Agnes Ward, Stratford, ON

PREP: 25 MIN. + RISING • **BAKE:** 35 MIN.
MAKES: 2 LOAVES (12 PIECES EACH)

- 1 Tbsp. active dry yeast
- ½ cup warm water (110° to 115°)
- 2 cups warm 2% milk (110° to 115°)
- 2 large eggs, room temperature
- 2 Tbsp. butter, softened
- 1 Tbsp. sugar
- 2 tsp. salt
- 7 to 7½ cups all-purpose flour
- 2 cups shredded sharp cheddar cheese

1. In a large bowl, dissolve yeast in warm water. Add milk, eggs, butter, sugar, salt and 3 cups flour; beat on medium speed 2 minutes. Stir in enough remaining flour to form a soft dough.
2. Turn dough onto a floured surface; knead until smooth and elastic, roughly 6-8 minutes. Place in a greased bowl, turning once to grease the top. Cover; let rise in a warm place until doubled, about 1 hour.
3. Punch dough down. Turn onto a lightly floured surface; knead in cheese. Divide dough in half; shape each portion into a 6-in. round loaf. Place on greased baking sheets. Cover with kitchen towels; let dough rise in a warm place until doubled, about 45 minutes. Preheat oven to 350°.
4. Bake until golden brown, roughly 35-40 minutes. Remove from pans to wire racks to cool.

1 PIECE: 199 cal., 5g fat (3g sat. fat), 29mg chol., 282mg sod., 30g carb. (2g sugars, 1g fiber), 7g pro.

DOUBLE-BERRY QUICK BREAD

Here's a quick bread that's healthy, fast and easy! This recipe is a favorite when prep time is tight and I have small amounts of different kinds of berries to use up.
—Jennifer Coduto, Kent, OH

PREP: 15 MIN. • **BAKE:** 50 MIN. + COOLING
MAKES: 1 LOAF (12 PIECES)

- **1½ cups all-purpose flour**
- **½ cup whole wheat flour**
- **½ cup sugar**
- **1½ tsp. baking powder**
- **½ tsp. salt**
- **¼ tsp. baking soda**
- **2 large egg whites**
- **1 large egg**
- **½ cup fat-free milk**
- **½ cup reduced-fat sour cream**
- **¼ cup unsweetened applesauce**
- **¼ cup canola oil**
- **2 tsp. vanilla extract**
- **1 cup fresh raspberries**
- **1 cup fresh blackberries**

1. Preheat oven to 375°. In a large bowl, whisk the first 6 ingredients. In another bowl, whisk egg whites, egg, milk, sour cream, applesauce, oil and vanilla until blended. Add to flour mixture; stir just until moistened. Gently fold in berries.
2. Transfer batter to a 9x5-in. loaf pan coated with cooking spray. Bake until a toothpick inserted in center comes out clean, 50-60 minutes. Cool in pan for 10 minutes before removing to a wire rack to cool.

1 PIECE: 188 cal., 6g fat (1g sat. fat), 19mg chol., 201mg sod., 28g carb. (11g sugars, 2g fiber), 5g pro. **DIABETIC EXCHANGES:** 2 starch, 1 fat.

CINNAMON ROLLS WITH COOKIE BUTTER FILLING

I created this recipe when I had a jar of cookie butter on hand and I was craving cinnamon rolls. Using frozen bread dough cuts down on time and effort, and the cookie butter makes a nice even filling with a touch of something special.
—Kallee Krong-McCreery, Escondido, CA

PREP: 20 MIN. + RISING • **BAKE:** 15 MIN.
MAKES: 1 DOZEN

- **½ cup Biscoff creamy cookie spread**
- **3 Tbsp. butter, softened**
- **½ tsp. vanilla extract**
- **⅓ cup sugar**
- **1 Tbsp. ground cinnamon**
- **1 loaf (1 lb.) frozen bread dough, thawed**

ICING

- **1⅓ cups confectioners' sugar**
- **1 to 2 Tbsp. 2% milk**
- **2 tsp. light corn syrup**
- **1 tsp. vanilla extract**

1. In a bowl, mix the first 5 ingredients. On a lightly floured surface, roll dough into a 12x7-in. rectangle. Spread butter mixture over dough to within ½ in. of edges. Roll up jelly-roll style, starting with a long side; pinch seam to seal. Cut into 12 slices. Arrange in a greased 13x9-in. baking pan, cut side down. Cover and let rise in a warm place until doubled, about 45 minutes.
2. Preheat oven to 350°. Bake until edges are lightly browned, 15-20 minutes. Place pan on a wire rack. Combine icing ingredients; drizzle over warm rolls. Let stand until set.

1 ROLL: 272 cal., 8g fat (3g sat. fat), 8mg chol., 236mg sod., 44g carb. (25g sugars, 2g fiber), 4g pro.

CONTEST-WINNING PUMPKIN COFFEE CAKE

It's tough to resist a second piece of this delightful treat with its comforting flavor. It's a breeze to throw together because it calls for pound cake mix and canned pumpkin.
—Sarah Steele, Moulton, AL

PREP: 15 MIN. • **BAKE:** 35 MIN. + COOLING
MAKES: 9 SERVINGS

- **1 pkg. (16 oz.) pound cake mix**
- **¾ cup canned pumpkin**
- **6 Tbsp. water**
- **2 large eggs, room temperature**
- **2 tsp. pumpkin pie spice**
- **1 tsp. baking soda**

TOPPING

- **½ cup chopped walnuts**
- **½ cup packed brown sugar**
- **¼ cup all-purpose flour**
- **3 tsp. butter, melted**

1. In a large bowl, combine the first 6 ingredients; beat on low speed for 30 seconds. Beat on medium speed for 2 minutes. Pour half the pumpkin mixture into a greased 9-in. square baking pan.
2. In a small bowl, combine the topping ingredients; sprinkle half over the batter. Carefully spread with remaining batter. Sprinkle with remaining topping (pan will be full).
3. Bake at 350° for 35-40 minutes or until a toothpick inserted in the center comes out clean. Cool on a wire rack.

1 PIECE: 385 cal., 18g fat (5g sat. fat), 79mg chol., 366mg sod., 51g carb. (35g sugars, 1g fiber), 7g pro.

BRAIDED ONION-POTATO LOAF

Mashed potato in a bread recipe? Absolutely! The potato's starch absorbs liquid during kneading, so the bread finishes with a crusty brown exterior and a flavorful, moist interior that helps the bread stay fresh longer.
—Joan Ranzini, Waynesboro, VA

PREP: 20 MIN. + RISING • **BAKE:** 25 MIN.
MAKES: 1 LOAF (16 PIECES)

- **1 large Yukon Gold potato, peeled and cubed**
- **1 small onion, chopped**
- **1 cup warm 2% milk (70° to 80°)**
- **1 large egg, room temperature**
- **2 Tbsp. butter**
- **1 Tbsp. honey**
- **¼ cup grated Parmesan cheese**
- **¼ cup chopped fresh parsley**
- **1½ tsp. salt**
- **¼ tsp. pepper**
- **4 cups bread flour**
- **1 pkg. (¼ oz.) active dry yeast**

TOPPING

- **1 large egg, lightly beaten**
- **Additional grated Parmesan cheese**

1. Place potato and onion in a small saucepan and cover with water. Bring to a boil. Reduce heat; cover and cook for 10-15 minutes or until vegetables are tender. Drain; mash until the potatoes are smooth (about ¾ cup).
2. In bread machine pan, place the milk, mashed potato, egg, butter, honey, cheese, parsley, salt, pepper, flour and yeast in order suggested by manufacturer. Select the dough setting (check dough after 5 minutes of mixing; add 1 to 2 Tbsp. water or flour if needed).
3. When cycle is completed, turn dough onto a lightly floured surface. Divide into thirds. Shape each into an 18-in. rope. Place ropes on a greased baking sheet and braid; pinch the ends to seal and tuck under.
4. Cover with a clean kitchen towel and let rise in a warm place until doubled, about 1 hour. Uncover; brush top with beaten egg. Sprinkle with additional cheese. Bake at 350° for 25-35 minutes or until golden brown. Remove from pan to a wire rack.

1 PIECE: 183 cal., 3g fat (2g sat. fat), 22mg chol., 271mg sod., 32g carb. (2g sugars, 1g fiber), 6g pro.

CONTEST-WINNING POTATO PAN ROLLS

Beautiful color and light-as-a-feather texture make these rolls our family's favorite for holiday meals. I won the reserve champion award at a 4-H yeast bread competition with this recipe.
—LeAnne Hofferichter-Tieken, Floresville, TX

PREP: 55 MIN. + RISING • **BAKE:** 20 MIN.
MAKES: 2½ DOZEN

- **2 medium potatoes, peeled and quartered**
- **1½ cups water**
- **2 pkg. (¼ oz. each) active dry yeast**
- **1 tsp. sugar**
- **½ cup butter, melted**
- **½ cup honey**
- **¼ cup canola oil**
- **2 large eggs, room temperature**
- **2 tsp. salt**
- **6 to 7 cups all-purpose flour**

1. In a large saucepan, bring potatoes and water to a boil. Reduce heat; cover and simmer for 15-20 minutes or until tender. Drain, reserving 1 cup cooking liquid; cool liquid to 110° to 115°. Mash potatoes; set aside 1 cup to cool to 110°-115° (save remaining potatoes for another use).
2. In a large bowl, dissolve yeast and sugar in reserved potato liquid; let stand for 5 minutes. Add the reserved mashed potatoes, butter, honey, oil, eggs, salt and 1½ cups flour; beat until smooth. Stir in enough of the remaining flour to form a soft dough.
3. Turn onto a floured surface; knead until smooth and elastic, 6-8 minutes. Place in a greased bowl, turning once to grease top. Cover and let rise in a warm place until doubled, about 1 hour.
4. Punch dough down and turn onto a floured surface; divide into 30 pieces. Shape each piece into a ball. Place 10 balls each in 3 greased 9-in. round baking pans. Cover and let rise until doubled, about 30 minutes.
5. Meanwhile, preheat oven to 400°. Bake until golden brown, 20-25 minutes. Remove from pans to wire racks to cool.

1 ROLL: 165 cal., 5g fat (2g sat. fat), 22mg chol., 193mg sod., 26g carb. (5g sugars, 1g fiber), 3g pro.

BLUEBERRY-ORANGE MUFFINS

This recipe was given to me years ago, and I've used it often since. In fact, it's so good that it won first prize at a county fair! Blueberries are plentiful in the Midwest, and this is a fragrant and fruity way to prepare them.
—Irene Parry, Kenosha, WI

TAKES: 30 MIN. • **MAKES:** 2 DOZEN

- **1 cup quick-cooking oats**
- **1 cup orange juice**
- **1 tsp. grated orange zest**
- **1 cup canola oil**
- **3 large eggs, room temperature, beaten**
- **3 cups all-purpose flour**
- **1 cup sugar**
- **4 tsp. baking powder**
- **1 tsp. salt**
- **½ tsp. baking soda**
- **3 to 4 cups fresh blueberries**

TOPPING

- **½ cup finely chopped nuts**
- **3 Tbsp. sugar**
- **½ tsp. ground cinnamon**

1. Mix oats, orange juice and zest. Blend in oil and eggs. Stir together flour, sugar, baking powder, salt and baking soda. Add oat mixture; mix lightly. Fold in the blueberries. Spoon the batter into 24 paper-lined muffin tins, filling two-thirds full. Combine topping ingredients; sprinkle over batter.
2. Bake at 400° for 15-18 minutes or until lightly browned.
3. Cool for 5 minutes before removing to a wire rack.

HEALTH TIP: To make these fruity muffins healthier, swap half of the all-purpose flour for whole wheat flour, and half of the oil for ½ cup unsweetened applesauce.

1 MUFFIN: 228 cal., 12g fat (2g sat. fat), 27mg chol., 200mg sod., 28g carb. (13g sugars, 1g fiber), 4g pro.

HONEY BEER BREAD

It's true—this yummy bread requires only four ingredients! Simply combine self-rising flour, sugar, honey and beer, pour the batter into the pan and bake.
—Cak Marshall, Salem, OR

PREP: 5 MIN. • **BAKE:** 45 MIN. + COOLING
MAKES: 1 LOAF (12 PIECES)

- **3 cups self-rising flour**
- **3 Tbsp. sugar**
- **⅓ cup honey**
- **1 bottle (12 oz.) beer**

1. Preheat oven to 350°. In a large bowl, whisk flour and sugar. Stir in honey and beer just until moistened.
2. Transfer to a greased 8x4-in. loaf pan. Bake 45-50 minutes or until a toothpick inserted in center comes out clean. Cool in pan 10 minutes before removing to a wire rack to cool.

1 PIECE: 163 cal., 0 fat (0 sat. fat), 0 chol., 374mg sod., 35g carb. (12g sugars, 1g fiber), 3g pro.

1) GLUTEN-FREE BANANA BREAD

Tired of gluten-free baked goods that are dry and crumbly? This banana bread tastes like the real thing and goes over well with everyone.
—Gladys Arnold, Pittsburgh, PA

PREP: 20 MIN. • **BAKE:** 45 MIN. + COOLING
MAKES: 2 LOAVES (12 PIECES EACH)

- **2 cups gluten-free all-purpose baking flour**
- **1 tsp. baking soda**
- **¼ tsp. salt**
- **4 large eggs, room temperature**
- **2 cups mashed ripe bananas (4-5 medium)**
- **1 cup sugar**
- **½ cup unsweetened applesauce**
- **⅓ cup canola oil**
- **1 tsp. vanilla extract**
- **½ cup chopped walnuts**

1. Preheat oven to 350°. In a large bowl, combine flour, baking soda and salt. In a small bowl, whisk eggs, bananas, sugar, applesauce, oil and vanilla. Stir into dry ingredients just until moistened.
2. Transfer to 2 greased 8x4-in. loaf pans. Sprinkle with the walnuts. Bake until a toothpick inserted in the center comes out clean, 45-55 minutes. Cool for 10 minutes before removing from pans to wire racks.

NOTE: Read all ingredient labels for possible gluten content prior to use. Ingredient formulas can change, and production facilities vary among brands. If you're concerned that your brand may contain gluten, contact the company.
1 PIECE: 140 cal., 6g fat (1g sat. fat), 35mg chol., 89mg sod., 21g carb. (11g sugars, 2g fiber), 3g pro.

2) MAKEOVER BANANA NUT BREAD

This slimmed-down banana bread is one of our favorite ways to enjoy the classic treat. In addition to swapping out the majority of the butter for applesauce, the amount of sugar is decreased, too, by adding a little honey and using more banana. No one will ever guess this bread is low in fat!
—*Taste of Home* Test Kitchen

PREP: 15 MIN. • **BAKE:** 1 HOUR
MAKES: 1 LOAF (16 PIECES)

- **2 Tbsp. butter, softened**
- **¾ cup sugar**
- **1 large egg, room temperature**
- **1 large egg white**
- **2 cups mashed ripe bananas (about 4 medium)**
- **¼ cup unsweetened applesauce**
- **¼ cup honey**
- **1 tsp. vanilla or rum extract**
- **1⅓ cups all-purpose flour**
- **⅔ cup whole wheat flour**
- **1 tsp. baking soda**
- **½ tsp. salt**
- **¼ cup chopped pecans**

1. In a large bowl, beat butter and sugar for 2 minutes or until crumbly. Beat in egg, then egg white, beating well after each addition. Beat on high speed until light and fluffy. Stir in the bananas, applesauce, honey and extract. Combine the flours, baking soda and salt; gradually add to banana mixture just until moistened.
2. Pour into a 9x5-in. loaf pan coated with cooking spray. Sprinkle with nuts. Bake at 325° for 60-65 minutes or until a toothpick inserted in the center comes out clean. Cool for 10 minutes before removing from pan to a wire rack to cool.

1 PIECE: 165 cal., 3g fat (1g sat. fat), 15mg chol., 173mg sod., 32g carb. (18g sugars, 2g fiber), 3g pro.

3) VEGAN BANANA NUT BREAD

I created this recipe when I was vegetarian and didn't eat eggs. It's packed with fiber, omega-3s and soy protein, but tastes delicious! Silken tofu makes a wonderful egg substitute.
—Brittany Carrington, Tehachapi, CA

PREP: 20 MIN. • **BAKE:** 50 MIN. + COOLING
MAKES: 1 LOAF (12 PIECES)

- **1 cup all-purpose flour**
- **1 cup whole wheat flour**
- **1 tsp. baking powder**
- **½ tsp. baking soda**
- **¼ tsp. salt**
- **1 cup sugar**
- **1 cup mashed ripe bananas (2 medium)**
- **¾ cup silken soft tofu**
- **¼ cup canola oil**
- **1 tsp. vanilla extract**
- **½ cup chopped walnuts**

1. In a large bowl, combine the first 5 ingredients. In a small bowl, beat the sugar, bananas, tofu, oil and and vanilla. Beat into dry ingredients just until moistened. Fold in walnuts.

2. Transfer to an 8x4-in. loaf pan coated with cooking spray. Bake at 350° for 50-55 minutes or until a toothpick inserted in the center of bread comes out clean. Cool for 10 minutes before removing from pan to a wire rack.

NOTE: Tofu is made from soybeans and does not contain animal products, yet it is high in protein. This makes it popular in vegetarian recipes, but it's nutritious and tasty in conventional recipes, too.

1 PIECE: 234 cal., 9g fat (1g sat. fat), 0 chol., 140mg sod., 37g carb. (19g sugars, 2g fiber), 4g pro.

DID YOU KNOW?

There are two types of tofu—fresh and silken. Fresh is packed in water and is located in the produce or dairy section in grocery stores. It is ideal for slicing and adding to stir-fries and soups. Silken soft tofu, named for its silky-smooth texture, is ideal for smoothies, sauces, dips and other dishes where a creamy consistency is desired. Silken tofu, which does not have to be refrigerated, is located in the Asian or health foods section.

4) CLASSIC BANANA BREAD

Whenever I pass a display of bananas in the grocery store, I can almost smell the amazing aroma of this bread baking in my oven!
—Gert Kaiser, Kenosha, WI

PREP: 15 MIN. • **BAKE:** 1¼ HOURS + COOLING
MAKES: 1 LOAF (16 PIECES)

- **1¾ cups all-purpose flour**
- **1½ cups sugar**
- **1 tsp. baking soda**
- **½ tsp. salt**
- **2 large eggs, room temperature**
- **2 medium ripe bananas, mashed (1 cup)**
- **½ cup canola oil**
- **¼ cup plus 1 Tbsp. buttermilk**
- **1 tsp. vanilla extract**
- **1 cup chopped walnuts**

1. Preheat oven to 350°. In a large bowl, stir together flour, sugar, baking soda and salt. In another bowl, combine the eggs, bananas, oil, buttermilk and vanilla; add to flour mixture, stirring just until combined. Fold in nuts.

2. Pour into a greased or parchment-lined 9x5-in. loaf pan. If desired, sprinkle with additional walnuts. Bake until a toothpick comes out clean, 1¼ to 1½ hours. Cool in pan for 15 minutes before removing to a wire rack.

1 PIECE: 255 cal., 12g fat (1g sat. fat), 27mg chol., 166mg sod., 34g carb. (21g sugars, 1g fiber), 4g pro.

Cakes, Pies & Desserts

Indulge your craving for something sweet with this collection of exquisite cakes, pies, tarts, cheesecakes and other luscious desserts.

AIR-FRYER CARROT COFFEE CAKE

One of the greatest things about the air fryer is it's conducive to making small, quick desserts like this carrot cake.
—Leigh Rys, Herndon, VA

PREP: 15 MIN. • **BAKE:** 35 MIN.
MAKES: 6 SERVINGS

- **1 large egg, lightly beaten, room temperature**
- **½ cup buttermilk**
- **⅓ cup sugar plus 2 Tbsp. sugar, divided**
- **3 Tbsp. canola oil**
- **2 Tbsp. dark brown sugar**
- **1 tsp. grated orange zest**
- **1 tsp. vanilla extract**
- **⅔ cup all-purpose flour**
- **⅓ cup white whole wheat flour**
- **1 tsp. baking powder**
- **2 tsp. pumpkin pie spice, divided**
- **¼ tsp. baking soda**
- **¼ tsp. salt**
- **1 cup shredded carrots**
- **¼ cup dried cranberries**
- **⅓ cup chopped walnuts, toasted**

1. Preheat air fryer to 350°. Grease and flour a 6-in. round baking pan. In a large bowl, whisk egg, buttermilk, ⅓ cup sugar, oil, brown sugar, orange zest and vanilla. In another bowl, whisk flours, baking powder, 1 tsp. pumpkin pie spice, baking soda and salt. Gradually beat into the egg mixture. Fold in carrots and dried cranberries. Pour into prepared pan.
2. In a small bowl, combine the walnuts, remaining 2 Tbsp. sugar and remaining 1 tsp. pumpkin spice. Sprinkle evenly over batter. Gently place pan in the basket of a large air fryer.
3. Cook until a toothpick inserted in center comes out clean, 35-40 minutes. Cover tightly with foil if top gets too dark. Cool in pan on a wire rack for 10 minutes before removing from pan. Serve warm.
1 PIECE: 316 cal., 13g fat (1g sat. fat), 32mg chol., 297mg sod., 46g carb. (27g sugars, 3g fiber), 6g pro.

TEST KITCHEN TIP
Using a room temperature egg helps the cake ingredients mix more evenly and achieve a higher volume.

COWABUNGA ROOT BEER CUPCAKES

I developed these cupcakes for my daughter's first birthday. The root beer flavor adds a nostalgic touch.
—Mindy Carswell, Walker, MI

PREP: 10 MIN. • **BAKE:** 15 MIN. + COOLING
MAKES: 24 SERVINGS

- **1 pkg. butter recipe golden cake mix (regular size)**
- **4 tsp. root beer concentrate, divided**
- **1 carton (12 oz.) frozen whipped topping, thawed**
- **Vanilla ice cream**

1. Prepare and bake cupcakes according to package directions, adding 2 tsp. root beer concentrate when mixing batter. Remove to wire racks to cool completely.
2. In a small bowl, mix whipped topping and the remaining 2 tsp. root beer concentrate until blended; spread over cupcakes. Serve with ice cream.
NOTE: This recipe was tested with McCormick root beer concentrate.
1 CUPCAKE: 163 cal., 7g fat (5g sat. fat), 30mg chol., 176mg sod., 21g carb. (13g sugars, 0 fiber), 2g pro.

TEST KITCHEN TIP

Everyone loves a good old-fashioned root beer float. Make these cupcakes even more reminiscent of the classic treat by garnishing each one with cut straws and a stemmed maraschino cherry. And don't forget a scoop of vanilla ice cream!

CHEESECAKE ROLLS

For an easy treat, fill flaky canned biscuits with cream cheese, fruit and honey. Any frozen berry can be used for the filling.
—Jennifer Stalcup, Vancouver, WA

PREP: 20 MIN. • **BAKE:** 20 MIN. + COOLING
MAKES: 8 SERVINGS

- **1 tube (16.3 oz.) large refrigerated flaky biscuits, such as Pillsbury Grands!**
- **1 cup whipped cream cheese**
- **2 Tbsp. honey**
- **¾ cup frozen wild unsweetened blueberries**
- **1 Tbsp. butter, melted**
- **1 tsp. sugar**
- **⅓ cup confectioners' sugar**
- **2 Tbsp. 2% milk**
- **½ tsp. lemon juice**

1. Preheat oven to 350°. On a lightly floured surface, separate biscuits and flatten each to a 5-in. circle. In a small bowl, combine cream cheese and honey; gently fold in blueberries. Place 2 Tbsp. mixture in center of each circle. Bring edges of dough together above filling; twist and pinch to seal.
2. Place on parchment-lined baking sheets, seam side down. Brush with butter; sprinkle with granulated sugar.
3. Bake until golden brown, 18-21 minutes. Remove from pans to wire racks to cool for 10 minutes. Meanwhile, whisk together confectioners' sugar, milk and lemon juice; brush over rolls. Cool completely. Refrigerate until chilled if desired. Sprinkle with additional confectioners' sugar. Refrigerate leftovers.
NOTE: Use frozen blueberries without thawing to avoid discoloring the batter.
1 ROLL: 299 cal., 14g fat (8g sat. fat), 24mg chol., 535mg sod., 38g carb. (16g sugars, 1g fiber), 4g pro.

APPLE PIE

I remember coming home sullen one day because we'd lost a softball game. Grandma, in her wisdom, suggested that a slice of hot apple pie would make me feel better. She was right!
—Maggie Greene, Granite Falls, WA

PREP: 20 MIN. • **BAKE:** 45 MIN.
MAKES: 8 SERVINGS

- **½ cup sugar**
- **½ cup packed brown sugar**
- **3 Tbsp. all-purpose flour**
- **1 tsp. ground cinnamon**
- **¼ tsp. ground ginger**
- **¼ tsp. ground nutmeg**
- **6 to 7 cups thinly sliced peeled tart apples**
- **1 Tbsp. lemon juice**
- **Dough for double-crust pie**
- **1 Tbsp. butter**
- **1 large egg white**
- **Optional: Turbinado or coarse sugar, ground cinnamon, vanilla bean ice cream and caramel sauce**

1. Preheat oven to 375°. In a small bowl, combine sugars, flour and spices. In a large bowl, toss apples with lemon juice. Add the sugar mixture; toss to coat.
2. On a lightly floured surface, roll half of the dough to a ⅛-in.-thick circle; transfer to a 9-in. pie plate. Trim even with rim. Add the filling; dot with butter. Roll the remaining dough to a ⅛-in.-thick circle. Place over filling. Trim, seal and flute edge. Cut slits in top. Beat the egg white until foamy; brush over crust. If desired, sprinkle with turbinado sugar and ground cinnamon. Cover edge loosely with foil.
3. Bake 25 minutes. Remove foil; bake until crust is golden brown and filling is bubbly, 20-25 minutes longer. Cool on a wire rack. If desired, serve with ice cream and caramel sauce.
NOTE: To make pie pastry, combine 2½ cups all-purpose flour and ½ tsp. salt; cut in 1 cup cold butter until crumbly. Gradually add ⅓ to ⅔ cup ice water, tossing with fork until dough holds together when pressed. Divide dough in half. Shape each into a disk; wrap and refrigerate 1 hour.
1 PIECE: 414 cal., 16g fat (7g sat. fat), 14mg chol., 227mg sod., 67g carb. (38g sugars, 2g fiber), 3g pro.

FRUIT JUICE POPS

I've relied on this recipe for years when my kids craved a refreshing treat. They enjoyed these pops more than store-bought ones. The pops taste great with either pineapple or orange juice. Try freezing and serving in cups made from hollowed-out oranges.
—Barbara Stewart, Garland, TX

PREP: 25 MIN. + FREEZING
MAKES: ABOUT 2½ DOZEN

- **2 cups water**
- **1½ cups sugar**
- **4 cups unsweetened apple juice**
- **1 cup unsweetened pineapple or orange juice**
- **½ cup lemon juice**
- **30 freezer pop molds or 20 paper cups (3 oz. each) and wooden pop sticks**

1. In a large saucepan, combine water and sugar; bring to a boil. Reduce heat; simmer, uncovered, 3-4 minutes or until sugar is dissolved, stirring occasionally. Remove from heat; stir in juices.
2. Fill molds with ¼ cup juice mixture or cups with ⅓ cup juice mixture. Top molds with holders. If using cups, top with foil and insert sticks through foil. Freeze until firm.
1 POP: 60 cal., 0 fat (0 sat. fat), 0 chol., 2mg sod., 15g carb. (14g sugars, 0 fiber), 0 pro.

PEANUT BUTTER ROCKY ROAD CHEESECAKE

My classic chocolate and peanut butter pairing upgrades a traditional cheesecake filling to pure creamy, crunchy bliss.
—Jacyn Siebert, San Francisco, CA

PREP: 30 MIN. • **BAKE:** 55 MIN. + CHILLING
MAKES: 16 SERVINGS

- **2 cups graham cracker crumbs**
- **½ cup butter, melted**
- **¼ cup sugar**

FILLING

- **4 pkg. (8 oz. each) cream cheese, softened**
- **1½ cups sugar**
- **3 Tbsp. vanilla extract**
- **⅛ tsp. salt**
- **4 large eggs, room temperature, lightly beaten**

TOPPING

- **2 Tbsp. creamy peanut butter**
- **2 Tbsp. honey**
- **1 jar (7 oz.) marshmallow creme**
- **½ cup hot fudge ice cream topping, warmed slightly**
- **½ cup chopped salted peanuts**

1. Preheat oven to 325°. Mix cracker crumbs, butter and sugar; press onto bottom and 1 in. up side of a greased 9-in. springform pan.

2. In a large bowl, beat cream cheese and sugar until smooth. Beat in the vanilla and salt. Add eggs; beat on low speed just until blended. Pour into the crust. Place on a baking sheet.

3. Bake until the center is almost set, 55-60 minutes. Cool on a wire rack 10 minutes. Loosen side from pan with a knife. Cool 1 hour longer. Refrigerate overnight, covering when completely cooled.

4. Remove rim from pan. In a microwave, warm peanut butter and honey; mix until smooth. Drop spoonfuls of marshmallow creme, fudge topping and peanut butter mixture alternately over the top of the cheesecake. Swirl together using a toothpick or skewer. Sprinkle top with chopped peanuts.

1 PIECE: 533 cal., 32g fat (17g sat. fat), 119mg chol., 363mg sod., 52g carb. (42g sugars, 1g fiber), 8g pro.

CARROT FRUITCAKE

Even those who don't care for fruitcake love this special holiday dessert. It's a fun way to dress up traditional carrot cake. Try it—your friends and family will agree.
—Ann Parden, Chunchula, AL

PREP: 20 MIN.
BAKE: 1 HOUR 15 MIN. + COOLING
MAKES: 16 SERVINGS

- **1½ cups chopped nuts**
- **1 cup chopped mixed candied fruit**
- **1 cup chopped dates**
- **1 cup raisins**
- **3 cups all-purpose flour, divided**
- **2 cups sugar**
- **1½ cups canola oil**
- **4 large eggs**
- **2 tsp. baking powder**
- **2 tsp. baking soda**
- **2 tsp. ground cinnamon**
- **1 tsp. salt**
- **3 cups finely shredded carrots**

ICING

- **1 cup confectioners' sugar**
- **1 to 2 Tbsp. 2% milk**

1. In a small bowl, combine the nuts, candied fruit, dates and raisins. Add ½ cup flour; toss to coat.
2. In a large bowl, combine sugar and oil. Add eggs, 1 at a time, beating well after each addition. In another bowl, mix the remaining 2 ½ cups flour, baking powder, baking soda, cinnamon and salt. Gradually add to sugar mixture, beating until smooth. (Batter will be stiff.) Fold in carrots and nut mixture. Transfer to a greased and floured 10-in. tube pan.
3. Bake at 350° for 75-80 minutes or until a toothpick inserted in center comes out clean. Cool in the pan for 15 minutes before removing to a wire rack to cool completely.
4. In a small bowl, mix confectioners' sugar and enough milk to reach desired consistency; drizzle over cake.
1 PIECE: 565 cal., 29g fat (3g sat. fat), 53mg chol., 395mg sod., 75g carb. (49g sugars, 4g fiber), 8g pro.

CHOCOLATE LOVER'S CREAM PIE

This simple cream pie uses Nutella, a sweet hazelnut-cocoa spread. Finding true love in a dessert has never been easier.
—Jenn Stewart, Lavergne, TN

PREP: 20 MIN. + CHILLING
MAKES: 8 SERVINGS

- **2 cups heavy whipping cream**
- **3 Tbsp. sugar**
- **½ tsp. vanilla extract**
- **1 pkg. (8 oz.) cream cheese, softened**
- **¾ cup confectioners' sugar**
- **⅔ cup Nutella**
- **1 chocolate crumb crust (9 in.)**
- **Grated chocolate**

1. In a large bowl, beat the cream until it begins to thicken. Add sugar and vanilla; beat until stiff peaks form.
2. In another bowl, beat the cream cheese, confectioners' sugar and Nutella until smooth. Fold in half of the whipped cream. Spoon into crust. Spread remaining whipped cream over the top. Garnish with chocolate. Refrigerate for at least 1 hour. Store leftovers in the refrigerator.
1 PIECE: 601 cal., 44g fat (22g sat. fat), 113mg chol., 218mg sod., 49g carb. (37g sugars, 2g fiber), 6g pro.

FROSTED CHOCOLATE CAKE

Here's my mother's oldest and most popular chocolate cake recipe. I always thought it deserved a fancier name, but Mom said a flashy name wouldn't make it taste better. No matter what you choose to call it, you'll agree it's simply the best!
—Beth Bristow, West Plains, MO

PREP: 40 MIN. • **BAKE:** 25 MIN. + COOLING
MAKES: 16 SERVINGS

- **4 large eggs, separated**
- **½ cup baking cocoa**
- **½ cup boiling water**
- **½ cup butter, softened**
- **1 cup packed brown sugar**
- **1 cup sugar, divided**
- **1 tsp. vanilla extract**
- **2½ cups all-purpose flour**
- **1 tsp. baking soda**
- **1 tsp. cream of tartar**
- **¼ tsp. salt**
- **1 cup buttermilk**

FROSTING

- **¾ cup butter, melted**
- **¾ tsp. vanilla extract**
- **6 cups confectioners' sugar**
- **3 Tbsp. whole milk**
- **Dark or additional regular baking cocoa, optional**

1. Place egg whites in a large bowl; let stand at room temperature 30 minutes. In a small bowl, mix cocoa and boiling water until smooth; cool slightly. Line bottoms of 2 greased 9-in. round baking pans with parchment; grease parchment.
2. Preheat oven to 375°. Cream butter, brown sugar and ¾ cup sugar until light and fluffy. Beat in vanilla and 1 egg yolk at a time. In another bowl, whisk together flour, baking soda, cream of tartar and salt. Add to creamed mixture alternately with buttermilk, beating after each addition. Stir in cocoa mixture.
3. With clean beaters, beat egg whites on medium speed until soft peaks form. Gradually add remaining ¼ cup sugar, 1 Tbsp. at a time, beating on high after each addition until sugar is dissolved. Continue beating until stiff peaks form. Fold into batter. Transfer to prepared pans. Bake until a toothpick inserted in center comes out clean, 23-28 minutes.
4. Cool cake layers in pans 10 minutes before removing to wire racks; remove parchment. Cool completely.
5. Beat together the first 4 frosting ingredients. Spread between layers and over top and sides of cake. If desired, dust top lightly with cocoa.
1 PIECE: 510 cal., 16g fat (10g sat. fat), 86mg chol., 283mg sod., 89g carb. (71g sugars, 1g fiber), 5g pro.

LEMON PUDDING CAKE

My husband, Lloyd, loves this cake because it tastes like lemon meringue pie. The cake is no-fuss and makes just enough for two..
—Dawn Fagerstrom, Warren, MN

PREP: 15 MIN. • **BAKE:** 40 MIN.
MAKES: 2 SERVINGS

- **1 large egg, separated, room temperature**
- **½ cup sugar**
- **⅓ cup whole milk**
- **2 Tbsp. all-purpose flour**
- **2 Tbsp. lemon juice**
- **1 tsp. grated lemon zest**
- **⅛ tsp. salt**
- **Optional: Confectioners' sugar, lemon slices and whipped cream**

1. Preheat oven to 325°. In a bowl, beat egg yolk. Add sugar, milk, flour, lemon juice, zest and salt; beat until smooth. Beat egg white until stiff peaks form; gently fold into lemon mixture. Pour into 2 ungreased 6-oz. custard cups (cups will be very full).
2. Place the cups in an 8-in. square baking pan. Pour boiling water into pan to a depth of 1 in. Bake until a knife inserted in the center comes out clean and top is golden, 40-45 minutes. If desired, top with confectioners' sugar, lemon slices and whipped cream.
1 CAKE: 288 cal., 4g fat (2g sat. fat), 112mg chol., 200mg sod., 60g carb. (51g sugars, 0 fiber), 5g pro.

BERRY RHUBARB FOOL

A fool is a British dessert that's usually made with custard. I modified it to create a quicker version. My kids love it because it doesn't taste like rhubarb—so I guess it's well named!
—Cheryl Miller, Fort Collins, CO

PREP: 30 MIN. + CHILLING
MAKES: 6 SERVINGS

- **3 cups sliced fresh or frozen rhubarb (1-in. pieces)**
- **⅓ cup sugar**
- **¼ cup orange juice**
- **Dash salt**
- **1 cup heavy whipping cream**
- **2 cups fresh strawberries, halved**

1. In a large saucepan, combine rhubarb, sugar, orange juice and salt. Bring to a boil. Reduce heat; simmer, covered, for 6-8 minutes or until rhubarb is tender. Cool slightly.
2. Process rhubarb mixture in a blender until smooth. Transfer mixture to a bowl; refrigerate, covered, until cold.
3. Just before serving, in a small bowl, whip cream until soft peaks form. In parfait glasses, alternately layer whipped cream, berries and rhubarb mixture.
1 CUP: 212 cal., 15g fat (9g sat. fat), 54mg chol., 42mg sod., 19g carb. (17g sugars, 2g fiber), 2g pro.

THOMAS FAGLON
Somerset, NJ

CHOCOLATE ESPRESSO-NUT TORTE

I love chocolate and nuts, and they come together deliciously in this torte. Serve it with sweetened whipped cream or your favorite ice cream.
—Thomas Faglon, Somerset, NJ

PREP: 40 MIN. • **BAKE:** 35 MIN. + CHILLING
MAKES: 14 SERVINGS

- **5 large eggs, separated**
- **1 tsp. baking cocoa**
- **1 cup hazelnuts, toasted and skins removed**
- **3 Tbsp. dark brown sugar**
- **½ cup butter, softened**
- **⅔ cup sugar**
- **6 oz. bittersweet chocolate, melted and cooled**
- **1 tsp. instant espresso powder**
- **1 tsp. almond extract**
- **¼ tsp. salt**

GANACHE

- **6 oz. bittersweet chocolate, chopped**
- **½ cup heavy whipping cream**
- **½ cup finely chopped almonds, toasted**

1. Place egg whites in a bowl; let stand at room temperature for 30 minutes. Line the bottom of a greased 9-in springform pan with waxed paper; grease the paper and dust with cocoa.
2. Place hazelnuts and brown sugar in a food processor; cover and process until ground. In a second large bowl, cream butter and sugar until light and fluffy, 5-7 minutes. Add egg yolks, 1 at a time, beating well after each addition. Beat in the melted chocolate, espresso powder, extract and salt. Gradually add the hazelnut mixture.
3. In the first large bowl, using clean beaters, beat the egg whites until stiff peaks form. Fold into batter. Spread into the prepared pan. Place the pan on a baking sheet.
4. Bake at 375° for 35-40 minutes or until a toothpick inserted in the center comes out with a few moist crumbs. Cool on a wire rack to room temperature. Remove side of pan and invert onto a serving plate.
5. To make ganache, place chocolate in a small bowl. In a small saucepan, bring cream just to a boil. Pour over chocolate; whisk until smooth. Cool, stirring occasionally, to room temperature or until ganache reaches a spreading consistency, about 30 minutes.
6. Spread ganache over top and side of cake; press almonds onto sides. Cover and refrigerate for 30 minutes or until set.
1 PIECE: 387 cal., 32g fat (13g sat. fat), 104mg chol., 118mg sod., 28g carb. (22g sugars, 4g fiber), 7g pro.

SOUR CREAM-LEMON PIE

I first tasted this pie at a restaurant. I found a similar recipe and now it's my hubby's favorite.
—Martha Sorensen, Fallon, NV

PREP: 25 MIN. + CHILLING
COOK: 10 MIN. + COOLING
MAKES: 8 SERVINGS

- **Dough for single-crust pie**
- **1 cup sugar**
- **3 Tbsp. plus 1½ tsp. cornstarch**
- **1 cup whole milk**
- **½ cup lemon juice**
- **3 large egg yolks, lightly beaten**
- **¼ cup butter, cubed**
- **1 Tbsp. grated lemon zest**
- **1 cup sour cream**
- **1 cup heavy whipping cream, whipped**

1. On a lightly floured surface, roll dough to a ⅛-in.-thick circle; transfer to a 9-in. pie plate. Trim to ½ in. beyond rim of plate; flute edge. Refrigerate 30 minutes. Preheat oven to 425°.
2. Line crust with a double thickness of foil. Fill with pie weights, dried beans or uncooked rice. Bake on a lower oven rack until edge of crust is golden brown, 20-25 minutes. Remove foil and weights; bake until bottom is golden brown, 3-6 minutes longer. Cool on a wire rack.
3. In a large heavy saucepan, mix sugar and cornstarch. Whisk in milk and lemon juice until smooth. Cook and stir over medium-high heat until thickened and bubbly. Reduce heat to low; cook and stir 2 minutes longer. Remove from heat.
4. In a small bowl, whisk a small amount of hot mixture into egg yolks; return all to the pan, whisking constantly. Bring to a gentle boil; cook and stir for 2 minutes. Remove from the heat. Stir in butter and lemon zest. Cool without stirring.
5. Stir in sour cream. Add filling to crust. Top with whipped cream. Store pie in the refrigerator.
NOTE: To make pie pastry, combine 1¼ cups all-purpose flour and ¼ tsp. salt; cut in ½ cup cold butter until crumbly. Gradually add 3-5 Tbsp. ice water, tossing with a fork until the dough holds together when pressed. Shape into a disk; wrap and refrigerate 1 hour.
1 PIECE: 437 cal., 26g fat (15g sat. fat), 145mg chol., 197mg sod., 46g carb. (29g sugars, 0 fiber), 4g pro.

CHOCOLATE CHIP CHEESE BALL

Your guests are in for a sweet surprise when they try this unique cheese ball that tastes just like cookie dough! Rolled in chopped pecans, the chip-studded spread is wonderful on regular or chocolate-flavored graham crackers. I especially like it because it can be assembled in a wink.
—Kelly Glascock, Syracuse, MO

PREP: 15 MIN. + CHILLING
MAKES: 16 SERVINGS

- **1 pkg. (8 oz.) cream cheese, softened**
- **½ cup butter, softened**
- **¼ tsp. vanilla extract**
- **¾ cup confectioners' sugar**
- **2 Tbsp. brown sugar**
- **¾ cup miniature semisweet chocolate chips**
- **¾ cup finely chopped pecans**
- **Graham crackers**

1. Beat the cream cheese, butter and vanilla until smooth; beat in the sugars just until blended. Stir in the chocolate chips. Refrigerate, covered, until firm enough to shape, about 2 hours.
2. Shape mixture into a ball. Wrap and refrigerate at least 1 hour.
3. To serve, roll cheese ball in pecans. Serve with graham crackers.
HEALTH TIP: This indulgent spread can be made with reduced-fat cream cheese, but it will be too soft to shape into a ball. Instead, serve in it a shallow dish and sprinkle with the chips and pecans. It's still completely delicious, but with fewer calories and less fat.
2 TBSP.: 203 cal., 17g fat (8g sat. fat), 30mg chol., 92mg sod., 14g carb. (12g sugars, 1g fiber), 2g pro.

LEMON RICOTTA CAKE

This recipe is a family gem that was passed down from my grandmother and mother. Garnished with shaved lemon peel, this moist four-layer cake is the perfect dessert when you want to impress.

—Nanette Slaughter, Sammamish, WA

PREP: 1 HOUR + CHILLING
BAKE: 30 MIN. + COOLING
MAKES: 16 SERVINGS

- **3 large eggs, room temperature**
- **2 large egg yolks, room temperature**
- **⅔ cup sugar**
- **⅓ cup lemon juice**
- **⅓ cup butter, cubed**

CAKE BATTER

- **1 cup butter, softened**
- **2 cups sugar**
- **3 large eggs, room temperature**
- **1 cup ricotta cheese**
- **1 cup buttermilk**
- **1 Tbsp. grated lemon zest**
- **1½ tsp. vanilla extract**
- **1 tsp. lemon juice**
- **3 cups all-purpose flour**
- **½ tsp. baking powder**
- **½ tsp. baking soda**
- **½ tsp. salt**

SUGARED LEMON ZEST

- **6 medium lemons**
- **¼ cup sugar**

FROSTING

- **⅔ cup butter, softened**
- **5½ cups confectioners' sugar**
- **⅓ cup 2% milk**
- **1½ tsp. grated lemon zest**
- **1½ tsp. vanilla extract**
- **⅛ tsp. salt**
- **Colored sugar, optional**

1. For the lemon curd, in a small bowl, combine eggs and egg yolks. In a heavy saucepan, cook and stir the sugar, lemon juice and butter over medium heat until smooth. Stir a small amount of hot mixture into eggs; return all to the pan, stirring constantly. Bring to a gentle boil; cook and stir until thickened, about 2 minutes. Cool slightly. Cover and chill until it's thickened, about 1½ hours or overnight.

2. Preheat oven to 350°. In a large bowl, cream butter and sugar until light and fluffy, 5-7 minutes. Add eggs, 1 at a time, beating well after each addition. Combine the ricotta cheese, buttermilk, lemon zest, vanilla and lemon juice. Combine the flour, baking powder, baking soda and salt; add to the creamed mixture alternately with the buttermilk mixture, beating well after each addition.

3. Pour into 2 greased and floured 9-in. round baking pans. Bake until a toothpick inserted in the center comes out clean, 30-35 minutes. Cool for 10 minutes before removing from pans to wire racks to cool completely.

4. Using a citrus zester, remove zest from lemons in long narrow strips; toss with sugar. Let stand for 30 minutes. (Save fruit for another use.) Meanwhile, to make the frosting, in a large bowl, cream butter until light and fluffy. Add the confectioners' sugar, milk, grated lemon zest, vanilla and salt; beat until smooth.

5. Cut each cake in half horizontally. Place 1 cake layer on a serving plate. Pipe a circle of frosting around edge of cake. Spread a third of the lemon curd inside frosting. Repeat layers twice. Top with remaining cake layer. Frost top and sides. If desired, pipe a decorative border of frosting using a star tip, and decorate sides of cake with colored sugar. Garnish with lemon zest strips. Store in the refrigerator.

1 PIECE: 657 cal., 27g fat (16g sat. fat), 172mg chol., 370mg sod., 98g carb. (77g sugars, 1g fiber), 8g pro.

CHOCOLATE ALMOND SILK PIE

I've been baking since I was 9 years old. Back then, my friends and I would get together on Saturdays to make chocolate chip cookies. Of all the cooking I do today, I still enjoy baking best. This silky chocolate pie is one of my favorite desserts.
—Diane Larson, Roland, IA

PREP: 20 MIN. + CHILLING
COOK: 30 MIN. + COOLING
MAKES: 10 SERVINGS

- **2/3 cup all-purpose flour**
- **1/4 cup butter, softened**
- **3 Tbsp. finely chopped almonds, toasted**
- **2 Tbsp. confectioners' sugar**
- **1/8 tsp. vanilla extract**

FILLING

- **3/4 cup sugar**
- **3 large eggs**
- **3 oz. unsweetened chocolate, coarsely chopped**
- **1/8 tsp. almond extract**
- **1/2 cup butter, softened**
- **Sweetened whipped cream and toasted sliced almonds, optional**

1. In a small bowl, combine the first 5 ingredients. Beat on low speed until well combined, 2-3 minutes. Press onto the bottom and up the side of a greased 9-in. pie plate. Bake at 400° for 8-10 minutes or until golden. Cool on a wire rack.

2. For filling, combine sugar and eggs in a small saucepan until well blended. Cook over low heat, stirring constantly until mixture coats the back of a metal spoon and reaches 160°. Remove from the heat. Stir in chocolate and almond extract until smooth. Cool to lukewarm (90°), stirring mixture occasionally.

3. In a large bowl, cream butter until light and fluffy. Add cooled egg mixture; beat on high speed for 5 minutes. Pour into cooled pie shell. Refrigerate for at least 6 hours before serving. Garnish with whipped cream and almonds if desired. Refrigerate leftovers.

1 PIECE: 293 cal., 21g fat (12g sat. fat), 100mg chol., 120mg sod., 26g carb. (17g sugars, 2g fiber), 5g pro.

SWEET POTATO PIE

This creamy sweet potato pie is subtly spiced and slices beautifully. We suggest baking up a few of these pies around the holidays to give to friends and family.
—North Carolina Sweet Potato Commission, Benson, NC

PREP: 30 MIN. • **BAKE:** 50 MIN. + COOLING
MAKES: 8 SERVINGS

- **Dough for single-crust pie**
- **2 medium sweet potatoes (about 1½ lbs.), peeled and cubed**
- **⅓ cup butter, softened**
- **½ cup sugar**
- **2 large eggs, room temperature, lightly beaten**
- **¾ cup evaporated milk**
- **1 tsp. vanilla extract**
- **½ tsp. ground cinnamon**
- **½ tsp. ground nutmeg**
- **¼ tsp. salt**

1. Preheat oven to 425°. On a lightly floured surface, roll dough to a ⅛-in.-thick circle; transfer to a 9-in. pie plate. Trim crust to ½ in. beyond rim of plate; flute edge. Refrigerate while preparing filling
2. Place sweet potatoes in a medium saucepan; add water to cover. Bring to a boil. Reduce heat; cook, uncovered, until tender, 13-15 minutes. Drain potatoes; return to pan. Mash until very smooth; cool to room temperature.
3. In a bowl, cream butter and sugar. Add the eggs; mix well. Add the milk, 2 cups mashed sweet potatoes, vanilla, cinnamon, nutmeg and salt; mix well. Pour into crust. Bake for 15 minutes. Reduce heat to 350°; bake until set or a knife inserted in the center comes out clean, 35-40 minutes. Cool on a wire rack. Refrigerate leftovers.
NOTE: To make pie pastry, combine 1¼ cups all-purpose flour and ¼ tsp. salt; cut in ½ cup cold butter until crumbly. Gradually add 3-5 Tbsp. ice water, tossing with a fork until the dough holds together when pressed. Shape into a disk; wrap and refrigerate 1 hour.
1 PIECE: 372 cal., 18g fat (9g sat. fat), 86mg chol., 300mg sod., 48g carb. (25g sugars, 2g fiber), 6g pro.

DARK CHOCOLATE PECAN CAKE

Made in a single loaf pan, this doubly good chocolate cake has a nutty praline layer and two layers of fluffy whipped cream. This is one of my husband's favorite cakes.
—Laura Draper, Garfield, WA

PREP: 30 MIN. • **BAKE:** 25 MIN. + COOLING
MAKES: 2 SERVINGS

- **1 Tbsp. butter**
- **3 Tbsp. brown sugar**
- **1½ tsp. heavy whipping cream**
- **3 Tbsp. chopped pecans**

BATTER

- **2 Tbsp. shortening**
- **¼ cup sugar**
- **2 Tbsp. beaten egg**
- **⅛ tsp. vanilla extract**
- **6 Tbsp. cake flour**
- **2 Tbsp. baking cocoa**
- **¼ tsp. baking soda**
- **⅛ tsp. baking powder**
- **⅛ tsp. salt**
- **3 Tbsp. water**

TOPPING

- **¼ cup heavy whipping cream**
- **2 tsp. confectioners' sugar**
- **⅛ tsp. vanilla extract**
- **Optional: Chocolate curls and chopped pecans**

1. Line a 5¾x3x2-in. loaf pan with parchment; coat with cooking spray. In a small saucepan, melt butter; stir in brown sugar and cream. Cook and stir over low heat until sugar dissolves. Pour into the prepared pan. Top with pecans. Cover and refrigerate.
2. In a small bowl, cream shortening and sugar until light and fluffy. Beat in egg and vanilla. Combine the flour, cocoa, baking soda, baking powder and salt; add to the creamed mixture alternately with water. Beat just until combined.
3. Pour over pecans in pan. Bake at 325° until a toothpick comes out clean, 25-30 minutes. Cool completely in pan.
4. In a small bowl, beat cream until it begins to thicken. Add confectioners' sugar and vanilla; beat until stiff peaks form. Remove cake from pan; split into 2 horizontal layers. Place bottom cake layer, nut side up, on a serving plate. Spread with half of the topping. Top with remaining layer and topping. If desired, garnish with chocolate curls and chopped pecans.
½ CAKE: 669 cal., 40g fat (15g sat. fat), 126mg chol., 428mg sod., 73g carb. (49g sugars, 3g fiber), 7g pro.

ITALIAN MERINGUE BUTTERCREAM

I spread this creamy meringue buttercream on my lemon-raspberry cupcakes. It's not as sweet as American buttercream, so it nicely complements the sweetness of the cupcakes.
—Katelyn Craft, Stamford, NY

PREP: 35 MIN. • **COOK:** 10 MIN.
MAKES: 4 CUPS

- **1 cup sugar, divided**
- **¼ cup water**
- **4 large egg whites, room temperature**
- **2 cups unsalted butter, cubed, room temperature**
- **1½ tsp. vanilla extract**

1. In a small heavy saucepan, combine ¾ cup sugar and water. Bring to a boil; cook over medium-high heat until a thermometer reads 250° (hard-ball stage), 8 to 10 minutes. Meanwhile, using a stand mixer, beat the egg whites in a large bowl on high speed until foamy. Gradually add remaining ¼ cup sugar, 1 Tbsp. at a time, beating on high after each addition, until sugar is dissolved and soft peaks form.
2. Slowly pour hot sugar syrup over egg whites while beating continuously. Continue beating on high speed until mixture cools to room temperature, roughly 15 to 20 minutes.
3. Gradually add butter, a few Tbsp. at a time, beating on medium after each addition until smooth. Beat in vanilla.
2 TBSP.: 63 cal., 6g fat (4g sat. fat), 15mg chol., 1mg sod., 3g carb. (3g sugars, 0 fiber), 0 pro.

GINGERBREAD PUMPKIN TRIFLE

I spice up special dinners with this towering dessert. A delicious alternative to pumpkin pie, it's my favorite potluck contribution.
—Deborah Hahn, Belle, MO

PREP: 1 HOUR + CHILLING
MAKES: 16 SERVINGS

- **½ cup shortening**
- **⅓ cup sugar**
- **1 cup molasses**
- **1 large egg, room temperature**
- **2⅓ cups all-purpose flour**
- **1 tsp. baking soda**
- **1 tsp. ground ginger**
- **1 tsp. ground cinnamon**
- **¾ tsp. salt**
- **¾ cup hot water**

FILLING/TOPPING

- **2 cups cold 2% milk**
- **1 pkg. (3.4 oz.) instant vanilla pudding mix**
- **1 can (15 oz.) pumpkin**
- **½ cup packed brown sugar**
- **1 tsp. vanilla extract**
- **½ tsp. ground cinnamon**
- **2 cups heavy whipping cream**
- **⅓ cup sugar**
- **1 tsp. rum extract**

1. In a large bowl, cream shortening and sugar until light and fluffy, 5-7 minutes. Beat in molasses and egg. Combine flour, baking soda, ginger, cinnamon and salt; add to creamed mixture alternately with hot water, beating well after each addition.
2. Pour into a greased 13x9-in. baking pan. Bake at 350° for 25-30 minutes or until a toothpick inserted in the center of the cake comes out clean. Cool on a wire rack. Cut gingerbread into ½-in. to 1-in. cubes.
3. In a large bowl, whisk milk and pudding mix for 2 minutes. Let stand for 2 minutes or until soft-set. Combine the pumpkin, brown sugar, vanilla and cinnamon; stir into pudding. In another bowl, beat cream until it begins to thicken. Add sugar and extract; beat until stiff peaks form.
4. Set aside ¼ cup gingerbread cubes. In a 4-qt. trifle bowl or glass serving bowl, layer a third of the remaining gingerbread cubes; top with a third of the pumpkin mixture and whipped cream. Repeat the layers twice. Crumble the reserved gingerbread; sprinkle over the top. Cover and refrigerate for at least 1 hour before serving.
1 CUP: 400 cal., 19g fat (9g sat. fat), 57mg chol., 314mg sod., 55g carb. (34g sugars, 2g fiber), 4g pro.

NUTTY CHEESECAKE SQUARES

These bars are easy enough to make for everyday occasions but special enough to serve company. They also travel well to potlucks and picnics.
—Ruth Simon, Buffalo, NY

PREP: 20 MIN. • **BAKE:** 20 MIN. + COOLING
MAKES: 20 SERVINGS

- **2 cups all-purpose flour**
- **1 cup finely chopped walnuts**
- **⅔ cup packed brown sugar**
- **½ tsp. salt**
- **⅔ cup cold butter**

FILLING

- **2 pkg. (8 oz. each) cream cheese, softened**
- **½ cup sugar**
- **2 large eggs, room temperature, lightly beaten**
- **¼ cup 2% milk**
- **1 tsp. vanilla extract**

1. In a large bowl, combine flour, walnuts, brown sugar and salt; cut in the butter until mixture resembles coarse crumbs. Set half aside; press remaining crumb mixture onto the bottom of a greased 13x9-in. baking pan. Bake at 350° for 10-15 minutes or until lightly browned.
2. In a large bowl, beat filling ingredients until smooth; pour over crust. Sprinkle with reserved crumb mixture.
3. Bake at 350° for 20-25 minutes or until a knife inserted in the center comes out clean. Cool on a wire rack for 1 hour. Store in the refrigerator.

1 PIECE: 233 cal., 14g fat (7g sat. fat), 50mg chol., 165mg sod., 23g carb. (13g sugars, 1g fiber), 4g pro.

STRAWBERRY CHEESECAKE

The creamy texture and lovely look of this cheesecake always garners compliments.
—L.C. Herschap, Luling, TX

PREP: 30 MIN. • **BAKE:** 50 MIN. + CHILLING
MAKES: 16 SERVINGS

CRUST

- **¾ cup ground pecans**
- **¾ cup graham cracker crumbs**
- **3 Tbsp. butter, melted**

FILLING

- **4 pkg. (8 oz. each) cream cheese, softened**
- **1¼ cups sugar**
- **1 Tbsp. lemon juice**
- **2 tsp. vanilla extract**
- **4 large eggs, room temperature, lightly beaten**

TOPPING

- **2 cups sour cream**
- **¼ cup sugar**
- **1 tsp. vanilla extract**

STRAWBERRY GLAZE

- **2 Tbsp. cornstarch**
- **¼ cup water**
- **1 jar (12 oz.) strawberry jelly**
- **3 Tbsp. orange-flavored liqueur or lemon juice**
- **Red food coloring, optional**
- **1 qt. whole fresh strawberries, halved**

1. Preheat oven to 350°. Combine pecans, crumbs and butter. Press onto the bottom of a 10-in. springform pan.
2. In a large bowl, beat cream cheese and sugar until smooth. Beat in lemon juice and vanilla. Add eggs; beat on low speed just until blended. Spoon over crust.
3. Bake until the filling is almost set, 45-50 minutes. Cool on a wire rack for 15 minutes. Meanwhile, for the topping, combine sour cream, sugar and vanilla. Spread over the cheesecake and return to oven for 5 minutes. Cool on a wire rack for 1 hour. Refrigerate overnight, covering when completely cooled.
4. Several hours before serving, prepare glaze. In a saucepan, combine cornstarch and water until smooth. Add strawberry jelly and cook over medium-high heat, stirring constantly, until jelly is melted and mixture has thickened. Remove from the heat; stir in liqueur and, if desired, food coloring. Cool to room temperature.
5. Just before serving, loosen and remove the side of the springform pan. Arrange strawberries on top with pointed ends up. Spoon glaze over the berries, allowing some to drip down sides of cake. Serve cheesecake immediately.

1 PIECE: 453 cal., 22g fat (11g sat. fat), 126mg chol., 159mg sod., 56g carb. (48g sugars, 2g fiber), 6g pro.

BANANA PUDDING TART

Here's a tart version of the classic banana pudding. Use the entire box of vanilla wafers, reserving ¼ cup crumbs to sprinkle on the whipped cream topping. I add a dash of chai spice to make it interesting!
—Tania Gordon, Chicago, IL

PREP: 30 MIN. + CHILLING
BAKE: 25 MIN. + COOLING
MAKES: 14 SERVINGS

- **5 medium bananas**
- **2 cups crushed vanilla wafers (about 60 wafers)**
- **5 Tbsp. butter, softened**
- **1 can (14 oz.) sweetened condensed milk**
- **¼ cup packed light brown sugar**
- **2 large eggs, room temperature**
- **3 large egg yolks, room temperature**
- **1 tsp. ground cinnamon**
- **½ tsp. ground nutmeg**
- **1 cup heavy whipping cream, whipped**

1. Preheat oven to 350°. Place bananas on a foil-lined rimmed baking sheet. Bake until tender and skins are dark brown, 25-30 minutes. Let cool for 15 minutes.
2. Meanwhile, mix the wafers and butter. Press crumbs onto bottom and up side of an ungreased 11-in. tart pan. Refrigerate 30 minutes.
3. Peel bananas; place in a large bowl. Add the milk, brown sugar, eggs and yolks, cinnamon and nutmeg; mix until combined. Pour filling into chilled crust. Place pan on a baking sheet. Bake until filling is set, 25-30 minutes.
4. Cool 1 hour on a wire rack. Refrigerate at least 4 hours before serving. Top with whipped cream and additional crushed vanilla wafers if desired.
1 PIECE: 336 cal., 18g fat (10g sat. fat), 109mg chol., 148mg sod., 41g carb. (31g sugars, 1g fiber), 5g pro.

TEST KITCHEN TIP

To keep bananas from turning brown, brush or spritz a small amount of lemon juice or other citrus acid onto the bananas after peeling them. This will help slow the browning process. Just be sure to not spritz too much lemon juice, as this could alter the flavor of the tart.

FROZEN PEANUT BUTTER & CHOCOLATE TERRINE

This terrine can be made ahead of time and stored in the freezer. When served, it cuts easily and has that wow factor with the lovely layers of banana, peanut butter and chocolate.
—Jennifer Jackson, Keller, TX

PREP: 30 MIN. + FREEZING
MAKES: 12 SERVINGS

- **15 Nutter Butter cookies, crushed (about 2 cups), divided**
- **1 carton (16 oz.) mascarpone cheese**
- **1 cup sugar**
- **2 tsp. vanilla extract**
- **1 carton (8 oz.) frozen whipped topping, thawed**
- **1 medium banana, sliced**
- **1 cup semisweet chocolate chips, melted and cooled slightly**
- **1 Tbsp. baking cocoa**
- **1 cup chunky peanut butter**

1. Line a 9x5-in. loaf pan with plastic wrap, letting edges extend up all the sides. Sprinkle with a third of the crushed cookies.
2. In a large bowl, mix the mascarpone cheese, sugar and vanilla; fold in whipped topping. Divide mixture evenly among 3 bowls.
3. To 1 portion of cheese mixture, fold in sliced banana; add to loaf pan, spreading evenly. Repeat cookie layer. To second portion, stir in melted chocolate and cocoa; add to loaf pan. Sprinkle with the remaining cookies. To third portion, stir in peanut butter. Spread over the top.
4. Freeze, covered, until firm, for at least 5 hours. To serve, invert terrine onto a platter; remove plastic wrap and cut into slices.
1 PIECE: 568 cal., 39g fat (18g sat. fat), 47mg chol., 190mg sod., 49g carb. (38g sugars, 3g fiber), 10g pro.

PINA COLADA CUPCAKES

Bring these colorful treats to your next picnic or potluck. Serve them as regular cupcakes or cut them, unfrosted, into chunks and layer into individual dishes to make mini trifles.
—Jennifer Gilbert, Brighton, MI

PREP TIME: 10 MIN. • **COOK TIME:** 30 MIN.
MAKES: 2 DOZEN

- 3 **large eggs, lightly beaten, room temperature**
- ½ **cup unsweetened pineapple juice**
- ½ **cup canola oil**
- 1 **cup canned coconut milk**
- 2 **tsp. rum extract**
- 3 **cups all-purpose flour**
- 2 **cups sugar**
- 2 **tsp. baking powder**
- ½ **tsp. baking soda**
- ½ **tsp. salt**

FROSTING

- 1 **cup butter, softened**
- 3 **Tbsp. canned coconut milk**
- 1 **tsp. rum extract**
- 3½ **cups confectioners' sugar**
- **Optional: Toasted sweetened shredded coconut, maraschino cherries, pineapple wedges**

1. Preheat oven to 350°. Line 24 muffin cups with foil liners. In a large bowl, whisk eggs, juice, milk, oil and extract until well blended. In another bowl, whisk flour, sugar, baking powder, baking soda and salt; gradually beat into egg mixture.
2. Fill prepared cups two-thirds full. Bake until a toothpick inserted in center comes out clean, 18-20 minutes. Cool in pans 10 minutes before removing to wire racks to cool completely.
3. In a large bowl, beat the butter until creamy. Beat in coconut milk and rum extract. Gradually beat in confectioners' sugar until smooth. Spread frosting over cupcakes. If desired, garnish with coconut, cherries and pineapple wedges.

1 CUPCAKE: 330 cal., 15g fat (7g sat. fat), 44mg chol., 189mg sod., 47g carb. (35g sugars, 0 fiber), 3g pro.

JENNIFER GILBERT
Brighton, MI

CREAMY PINEAPPLE PIE

Here's a light and refreshing dessert that's quick to make and impressive to serve. It makes a sweet ending to a summer meal.
—Sharon Bickett, Chester, SC

TAKES: 10 MIN. • **MAKES:** 8 SERVINGS

- 1 **can (14 oz.) sweetened condensed milk**
- 1 **can (8 oz.) crushed pineapple, undrained**
- ¼ **cup lemon juice**
- 1 **carton (8 oz.) frozen whipped topping, thawed**
- 1 **graham cracker crust (9 in.)**
- **Optional: Chopped toasted macadamia nuts and additional crushed pineapple**

Combine milk, pineapple and lemon juice; fold in whipped topping. Pour filling into prepared crust. Refrigerate until serving. If desired, serve with toasted macadamia nuts and additional crushed pineapple.

NOTE: To make a 9-in. graham cracker crust, combine 1½ cups crushed graham cracker crumbs (24 squares), ¼ sugar and ⅓ cup melted butter. Press onto the bottom and up the sides of an ungreased 9-in. pie plate. Bake at 375° until lightly browned, 8-10 minutes. Cool crust on a wire rack before filling

1 PIECE: 367 cal., 14g fat (9g sat. fat), 17mg chol., 185mg sod., 54g carb. (46g sugars, 1g fiber), 5g pro.

1 FAVORITE 4 WAYS *Fruit Pies*

1) STRAWBERRY CRUMBLE PIE

We host an annual pie-making party before our big pig roast celebration on Labor Day. The pies, including this strawberry delight, take center stage at the end of the meal.
—Beth Howard, Donnellson, IA

PREP: 15 MIN. + CHILLING • **BAKE:** 45 MIN.
MAKES: 8 SERVINGS

- **1¼ cups all-purpose flour**
- **Dash salt**
- **¼ cup shortening**
- **¼ cup cold butter, cubed**
- **3 to 4 Tbsp. ice water**

FILLING

- **1 cup sugar**
- **¼ cup quick-cooking tapioca**
- **Dash salt**
- **6 cups halved fresh strawberries**

CRUMBLE

- **1 cup all-purpose flour**
- **½ cup packed brown sugar**
- **½ cup cold butter, cubed**

1. In a large bowl, mix flour and salt; cut in shortening and butter until crumbly. Gradually add ice water, tossing with a fork until dough holds together when pressed. Shape into a disk; wrap. Refrigerate 1 hour or overnight.
2. Preheat oven to 425°. In a large bowl, mix the sugar, tapioca and salt; add the strawberries and toss to coat. On a lightly floured surface, roll the dough to an ⅛-in.-thick circle; transfer to a 9-in. pie plate. Trim crust to ½ in. beyond rim of plate; flute edge. Add filling. For topping, in a small bowl, combine flour and brown sugar; cut in butter until crumbly. Sprinkle over filling. Place pie plate on a rimmed baking sheet.
3. Bake 20-25 minutes. Reduce oven to 375°. Bake until crust is golden brown and filling is bubbly, 25-30 minutes longer. Cool on a wire rack.
1 PIECE: 542 cal., 24g fat (13g sat. fat), 46mg chol., 509mg sod., 79g carb. (44g sugars, 3g fiber), 5g pro.

2) CAST-IRON BLUEBARB PIE

Blueberries provide a sweet counterpoint to tart rhubarb in this fabulous summertime pie topped with a flaky homemade crust.
—Steve Gyuro, Franklin, WI

PREP: 50 MIN. + CHILLING
BAKE: 40 MIN. + COOLING
MAKES: 8 SERVINGS

- **2 cups all-purpose flour**
- **1 tsp. salt**
- **⅔ cup shortening**
- **6 to 8 Tbsp. ice water**

FILLING

- **1½ cups sugar**
- **3 Tbsp. quick-cooking tapioca**
- **¼ tsp. salt**
- **4 cups sliced fresh or frozen rhubarb, thawed**
- **2 cups fresh or frozen blueberries, thawed**
- **1 Tbsp. butter**
- **1 tsp. 2% milk**
- **Coarse sugar or sugar, optional**

1. In a small bowl, combine flour and salt; cut in the shortening until crumbly. Gradually add water, tossing with a fork until dough forms a ball. Divide dough in half, with 1 portion slightly larger than the other. Wrap separately; refrigerate for 4 hours or until easy to handle.
2. On a lightly floured surface, roll out larger portion of dough to fit a 9-in. cast-iron skillet or deep-dish pie plate. Transfer crust to pie plate. Trim crust even with rim of plate.
3. In a large bowl combine sugar, tapioca and salt. Add rhubarb and blueberries; toss to coat. Let stand for 15 minutes. Transfer filling to crust. Dot with butter.
4. Roll out remaining dough to fit top of pie. Place over filling. Trim, seal and flute edge. Cut slits in crust. If desired, make additional dough and use to create cutouts to decorate top of pie. Brush with milk; sprinkle with coarse sugar if desired.
5. Bake at 400° until crust is golden brown and filling is bubbly, 40-45 minutes. Cover edge with foil during the last 15 minutes to prevent overbrowning if necessary. Cool on a wire rack.
1 PIECE: 471 cal., 18g fat (5g sat. fat), 4mg chol., 383mg sod., 74g carb. (43g sugars, 3g fiber), 4g pro.

3) BUTTERMILK LEMON MERINGUE PIE

Lemon lovers everywhere will agree—this wonderful pie with a little tang beats standard lemon meringue every time. Compliments roll in whenever I serve it.
—Ellen Riley, Murfreesboro, TN

PREP: 30 MIN. • **BAKE:** 15 MIN. + CHILLING
MAKES: 8 SERVINGS

- **1½ cups graham cracker crumbs**
- **¼ cup sugar**
- **⅓ cup butter, melted**

FILLING

- **¾ cup sugar**
- **3 Tbsp. cornstarch**
- **1½ cups buttermilk**
- **3 large egg yolks**
- **2 Tbsp. butter**
- **2 Tbsp. lemon juice**
- **2 tsp. grated lemon zest**

MERINGUE

- **3 large egg whites, room temperature**
- **½ tsp. vanilla extract**
- **¼ tsp. cream of tartar**
- **6 Tbsp. sugar**

1. Combine the cracker crumbs, sugar and butter; press onto the bottom and up the sides of an ungreased 9-in. pie plate. Bake at 350° for 10-12 minutes or until crust is lightly browned. Cool on a wire rack.
2. For filling, in a large saucepan, combine sugar and cornstarch. Stir in buttermilk until smooth. Cook and stir over medium-high heat until thickened and bubbly. Reduce the heat to low; cook and stir for 2 minutes longer. Remove from the heat. Stir 1 cup of hot mixture into egg yolks; return all to pan, stirring constantly. Bring to a gentle boil; cook and stir for 2 minutes longer. Remove from the heat. Stir in the butter. Gently stir in lemon juice and zest. Pour hot filling into pastry shell.
3. For meringue, in a small mixing bowl, beat the egg whites, vanilla and cream of tartar on medium speed until soft peaks form. Gradually beat in the sugar, 1 Tbsp. at a time, on high until stiff peaks form. Spread over hot filling, sealing edges to the crust.
4. Bake at 350° until golden brown, 15-20 minutes. Cool on a wire rack for 1 hour; refrigerate for 1-2 hours before serving. Refrigerate leftovers.
1 PIECE: 350 cal., 14g fat (8g sat. fat), 106mg chol., 242mg sod., 52g carb. (42g sugars, 1g fiber), 5g pro.

4) CRANBERRY APPLE SHEET PIE

My husband loves pie, so I made one with apples, raspberries and cranberries. It's so good, I bend the rules and let the grandkids enjoy it for breakfast.
—Brenda Smith, Curran, MI

PREP: 45 MIN. +CHILLING
BAKE: 45 MIN. + COOLING • **MAKES:** 2 DOZEN

- **Dough for 2 double-crust pies**
- **2¼ cups sugar**
- **⅓ cup all-purpose flour**
- **7 medium tart apples, peeled and sliced (about 8 cups)**
- **3 cups fresh or frozen cranberries**
- **2 tsp. grated orange zest**
- **1½ tsp. ground nutmeg**
- **1½ tsp. ground cinnamon**
- **6 cups frozen or fresh raspberries**
- **Optional: Egg wash, additional sugar or coarse sugar, and whipped cream**

1. Divide dough into 2 portions so that one portion is slightly larger than the other; wrap and refrigerate 1 hour or overnight.
2. Roll out the larger portion of dough between 2 pieces of waxed paper into a 18x13-in. rectangle. Remove top sheet of waxed paper; place a 15x10x1-in. baking pan upside down over crust. Lifting with waxed paper, carefully invert crust into pan. Remove waxed paper; press crust onto bottom and up sides of pan. Allow to chill while preparing filling.
3. In a Dutch oven, mix sugar and flour; stir in apples, cranberries, orange zest and spices. Bring to a boil over medium-high heat. Reduce the heat; simmer, uncovered, 10-12 minutes or until the apples are tender and the juices are thickened, stirring occasionally. Remove from heat; stir in raspberries. Set aside to cool completely.
4. Preheat oven to 375°. Add the filling to prepared crust.
5. On a well-floured surface, roll the remaining dough into a ⅛-in.-thick rectangle; cut into 1½-in.-wide strips. Arrange strips over filling, sealing ends to bottom crust. If desired, brush crust with egg wash; sprinkle with additional sugar or coarse sugar.
6. Bake pie on lowest oven rack for 45-50 minutes or until the crust is golden brown and filling is bubbly. Cool on a wire rack. If desired, serve with whipped cream.
NOTE: To make pie pastry, combine 2½ cups all-purpose flour and ½ tsp. salt; cut in 1 cup cold butter until crumbly. Gradually add ⅓ to ⅔ cup ice water, tossing with a fork until the dough holds together when pressed. Divide dough in half. Shape each into a disk; wrap and refrigerate 1 hour.
1 PIECE: 352 cal., 16g fat (10g sat. fat), 40mg chol., 207mg sod., 51g carb. (25g sugars, 4g fiber), 4g pro.

Cookies & Candies

Tasty treats in small bites—these delectable cookies, candies, brownies and bars are just what you need for bake sales, holiday platters or a sweet snack whenever a craving calls.

CHOCOLATE-DRIZZLED RAVIOLI COOKIES

My daughter Madalyn came up with these must-have treats. Even her teachers were asking her to make them and share the recipe!
—Sarah Sandifer, Bamberg, SC

PREP: 45 MIN. + CHILLING
BAKE: 15 MIN./BATCH + COOLING
MAKES: ABOUT 3½ DOZEN

- **1 cup shortening**
- **1⅓ cups sugar**
- **2 large eggs, room temperature**
- **1 tsp. vanilla extract**
- **2½ cups all-purpose flour**
- **1 tsp. baking powder**
- **½ tsp. salt**

FILLING

- **12 Oreo cookies**
- **1 pkg. (8 oz.) cream cheese, softened**
- **¼ cup confectioners' sugar**
- **½ tsp. coconut extract**

DRIZZLE

- **1 cup semisweet chocolate chips**
- **2 tsp. shortening**

1. In a large bowl, cream shortening and sugar 5-7 minutes or until light and fluffy. Beat in eggs and vanilla. In another bowl, whisk the flour, baking powder and salt; gradually beat into creamed mixture.
2. Divide the dough in half. Shape each into a disk; wrap. Refrigerate until firm enough to roll, about 30 minutes.
3. For filling, place the Oreos in a food processor; process until finely crushed. Add cream cheese, confectioners' sugar and extract; process until blended.
4. Preheat the oven to 350°. On a lightly floured surface, roll 1 portion of dough to ⅛-in. thickness. Cut with a floured 2-in. round cookie cutter. Place about 1½ tsp. filling in the center of half of the cookies. Cover with the remaining cookies. Press edges with a fork to seal. Place 1 in. apart on greased baking sheets. Repeat with remaining dough and filling.
5. Bake 15-20 minutes or until the edges are light brown. Cool on pans 2 minutes. Remove to wire racks to cool completely.
6. In a microwave, melt chocolate chips and shortening; stir until smooth. Drizzle over cookies; let stand until set. Store in an airtight container in the refrigerator.

1 COOKIE: 155 cal., 9g fat (3g sat. fat), 15mg chol., 75mg sod., 18g carb. (11g sugars, 1g fiber), 2g pro.

CHOCOLATE SCOTCHEROOS

One of my students gave me this recipe. The cereal treats are easy to make and have become a family favorite.
—Lois Mays, Covington, PA

PREP: 25 MIN. + CHILLING • **MAKES:** 2 DOZEN

- **1 cup sugar**
- **1 cup light corn syrup**
- **1 cup creamy peanut butter**
- **6 cups crisp rice cereal**
- **3/4 cup butterscotch chips**
- **3/4 cup semisweet chocolate chips**
- **3/4 tsp. shortening**

1. In a large saucepan, bring sugar and corn syrup to a boil. Cook and stir until sugar is dissolved; stir in peanut butter.
2. Remove from the heat. Add cereal and mix well. Press mixture into a greased 13x9-in. pan.
3. In a microwave-safe bowl, melt chips and shortening; stir until smooth. Spread over cereal mixture. Cover and refrigerate for at least 1 hour before cutting.

1 BAR: 232 cal., 9g fat (4g sat. fat), 0 chol., 98mg sod., 36g carb. (29g sugars, 1g fiber), 4g pro.

TEST KITCHEN TIP

To keep these bars from getting too hard, once the sugar and corn syrup come to a boil, reduce the heat or remove the pan from heat. You don't want to overheat it or else the sugar mixture will harden over time, and you won't get a soft and chewy bar.

MARTHA WASHINGTON CANDY

Passed down by my grandmother and mother, this Martha Washington candy recipe is a cherished family tradition. We've even had each grandchild and great-grandchild take a turn stirring the candy mixture!
—Cindi Boger, Ardmore, AL

PREP: 45 MIN. + CHILLING
MAKES: ABOUT 5½ DOZEN

- **1 cup butter, softened**
- **4 cups confectioners' sugar**
- **1 can (14 oz.) sweetened condensed milk**
- **1 tsp. vanilla extract**
- **3 cups sweetened shredded coconut**
- **2 cups chopped pecans, toasted**
- **6 cups semisweet chocolate chips**
- **1/4 cup shortening**
- **Additional sweetened shredded coconut, optional**

1. In a bowl, beat butter, confectioners' sugar, milk and vanilla until blended. Stir in coconut and pecans. Divide dough in half; refrigerate, covered, 1 hour.
2. Working with half the dough at a time, shape mixture into 1-in. balls; place the balls on waxed paper-lined baking sheets. Refrigerate 30 minutes longer.
3. In top of a double boiler or a metal bowl over barely simmering water, melt the chocolate chips and shortening; stir until smooth. Dip balls in melted chocolate; allow excess to drip off. Return to waxed paper. Top with some additional coconut if desired. Refrigerate until set. Store in an airtight container in the refrigerator until ready to serve.

FREEZE OPTION: Freeze candy, layered between pieces of waxed paper, in freezer containers. To use, thaw in refrigerator 2 hours before serving.

1 PIECE: 196 cal., 13g fat (7g sat. fat), 9mg chol., 43mg sod., 23g carb. (21g sugars, 1g fiber), 2g pro.

NANCY ZIMMERMAN
Cape May Court House, NJ

LEMONY COCONUT BARS

These chewy bars with a hint of citrus make a refreshing addition to cookie trays. Try lime juice and zest for a zingy twist.
—Nancy Zimmerman,
Cape May Court House, NJ

PREP: 25 MIN.
BAKE: 25 MIN. + COOLING
MAKES: 2 DOZEN

- **½ cup butter, softened**
- **½ cup packed light brown sugar**
- **1½ cups all-purpose flour**

FILLING

- **2 large eggs**
- **1 cup packed light brown sugar**
- **½ tsp. grated lemon zest**
- **½ tsp. vanilla extract**
- **¼ tsp. lemon extract**
- **2 Tbsp. all-purpose flour**
- **½ tsp. baking powder**
- **¼ tsp. salt**
- **1½ cups sweetened shredded coconut**
- **1 cup chopped pecans or walnuts**

GLAZE

- **1 cup confectioners' sugar**
- **1 Tbsp. butter, melted**
- **½ tsp. grated lemon zest**
- **3 Tbsp. lemon juice**

1. Preheat oven to 350°. In a bowl, cream the butter and sugar until light and fluffy, 5-7 minutes; gradually beat in the flour, mixing well.
2. Press onto bottom of a greased 13x9-in. baking pan. Bake until edges are golden brown, 8-10 minutes. Cool on a wire rack.
3. For filling, in a large bowl, beat eggs, brown sugar, lemon zest and extracts until blended. In a small bowl, mix flour, baking powder and salt; stir into the egg mixture. Stir in the coconut and pecans. Spread over crust.
4. Bake until golden brown, 17-20 minutes. Cool bars for 10 minutes on a wire rack. Meanwhile, in a small bowl, mix glaze ingredients until smooth; drizzle glaze over warm filling. Cool completely. Cut into bars.

1 BAR: 208 cal., 10g fat (5g sat. fat), 27mg chol., 96mg sod., 29g carb. (21g sugars, 1g fiber), 2g pro.

PEANUT BUTTER OATMEAL-CHIP COOKIES

This cookie is my husband's favorite, my classes' favorite, my colleagues' favorite and, no surprise, my favorite too. The recipe makes a big batch—holiday gifts, here we come!
—Dana Chew, Okemah, OK

PREP: 35 MIN.
BAKE: 10 MIN./BATCH
MAKES: ABOUT 11 DOZEN

- **2½ cups butter, softened**
- **½ cup creamy peanut butter**
- **2 cups sugar**
- **2 cups packed brown sugar**
- **4 large eggs, room temperature**
- **2 tsp. vanilla extract**
- **6 cups all-purpose flour**
- **2 tsp. salt**
- **2 tsp. baking soda**
- **½ tsp. baking powder**
- **2 cups semisweet chocolate chips**
- **1⅔ cups (11 oz.) peanut butter and milk chocolate chips**
- **1 cup quick-cooking oats**

1. Preheat oven to 375°. Cream butter, peanut butter and sugars until light and fluffy, 5-7 minutes. Beat in the eggs and vanilla. In a separate bowl, whisk flour, salt, baking soda and baking powder; gradually beat into creamed mixture.
2. Stir in chips and oats. Drop by rounded tablespoonfuls 2 in. apart onto ungreased baking sheets. Bake until golden brown, 9-12 minutes. Cool for 2 minutes before removing from pans to wire racks. Store in an airtight container.

1 COOKIE: 109 cal., 6g fat (3g sat. fat), 16mg chol., 93mg sod., 14g carb. (8g sugars, 0 fiber), 1g pro.

BAKLAVA THUMBPRINT COOKIES

The topping on my sister-in-law's peach cobbler was so delicious that I asked for the recipe, then decided to use that to top a cookie I developed with the flavors of baklava. My adult son tried one and immediately ate two more—which is unusual for him! It's a good recipe to mix up the night before and bake fresh the next day for company.
—Sharon Eshelman, Harrington, DE

PREP: 30 MIN. + CHILLING
BAKE: 15 MIN./BATCH
MAKES: 2 DOZEN

- **1 cup sugar**
- **½ cup butter, softened**
- **2 large eggs, room temperature**
- **1 tsp. almond extract**
- **1 tsp. vanilla extract**
- **2¼ cups all-purpose flour**
- **1 tsp. baking powder**
- **½ tsp. salt**

TOPPING

- **3 Tbsp. sugar**
- **2 tsp. ground cinnamon**
- **½ cup honey**
- **¾ cup chopped walnuts**

1. In a large bowl, cream sugar and butter until blended. Beat in eggs, 1 at a time, and extracts. In another bowl, whisk flour, baking powder and salt; gradually beat into creamed mixture. Wrap the dough; refrigerate until firm enough to form into balls, about 30 minutes.
2. Preheat oven to 375°. For topping, combine sugar and cinnamon; set aside. Shape dough into 1-in. balls; refrigerate again if dough becomes too warm. Place 2½ in. apart on parchment-lined baking sheets. Bake 8 minutes. Press a deep indentation in center of each cookie with the back of a rounded teaspoon. Fill each with honey and walnuts; sprinkle with the cinnamon sugar. Return to oven and bake until edges begin to brown, 7-9 minutes longer. Cool on pans 1 minute. Remove to wire racks to cool. Store cookies in an airtight container.

1 COOKIE: 168 cal., 7g fat (3g sat. fat), 26mg chol., 106mg sod., 25g carb. (16g sugars, 1g fiber), 2g pro.

PEPPERMINT BROWNIES

My grandmother encouraged me to enter these brownies in the county fair some years ago, and they earned top honors! They are a delicious treat to serve during the holidays.
—Marcy Greenblatt, Redding, CA

PREP: 15 MIN. • **BAKE:** 35 MIN. + COOLING.
MAKES: 2 DOZEN

1⅓ cups all-purpose flour
1 cup baking cocoa
1 tsp. salt
1 tsp. baking powder
¾ cup canola oil
2 cups sugar
4 large eggs, room temperature
2 tsp. vanilla extract
⅔ cup crushed peppermint candies

GLAZE

1 cup semisweet chocolate chips
1 Tbsp. shortening
2 Tbsp. crushed peppermint candies

1. Preheat oven to 350°. Line a 13x9-in. baking pan with foil and grease the foil; set pan aside.
2. In a large bowl, whisk together the first 4 ingredients. In a large bowl, beat oil and sugar until blended. Add eggs, 1 at a time, beating well after each addition. Beat in vanilla. Gradually add flour mixture; stir in crushed peppermint candies. Spread into prepared pan.
3. Bake until a toothpick inserted in center comes out clean, 35-40 minutes. Cool in pan on a wire rack.
4. In a microwave, melt chocolate chips and shortening; stir until smooth. Spread glaze over the brownies; sprinkle with candies. Cut into bars.

1 BROWNIE: 222 cal., 11g fat (3g sat. fat), 35mg chol., 128mg sod., 31g carb. (22g sugars, 1g fiber), 3g pro.

READER REVIEW

"I made these brownies for my family and they raved over them. The peppermint is a perfect amount—not too overwhelming."

JSHOCINSKI, TASTEOFHOME.COM

PEANUT BUTTER SNOWBALLS

These creamy treats showcase the delectable combination of white chocolate and peanut butter. I once prepared them for a bake sale at my granddaughter's school, and I've also put them in gift boxes to share with friends and neighbors at Christmastime.
—Wanda Regula, Birmingham, MI

PREP: 15 MIN. + FREEZING
MAKES: 2½ DOZEN

1 cup confectioners' sugar
½ cup creamy peanut butter
3 Tbsp. butter, softened
1 lb. white candy coating, coarsely chopped
Chopped peanuts, optional

1. In a bowl, combine the sugar, peanut butter and butter. Chill in the freezer for 30 minutes or until the mixture is easy to handle. Shape into 1-in. balls and place on a waxed paper-lined baking sheet. Freeze for 30 minutes or until firm.
2. Meanwhile, melt the candy coating in a microwave-safe bowl. Dip each ball and place on waxed paper to harden. If desired, sprinkle with chopped peanuts.

1 PIECE: 132 cal., 8g fat (5g sat. fat), 3mg chol., 27mg sod., 16g carb. (15g sugars, 0 fiber), 1g pro.

LORRAINE CALAND
Shuniah, ON

ORANGE PISTACHIO COOKIES

I had never tried pistachios until I visited a friend who served me these cookies. I was in love! I made the recipe my own, and now my family can't get enough of them.
—Lorraine Caland, Shuniah, ON

PREP: 20 MIN. + CHILLING
BAKE: 10 MIN./BATCH + COOLING
MAKES: ABOUT 4½ DOZEN

- **¾ cup butter, softened**
- **1 cup sugar**
- **1 large egg, room temperature**
- **1 Tbsp. grated orange zest**
- **1 tsp. vanilla extract**
- **2 cups all-purpose flour**
- **¼ cup cornstarch**
- **½ cup pistachios, toasted and finely chopped**

ICING

- **2¼ cups confectioners' sugar**
- **¼ cup orange juice**
- **1 Tbsp. butter, melted**
- **Additional pistachios, toasted and finely chopped, optional**

1. In a large bowl, cream the butter and sugar until light and fluffy, 5-7 minutes. Beat in the egg, orange zest and vanilla. In another bowl, whisk the flour and cornstarch; gradually beat into the creamed mixture.
2. Divide the dough in half. Roughly shape each portion into a 7-in. roll along the long end of a 14x8-in. sheet of waxed paper. Tightly roll waxed paper over dough, using the waxed paper to mold the dough into a smooth roll. Place waxed paper-covered roll in an airtight container; freeze for 30 minutes or until firm, or refrigerate overnight.
3. Preheat the oven to 350°. Sprinkle pistachios on a rimmed baking sheet. Unwrap and roll each roll of dough in pistachios. Cut the dough crosswise into ¼-in. slices. Place slices ½ in. apart on parchment-lined baking sheets. Bake for 6-8 minutes or until the bottoms are light brown. Cool slightly on pan. Remove from pans to wire racks to cool completely.
4. In a bowl, combine the confectioners' sugar, orange juice and butter until smooth. Spread over cookies. If desired, sprinkle with additional pistachios. Let stand until set.

NOTE: To toast nuts, bake in a shallow pan in a 350° oven for 5-10 minutes or cook in a skillet over low heat until lightly browned, stirring occasionally.

1 COOKIE: 83 cal., 3g fat (2g sat. fat), 10mg chol., 27mg sod., 13g carb. (9g sugars, 0 fiber), 1g pro.

FROSTED PUMPKIN CRANBERRY BARS

With tangy dried cranberries tucked inside and a creamy brown butter frosting, these mildly spiced pumpkin bars are doubly delightful. It's a good thing the recipe makes lots, because once you taste one, you won't be able to resist going back for more!
—Barbara Nowakowski, Mesa, AZ

PREP: 15 MIN. • **BAKE:** 20 MIN. + COOLING
MAKES: ABOUT 4 DOZEN

- **1½ cups all-purpose flour**
- **1¼ cups sugar**
- **2 tsp. baking powder**
- **2 tsp. ground cinnamon**
- **1 tsp. baking soda**
- **½ tsp. ground ginger**
- **3 large eggs, room temperature**
- **1 can (15 oz.) pumpkin**
- **¾ cup butter, melted**
- **¾ cup chopped dried cranberries**

BROWN BUTTER FROSTING

- **½ cup butter**
- **4 cups confectioners' sugar**
- **1 tsp. vanilla extract**
- **4 to 6 Tbsp. whole milk**
- **Additional dried cranberries, optional**

1. In a large bowl, combine the first 6 ingredients. In another bowl, whisk the eggs, pumpkin and butter; stir into the dry ingredients until well combined. Stir in cranberries.
2. Spread into a greased 15x10x1-in. baking pan. Bake at 350° until a toothpick inserted in the center comes out clean, 20-25 minutes. Cool on a wire rack.
3. For frosting, in a large heavy saucepan, cook the butter over medium heat for 5-7 minutes or until golden brown. Pour into a large bowl; beat in confectioners' sugar, vanilla and enough milk to reach spreading consistency. Frost bars. If desired, sprinkle with finely chopped dried cranberries.

1 SERVING: 130 cal., 5g fat (3g sat. fat), 26mg chol., 96mg sod., 21g carb. (16g sugars, 1g fiber), 1g pro.

MACADAMIA NUT COOKIES

I host a mainland luau every year. These rich cookies are full of Hawaiian macadamia nuts and chocolate chips.
—Mary Gaylord, Balsam Lake, WI

PREP: 20 MIN. + CHILLING
BAKE: 10 MIN./BATCH + COOLING
MAKES: ABOUT 6 DOZEN

- **1 cup butter, softened**
- **¾ cup sugar**
- **¾ cup packed brown sugar**
- **2 large eggs, room temperature**
- **1 tsp. vanilla extract**
- **2¼ cups all-purpose flour**
- **1 tsp. baking soda**
- **1 tsp. salt**
- **2 jars (3½ oz. each) macadamia nuts, chopped**
- **2 cups semisweet chocolate chips**
- **1 cup (6 oz.) white baking chips**

1. In a large bowl, cream the butter and sugars for 5-7 minutes or until light and fluffy. Add the eggs and vanilla; beat on medium speed for 2 minutes. Combine the flour, baking soda and salt; add to creamed mixture and beat for 2 minutes. Stir in nuts and chocolate chips. Cover and refrigerate for several hours or overnight.
2. Drop by tablespoonfuls 2 in. apart onto ungreased baking sheets. Bake at 375° for 10-12 minutes or until golden brown. Cool on pans for 1 minute before removing to wire racks; cool completely.

2 COOKIES: 201 cal., 12g fat (6g sat. fat), 26mg chol., 170mg sod., 24g carb. (14g sugars, 1g fiber), 2g pro.

STRAWBERRY COOKIE CUPS

I learned to bake beside my mother and grandmother. When I was on break from college, I knew just how to entertain myself: I made cookies. Sharing this recipe with my mom and grandmother was a proud moment.
—Andrea Zulauf, Livonia, NY

PREP: 45 MIN. + CHILLING
BAKE: 10 MIN./BATCH + COOLING
MAKES: ABOUT 4 DOZEN

- **1 cup butter, softened**
- **1½ cups confectioners' sugar**
- **1 large egg, room temperature**
- **1½ tsp. vanilla extract**
- **2½ cups all-purpose flour**
- **1½ oz. strawberry gelatin**
- **1 tsp. baking soda**
- **1 tsp. cream of tartar**

FILLING

- **1 pkg. (8 oz.) cream cheese, softened**
- **1½ cups confectioners' sugar**

1. Preheat oven to 375°. In a large bowl, beat butter and confectioners' sugar until blended. Beat in the egg and vanilla. In another bowl, whisk flour, gelatin, baking soda and cream of tartar; gradually beat into creamed mixture.
2. Divide the dough in half. Shape each into a disk; wrap and refrigerate until firm enough to roll, about 30 minutes.
3. On a lightly floured surface, roll the first portion of dough to ⅛-in. thickness. Cut with a floured 2¾-in. flower-shaped cookie cutter. Press flower cutouts onto bottoms and up the sides of ungreased mini-muffin cups.
4. Bake 6-8 minutes or until the edges are brown. With the end of a wooden spoon handle, reshape the puffed cookie cups. Cool 5 minutes. Remove from pans to wire racks to cool completely. Repeat with the second portion of dough.
5. In a small bowl, beat cream cheese until smooth. Gradually beat in confectioners' sugar. Pipe into cookie cups. Store in an airtight container in the refrigerator.

FREEZE OPTION: Transfer wrapped disks to a freezer container; freeze. To use, thaw dough in refrigerator until soft enough to roll. Prepare filling and cookies. Bake and decorate as directed.

1 COOKIE: 109 cal., 6g fat (3g sat. fat), 19mg chol., 75mg sod., 14g carb. (8g sugars, 0 fiber), 1g pro.

BUTTERY SPRITZ COOKIES

This eye-catching spritz always makes an appearance on my Christmas cookie tray. The dough is easy to work with, so it's fun to make these into a variety of festive shapes.
—Beverly Launius, Sandwich, IL

PREP: 20 MIN.
BAKE: 10 MIN./BATCH + COOLING
MAKES: ABOUT 7½ DOZEN

- **1 cup butter, softened**
- **2¼ cups confectioners' sugar, divided**
- **½ tsp. salt**
- **1 large egg, room temperature**
- **1 tsp. vanilla extract**
- **½ tsp. almond extract**
- **2½ cups all-purpose flour**
- **Melted semisweet chocolate, optional**
- **2 to 3 Tbsp. water**
- **Colored sugar and sprinkles**

1. Preheat oven to 375°. In a large bowl, cream butter, 1¼ cups confectioners' sugar and salt until light and fluffy, 5-7 minutes. Beat in egg and extracts. Gradually beat flour into the creamed mixture.
2. Using a cookie press fitted with a disk of your choice, press dough 2 in. apart onto ungreased baking sheets. Bake until set, 6-8 minutes (do not brown). Remove to wire racks to cool completely.
3. If desired, dip in melted chocolate and let stand until set or, in a small bowl, mix remaining 1 cup confectioners' sugar and enough water to reach the desired glaze consistency. Dip cookies in glaze; decorate as desired. Let stand until set.

1 COOKIE: 43 cal., 2g fat (1g sat. fat), 7mg chol., 30mg sod., 6g carb. (3g sugars, 0 fiber), 0 pro.

MINIATURE PEANUT BUTTER TREATS

I have three children and eight grandchildren, and every one of them loves these peanut butter "thingies," as the kids like to call them.
—Jodie McCoy, Tulsa, OK

PREP: 20 MIN. + CHILLING
BAKE: 10 MIN./BATCH + COOLING
MAKES: 3½ DOZEN

COOKIE

- **½ cup butter, softened**
- **½ cup sugar**
- **½ cup packed brown sugar**
- **1 large egg, room temperature**
- **½ cup creamy peanut butter**
- **½ tsp. vanilla extract**
- **1¼ cups all-purpose flour**
- **¾ tsp. baking soda**
- **½ tsp. salt**

FILLING

- **42 miniature peanut butter-chocolate cups**

1. In a bowl, combine the butter, sugars, egg, peanut butter and vanilla; beat until smooth. Combine the flour, baking soda and salt; gradually add to the creamed mixture. Cover and chill for 1 hour or until easy to handle.
2. Roll into 42 walnut-sized balls; place in greased miniature muffin cups. Bake at 375° for 8-9 minutes.
3. Remove from the oven; gently press 1 peanut butter cup into each cookie, forming a depression. Cool 10 minutes before removing treats to wire racks to cool completely.

1 PIECE: 108 cal., 6g fat (3g sat. fat), 11mg chol., 108mg sod., 12g carb. (9g sugars, 1g fiber), 2g pro.

BAVARIAN MINT FUDGE

My sister-in-law sent this chocolate candy to us one Christmas, and it's been a traditional holiday treat in our home ever since. With just six ingredients, it couldn't be easier to make.
—Sue Tucker, Edgemoor, SC

PREP: 20 MIN. + CHILLING • **MAKES:** 2½ LBS.

- **1½ tsp. plus 1 Tbsp. butter, divided**
- **2 cups semisweet chocolate chips**
- **1 pkg. (11½ oz.) milk chocolate chips**
- **1 can (14 oz.) sweetened condensed milk**
- **1 tsp. peppermint extract**
- **1 tsp. vanilla extract**

1. Line an 11x7-in. baking pan with foil. Grease the foil with 1½ tsp. butter; set aside.
2. In a microwave-safe bowl, combine chocolate chips, milk and the remaining 1 Tbsp. butter. Microwave on high for 1 minute; stir. Microwave on high, stirring every 30 seconds until chips are just melted, 1-2 minutes longer. Stir in the extracts (fudge mixture will not be glossy). Spread into prepared pan. Refrigerate until set.
3. Using the foil, lift fudge out of the pan. Discard foil; cut fudge into 1-in. squares. Store in the refrigerator.

1 PIECE: 62 cal., 3g fat (2g sat. fat), 3mg chol., 12mg sod., 8g carb. (7g sugars, 0 fiber), 1g pro.

READER REVIEW

"I have made this fudge for many, many years and everyone wants the recipe. It's so creamy and wonderful, not to mention easy!"

SJ6906, TASTEOFHOME.COM

5i

ROSEMARY SHORTBREAD COOKIES

With the perfect hint of rosemary and a classic buttery texture, these delicate cookies look and taste elegant. The fact that they're very easy to prepare can be our little secret.
—Amavida Coffee, Rosemary Beach, FL

PREP: 30 MIN. + CHILLING
BAKE: 15 MIN./BATCH
MAKES: 5½ DOZEN

- **1 cup butter, softened**
- **½ cup confectioners' sugar**
- **2 cups all-purpose flour**
- **2 Tbsp. minced fresh rosemary**
- **½ tsp. sea salt**

1. In a large bowl, cream the butter and confectioners' sugar until light and fluffy, 5-7 minutes. Combine the flour, rosemary and salt; gradually add to the creamed mixture and mix well.
2. Shape into two 8¼-in. rolls and wrap. Refrigerate rolls overnight. Cut into ¼-in. slices. Place dough slices 2 in. apart on ungreased baking sheets.
3. Bake at 350° for 11-13 minutes or until edges begin to brown. Cool for 1 minute before removing from pans to wire racks. Store in an airtight container.

1 COOKIE: 42 cal., 3g fat (2g sat. fat), 7mg chol., 38mg sod., 4g carb. (1g sugars, 0 fiber), 0 pro.

CARAMEL-PECAN COOKIE BUTTER BARS

I love cookie butter and spread it on toast, vanilla wafers and graham crackers. One day I was thinking about another way to use it. I came up with these bars, and they were an instant hit! These cookies freeze well—they are so tempting to remove from the freezer one by one until there are no more left.
—Sherry Little, Cabot, AR

PREP: 15 MIN. • **BAKE:** 15 MIN. + COOLING
MAKES: 2 DOZEN

- **½ cup butter, softened**
- **½ cup sugar**
- **½ cup packed brown sugar**
- **½ cup Biscoff creamy cookie spread**
- **1 large egg, room temperature**
- **1¼ cups self-rising flour**
- **2 cups pecan halves, coarsely chopped**
- **1 pkg. (11 oz.) caramels**
- **3 Tbsp. half-and-half cream**
- **1 tsp. vanilla extract**
- **1 cup (6 oz.) dark chocolate chips**
- **1 Tbsp. shortening**

1. Preheat oven to 375°. In a large bowl, cream butter, sugars and cookie butter until light and fluffy, 5-7 minutes. Beat in egg. Gradually beat in flour. Spread onto bottom of greased 13x9-in. baking pan. Sprinkle with pecans; press lightly into dough. Bake until the edges are lightly browned, 15-20 minutes.
2. Meanwhile, in a large saucepan, combine caramels and cream. Cook and stir over medium-low heat until caramels are melted. Remove from the heat; stir in vanilla. Pour over crust. Cool completely in pan on a wire rack.
3. In a microwave, melt chocolate chips and shortening; stir until smooth. Drizzle over bars; let stand until set. Cut into bars.

1 BAR: 285 cal., 17g fat (6g sat. fat), 20mg chol., 149mg sod., 34g carb. (25g sugars, 2g fiber), 3g pro.

AGNES WARD
Stratford, ON

WHITE CHOCOLATE RASPBERRY THUMBPRINTS

When I pass around the cookie tray, all eyes land on these fancy thumbprints. The white chocolate filling and dab of jewel-toned jam will satisfy any sweet tooth.
—Agnes Ward, Stratford, ON

PREP: 25 MIN. + CHILLING
BAKE: 10 MIN./BATCH + COOLING
MAKES: ABOUT 3 DOZEN

- ¾ cup butter, softened
- ½ cup packed brown sugar
- 2 large eggs, separated, room temperature
- 1¼ cups all-purpose flour
- ¼ cup baking cocoa
- 1¼ cups finely chopped pecans or walnuts

FILLING

- 4 oz. white baking chocolate, coarsely chopped
- 2 Tbsp. butter
- ¼ cup seedless raspberry jam

1. In a large bowl, cream butter and brown sugar until light and fluffy, 5-7 minutes. Beat in egg yolks. Combine the flour and cocoa; gradually add to creamed mixture and mix well. Cover and refrigerate for 1-2 hours or until easy to handle.
2. In a shallow bowl, whisk the egg whites until foamy. Place nuts in another shallow bowl. Shape dough into 1-in. balls. Dip into egg whites, then roll in nuts.
3. Using a wooden spoon handle, make an indentation in center of each cookie. Place 1 in. apart on greased baking sheets. Bake at 350° until set, 8-10 minutes. Remove to wire racks to cool completely.
4. In a microwave, melt white chocolate and butter; stir until smooth. Spoon about ½ tsp. into each cookie. Top each with about ¼ tsp. jam. Store the cookies in an airtight container.

1 COOKIE: 120 cal., 8g fat (4g sat. fat), 22mg chol., 43mg sod., 11g carb. (7g sugars, 1g fiber), 2g pro.

CANDY BAR BROWNIES

Two kinds of candy bars baked into these brownies make them an extra special treat.
—Sharon Evans, Clear Lake, IA

PREP: 15 MIN. • **BAKE:** 30 MIN. + COOLING
MAKES: 3 DOZEN

- ¾ cup butter, melted
- 2 cups sugar
- 4 large eggs, room temperature
- 2 tsp. vanilla extract
- 1½ cups all-purpose flour
- ⅓ cup baking cocoa
- ½ tsp. baking powder
- ¼ tsp. salt
- 4 Snickers bars (2.07 oz. each), cut into ¼-in. pieces
- 3 plain milk chocolate candy bars (1.55 oz. each), coarsely chopped

1. In a large bowl, combine the butter, sugar, eggs and vanilla. In a small bowl, combine the flour, cocoa, baking powder and salt; set aside ¼ cup. Stir remaining dry ingredients into the egg mixture until well combined. Toss Snickers pieces with reserved flour mixture; stir into batter.
2. Transfer batter to a greased 13x9-in. baking pan. Sprinkle with milk chocolate candy bar pieces. Bake at 350° until a toothpick inserted in the center comes out clean (do not overbake), 30-35 minutes. Cool on a wire rack. Chill before cutting.

1 BROWNIE: 121 cal., 5g fat (3g sat. fat), 34mg chol., 73mg sod., 17g carb. (12g sugars, 0 fiber), 2g pro.

TEST KITCHEN TIP

For perfectly sized brownies or bars, lay a clean ruler on top of the bars and make cut marks with the tip of the knife. Use the edge of the ruler as a cutting guide.

CHOCOLATE-PEANUT BUTTER CUP COOKIES

If you want to enjoy one of these soft chocolate chip peanut butter cup cookies the day after you make them, you'd better find a good hiding spot. They disappear fast!
—Jennifer Krey, Clarence, NY

PREP: 25 MIN. • **BAKE:** 10 MIN./BATCH
MAKES: 4 DOZEN

- **1 cup butter, softened**
- **¾ cup creamy peanut butter**
- **1 cup packed brown sugar**
- **½ cup sugar**
- **2 large egg yolks, room temperature**
- **¼ cup 2% milk**
- **2 tsp. vanilla extract**
- **2⅓ cups all-purpose flour**
- **⅓ cup baking cocoa**
- **1 tsp. baking soda**
- **1 cup milk chocolate chips**
- **1 cup peanut butter chips**
- **6 pkg. (1½ oz. each) peanut butter cups, chopped**

1. Preheat oven to 350°. In a large bowl, cream butter, peanut butter and sugars until light and fluffy, 5-7 minutes. Beat in egg yolks, milk and vanilla. Combine flour, cocoa and baking soda; gradually add to creamed mixture and mix well. Stir in the chips and peanut butter cup pieces.
2. Drop heaping tablespoons 2 in. apart onto ungreased baking sheets. Bake until set (do not overbake), 8-10 minutes. Cool for 2 minutes before removing from pans to wire racks. Store the cookies in an airtight container.

1 COOKIE: 170 cal., 10g fat (4g sat. fat), 20mg chol., 100mg sod., 18g carb. (12g sugars, 1g fiber), 3g pro.

M&M OAT BARS

These irresistible bars sweeten any occasion. Switch up the colors of the M&M's to match the season or holiday.
—Renee Schwebach, Dumont, MN

PREP: 20 MIN. • **BAKE:** 10 MIN. + COOLING
MAKES: 6 DOZEN

- **½ cup butter, softened**
- **1 cup packed brown sugar**
- **1 large egg, room temperature**
- **1 tsp. vanilla extract**
- **1¼ cups all-purpose flour**
- **½ tsp. baking soda**
- **½ tsp. salt**
- **2 cups quick-cooking oats**
- **1 pkg. (14 oz.) caramels**
- **3 Tbsp. water**
- **1 cup miniature semisweet chocolate chips**
- **1 cup chopped walnuts**
- **1 cup plain M&M's**
- **3 oz. white candy coating**

1. In a large bowl, cream butter and brown sugar until light and fluffy, 5-7 minutes. Beat in egg and vanilla. Combine the flour, baking soda and salt; add to the creamed mixture and mix well. Stir in oats.
2. Press into a greased 15x10x1-in. baking pan. Bake at 350° until golden brown, 10-15 minutes. Cool on a wire rack.
3. In a microwave, melt caramels with water; stir until smooth. Spread over crust. Sprinkle with the chips, nuts and M&M's. Gently press into the caramel mixture. Melt candy coating; drizzle over the top. Let stand 5 minutes or until set. Cut into bars.

1 BAR: 104 cal., 5g fat (2g sat. fat), 7mg chol., 56mg sod., 15g carb. (11g sugars, 1g fiber), 2g pro.

CRISPY PEANUT BUTTER BALLS

I make more than 40 different types of treats during the holidays for friends and family. These crispy peanut butter balls are one of my favorite candies to give away as gifts.
—Liz David, St. Catharines, ON

PREP: 40 MIN. + CHILLING
MAKES: 6 DOZEN

- **2 cups creamy peanut butter**
- **½ cup butter, softened**
- **3¾ cups confectioners' sugar**
- **3 cups crisp rice cereal**
- **4 cups semisweet chocolate chips**
- **¼ cup plus 1 tsp. shortening, divided**
- **⅓ cup white baking chips**

1. In a large bowl, beat peanut butter and butter until blended; gradually beat in the confectioners' sugar until smooth. Stir in cereal. Shape into 1-in. balls. Refrigerate until chilled.
2. In a microwave, melt chocolate chips and ¼ cup shortening; stir until smooth. Dip balls into chocolate; allow excess to drip off. Place on a waxed paper-lined pan. Let stand until set.
3. In a microwave, melt the white baking chips and remaining shortening. Stir until smooth. Drizzle over candies. Refrigerate until set.

NOTE: Reduced-fat peanut butter is not recommended for this recipe.

1 PIECE: 133 cal., 8g fat (3g sat. fat), 3mg chol., 54mg sod., 14g carb. (12g sugars, 1g fiber), 2g pro.

CHOCOLATE CARAMEL KISS COOKIES

I make this cookie every Christmas with my family. With cinnamon in the batter and a caramel kiss on top, it's a fun twist on the classic peanut butter blossom. We love the cinnamon-caramel combination, but you could switch out the kiss with a different festive flavor.
—Kristen Heigl, Staten Island, NY

PREP: 15 MIN.
BAKE: 10 MIN./BATCH + COOLING
MAKES: ABOUT 2 DOZEN

- **½ cup butter, softened**
- **½ cup packed brown sugar**
- **1 cup sugar, divided**
- **1 large egg plus 1 large egg yolk, room temperature**
- **1½ tsp. vanilla extract**
- **1¼ cups all-purpose flour**
- **¾ cup baking cocoa**
- **1 tsp. baking soda**
- **1 tsp. ground cinnamon**
- **¾ tsp. salt**
- **24 caramel-filled milk chocolate kisses**

1. Preheat oven to 350°. Cream butter, brown sugar and ½ cup sugar until light and fluffy, 5-7 minutes. Beat in the egg, egg yolk and vanilla. In another bowl, whisk the next 5 ingredients; gradually beat into creamed mixture.
2. Shape rounded tablespoons of dough into balls. Roll in remaining sugar. Place 2 in. apart on ungreased baking sheets. Bake 8-10 minutes or until edges begin to brown. Immediately press a chocolate kiss into center of each cookie (cookie will crack around edges). Cool on pans for 2 minutes. Remove to wire racks to cool.

1 COOKIE: 143 cal., 6g fat (3g sat. fat), 27mg chol., 170mg sod., 23g carb. (15g sugars, 1g fiber), 2g pro.

RICH PISTACHIO BRITTLE

Here's a fun twist on traditional brittle. The pistachios add texture and a wonderful taste to the rich, buttery candy.
—Valonda Seward, Coarsegold, CA

PREP: 10 MIN. • **COOK:** 30 MIN. + COOLING
MAKES: ABOUT 1½ LBS.

- **1¼ cups sugar**
- **⅓ cup water**
- **⅓ cup light corn syrup**
- **1 tsp. salt**
- **½ cup butter, cubed**
- **2 cups pistachios, toasted**
- **½ tsp. baking soda**
- **½ tsp. vanilla extract**

1. Butter a 15x10x1-in. pan, set aside. In a large saucepan, combine the sugar, water, corn syrup and salt. Cook over medium heat until a candy thermometer reads 240° (soft-ball stage). Carefully add butter and pistachios; cook and stir until mixture reaches 284° (soft-crack stage).
2. Remove from the heat; stir in baking soda and vanilla. Immediately pour into prepared pan. Spread to ¼-in. thickness. Cool before breaking into pieces. Store in an airtight container.

1 OZ.: 161 cal., 9g fat (3g sat. fat), 11mg chol., 215mg sod., 18g carb. (14g sugars, 1g fiber), 3g pro.

CINNAMON TWIRL COOKIES

These rolled cookies are tasty and fun to make with your family. The sugary mix of walnuts and cinnamon is a light, sweet filling that will leave everyone wanting another bite.
—Phyllis Cappuccio, Boston, MA

PREP: 40 MIN. + CHILLING
BAKE: 20 MIN./BATCH + COOLING
MAKES: 64 COOKIES

- **1 cup margarine, softened**
- **1 cup sour cream**
- **1 large egg yolk, room temperature**
- **2½ cups all-purpose flour**
- **Dash salt**

FILLING

- **1 cup finely chopped walnuts**
- **1 cup sugar**
- **2½ tsp. ground cinnamon**
- **Confectioners' sugar**

1. In a large bowl, beat margarine and sour cream until blended. Add egg yolk; mix well. Combine flour and salt; add to margarine mixture and mix well (dough will be sticky). Cover and refrigerate for 4 hours or overnight.
2. Preheat oven to 350°. Divide dough into eighths. On a well-floured surface, roll each portion into a 10-in. circle. Cut each dough circle into 8 triangles. Combine the walnuts, sugar and cinnamon; sprinkle over each triangle.
3. Roll up triangles from the wide ends and place point side down 1 in. apart on parchment-lined baking sheets. Bake until lightly browned, 20-22 minutes. Remove cookies to wire racks to cool. Dust with confectioners' sugar. Store cookies in an airtight container.

1 COOKIE: 68 cal., 5g fat (1g sat. fat), 4mg chol., 37mg sod., 6g carb. (2g sugars, 0 fiber), 1g pro.

FROSTED CASHEW COOKIES

We savor these cookies every Christmas, but they're special year-round with coffee or tucked into a lunchbox. I won a ribbon with these cookies at my county fair.
—Sheila Wyum, Rutland, ND

PREP: 20 MIN.
BAKE: 10 MIN./BATCH + COOLING
MAKES: ABOUT 3 DOZEN

- **½ cup butter, softened**
- **1 cup packed brown sugar**
- **1 large egg, room temperature**
- **⅓ cup sour cream**
- **½ tsp. vanilla extract**
- **2 cups all-purpose flour**
- **¾ tsp. each baking powder, baking soda and salt**
- **1½ cups salted cashews, coarsely chopped**

BROWNED BUTTER FROSTING

- **½ cup butter, cubed**
- **3 Tbsp. half-and-half cream**
- **¼ tsp. vanilla extract**
- **2 cups confectioners' sugar**
- **Additional cashew halves, optional**

1. In a large bowl, cream the butter and brown sugar. Beat in the egg, sour cream and vanilla; mix well. Combine the flour, baking powder, baking soda and salt; add to creamed mixture and mix well. Stir in chopped cashews.
2. Drop by tablespoonfuls 2 in. apart onto greased baking sheets. Bake at 375° for 8-10 minutes or until lightly browned. Cool on a wire rack.
3. For the frosting, lightly brown butter in a small saucepan. Remove from the heat; add the cream and vanilla. Beat in the confectioners' sugar until thick and smooth. Frost cookies. Top each with a cashew half if desired.

2 EACH: 348 cal., 19g fat (9g sat. fat), 43mg chol., 381mg sod., 40g carb. (26g sugars, 1g fiber), 5g pro.

MAINE POTATO CANDY

Years ago, folks in Maine ate potatoes daily and used leftovers in bread, doughnuts and candy. With only five ingredients, this sweet old-fashioned treat couldn't be easier to make.
—Barbara Allen, Chelmsford, MA

PREP: 30 MIN. + CHILLING
MAKES: 40 SERVINGS

- **4 cups confectioners' sugar**
- **4 cups sweetened shredded coconut**
- **¾ cup cold mashed potatoes (without added milk and butter)**
- **1½ tsp. vanilla extract**
- **½ tsp. salt**
- **1 lb. dark chocolate candy coating, coarsely chopped**

1. In a large bowl, combine the first 5 ingredients. Line a 9-in. square pan with foil; butter the foil. Spread coconut mixture into the pan. Cover and chill overnight. Cut into 2x1-in. rectangles. Cover and freeze.
2. In a microwave, melt candy coating; stir until smooth. Dip bars in coating; allow excess to drip off. Place on waxed paper to set. Store in an airtight container.

1 PIECE: 155 cal., 7g fat (6g sat. fat), 0 chol., 55mg sod., 25g carb. (23g sugars, 1g fiber), 1g pro.

1 FAVORITE
4 WAYS
Brownies
1
2
3
4

1) BROWNIE BRITTLE

I love brownies in all forms. This one is crisp, almost like a cracker. It's great for snacking but is also amazing crumbled on top of a scoop of vanilla ice cream.
—James Schend, Pleasant Prairie, WI

PREP: 25 MIN. • **BAKE:** 20 MIN. + COOLING
MAKES: 1½ DOZEN

- **1 large egg, room temperature**
- **¼ cup canola oil**
- **½ cup sugar**
- **1 Tbsp. water**
- **½ tsp. vanilla extract**
- **⅓ cup all-purpose flour**
- **3 Tbsp. baking cocoa**
- **¼ tsp. salt**
- **¼ tsp. baking powder**
- **1 tsp. instant espresso powder, optional**
- **Optional: Chopped walnuts, pecans, hazelnuts or peanuts**

DRIZZLE

- **¼ cup semisweet chocolate chips**
- **1 tsp. canola oil**

1. Preheat oven to 350°. In a large bowl, beat the eggs, oil, sugar, water and vanilla. Whisk together flour, cocoa, salt, baking powder and, if desired, espresso powder; stir into the egg mixture until blended.
2. Spread into a greased or parchment paper-lined 15x10x1-in. baking pan. Top with chopped nuts if desired. Bake until very firm to the touch, 12-15 minutes. Cool on a wire rack. Break into pieces.
3. In a microwave, melt chocolate chips and oil; stir until smooth. Drizzle over pieces. Let stand until set.

1 PIECE: 78 cal., 4g fat (1g sat. fat), 10mg chol., 44mg sod., 9g carb. (7g sugars, 0 fiber), 1g pro.

TEST KITCHEN TIP

When spreading the batter into the 15x10x1-in. baking pan, spread it in a very thin layer and spread it out as evenly as possible. Use an offset spatula to smooth out any lumps.

2) CHEWY BROWNIES

Corn syrup helps keep these brownies moist and fudgy.
—Sheila Wood, Macksville, KS

PREP: 10 MIN. • **BAKE:** 25 MIN.
MAKES: ABOUT 3 DOZEN

- **2 cups sugar**
- **1½ cups all-purpose flour**
- **⅓ cup baking cocoa**
- **1½ tsp. salt**
- **1 tsp. baking powder**
- **1 cup vegetable oil**
- **4 large eggs, room temperature**
- **2 Tbsp. light corn syrup**
- **1 tsp. vanilla extract**
- **1 cup chopped nuts, optional**
- **Confectioners' sugar, optional**

1. In a bowl, combine sugar, flour, cocoa, salt and baking powder. Combine the oil, eggs, corn syrup and vanilla; add to dry ingredients. Fold in nuts if desired. Spread into a greased 13x9-in. baking pan.
2. Bake at 350° for 25-27 minutes or until a toothpick inserted in the center comes out clean. Dust with confectioners' sugar while warm if desired.

1 BROWNIE: 129 cal., 7g fat (1g sat. fat), 24mg chol., 118mg sod., 16g carb. (11g sugars, 0 fiber), 1g pro.

3) CHOCOLATE FUDGE BROWNIES

My children always looked forward to these after-school snacks. They're so fudgy, they don't need icing.
—Hazel Fritchie, Palestine, IL

PREP: 15 MIN. • **BAKE:** 35 MIN. + COOLING
MAKES: 16 SERVINGS

- **1 cup butter, cubed**
- **6 oz. unsweetened chocolate, chopped**
- **4 large eggs, room temperature**
- **2 cups sugar**
- **1 tsp. vanilla extract**
- **½ tsp. salt**
- **1 cup all-purpose flour**
- **2 cups chopped walnuts**
- **Confectioners' sugar, optional**

1. Preheat the oven to 350°. In a small saucepan, melt butter and chocolate over low heat. Cool slightly.
2. In a large bowl, beat eggs, sugar, vanilla and salt until blended. Stir in chocolate mixture. Add flour, mixing well. Stir in walnuts.
3. Spread into a greased 9-in. square baking pan. Bake 35-40 minutes or until a toothpick inserted in center comes out with moist crumbs (do not overbake).
4. Cool completely in pan on a wire rack. If desired, dust with confectioners' sugar. Cut into bars.

1 BROWNIE: 410 cal., 28g fat (12g sat. fat), 77mg chol., 186mg sod., 36g carb. (26g sugars, 3g fiber), 6g pro.

4) COCOA CAKE BROWNIES

These fudgy brownies are delicious. People say these have a texture somewhere between chewy and cakelike brownies.
—Helen Turner, Upland, IN

TAKES: 30 MIN. • **MAKES:** ABOUT 2½ DOZEN

- **1 cup butter, melted**
- **1 cup sugar**
- **4 large eggs, room temperature**
- **2 tsp. vanilla extract**
- **1 cup all-purpose flour**
- **7 Tbsp. baking cocoa**
- **1 tsp. baking powder**
- **½ tsp. salt**

1. In a large bowl, combine the butter and sugar. Add eggs, 1 at a time, stirring well after each addition. Beat in the vanilla. Combine the flour, cocoa, baking powder and salt; gradually add to butter mixture just until moistened.
2. Transfer to a greased 13x9-in. baking pan. Bake at 350° for 20-25 minutes or until a toothpick inserted in the center comes out clean (do not overbake). Cool on a wire rack.

1 BROWNIE: 109 cal., 7g fat (4g sat. fat), 45mg chol., 123mg sod., 11g carb. (7g sugars, 0 fiber), 2g pro.

Seasonal Specialties

No matter what the season, you'll find so many reasons to celebrate! From summer's fresh bounty to winter's coziest comfort foods, these recipes will turn your gatherings into memorable occasions.

TRIPLE-CHOCOLATE PEPPERMINT TREATS

Santa is sure to stop by your house if you leave these minty chocolate cookies waiting for him. They're quick and easy for the whole family to make together.
—Teresa Ralston, New Albany, OH

PREP: 40 MIN.
BAKE: 10 MIN./BATCH + COOLING
MAKES: ABOUT 6½ DOZEN

- **1 cup butter, softened**
- **1 cup packed brown sugar**
- **½ cup sugar**
- **2 large eggs, room temperature**
- **2 tsp. vanilla extract**
- **2½ cups all-purpose flour**
- **¾ cup baking cocoa**
- **1 tsp. salt**
- **1 tsp. baking soda**
- **1 cup semisweet chocolate chips**
- **½ cup 60% cacao bittersweet chocolate baking chips**

WHITE CHOCOLATE FROSTING

- **½ cup white baking chips**
- **4 oz. cream cheese, softened**
- **3 cups confectioners' sugar**
- **2 to 3 Tbsp. 2% milk**
- **⅓ to ½ cup crushed peppermint candies**

1. Preheat oven to 375°. Cream together butter and sugars until light and fluffy, 5-7 minutes. Beat in eggs and vanilla. In a separate bowl, whisk flour, cocoa, salt and baking soda; gradually beat into the creamed mixture. Stir in semisweet and bittersweet chocolate chips.
2. Drop dough by rounded teaspoonfuls 2 in. apart onto ungreased baking sheets. Bake until set, roughly 8-10 minutes. Cool for 2 minutes before removing to wire racks to cool completely.
3. For frosting, melt white baking chips in a microwave; stir chips until smooth. In another bowl, beat cream cheese and confectioners' sugar until smooth. Beat in melted chips. Add enough milk to reach desired consistency. Frost cookies; sprinkle with peppermint candies.

1 COOKIE: 99 cal., 4g fat (3g sat. fat), 12mg chol., 72mg sod., 15g carb. (11g sugars, 0 fiber), 1g pro.

VALENTINE'S DAY

SONYA LABBE
West Hollywood, CA

SO-EASY COQ AU VIN

Here's my adaptation of the beloved French dish. I substituted boneless skinless chicken breasts for a lighter version with the same taste. It's perfect for a romantic dinner.
—Sonya Labbe, West Hollywood, CA

PREP: 20 MIN. • **COOK:** 5 HOURS
MAKES: 4 SERVINGS

- **3 bacon strips, chopped**
- **4 boneless skinless chicken breast halves (4 oz. each)**
- **½ lb. sliced fresh mushrooms**
- **1 medium onion, chopped**
- **4 garlic cloves, minced**
- **1 bay leaf**
- **⅓ cup all-purpose flour**
- **½ cup red wine**
- **½ cup chicken broth**
- **½ tsp. dried thyme**
- **¼ tsp. pepper**
- **Hot cooked noodles, optional**

1. In large skillet, cook bacon over medium heat until crisp, stirring occasionally. Remove with a slotted spoon; drain on paper towels. Brown chicken on both sides in drippings over medium heat. Transfer chicken to a 3-qt. slow cooker.
2. Add mushrooms, onion and garlic to skillet; cook and stir just until tender, 1-2 minutes. Spoon over chicken; add bay leaf.
3. In a small bowl, whisk the flour, wine, broth, thyme and pepper until smooth; pour over chicken.
4. Cover; cook on low until chicken is tender, 5-6 hours. Discard bay leaf. If desired, serve with noodles. Top with bacon.

1 CHICKEN BREAST HALF WITH ½ CUP MUSHROOM SAUCE: 299 cal., 11g fat (3g sat. fat), 75mg chol., 324mg sod., 16g carb. (4g sugars, 2g fiber), 28g pro. **DIABETIC EXCHANGES:** 3 lean meat, 1½ fat, 1 vegetable, ½ starch.

CHEDDAR MASHED CAULIFLOWER

Want an alternative to mashed potatoes? Try cauliflower jazzed up with cheddar cheese and rosemary.
—Chrystal Baker, Studio City, CA

TAKES: 15 MIN. • **MAKES:** 6 SERVINGS

- **2 medium heads cauliflower, broken into florets**
- **⅓ cup 2% milk**
- **1 Tbsp. minced fresh rosemary**
- **½ tsp. salt**
- **1 cup shredded sharp cheddar cheese**
- **Coarsely ground black pepper, optional**

In a Dutch oven, bring 1 in. of water to a boil. Add cauliflower; cover and cook until tender, 5-10 minutes. Drain. Mash the cauliflower with the milk, rosemary and salt. Stir in cheese until melted. If desired, top with additional fresh rosemary and coarsely ground black pepper.

¾ CUP: 122 cal., 6g fat (4g sat. fat), 21mg chol., 374mg sod., 12g carb. (5g sugars, 5g fiber), 8g pro.

STRAWBERRY JAM CAKE

When I'm tasked with baking a cake, this is my go-to recipe because everyone is crazy about it. Every year I make it for a charity raffle we have at work for Relay for Life. No matter the occasion, it's a great way to show some love.
—Tammy Urbina, Warner Robins, GA

PREP: 35 MIN. • **BAKE:** 25 MIN. + COOLING
MAKES: 12 SERVINGS

1 cup butter, softened
1¾ cups sugar
5 large egg whites, room temperature
2 cups pureed strawberries
½ cup sour cream
1 tsp. strawberry extract, optional
3 cups cake flour
2½ tsp. baking powder
¼ tsp. baking soda
¼ tsp. salt

FROSTING

1 pkg. (8 oz.) cream cheese, softened
¼ cup butter, softened
6 cups confectioners' sugar
¼ cup pureed strawberries
½ tsp. strawberry extract, optional
1 to 3 drops red food coloring, optional
½ cup seedless strawberry jam, divided
Halved or sliced fresh strawberries, optional

1. Grease and flour three 9-in. round baking pans.
2. In a large bowl, cream butter and sugar until light and fluffy, 5-7 minutes. Add egg whites, 1 at a time, beating well after each addition. Beat in the strawberries, sour cream and, if desired, extract. Combine the flour, baking powder, baking soda and salt; add to the creamed mixture. Transfer batter to prepared pans.
3. Bake at 350° until a toothpick inserted in the center of the cake comes out clean, 22-26 minutes. Cool for 10 minutes before removing from pans to wire racks to cool completely.
4. For frosting, in a large bowl, beat the cream cheese and butter until fluffy. Add the confectioners' sugar, strawberries and, if desired, the extract and red food coloring; beat until smooth.
5. Place bottom cake layer on a serving plate; top with ¼ cup jam and ½ cup frosting. Repeat layers. Top with the remaining cake layer. Spread remaining frosting over the top and sides of cake. Garnish with strawberries if desired.

1 PIECE: 783 cal., 28g fat (17g sat. fat), 72mg chol., 416mg sod., 130g carb. (99g sugars, 1g fiber), 6g pro.

CHOCOLATE PECAN FONDUE

Try this chocolate fondue on Valentine's Day. Our favorite dippers include fruit, cookies, marshmallows and pound cake.
—Suzanne McKinley, Lyons, GA

TAKES: 15 MIN. • **MAKES:** 1⅓ CUPS

½ cup half-and-half cream
2 Tbsp. honey
9 oz. semisweet chocolate, broken into small pieces
¼ cup finely chopped pecans
1 tsp. vanilla extract
Fresh fruit and shortbread cookies

1. In a heavy saucepan over low heat, combine cream and honey; heat until warm. Add chocolate; stir until melted. Stir in pecans and vanilla.
2. Transfer to a fondue pot or a 1½-qt. slow cooker and keep warm. Serve with fruit and cookies.

2 TBSP.: 178 cal., 12g fat (6g sat. fat), 6mg chol., 6mg sod., 19g carb. (17g sugars, 2g fiber), 3g pro.

MARDI GRAS

SPRINGTIME BEIGNETS & BERRIES

I've always loved beignets but never thought I could make them myself. Turns out they're easy! Sometimes I'll even make a quick berry whipped cream and pipe it inside for a fun surprise.
—Kathi Hemmer, Grand Junction, CO

PREP: 25 MIN. + CHILLING • **COOK:** 25 MIN.
MAKES: 4 DOZEN

- **¼ cup butter, room temperature**
- **¾ cup sugar**
- **½ tsp. salt**
- **½ tsp. ground cinnamon**
- **½ cup plus 2 Tbsp. warm water (120° to 130°), divided**
- **½ cup evaporated milk**
- **1 pkg. (¼ oz.) quick-rise yeast**
- **1 large egg**
- **3¼ to 3¾ cups all-purpose flour**
- **Oil for deep-fat frying**
- **Confectioners' sugar**
- **Berries and whipped topping, optional**

1. Beat butter, sugar, salt and cinnamon until crumbly. Beat in ½ cup water and evaporated milk. In another bowl, dissolve yeast in remaining 2 Tbsp. water; add to milk mixture. Beat in egg until blended.
2. Add 2 cups flour; mix until well blended. Stir in enough remaining flour to form a soft dough (dough will be sticky). Place in a greased bowl, turning once to grease the top. Cover and refrigerate 4 hours or overnight.
3. Bring dough to room temperature. On a floured surface, roll dough into a 16x12-in. rectangle. Cut into 2-in. squares. In a deep cast-iron skillet or deep- fat fryer, heat oil to 375°. Drop beignets, a few at a time, into hot oil. Fry until golden brown, about 1 minute per side. Drain on paper towels. Dust beignets with confectioners' sugar. If desired, serve with assorted berries and whipped topping.

1 BEIGNET: 74 cal., 3g fat (1g sat. fat), 7mg chol., 36mg sod., 10g carb. (3g sugars, trace fiber), 1g pro.

PASSION FRUIT HURRICANES

Our version of the famous New Orleans beverage uses real fruit juice. They're aptly named because each sip packs a punch!
—*Taste of Home* Test Kitchen

TAKES: 10 MIN. • **MAKES:** 6 SERVINGS

- **2 cups passion fruit juice**
- **1 cup plus 2 Tbsp. sugar**
- **¾ cup lime juice**
- **¾ cup light rum**
- **¾ cup dark rum**
- **3 Tbsp. grenadine syrup**
- **6 to 8 cups ice cubes**
- **Orange slices, starfruit slices and maraschino cherries**

1. In a pitcher, combine the fruit juice, sugar, lime juice, rum and grenadine; stir until sugar is dissolved.
2. Pour into hurricane or highball glasses filled with ice. Serve with orange slices, starfruit slices and cherries.

¾ CUP: 340 cal., 0 fat (0 sat. fat), 0 chol., 7mg sod., 55g carb. (50g sugars, 0 fiber), 0 pro.

ONE-POT RED BEANS & RICE

This is a one-pot meal that's ready in about 30 minutes. It's one of my husband's favorites and uses simple ingredients, so it's been a go-to recipe in our house for years.
—Janice Conklin, Stevensville, MT

TAKES: 30 MIN. • **MAKES:** 6 SERVINGS

- **1 Tbsp. olive oil**
- **2 celery ribs, sliced**
- **1 medium onion, chopped**
- **1 medium green pepper, chopped**
- **1 pkg. (14 oz.) smoked turkey sausage, sliced**
- **1 carton (32 oz.) reduced-sodium chicken broth**
- **1 can (16 oz.) kidney beans, rinsed and drained**
- **1¼ cups uncooked converted rice**
- **⅓ cup tomato paste**
- **1 bay leaf**
- **1½ tsp. Cajun seasoning**
- **¼ tsp. cayenne pepper**
- **Hot pepper sauce, optional**

1. In a Dutch oven, heat oil over medium-high heat. Add celery, onion and green pepper; cook and stir until crisp-tender, 3-4 minutes. Add sausage; cook until browned, 2-3 minutes.
2. Stir in broth, beans, rice, tomato paste, bay leaf, Cajun seasoning and cayenne pepper. Bring to a boil; reduce the heat. Simmer, uncovered, until rice is tender and liquid is absorbed, 15-20 minutes, stirring occasionally. Discard bay leaf. If desired, serve with pepper sauce.

1⅓ CUPS: 347 cal., 6g fat (2g sat. fat), 41mg chol., 1272mg sod., 50g carb. (6g sugars, 5g fiber), 22g pro.

AIR-FRYER SHRIMP PO'BOYS

My husband loves crispy coconut shrimp and po'boys, so I combined them with a spicy remoulade and voila! This air-fryer shrimp is a big hit with family and friends and is frequently requested. For catfish po'boys, substitute cornmeal for the coconut and add a few minutes to the cooking time.
—Marla Clark, Albuquerque, NM

PREP: 35 MIN. • **COOK:** 10 MIN./BATCH
MAKES: 4 SERVINGS

- **½ cup mayonnaise**
- **1 Tbsp. Creole mustard**
- **1 Tbsp. chopped cornichons or dill pickles**
- **1 Tbsp. minced shallot**
- **1½ tsp. lemon juice**
- **⅛ tsp. cayenne pepper**

COCONUT SHRIMP

- **1 cup all-purpose flour**
- **1 tsp. herbes de Provence**
- **½ tsp. sea salt**
- **½ tsp. garlic powder**
- **½ tsp. pepper**
- **¼ tsp. cayenne pepper**
- **1 large egg**
- **½ cup 2% milk**
- **1 tsp. hot pepper sauce**
- **2 cups sweetened shredded coconut**
- **1 lb. uncooked shrimp (26-30 per lb.), peeled and deveined**
- **Cooking spray**
- **4 hoagie buns, split**
- **2 cups shredded lettuce**
- **1 medium tomato, thinly sliced**

1. For remoulade, in a bowl, combine the first 6 ingredients. Refrigerate, covered, until serving.
2. Preheat air fryer to 375°. In a shallow bowl, mix flour, herbes de Provence, sea salt, garlic powder, pepper and cayenne. In a separate shallow bowl, whisk egg, milk and hot pepper sauce. Place coconut in a third shallow bowl. Dip shrimp in flour to coat both sides; shake off excess. Dip in egg mixture, then in coconut, patting to help adhere.
3. In batches, arrange shrimp in a single layer on greased tray in air-fryer basket; spritz with cooking spray. Cook until coconut is lightly browned and shrimp turn pink, 3-4 minutes on each side.
4. Spread the cut side of hoagie buns with remoulade. Top with shrimp, lettuce and tomato.

1 SANDWICH: 716 cal., 40g fat (16g sat. fat), 173mg chol., 944mg sod., 60g carb. (23g sugars, 4g fiber), 31g pro.

ST. PATRICK'S DAY

GLAZED CORNED BEEF

Our family is Dutch, not Irish, but that doesn't stop me from serving this delicious entree on St. Patrick's Day. The tender meat is topped with a simple, tangy glaze that is so tasty. Leftovers make excellent Reuben sandwiches.
—Perlene Hoekema, Lynden, WA

PREP: 3 HOURS • **BAKE:** 25 MIN. + STANDING
MAKES: 8 SERVINGS

- **1 corned beef brisket with spice packet (3 to 4 lbs.), trimmed**
- **1 medium onion, sliced**
- **1 celery rib, sliced**
- **¼ cup butter, cubed**
- **1 cup packed brown sugar**
- **⅔ cup ketchup**
- **⅓ cup white vinegar**
- **2 Tbsp. prepared mustard**
- **2 tsp. prepared horseradish**

1. Place corned beef and contents of seasoning packet in a Dutch oven; cover with water. Add onion and celery; bring to a boil. Reduce heat; cover and simmer for 2½ hours or until meat is tender.
2. Drain and discard liquid and vegetables. Place beef on a greased rack in a shallow roasting pan.
3. In a small saucepan, melt butter over medium heat. Stir in the remaining ingredients. Cook and stir until sugar is dissolved. Brush over beef.
4. Bake, uncovered, at 350° for roughly 25 minutes. Let stand for 10 minutes before slicing.

3 OZ. COOKED BEEF: 484 cal., 29g fat (11g sat. fat), 132mg chol., 1708mg sod., 35g carb. (33g sugars, 1g fiber), 22g pro.

EASY IRISH CREAM

Stir up this fast and easy recipe for a party or potluck. There's plenty of coffee flavor in every cozy cup.
—Anna Hansen, Park City, UT

TAKES: 15 MIN. • **MAKES:** 5 CUPS

- **2 cups half-and-half cream**
- **1 can (13.4 oz.) dulce de leche or sweetened condensed milk**
- **1¼ cups Irish whiskey**
- **¼ cup chocolate syrup**
- **2 Tbsp. instant coffee granules**
- **2 tsp. vanilla extract**
- **Hot brewed coffee or ice cubes**

Pulse first 6 ingredients in a blender until smooth. Stir 1-2 Tbsp. into a mug of hot coffee, or pour coffee and cream over ice.

½ CUP: 415 cal., 21g fat (13g sat. fat), 79mg chol., 116mg sod., 35g carb. (34g sugars, 0 fiber), 4g pro.

COLCANNON IRISH POTATOES

My mother came from Ireland as a teen and brought this homey recipe with her. It's a fantastic way to get my family to eat cooked cabbage—it's hidden in Grandma's potatoes!
—Marie Pagel, Lena, WI

TAKES: 30 MIN. • **MAKES:** 10 SERVINGS

- **2½ lbs. potatoes (about 6 medium), peeled and cut into 1-in. pieces**
- **2 cups chopped cabbage**
- **1 large onion, chopped**
- **1 tsp. salt**
- **¼ tsp. pepper**
- **¼ cup butter, softened**
- **1 cup 2% milk**

1. Place potatoes in a 6-qt. stockpot; add water to cover. Bring to a boil. Reduce heat to medium; cook, covered, until potatoes are almost tender, 8-10 minutes.
2. Add cabbage and onion; cook, covered, until the cabbage is tender, 5-7 minutes. Drain; return to pot. Add salt and pepper; mash to desired consistency, gradually adding butter and milk.

¾ CUP: 129 cal., 5g fat (3g sat. fat), 14mg chol., 290mg sod., 19g carb. (4g sugars, 2g fiber), 3g pro. **DIABETIC EXCHANGES:** 1 starch, 1 fat.

ST. PATRICK'S DAY CUPCAKES

These stir-and-bake cupcakes come together quickly. Pistachio pudding mix gives them a mild flavor and pretty pastel color that makes them perfect for St. Patrick's Day.
—Kathy Meyer, Almond, WI

PREP: 15 MIN. • **BAKE:** 20 MIN. + COOLING
MAKES: 1 DOZEN

- **1¾ cups all-purpose flour**
- **⅔ cup sugar**
- **1 pkg. (3.4 oz.) instant pistachio pudding mix**
- **2 tsp. baking powder**
- **½ tsp. salt**
- **2 large eggs, room temperature**
- **1¼ cups 2% milk**
- **½ cup canola oil**
- **1 tsp. vanilla extract**
- **1 can (16 oz.) cream cheese frosting**
- **Green food coloring and gold sprinkles, optional**

1. Preheat oven to 375°. In a large bowl, whisk flour, sugar, pudding mix, baking powder and salt. In a small bowl, beat the eggs, milk, oil and vanilla; add to dry ingredients and mix until blended.
2. Fill paper-lined muffin cups three-fourths full. Bake at 375° until a toothpick inserted in the center comes out clean, 18-22 minutes. Cool for 10 minutes before removing from pan to a wire rack to cool completely. Add food coloring to frosting if desired; frost cupcakes and decorate with sprinkles.

1 CUPCAKE: 410 cal., 17g fat (4g sat. fat), 33mg chol., 398mg sod., 59g carb. (40g sugars, 0 fiber), 4g pro.

RAINBOW FRUIT SALAD

When my children were young, I would often dress up fresh fruit in this easy-to-fix salad. Years later, my grandkids and great-grandkids love digging into the fruity layers. It goes well with barbecued meats or cold sandwiches.
—Jonnie Adams Sisler, Stevensville, MT

PREP: 20 MIN. + CHILLING
MAKES: 20 SERVINGS

- **2 large firm bananas, sliced**
- **2 Tbsp. lemon juice**
- **2 cups seeded cubed watermelon**
- **2 cups fresh or canned pineapple chunks**
- **1 pint fresh blueberries**
- **3 kiwifruit, peeled and sliced**
- **1 pint fresh strawberries, halved**
- **6 oz. cream cheese, softened**
- **⅓ cup confectioners' sugar**
- **2 Tbsp. fresh lime juice**
- **½ tsp. grated lime zest**
- **1 cup heavy whipping cream, whipped**

1. Toss bananas in lemon juice; place in a 4-qt. glass serving bowl. Add remaining fruit in layers.
2. In a bowl, beat the cream cheese until smooth. Gradually add sugar, lime juice and lime zest. Stir in a small amount of whipped cream; mix well. Fold in the remaining whipped cream. Spread over fruit. Chill until serving.

¾ CUP: 123 cal., 7g fat (5g sat. fat), 22mg chol., 31mg sod., 14g carb. (10g sugars, 2g fiber), 1g pro.

TEST KITCHEN TIP

It's best to store fruit salad in an airtight container in the refrigerator. The containers create the perfect level of moisture and humidity for cut fruit, helping the pieces stay fresher for longer. Or store individual fruit portions in reusable silicone bags for an easy grab-and-go snack.

EASTER

SPRINGTIME PENNE

With ham and asparagus in a creamy sauce, this simple pasta is tasty enough for even your pickiest guests. It's wonderful for Easter and is a good way to use up leftover ham.
—Cheryl Newendorp, Pella, IA

TAKES: 20 MIN. • **MAKES:** 5 SERVINGS

- **3 cups uncooked penne pasta**
- **1 lb. fresh asparagus, cut into 1-in. pieces**
- **1 large onion, chopped**
- **¼ cup butter**
- **½ lb. cubed fully cooked ham**
- **½ cup heavy whipping cream**
- **¼ tsp. pepper**
- **⅛ tsp. salt**
- **Shredded Parmesan cheese, optional**

1. Cook pasta according to package directions. Meanwhile, in a large skillet, saute asparagus and onion in butter for 5-8 minutes or until the asparagus is crisp-tender.
2. Add the ham, cream, pepper and salt; bring to a boil. Reduce heat; cook over low heat for 1 minute. Drain pasta. Add to the asparagus mixture; toss to coat. If desired, top with shredded Parmesan cheese.

HEALTH TIP: Although this pasta dish tastes light and fresh, it does contain butter and cream. Use just 2 Tbsp. of butter and half-and-half in place of heavy whipping cream to slim this dish down to just under 300 calories for each serving.

1½ CUPS: 389 cal., 21g fat (12g sat. fat), 75mg chol., 617mg sod., 37g carb. (4g sugars, 3g fiber), 16g pro.

SMOKED SALMON & DILL DEVILED EGGS

Take this perennial party food and give it an upscale twist with smoked salmon. Your guests will be delighted with the results.
—Jan Valdez, Chicago, IL

TAKES: 25 MIN. • **MAKES:** 16 APPETIZERS

- **8 hard-boiled large eggs**
- **1 pkg. (3 oz.) smoked salmon or lox, finely chopped**
- **6 Tbsp. sour cream**
- **1 Tbsp. chopped fresh dill or 1 tsp. dill weed**
- **1 tsp. cider vinegar**
- **1 tsp. Dijon mustard**
- **¼ tsp. cayenne pepper**

1. Cut eggs lengthwise in half. Remove yolks; set whites aside.
2. In a small bowl, mash yolks. Add the remaining ingredients; mix well. Spoon into egg whites. Refrigerate until serving.

1 STUFFED EGG HALF: 57 cal., 4g fat (2g sat. fat), 111mg chol., 147mg sod., 1g carb. (0 sugars, 0 fiber), 4g pro.

CAESAR SALAD

This crunchy, refreshing Caesar salad has a zippy, zesty dressing that provides a burst of flavor with each bite. It's a salad that will perk up any spring or summer meal.
—Schelby Thompson, Camden Wyoming, DE

TAKES: 10 MIN. • **MAKES:** 6 SERVINGS

- **1 large bunch romaine, torn**
- **¾ cup olive oil**
- **3 Tbsp. red wine vinegar**
- **1 tsp. Worcestershire sauce**
- **½ tsp. salt**
- **¼ tsp. ground mustard**
- **1 large garlic clove, minced**
- **½ fresh lemon**
- **Dash pepper**
- **¼ to ½ cup shredded Parmesan cheese**
- **Caesar-flavored or garlic croutons**

1. Place lettuce in a large salad bowl. Combine the next 6 ingredients in a blender; process until smooth. Pour over lettuce and toss to coat.
2. Squeeze lemon juice over lettuce. Sprinkle with pepper, cheese and croutons.

1 CUP: 265 cal., 28g fat (4g sat. fat), 2mg chol., 268mg sod., 3g carb. (1g sugars, 1g fiber), 2g pro.

EASTER NEST TORTE

In this delectable dessert, a luscious cake layer nestles rich mousse and chocolate twigs. Your guests won't be able to get enough of this unique Easter treat.
—*Taste of Home* Test Kitchen

PREP: 1 HOUR + CHILLING
BAKE: 15 MIN. + COOLING
MAKES: 16 SERVINGS

- **½ cup butter, softened**
- **½ cup sugar**
- **2 large eggs, room temperature**
- **½ cup all-purpose flour**
- **⅓ cup baking cocoa**
- **1 tsp. baking powder**
- **¼ tsp. salt**
- **8 oz. semisweet chocolate, melted**

FILLING

- **¼ cup sugar**
- **1 tsp. cornstarch**
- **1¼ cups 2% milk**
- **3 large egg yolks, lightly beaten**
- **1 envelope unflavored gelatin**
- **3 Tbsp. cold water**
- **7 oz. semisweet chocolate, chopped**
- **1¼ cups heavy whipping cream**
- **20 to 30 small candy Easter eggs**

1. In a large bowl, cream butter and sugar until light and fluffy, 5-7 minutes. Add eggs, 1 at a time, beating well after each addition. Combine the flour, cocoa, baking powder and salt; gradually add to creamed mixture and mix well.
2. Spread into a greased 9-in. springform pan. Bake at 350° for 15-20 minutes or until a toothpick inserted in the center comes out clean. Cool for 10 minutes. Carefully run a knife around edge of pan to loosen. Remove sides and bottom of pan. Cool completely on a wire rack.
3. From a large sheet of waxed paper, cut a 29x5-in. strip. Fold strip lengthwise in half. Place strip on a large sheet of waxed paper on a work surface. Spread melted chocolate evenly along 1 long edge of waxed paper strip; spread upward, making a wavy line to within ½ in. of other long edge. Let stand for 10-30 minutes until chocolate begins to set but is still pliable.
4. Carefully lift waxed paper strip and wrap chocolate strip around cake with straight edge on the bottom. Do not remove waxed paper. Refrigerate until chilled. Meanwhile, cover 3 baking sheets with waxed paper. Drizzle remaining melted chocolate from a spatula over waxed paper in both directions. Chill for 10 minutes. Peel off waxed paper; break the chocolate into 2- to 3-in. twigs.
5. For filling, in a small saucepan, combine the sugar and cornstarch. Stir in milk until smooth. Cook and stir over medium-high heat until slightly thickened and bubbly. Reduce heat; cook and stir 2 minutes longer. Remove from the heat. Stir a small amount of hot filling into egg yolks; return all to the pan, stirring constantly. Bring to a gentle boil; cook and stir 2 minutes longer. Remove from the heat.
6. In a small bowl, sprinkle gelatin over water; let stand for 1 minute. Stir into custard until gelatin is dissolved. Add chopped chocolate; stir until smooth. Cover surface with plastic wrap; cool to room temperature.
7. In a large bowl, beat cream until soft peaks form; fold into chocolate mixture. Carefully spoon over top of cake. Cover and refrigerate for 1-2 hours or until set. Remove waxed paper strip from side of cake. Position chocolate twigs around top of cake to create a nest. Arrange candy eggs in center.

1 PIECE: 385 cal., 24g fat (14g sat. fat), 96mg chol., 142mg sod., 28g carb. (20g sugars, 1g fiber), 6g pro.

EASTER SUGAR COOKIES

Cream cheese contributes to the rich taste of these melt-in-your-mouth cookies. They have such nice flavor, you can skip the frosting and sprinkle them with colored sugar for a change of pace.
—Julie Brunette, Green Bay, WI

PREP: 15 MIN. + CHILLING
BAKE: 10 MIN./BATCH
MAKES: 4 DOZEN

- **1 cup butter, softened**
- **3 oz. cream cheese, softened**
- **1 cup sugar**
- **1 large egg yolk, room temperature**
- **½ tsp. vanilla extract**
- **¼ tsp. almond extract**
- **2¼ cups all-purpose flour**
- **½ tsp. salt**
- **¼ tsp. baking soda**
- **Tinted frosting or colored sugar**

1. In a bowl, cream butter, cream cheese and sugar. Beat in egg yolk and extracts. Combine the flour, salt and baking soda; gradually add to creamed mixture. Cover and refrigerate for 3 hours or until easy to handle.
2. Preheat oven to 375°. On a lightly floured surface, roll out dough to ⅛-in. thickness. Cut with a 2½-in. cookie cutter dipped in flour. Place 1 in. apart on ungreased baking sheets. Bake until edges begin to brown, 8-10 minutes. Cool for 2 minutes before removing from pans to wire racks. Decorate as desired.

1 COOKIE: 79 cal., 5g fat (3g sat. fat), 16mg chol., 67mg sod., 9g carb. (4g sugars, 0 fiber), 1g pro.

CINCO DE MAYO

CONTEST-WINNING GRILLED CORN SALSA

Nothing beats the flavor of grilled vegetables, and this is a super way to use your garden bounty. I grill the veggies anytime I'm grilling something else, then whip up the salad and put it in the fridge to marinate. It's even better the next day.

—Teri Kman, Laporte, CO

PREP: 30 MIN.
GRILL: 10 MIN. PER BATCH + CHILLING
MAKES: 7½ CUPS

- **8 medium ears sweet corn, husks removed**
- **2 small yellow summer squash, cut into ½-in. slices**
- **1 medium sweet red pepper, cut into 4 wedges**
- **1 medium red onion, cut into ½-in. rings**
- **1 medium tomato, seeded and chopped**

BASIL VINAIGRETTE

- **½ cup olive oil**
- **⅓ cup white balsamic or cider vinegar**
- **12 fresh basil leaves, chopped**
- **1 tsp. salt**
- **1 tsp. garlic powder**
- **1 tsp. dried oregano**

1. Fill a Dutch-oven two-thirds full with water; bring to a boil. Add corn. Reduce heat; cover and simmer until crisp-tender, 5 minutes. Remove corn; cool slightly.
2. On a lightly oiled grill rack, grill the corn, squash, red pepper and onion, covered, over medium heat until lightly browned, turning occasionally, roughly 8-10 minutes.
3. Cut corn from cobs; cut the squash, red pepper and onion into bite-size pieces. Place grilled vegetables in a large bowl; add tomato.
4. In a small bowl, whisk the vinaigrette ingredients. Pour over vegetables; toss to coat. Cover and refrigerate until chilled. Serve with a slotted spoon.

¼ CUP: 60 cal., 4g fat (1g sat. fat), 0 chol., 84mg sod., 6g carb. (2g sugars, 1g fiber), 1g pro. **DIABETIC EXCHANGES:** ½ starch, ½ fat.

GRILLED PORK TACOS

My family raves about this moist pork with smoked paprika and pineapple. I dish up the tacos next to brown rice and a fresh salad of avocado and tomatoes.

—E. Gelesky, Bala Cynwyd, PA

TAKES: 30 MIN. • **MAKES:** 4 SERVINGS

- **1 lb. boneless pork ribeye chops, cut into ¾-in. cubes**
- **2 Tbsp. plus 2 tsp. lime juice, divided**
- **1 tsp. smoked or regular paprika**
- **½ tsp. salt**
- **¼ tsp. pepper**
- **¾ cup canned black beans, rinsed and drained**
- **½ cup canned unsweetened pineapple tidbits plus 1 Tbsp. reserved juice**
- **2 Tbsp. finely chopped red onion**
- **2 Tbsp. chopped fresh cilantro**
- **4 flour tortillas (6 to 8 in.), warmed**
- **Reduced-fat sour cream or plain yogurt, optional**

1. In a large bowl, toss pork with 2 Tbsp. lime juice and seasonings; let stand 5 minutes. Meanwhile, in a small bowl, mix beans, pineapple with reserved juice, onion, cilantro and remaining lime juice.
2. Thread pork onto 4 metal or soaked wooden skewers. Moisten a paper towel with cooking oil; using long-handled tongs, rub on the grill rack to coat lightly. Grill the kabobs, covered, over medium heat for 6-8 minutes or until tender, turning occasionally.
3. Remove pork from skewers; serve in tortillas. Top with bean mixture and, if desired, sour cream.

1 TACO WITH ¼ CUP SALSA: 383 cal., 16g fat (6g sat. fat), 66mg chol., 636mg sod., 31g carb. (6g sugars, 4g fiber), 27g pro. **DIABETIC EXCHANGES:** 3 starch, 3 medium-fat meat.

READER REVIEW

"Nice change from traditional tacos, and even better because they were grilled. Will be making again."

JUSTMBETH, TASTEOFHOME.COM

MEXICAN TEA COOKIES

Mexican tea cookies are a holiday favorite in our family. I updated the recipe by frosting them with a buttercream made with dulce de leche. They are a tender, crumbly cookie that everyone enjoys.
—David Ross, Spokane Valley, WA

PREP: 45 MIN. + CHILLING
BAKE: 10 MIN./BATCH + COOLING
MAKES: 3 DOZEN

- **1 cup butter, softened**
- **½ cup confectioners' sugar**
- **½ cup sugar**
- **1 large egg, room temperature**
- **1 tsp. vanilla extract**
- **3¼ cups all-purpose flour**
- **¾ cup finely chopped pecans**
- **1 tsp. baking powder**
- **¼ tsp. salt**
- **¼ tsp. ground cinnamon**

BUTTERCREAM

- **½ cup butter, softened**
- **1 Tbsp. heavy whipping cream**
- **1 tsp. vanilla extract**
- **2 cups confectioners' sugar**
- **½ cup dulce de leche**
- **2 Tbsp. ground pecans**

1. In a large bowl, cream the butter and sugars until light and fluffy, 5-7 minutes. Beat in egg and vanilla. In another bowl, whisk flour, pecans, baking powder, salt and cinnamon; gradually beat into creamed mixture; dough will be soft. Form dough into a disk; wrap and refrigerate 1 hour or until chilled.
2. Preheat oven to 350°. On a floured surface, roll dough to ¼-in. thickness. Cut with a floured 2-in. round cookie cutter; re-roll dough scraps as needed. Place 2 in. apart on parchment-lined baking sheets. Bake until until edges begin to lightly brown, 10-12 minutes. Remove from pans to wire racks to cool completely.
3. For buttercream, in a large bowl, beat butter, cream and vanilla until creamy. Beat in confectioners' sugar alternately with dulce de leche until smooth. Sprinkle cookies with additional confectioners' sugar. Pipe buttercream onto cookies; sprinkle with pecans. Store, covered, in refrigerator.

NOTE: This recipe was tested with Nestle La Lechera dulce de leche; look for it in the international foods section. If using Eagle Brand dulce de leche (caramel flavored sauce), thicken according to package directions before using.

1 COOKIE: 188 cal., 10g fat (5g sat. fat), 27mg chol., 101mg sod., 23g carb. (13g sugars, 1g fiber), 2g pro.

CHIPOTLE GUACAMOLE

My guacamole is so good because it has just a hint of smoke from the chipotle pepper. Stir in the chopped pepper or put a dollop in the center of the dip so people who aren't into the pepper can scoop around it.
—Gayle Sullivan, Salem, MA

PREP: 15 MIN. + CHILLING • **MAKES:** 3 CUPS

- **4 medium ripe avocados, peeled and pitted**
- **1 small tomato, seeded and chopped**
- **⅓ cup finely chopped red onion**
- **3 garlic cloves, minced**
- **2 Tbsp. lemon juice**
- **2 Tbsp. olive oil**
- **¼ tsp. salt**
- **1 to 2 Tbsp. minced fresh cilantro, optional**
- **1 finely chopped chipotle pepper in adobo sauce plus 1 tsp. adobo sauce**
- **Tortilla chips**

Mash avocados. Stir in next 6 ingredients and, if desired, cilantro. Dollop chipotle pepper and adobo sauce over center of guacamole. Refrigerate 1 hour. Serve with chips.

¼ CUP: 103 cal., 9g fat (1g sat. fat), 0 chol., 70mg sod., 5g carb. (1g sugars, 3g fiber), 1g pro.

MICHELADA

Like your drinks with a south-of-the-border vibe? Try this kicked-up beer cocktail that's a zesty mix of Mexican lager, lime juice and hot sauce. There are many variations, but this easy recipe is perfect for rookie mixologists.
—Ian Cliffe, Milwaukee, WI

TAKES: 5 MIN. • **MAKES:** 2 SERVINGS

- **Coarse salt**
- **Lime wedges**
- **Ice cubes**
- **6 dashes hot sauce, such as Valentina or Tabasco**
- **3 dashes Maggi seasoning or soy sauce**
- **1 to 3 dashes Worcestershire sauce**
- **¼ to ⅓ cup lime juice**
- **1 bottle (12 oz.) beer, such as Corona, Modelo or Tecate**

Place coarse salt in a shallow dish; run a lime wedge around rims of 2 cocktail glasses. Dip rims of glasses into salt, shaking off excess. Fill each glass with ice. In a small pitcher, combine hot sauce, Maggi seasoning, Worcestershire sauce and lime juice. Add beer. Pour into glasses over ice. Garnish with lime wedges. Serve immediately.

1 DRINK: 165 cal., 0 fat (0 sat. fat), 0 chol., 137mg sod., 17g carb. (12g sugars, 0 fiber), 1g pro.

MOTHER'S DAY

FRUITY CHICKEN SALAD MINI SANDWICHES

Chicken salad ranks among the classics, and this version is great for parties of all kinds. Feel free to substitute green grapes for the red, or toss in extra strawberries when they're in season. The filling can also be served on a bed of salad greens.

—Marcy Kamery, Blasdell, NY

TAKES: 25 MIN. • **MAKES:** 12 SERVINGS

- **6 cups chopped cooked chicken**
- **¾ cup sliced fresh strawberries**
- **½ cup halved seedless red grapes**
- **2 celery ribs, finely chopped**
- **⅓ cup chopped pecans, toasted**
- **¾ cup sour cream**
- **¾ cup mayonnaise**
- **⅓ cup chopped fresh basil**
- **2 tsp. lemon juice**
- **¾ tsp. salt**
- **¼ tsp. garlic powder**
- **¼ tsp. pepper**
- **24 potato dinner rolls or Hawaiian sweet rolls, split**

1. Place first 5 ingredients in a large bowl. In a small bowl, mix the sour cream, mayonnaise, basil, lemon juice and seasonings; stir into chicken mixture. Refrigerate, covered, until serving.
2. To serve, fill each roll with ⅓ cup chicken mixture.

NOTE: To toast nuts, bake in a shallow pan in a 350° oven for 5-10 minutes or cook in a skillet over low heat until lightly browned, stirring occasionally.

2 SANDWICHES: 524 cal., 23g fat (5g sat. fat), 67mg chol., 669mg sod., 49g carb. (8g sugars, 3g fiber), 29g pro.

MACARONI SALAD

When it's finally warm enough to grill, my mother asks me to make the family macaroni salad. To make it extra creamy, I keep a small amount of dressing separate and stir it in just before serving.

—Carly Curtin, Ellicott City, MD

PREP: 20 MIN. + CHILLING • **COOK:** 15 MIN.
MAKES: 16 SERVINGS

- **1 pkg. (16 oz.) elbow macaroni**
- **1 cup reduced-fat mayonnaise**
- **3 to 4 Tbsp. water or 2% milk**
- **2 Tbsp. red wine vinegar**
- **1 Tbsp. sugar**
- **1½ tsp. salt**
- **¼ tsp. garlic powder**
- **¼ tsp. pepper**
- **1 small sweet yellow, orange or red pepper, finely chopped**
- **1 small green pepper, finely chopped**
- **1 small onion, finely chopped**
- **1 celery rib, finely chopped**
- **2 Tbsp. minced fresh parsley**

1. Cook macaroni according to package directions. Drain; rinse with cold water and drain again.
2. In a small bowl, mix mayonnaise, water, vinegar, sugar and seasonings until blended. In a large bowl, combine the macaroni, peppers, onion and celery. Add 1 cup dressing; toss gently to coat. Refrigerate, covered, until cold, about 2 hours. Cover and refrigerate remaining dressing to add just before serving.
3. To serve, stir in the reserved dressing. Sprinkle with parsley.

¾ CUP: 160 cal., 6g fat (1g sat. fat), 5mg chol., 320mg sod., 24g carb. (3g sugars, 1g fiber), 4g pro. **DIABETIC EXCHANGES:** 1½ starch, 1 fat.

DILL VEGETABLE DIP

A friend gave me this zesty dip recipe many years ago. To make it mobile, spoon a serving of the dip in the bottom of a small cup, then garnish with fresh veggies.

—Karen Gardiner, Eutaw, AL

PREP: 5 MIN. + CHILLING • **MAKES:** 1½ CUPS

- **1 cup sour cream**
- **½ cup mayonnaise**
- **1 Tbsp. finely chopped onion**
- **2 tsp. dried parsley flakes**
- **1 tsp. dill weed**
- **1 tsp. seasoned salt**
- **Assorted fresh vegetables**

Combine the first 6 ingredients; mix well. Cover and refrigerate dip. Serve with fresh vegetables.

2 TBSP.: 107 cal., 11g fat (3g sat. fat), 17mg chol., 187mg sod., 1g carb. (1g sugars, 0 fiber), 1g pro.

STRAWBERRY MASCARPONE CAKE

Don't let the number of steps in this recipe fool you—it's easy to assemble. The cake bakes up high and fluffy, and the berries add a fresh fruity flavor. Cream cheese is a good substitute if you don't have mascarpone cheese handy.
—Carol Witczak, Tinley Park, IL

PREP: 1 HOUR + CHILLING
BAKE: 30 MIN. + COOLING
MAKES: 12 SERVINGS

- **6 cups fresh strawberries, halved (2 lbs.)**
- **2 Tbsp. sugar**
- **1 tsp. grated orange zest**
- **1 Tbsp. orange juice**
- **½ tsp. almond extract**

CAKE

- **6 large eggs, separated, room temperature**
- **2 cups cake flour**
- **2 tsp. baking powder**
- **¼ tsp. salt**
- **1½ cups sugar, divided**
- **½ cup canola oil**
- **¼ cup water**
- **1 Tbsp. grated orange zest**
- **½ tsp. almond extract**

WHIPPED CREAM

- **2 cups heavy whipping cream**
- **⅓ cup confectioners' sugar**
- **2 tsp. vanilla extract**

FILLING

- **1 cup mascarpone cheese**
- **½ cup heavy whipping cream**

1. In a large bowl, combine the first 5 ingredients. Refrigerate, covered, at least 30 minutes.
2. Place egg whites in a large bowl; let stand at room temperature 30 minutes. Meanwhile, preheat oven to 350°. Grease bottoms of two 8-in. round baking pans; line with parchment. Sift flour, baking powder and salt together twice; place in another large bowl.
3. In a small bowl, whisk the egg yolks, 1¼ cups sugar, oil, water, orange zest and almond extract until blended. Add to flour mixture; beat until well blended.
4. With clean beaters, beat egg whites on medium speed until soft peaks form. Gradually add remaining ¼ cup sugar, 1 Tbsp. at a time, beating on high after each addition until sugar is dissolved. Continue beating until soft glossy peaks form. Fold a fourth of the egg whites into batter, then fold in remaining whites.
5. Gently transfer batter to prepared pans. Bake on lowest oven rack until top springs back when lightly touched, 30-35 minutes. Cool cakes in pans for 10 minutes before removing to wire racks; remove the parchment. Cool completely.
6. Meanwhile, for whipped cream, in a large bowl, beat cream until it begins to thicken. Add the confectioners' sugar and vanilla; beat until soft peaks form. Refrigerate, covered, at least 1 hour. For the filling, in a small bowl, beat mascarpone cheese and cream until stiff peaks form. Refrigerate until assembling.
7. Drain strawberries, reserving juice mixture. Using a serrated knife, trim tops of cakes if domed. Place 1 cake layer on a serving plate. Brush with half of reserved juice mixture; spread with ¾ cup filling. Arrange half the strawberries over the top, creating an even layer; spread with remaining filling. Brush remaining cake layer with remaining juice mixture; place layer over filling, brushed side down.
8. Gently stir whipped cream; spread over top and side of cake. Just before serving, arrange the remaining strawberries over the cake.

1 PIECE: 677 cal., 48g fat (22g sat. fat), 196mg chol., 200mg sod., 56g carb. (36g sugars, 2g fiber), 10g pro.

SWEDISH BUTTER COOKIES

It's impossible to eat just one of these treats. Naturally, they're a favorite with my Swedish husband and children—but anyone with a sweet tooth will appreciate them. My recipe is well-traveled among our friends and neighbors. Folks just can't get enough!
—Sue Soderland, Elgin, IL

PREP: 10 MIN.
BAKE: 25 MIN./BATCH
MAKES: ABOUT 6 DOZEN

- **1 cup butter, softened**
- **1 cup sugar**
- **2 tsp. maple syrup**
- **2 cups all-purpose flour**
- **1 tsp. baking soda**
- **Confectioners' sugar**

1. Preheat oven to 300°. In a large bowl, cream butter and sugar until light and fluffy, 5-7 minutes. Add syrup. Combine flour and baking soda; gradually add to creamed mixture and mix well.
2. Divide dough into 8 portions. Roll each portion into a 9-in. log. Place 3 in. apart on ungreased baking sheets. Bake for 25 minutes or until lightly browned. Cut into 1-in. slices. Remove to wire racks. Dust with confectioners' sugar.

1 COOKIE: 47 cal., 3g fat (2g sat. fat), 7mg chol., 38mg sod., 6g carb. (3g sugars, 0 fiber), 0 pro.

JUNETEENTH

TEXAS-STYLE BRISKET

This is the quintessential brisket here in the Lone Star State. Grilling with wood chips takes a little extra effort, but I promise, you'll be glad you did. Each bite tastes like heaven on a plate. Even my husband's six-generation Texas family is impressed!
—Renee Morgan, Taylor, TX

PREP: 35 MIN. + CHILLING
COOK: 6 HOURS + STANDING
MAKES: 20 SERVINGS

- **1 whole fresh beef brisket (12 to 14 lbs.)**
- **½ cup pepper**
- **¼ cup kosher salt**
- **Large disposable foil pan**
- **About 6 cups wood chips, preferably oak**

1. Trim fat on brisket to ½-in. thickness. Rub brisket with pepper and salt; place in a large disposable foil pan, fat side up. Refrigerate, covered, several hours or overnight. Meanwhile, soak wood chips in water.

2. To prepare the grill for slow indirect cooking, adjust grill vents so top vent is half open and bottom vent is open only a quarter of the way. Make 2 arrangements of 45 unlit coals on opposite sides of the grill, leaving center of the grill open. Light 20 additional coals until ash-covered; distribute over the unlit coals. Sprinkle 2 cups of soaked wood chips over the lit coals.

3. Replace grill rack. Close grill and allow temperature in grill to reach 275°, about 15 minutes.

4. Place foil pan with brisket in center of grill rack; cover grill and cook 3 hours (do not open grill). Check temperature of grill periodically to maintain a temperature of 275° throughout cooking. Heat level may be adjusted by opening vents to raise the temperature and closing vents partway to decrease temperature.

5. Add another 10 unlit coals and 1 cup wood chips to each side of the grill. Cook brisket, covered, 3-4 hours longer or until fork-tender (a thermometer inserted in brisket should read about 190°); add coals and wood chips as needed to maintain a grill temperature of 275°.

6. Remove brisket from grill. Cover tightly with foil; let stand 30-60 minutes. Cut brisket across the grain into slices.

5 OZ. COOKED BEEF: 351 cal., 12g fat (4g sat. fat), 116mg chol., 1243mg sod., 2g carb. (0 sugars, 1g fiber), 56g pro.

BLACK-EYED PEAS WITH COLLARD GREENS

Here's a side dish that's considered a staple in the South. Enjoy the greens alongside your favorite grilled or salt-cured meats.
—Athena Russell, Greenville, SC

TAKES: 25 MIN. • **MAKES:** 6 SERVINGS

- **2 Tbsp. olive oil**
- **1 garlic clove, minced**
- **8 cups chopped collard greens**
- **½ tsp. salt**
- **¼ tsp. cayenne pepper**
- **2 cans (15½ oz. each) black-eyed peas, rinsed and drained**
- **4 plum tomatoes, seeded and chopped**
- **¼ cup lemon juice**
- **2 Tbsp. grated Parmesan cheese**

In a Dutch oven, heat oil over medium heat. Add garlic; cook and stir 1 minute. Add collard greens, salt and cayenne; cook and stir 6-8 minutes or until greens are tender. Add peas, tomatoes and lemon juice; heat through. Sprinkle servings with cheese.

¾ CUP: 177 cal., 5g fat (1g sat. fat), 1mg chol., 412mg sod., 24g carb. (3g sugars, 6g fiber), 9g pro.

BLUE RIBBON RED VELVET CAKE

This two-layer beauty features a striking red interior. It calls for more baking cocoa than most red velvet cakes, making it even more chocolaty. I'm proud to say that this recipe won a blue ribbon in the holiday cake division at the 2006 Alaska State Fair. I think this cake will be a winner in your house, too!
—Cindi DeClue, Anchorage, AK

PREP: 35 MIN. • **BAKE:** 25 MIN. + COOLING
MAKES: 16 SERVINGS

- **1½ cups canola oil**
- **1 cup buttermilk**
- **2 large eggs, room temperature**
- **2 Tbsp. red food coloring**
- **1 tsp. white vinegar**
- **2½ cups all-purpose flour**
- **1½ cups sugar**
- **3 Tbsp. baking cocoa**
- **1 tsp. baking soda**

FROSTING

- **1 pkg. (8 oz.) cream cheese, softened**
- **½ cup butter, softened**
- **2 tsp. vanilla extract**
- **3¾ cups confectioners' sugar**

1. Preheat oven to 350°. Line the bottoms of 2 greased 9-in. round cake pans with parchment; grease parchment. Beat the first 5 ingredients until well blended. In another bowl, whisk together flour, sugar, baking cocoa and baking soda; gradually beat into oil mixture.
2. Transfer batter to prepared pans. Bake until a toothpick inserted in center comes out clean, 25-30 minutes. Cool in pans for 10 minutes before removing to wire racks; remove parchment. Cool completely.
3. Beat cream cheese, butter and vanilla until blended. Gradually beat in the confectioners' sugar until smooth. Using a long serrated knife, trim tops of cakes; set tops aside. Place 1 cake layer on a serving plate. Spread with ¾ cup frosting. Top with remaining cake layer, bottom side up. Frost the top and side with the remaining frosting.
4. Break cake tops into pieces. Pulse in a food processor until fine crumbs form. Decorate cake with crumbs as desired.

1 PIECE: 559 cal., 33g fat (8g sat. fat), 53mg chol., 208mg sod., 64g carb. (48g sugars, 1g fiber), 4g pro.

STRAWBERRY COOLER

This refreshing beverage is easy to double. Just make two batches ahead of time, and add ginger ale and ice when you're ready for more!
—Judy Robertson, Southington, CT

TAKES: 10 MIN. • **MAKES:** 8 SERVINGS

- **3 cups water**
- **5 cups sliced fresh strawberries**
- **¾ to 1 cup sugar**
- **¼ cup lemon juice**
- **2 tsp. grated lemon zest**
- **1 cup ginger ale**
- **Crushed ice**
- **Additional strawberries, optional**

In a blender, process the water, sliced strawberries, sugar, and lemon juice and zest in batches until smooth. Strain out the berry seeds if desired. Pour mixture into a pitcher; stir in the ginger ale. Serve in chilled glasses over ice. If desired, garnish with strawberries.

1 CUP: 116 cal., 0 fat (0 sat. fat), 0 chol., 3mg sod., 29g carb. (26g sugars, 2g fiber), 1g pro.

FATHER'S DAY

PEACHY PORK RIBS

These meaty ribs make great picnic fare. Bake them first in the oven so the pork gets tender, then finish them off on the grill with a fruity basting sauce.
—Tom Arnold, Milwaukee, WI

PREP: 20 MIN. • **COOK:** 2 HOURS 10 MIN.
MAKES: 4 SERVINGS

- 2 **racks pork baby back ribs (4 lbs.), cut into serving-size pieces**
- ½ **cup water**
- 3 **medium ripe peaches, peeled and cubed**
- 2 **Tbsp. chopped onion**
- 2 **Tbsp. butter**
- 1 **garlic clove, minced**
- 3 **Tbsp. lemon juice**
- 2 **Tbsp. orange juice concentrate**
- 1 **Tbsp. brown sugar**
- 2 **tsp. soy sauce**
- ½ **tsp. ground mustard**
- ¼ **tsp. salt**
- ¼ **tsp. pepper**

1. Place ribs in a shallow roasting pan; add water. Cover and bake at 325° for 2 hours.
2. Meanwhile, for sauce, place peaches in a blender; cover and process until blended. In a small saucepan, saute onion in butter until tender. Add garlic; cook for 1 minute longer. Stir in the lemon juice, orange juice concentrate, brown sugar, soy sauce, mustard, salt, pepper and peach puree; heat through.
3. Drain ribs. Spoon some of the sauce over ribs. Grill ribs on a lightly oiled rack, covered, over medium heat until browned, 8-10 minutes, turning occasionally and brushing with sauce.

1 SERVING: 884 cal., 67g fat (26g sat. fat), 260mg chol., 553mg sod., 16g carb. (13g sugars, 1g fiber), 52g pro.

5i

FINGERLING POTATOES WITH FRESH PARSLEY & CHIVES

We use seasonings like adobo, Sazon, fresh parsley and minced chives when we grill potatoes. We've even smoked the potatoes in our portable smoker before grilling.
—Teri Rasey, Cadillac, MI

PREP: 30 MIN. + MARINATING
GRILL: 10 MIN. • **MAKES:** 6 SERVINGS

- 2 **lbs. fingerling potatoes**
- ¼ **cup olive oil**
- ½ **tsp. Goya Sazon without annatto**
- ½ **tsp. adobo seasoning**
- 2 **Tbsp. minced fresh parsley**
- 2 **Tbsp. minced chives**

1. Place potatoes in a 6-qt. stockpot; add water to cover. Bring to a boil. Reduce the heat; cook, uncovered, 15-20 minutes or until tender. Drain.
2. In a large bowl, combine olive oil and seasonings; reserve 1 Tbsp. of marinade. Add the potatoes; toss to coat. Let stand for 15 minutes.
3. Thread potatoes onto 4 metal or soaked wooden skewers. Grill, covered, over medium heat 8-10 minutes or until browned, turning once. Cool slightly.
4. Remove potatoes from skewers. Transfer the potatoes to a large bowl. Add reserved marinade and herbs; toss to coat.

1 SERVING: 215 cal., 9g fat (1g sat. fat), 0 chol., 172mg sod., 30g carb. (2g sugars, 3g fiber), 4g pro. **DIABETIC EXCHANGES:** 2 starch, 2 fat.

BARBARA CARLUCCI
Orange Park, FL

5i

MACAROON ICE CREAM TORTE

We love frozen treats. Featuring four kinds of chocolate, this torte is so pretty and decadent, people think it came from an ice cream shop.
—Barbara Carlucci, Orange Park, FL

PREP: 20 MIN. + FREEZING
MAKES: 16 SERVINGS

30 chocolate or plain macaroon cookies, crumbled
1 qt. coffee ice cream, softened if necessary
1 qt. chocolate ice cream, softened if necessary
1 cup milk chocolate toffee bits or 4 Heath candy bars (1.4 oz. each), coarsely chopped
Hot fudge topping, warmed

1. Sprinkle a third of the cookies into an ungreased 9-in. springform pan. Layer with 2 cups coffee ice cream, another third of the cookies, 2 cups chocolate ice cream and ½ cup toffee bits; repeat layers.
2. Freeze, covered, until firm. Torte may be frozen up to 2 months. Remove from freezer 10 minutes before slicing. Serve with fudge topping.

1 PIECE: 341 cal., 20g fat (11g sat. fat), 36mg chol., 110mg sod., 37g carb. (35g sugars, 2g fiber), 4g pro.

SWEET & SPICY BAKED BEANS

This recipe is a hit with guests and family. It's sweet, simple and delicious, and someone always asks for the recipe.
—Elliot Wesen, Arlington, TX

PREP: 15 MIN. • **BAKE:** 50 MIN.
MAKES: 14 SERVINGS

2 cans (28 oz. each) baked beans
1 can (20 oz.) unsweetened crushed pineapple, drained
1 cup spicy barbecue sauce
½ cup molasses
2 Tbsp. prepared mustard
½ tsp. pepper
¼ tsp. salt
1 can (6 oz.) french-fried onions, crushed, divided
5 bacon strips, cooked and crumbled, divided

1. In a large bowl, combine the first 7 ingredients. Stir in half the onions and bacon. Transfer mixture to a greased 13x9-in. baking dish.
2. Cover and bake at 350° for 45 minutes. Sprinkle with the remaining onions and bacon. Bake, uncovered, 5-10 minutes longer or until bubbly.

¾ CUP: 285 cal., 9g fat (3g sat. fat), 10mg chol., 860mg sod., 46g carb., 7g fiber, 7g pro.

5i

GRILLED MUSHROOM KABOBS

Earthy grilled mushrooms taste like flame-kissed goodness. The balsamic vinegar adds just enough tanginess to the savory side.
—Melissa Hoddinott, Sherwood Park, AB

PREP: 30 MIN. • **COOK:** 10 MIN.
MAKES: 4 SERVINGS

16 pearl onions
20 medium fresh mushrooms
⅓ cup balsamic vinegar
¼ cup butter, cubed
2 garlic cloves, minced
½ tsp. salt
½ tsp. pepper
Minced fresh parsley, optional

1. In a small saucepan, bring 6 cups water to a boil. Add pearl onions; boil 5 minutes. Drain and rinse with cold water. Peel.
2. On 4 metal or soaked wooden skewers, alternately thread mushrooms and onions, skewering mushrooms horizontally through cap. In a microwave-safe bowl, combine vinegar, butter, garlic, salt and pepper; microwave, covered, on high until butter is melted, 30-45 seconds. Whisk to combine. Reserve half of the vinegar mixture for serving. Brush kabobs with remaining vinegar mixture.
3. Grill kabobs, covered, over medium heat or broil 4 in. from heat until vegetables are tender, 10-12 minutes, turning occasionally and basting frequently with vinegar mixture. If desired, sprinkle with parsley; serve with reserved vinegar mixture.

1 KABOB: 161 cal., 12g fat (7g sat. fat), 31mg chol., 393mg sod., 13g carb. (7g sugars, 1g fiber), 3g pro.

FOURTH OF JULY

STEAK & SHRIMP KABOBS

You'll make any get-together special with these attractive kabobs. Cubes of marinated steak are skewered with shrimp, mushrooms, tomatoes, green peppers and onions, then grilled. For picnics, I assemble the kabobs at home and carry them in a large container.
—Karen Mergener, St. Croix, MN

PREP: 20 MIN. + MARINATING
GRILL: 15 MIN.
MAKES: 8 SERVINGS

- **1 cup teriyaki sauce**
- **1 can (6 oz.) pineapple juice**
- **½ cup packed brown sugar**
- **6 garlic cloves, minced**
- **¼ tsp. Worcestershire sauce**
- **⅛ tsp. pepper**
- **1 lb. beef top sirloin steak, cut into 1-in. cubes**
- **1 lb. uncooked shrimp (26-30 per lb.), peeled and deveined**
- **1 lb. whole fresh mushrooms**
- **2 large green peppers, cut into 1-in. pieces**
- **2 medium onions, halved and quartered**
- **1 pint cherry tomatoes**
- **1½ tsp. cornstarch**

1. In a large bowl, combine the first 6 ingredients. Pour half of the marinade into a shallow dish; add beef. Cover and refrigerate 8 hours or overnight, turning occasionally. Cover and refrigerate the remaining marinade.
2. Drain and discard marinade from beef. On metal or soaked wooden skewers, alternately thread the beef, shrimp, mushrooms, green peppers, onions and tomatoes. In a small saucepan, combine the cornstarch and reserved marinade until smooth. Bring to a boil; cook and stir until thickened, 1-2 minutes.
3. Prepare grill for indirect heat, using a drip pan. Place kabobs over drip pan and grill, covered, over indirect medium heat for 5 minutes. Turn kabobs and brush with thickened marinade. Cover and cook until the shrimp turn pink and beef reaches desired doneness, 5-10 minutes turning and brushing occasionally.

1 KABOB: 258 cal., 3g fat (1g sat. fat), 92mg chol., 1326mg sod., 30g carb. (24g sugars, 2g fiber), 26g pro.

FRIED POTATO SALAD

This recipe began with leftover fried potatoes I had on hand. We liked it so much that now I will fry potatoes just to make this salad. Sometimes I add grated sharp cheddar for a cheesy twist.
—Leann Stallard, Dryden, VA

PREP: 30 MIN.
COOK: 15 MIN./BATCH + COOLING
MAKES: 10 SERVINGS

- **8 medium potatoes, peeled and cut into ¼-in. pieces (about 8 cups)**
- **3 Tbsp. applewood seasoning rub**
- **½ cup canola oil**
- **1 small onion, finely chopped**
- **1 small green pepper, finely chopped**
- **2 cups Miracle Whip**
- **4 hard-boiled large eggs, chopped**
- **1 tsp. salt**
- **½ tsp. pepper**

1. Sprinkle potatoes with applewood seasoning. In a large skillet, heat oil over medium heat. Add potatoes in batches; cook, stirring frequently, until potatoes are tender, 15-20 minutes. Cool completely. Transfer to a large bowl.
2. Add remaining ingredients; gently toss to coat. Refrigerate until serving.

¾ CUP: 362 cal., 25g fat (3g sat. fat), 78mg chol., 585mg sod., 28g carb. (6g sugars, 2g fiber), 5g pro.

RED, WHITE & BLUE SUMMER SALAD

Caprese and fresh fruit always remind me of summer. In this salad, I combine traditional Caprese flavors with summer blueberries and peaches. I also add prosciutto for saltiness, creating a balanced, flavor-packed side dish.
—Emily Falke, Santa Barbara, CA

TAKES: 25 MIN. • **MAKES:** 12 SERVINGS

- **⅔ cup extra virgin olive oil**
- **½ cup julienned fresh basil**
- **⅓ cup white balsamic vinegar**
- **¼ cup julienned fresh mint leaves**
- **2 garlic cloves, minced**
- **2 tsp. Dijon mustard**
- **1 tsp. sea salt**
- **1 tsp. sugar**
- **1 tsp. pepper**
- **2 cups cherry tomatoes**
- **8 cups fresh arugula**
- **1 carton (8 oz.) fresh mozzarella cheese pearls, drained**
- **2 medium peaches, sliced**
- **2 cups fresh blueberries**
- **6 oz. thinly sliced prosciutto, julienned**
- **Additional mint leaves**

1. In a bowl, whisk the first 9 ingredients. Add tomatoes; let mixture stand while preparing salad.
2. In a large bowl, combine arugula, mozzarella, peach slices, blueberries and prosciutto. Pour tomato mixture over top; toss to coat. Garnish with additional mint leaves. Serve immediately.

1 CUP: 233 cal., 18g fat (5g sat. fat), 27mg chol., 486mg sod., 10g carb. (8g sugars, 2g fiber), 8g pro.

BERRIES & CREAM TORTE

It's easy to see why this fruity dessert always impresses dinner guests. I sometimes substitute sliced bananas for the berries.
—Tina Sawchuk, Ardmore, AB

PREP: 40 MIN.
BAKE: 10 MIN./BATCH + CHILLING
MAKES: 12 SERVINGS

- **1 cup butter, softened**
- **1 cup sugar**
- **2 large eggs, room temperature**
- **2 cups all-purpose flour**
- **2 tsp. baking powder**
- **½ tsp. salt**

FILLING

- **½ cup sugar**
- **4½ tsp. confectioners' sugar**
- **4½ tsp. cornstarch**
- **3 cups heavy whipping cream**
- **4 cups sliced fresh strawberries**
- **2 cups fresh blueberries**
- **2 cups fresh raspberries**

1. In a large bowl, cream butter and sugar. Add eggs, 1 at a time, beating well after each addition. Combine the flour, baking powder and salt; gradually add to the creamed mixture.
2. Line 2 baking sheets with parchment or greased aluminum foil; draw a 9¾-in. circle on each. Spoon a fourth of the batter onto each circle; spread evenly with a spoon to within ¼ in. of edge. Bake at 350° for 8-10 minutes or until edges are golden brown. Remove to wire racks to cool completely. Repeat with the remaining batter.
3. Combine the sugar, confectioner's sugar and cornstarch. In a large bowl, beat the cream and sugar mixture until stiff peaks form. To assemble, place 1 cookie layer on a large serving plate. Top with 1½ cups whipped cream mixture and 2 cups of mixed berries. Repeat layers twice. Top with remaining cookie layer and whipped cream mixture. Arrange the remaining berries on top. Cover and refrigerate for 4 hours.

1 PIECE: 572 cal., 39g fat (23g sat. fat), 158mg chol., 354mg sod., 54g carb. (33g sugars, 4g fiber), 5g pro.

OKTOBERFEST

GERMAN SAUERBRATEN

Our family loves it when Mom prepares this wonderful old-world dish. The tender beef has a bold blend of mouthwatering seasonings. It smells so good while it cooks in the oven—and it tastes even better!
—Cathy Eland, Highstown, NJ

PREP: 10 MIN. + MARINATING • **COOK:** 3 HRS.
MAKES: 14 SERVINGS

- **2 tsp. salt**
- **1 tsp. ground ginger**
- **1 beef top round roast (4 lbs.)**
- **2½ cups water**
- **2 cups cider vinegar**
- **⅓ cup sugar**
- **2 medium onions, sliced, divided**
- **2 Tbsp. mixed pickling spices, divided**
- **1 tsp. whole peppercorns, divided**
- **8 whole cloves, divided**
- **2 bay leaves, divided**
- **2 Tbsp. vegetable oil**
- **14 to 16 gingersnaps, crushed**

1. In a bowl, combine salt and ginger; rub over roast. Place in a deep glass bowl. In a large bowl, combine the water, vinegar and sugar. Pour half of the marinade into a large saucepan; add half of the onions, pickling spices, peppercorns, cloves and bay leaves. Bring to a boil. Pour over the roast; turn to coat. Cover and refrigerate for 2 days, turning twice a day.
2. To the remaining marinade, add the remaining onions, pickling spices, peppercorns, cloves and bay leaves. Cover and refrigerate.
3. Drain and discard marinade from roast; pat roast dry. In a Dutch oven over medium-high heat, brown roast in oil on all sides. Pour 1 cup of reserved marinade with all of the onions and seasonings over roast (cover and refrigerate remaining marinade). Bring to a boil. Reduce heat; cover and simmer for 3 hours or until meat is tender.
4. Strain cooking juices, discarding onions and seasonings. Add enough reserved marinade to the cooking juices to measure 3 cups. Pour into a large saucepan; bring to a boil. Add gingersnaps; reduce heat and simmer until gravy is thickened. Slice roast and serve with gravy.

4 OZ. COOKED BEEF WITH GRAVY: 233 cal., 7g fat (2g sat. fat), 72mg chol., 410mg sod., 11g carb. (6g sugars, 0 fiber), 30g pro.

BAVARIAN APPLE-SAUSAGE HASH

This traditional recipe reflects my German roots. In the cooler months, nothing is as comforting as a hearty hash. Include this as a side dish on an Oktoberfest or any holiday menu. It's also delicious as a brunch entree over cheddar grits or topped with a fried egg.
—Crystal Schlueter, Northglenn, CO

TAKES: 30 MIN. • **MAKES:** 4 SERVINGS

- **2 Tbsp. canola oil**
- **½ cup chopped onion**
- **4 fully cooked apple chicken sausages or flavor of your choice, sliced**
- **1½ cups thinly sliced Brussels sprouts**
- **1 large tart apple, peeled and chopped**
- **1 tsp. caraway seeds**
- **¼ tsp. salt**
- **⅛ tsp. pepper**
- **2 Tbsp. finely chopped walnuts**
- **1 Tbsp. brown sugar**
- **1 Tbsp. whole grain mustard**
- **1 Tbsp. cider vinegar**

1. In a large skillet, heat the oil over medium-high heat; saute onion until tender, 1-2 minutes. Add the sausages, Brussels sprouts, apple and seasonings; saute until lightly browned, 6-8 minutes.
2. Stir in walnuts, brown sugar, mustard and vinegar; cook and stir 2 minutes.

1 CUP: 310 cal., 17g fat (3g sat. fat), 60mg chol., 715mg sod., 25g carb. (19g sugars, 3g fiber), 16g pro.

BLAUKRAUT

This authentic German recipe is special to me because my mother used to make it for us when we were children. It's also become one of the most requested side dishes at our restaurant, Frankenmuth Bavarian Inn. Serve it alongside pork chops or your favorite German entree.
—Dorothy Zehnder, Frankenmuth, MI

PREP: 20 MIN. • **COOK:** 20 MIN.
MAKES: 10 SERVINGS

- **6 oz. bacon strips, chopped**
- **1 medium onion, chopped**
- **¼ tsp. liquid smoke, optional**
- **2 lbs. red cabbage (about 1 medium head), shredded**
- **3¼ cups water**
- **1½ cups white vinegar**
- **1 medium apple, sliced**
- **1 cup sugar**
- **1¼ tsp. salt**

1. In a Dutch oven, cook the bacon over medium heat for 5 minutes. Add onion; cook and stir until tender, 6-8 minutes. If desired, stir in liquid smoke.
2. Add cabbage, water, vinegar, apple, sugar and salt. Bring to a boil; reduce heat. Simmer, covered, until cabbage is crisp-tender, about 20 minutes, stirring every 10 minutes. Serve with a slotted spoon.

½ CUP: 189 cal., 7g fat (2g sat. fat), 11mg chol., 433mg sod., 30g carb. (26g sugars, 2g fiber), 4g pro.

EASY APPLE STRUDEL

My family loves it when I make this wonderful dessert. Old-fashioned strudel is too fattening and time-consuming, but this revised classic is just as good. We love it best served warm from the oven.
—Joanie Fuson, Indianapolis, IN

PREP: 30 MIN. • **BAKE:** 35 MIN.
MAKES: 6 SERVINGS

- **⅓ cup raisins**
- **2 Tbsp. water**
- **¼ tsp. almond extract**
- **3 cups coarsely chopped peeled apples**
- **⅓ cup plus 2 tsp. sugar, divided**
- **3 Tbsp. all-purpose flour**
- **¼ tsp. ground cinnamon**
- **2 Tbsp. butter, melted**
- **2 Tbsp. canola oil**
- **8 sheets phyllo dough (14x9-in. size)**
- **Confectioners' sugar, optional**

1. Preheat oven to 350°. Place raisins, water and extract in a large microwave-save bowl; microwave, uncovered, on high for 1½ minutes. Let stand 5 minutes. Drain. Add apples, ⅓ cup sugar, flour and cinnamon; toss to combine.
2. In a small bowl, mix melted butter and oil; remove 2 tsp. mixture for brushing top. Place 1 sheet of phyllo dough on a work surface; brush lightly with some of the butter mixture. (Keep remaining remaining phyllo covered with a damp towel to prevent it from drying out.) Layer with 7 additional phyllo sheets, brushing each layer with the butter mixture. Spread apple mixture over phyllo to within 2 in. of 1 long side.
3. Fold the short edges over filling. Roll up jelly-roll style, starting from the side with a 2-in. border. Transfer to a baking sheet coated with cooking spray. Brush with reserved butter mixture; sprinkle with remaining 2 tsp. sugar. With a sharp knife, cut diagonal slits in top of strudel.
4. Bake strudel until golden brown, 35-40 minutes. Cool on a wire rack. If desired, dust with confectioners' sugar before serving.

1 PIECE: 229 cal., 9g fat (3g sat. fat), 10mg chol., 92mg sod., 37g carb. (24g sugars, 2g fiber), 2g pro.

HALLOWEEN

HAM & CHEESE SPIDERS

These creepy spider-shaped sandwiches are sure to scare up some Halloween fun! Convenience items make them easy to prepare, and kids enjoy the classic ham-and-cheese combo.

—Kendra Barclay, De Kalb, IL

PREP: 30 MIN. • **BAKE:** 15 MIN.
MAKES: 5 SANDWICHES

- 1 cup chopped fully cooked ham
- 2 Tbsp. finely chopped onion
- 2 Tbsp. butter, softened
- 1½ tsp. prepared mustard
- 2 tubes (6 oz. each) small refrigerated flaky biscuits (5 count), divided
- 1 tube (11 oz.) refrigerated breadsticks
- 5 slices American cheese
- 1 large egg yolk
- 1 tsp. water
- 10 ripe olive slices (about 2 Tbsp.)
- 1 Tbsp. diced pimientos
- 1 tsp. poppy seeds

1. Preheat oven to 375°. Using small pieces of foil, make forty ½-in. foil balls for shaping spider legs; coat lightly with cooking spray.
2. For filling, mix first 4 ingredients. On greased baking sheets, pat 5 biscuits into 3½-in. circles. For legs, cut each of 10 breadsticks crosswise in half; cut each piece lengthwise in half. (Reserve the remaining breadsticks for another use.) Attach 8 legs to each biscuit, twisting and pressing onto pan to adhere. Tuck a foil ball under the center of each leg.
3. Spoon filling over biscuits. Fold cheese slices into quarters; place over top. Pat remaining biscuits into 4-in. circles; place over cheese, pressing edges to seal.
4. Whisk together egg yolk and water; brush over tops. Attach olives for eyes; fill centers with pimientos. Sprinkle with poppy seeds.
5. Bake until golden brown, 15-20 minutes. Serve warm.

½ SANDWICH: 264 cal., 12g fat (5g sat. fat), 35mg chol., 827mg sod., 28g carb. (5g sugars, 1g fiber), 10g pro.

COCONUT ORANGE SLICE COOKIES

Here's a family recipe that was handed down to me. The coconut and orange combination gives them a distinctive taste unlike any other cookie I've tried.

—Patricia Ann Stickler, Durand, MI

PREP: 25 MIN. • **BAKE:** 15 MIN./BATCH
MAKES: 2 DOZEN COOKIES

- 1 cup shortening
- 1 cup sugar
- 1 cup packed brown sugar
- 2 large eggs, room temperature
- 1 tsp. vanilla extract
- 2 cups all-purpose flour
- 1 tsp. baking powder
- 1 tsp. baking soda
- ½ tsp. salt
- 2 cups old-fashioned oats
- 2 cups orange candy slices, chopped
- 1 cup sweetened shredded coconut

1. Preheat oven to 350°. In a large bowl, cream shortening and sugars until light and fluffy, 5-7 minutes. Beat in eggs and vanilla. In another bowl, whisk flour, baking powder, baking soda and salt; gradually beat into creamed mixture. Stir in oats, orange candy and coconut.
2. Shape dough into 2-in. balls; place 3 in. apart on parchment-lined baking sheets. Bake until cookies are set and edges begin to brown, 15-18 minutes. Remove from pans to wire racks to cool. Store in an airtight container.

1 COOKIE: 285 cal., 10g fat (3g sat. fat), 16mg chol., 144mg sod., 46g carb. (30g sugars, 1g fiber), 3g pro.

FROSTED PISTACHIO BARS

Bar cookies are the best—so fast and easy. Go as spooky as you dare when decorating this pan for Halloween.
—Shannon Sheehy, Richmond, VA

PREP: 20 MIN. • **BAKE:** 20 MIN. + COOLING
MAKES: 2 DOZEN

- **2 cups all-purpose flour**
- **2 pkg. (3.4 oz. each) instant pistachio pudding mix**
- **½ cup sugar**
- **1 tsp. baking powder**
- **½ tsp. salt**
- **1 large egg, room temperature**
- **½ cup canola oil**
- **¼ cup water**
- **1 tsp. vanilla extract**
- **½ cup chopped pistachios, optional**

FROSTING

- **3 oz. cream cheese, softened**
- **¼ cup butter, softened**
- **1 tsp. vanilla extract**
- **⅛ tsp. salt**
- **3 cups confectioners' sugar**
- **Optional decorations: candy eyeballs, M&M's minis, milk chocolate M&M's, Life Savers hard candies and gummies, regular and mini peanut butter cups, licorice twists, shoestring licorice, Starburst fruit chews, mega and regular Smarties, Nerds, Runts, Snaps chewy candies, candy corn, tiny-size Chiclets gum, butterscotch hard candies, Rolo candies, Caramel Creams and PayDay candy bar**

1. Preheat oven to 350°. In a large bowl, whisk flour, pudding mix, sugar, baking powder and salt. In another bowl, whisk egg, oil, water and vanilla until blended; stir into flour mixture. If desired, stir in pistachios. (Dough will be stiff.)
2. Press dough into a greased 13x9-in. baking pan. Bake 20-25 minutes or until edges begin to brown. Cool completely in pan on a wire rack.
3. In a large bowl, beat cream cheese, butter, vanilla and salt until blended. Gradually beat in confectioners' sugar. Spread over top. Decorate as desired.
4. Cut into bars before serving. Store in the refrigerator.

1 BAR: 219 cal., 8g fat (2g sat. fat), 16mg chol., 227mg sod., 35g carb. (25g sugars, 0 fiber), 2g pro.

ANTI-VAMPIRE POTION (BUTTERNUT SQUASH & GARLIC SOUP)

I remember making this velvety soup with my mom. Butternut squash gives it warm color, and garlic wards off any unfriendly spirits. Use whipping cream in place of the half-and-half for an extra smooth texture.
—Steven Eder, Lebanon, PA

PREP: 15 MIN. • **COOK:** 25 MIN.
MAKES: 6 SERVINGS

- **2 Tbsp. butter**
- **1 medium onion, chopped**
- **8 garlic cloves, chopped**
- **1 tsp. ground cinnamon**
- **¼ to ½ tsp. ground nutmeg**
- **4 cups peeled butternut squash, cut in 1-in. cubes**
- **2 cups vegetable stock**
- **2 cups half-and-half cream**
- **Salt and pepper to taste**
- **8 cooked bacon strips, chopped**
- **1 pkg. (5.2 oz.) Boursin Garlic & Fine Herbs Gournay Cheese, crumbled**

1. In a large saucepan, melt butter over medium heat. Add onion and garlic; cook until tender, 3-4 minutes. Add cinnamon and nutmeg; cook 2 minutes.
2. Stir in squash and vegetable stock. Bring to a boil. Reduce heat; simmer, covered, until the squash is tender, 15-20 minutes.
3. Use an immersion blender or pulse soup in batches in blender until smooth. Return soup to pan; add half-and-half and salt and pepper to taste. Heat through, but do not boil. Serve immediately with bacon and crumbled cheese.

1 CUP: 388 cal., 28g fat (17g sat. fat), 92mg chol., 697mg sod., 21g carb. (7g sugars, 3g fiber), 12g pro.

MONSTER MUNCHIES

Looking for a fun munchie for your next Halloween shindig? Transform squash or pumpkin seeds into a spellbinding snack with ranch salad dressing mix.
—*Taste of Home* Test Kitchen

TAKES: 30 MIN. • **MAKES:** 3 CUPS

- **3 cups fresh pumpkin or squash seeds, washed and drained**
- **¼ cup vegetable oil**
- **¼ to ⅓ cup ranch salad dressing mix**

In a large skillet, saute seeds in oil for 5 minutes or until lightly browned. Using a slotted spoon, transfer seeds to an ungreased 15x10x1-in. baking pan. Sprinkle with salad dressing mix; stir to coat. Spread in a single layer. Bake at 325° for 10-15 minutes or until crisp. Store in an airtight container for up to 3 weeks.

¼ CUP: 350 cal., 23g fat (4g sat. fat), 0 chol., 481mg sod., 29g carb. (0 sugars, 9g fiber), 9g pro.

THANKSGIVING

APPLE-SAGE ROASTED TURKEY

A hint of apple flavor gives a slightly sweet spin to the dinner's main event. The lovely aroma wafting from your kitchen as this turkey cooks will have everybody talking.
—Suzy Horvath, Milwaukie, OR

PREP: 20 MIN.
BAKE: 35 HOURS + STANDING
MAKES: 14 SERVINGS

- ½ **cup apple cider or juice**
- ½ **cup apple jelly**
- ⅓ **cup butter, cubed**

TURKEY

- ⅓ **cup minced fresh sage**
- ¼ **cup butter, softened**
- 1 **turkey (14 to 16 lbs.)**
- 2 **Tbsp. apple cider or juice**
- 1½ **tsp. salt**
- 1½ **tsp. pepper**
- 2 **large apples, cut into wedges**
- 1 **large onion, cut into wedges**
- 8 **fresh sage leaves**

1. Preheat the oven to 325°. In a small saucepan, combine apple cider, jelly and butter. Cook and stir until butter is melted. Remove from heat and set aside.
2. In a small bowl, combine minced sage and butter. With fingers, carefully loosen skin from the turkey breast; rub butter mixture under the skin. Brush turkey with apple cider. Sprinkle salt and pepper over turkey and inside cavity.
3. Place the apples, onion and sage leaves inside the cavity. Tuck wings under turkey; tie drumsticks together. Place breast side up on a rack in a roasting pan.
4. Bake, uncovered, 3½ to 4 hours or until a thermometer inserted in thickest part of the thigh reads 170°-175°, basting occasionally with cider mixture. Cover loosely with foil if turkey browns too quickly. Cover and let stand 20 minutes before slicing.

FREEZE OPTION: Place sliced turkey in freezer containers; top with any cooking juices. Cool and freeze. To use, partially thaw in the refrigerator overnight. Heat through in a covered saucepan, gently stirring and adding a little broth or water if necessary.

9 OZ. COOKED TURKEY: 506 cal., 19g fat (9g sat. fat), 191mg chol., 466mg sod., 14g carb. (12g sugars, 1g fiber), 66g pro.

CLASSIC MAKE-AHEAD MASHED POTATOES

This holiday staple saves time on the day of the feast. No more frantically whipping the potatoes while hungry family and guests hang around the kitchen!
—Marty Rummel, Trout Lake, WA

PREP: 40 MIN. + CHILLING • **BAKE:** 55 MIN.
MAKES: 12 SERVINGS (¾ CUP EACH)

- 5 **lbs. potatoes, peeled and cut into wedges**
- 1 **pkg. (8 oz.) reduced-fat cream cheese, cubed**
- 2 **large egg whites, beaten**
- 1 **cup reduced-fat sour cream**
- 2 **tsp. onion powder**
- 1 **tsp. salt**
- ½ **tsp. pepper**
- 1 **Tbsp. butter, melted**

1. Place potatoes in a Dutch oven and cover with water. Bring to a boil. Reduce heat; cover and cook for 15-20 minutes or until tender. Drain.
2. In a large bowl, mash potatoes with cream cheese. Combine the egg whites, sour cream, onion powder, salt and pepper; stir into potatoes until blended. Transfer to a greased 3-qt. baking dish. Drizzle top with butter. Cover and refrigerate overnight.
3. Remove potatoes from the refrigerator 30 minutes before baking. Preheat oven to 350°. Cover and bake for 50 minutes. Uncover; bake 5-10 minutes longer or until a thermometer reads 160°.

¾ CUP: 220 cal., 7g fat (4g sat. fat), 22mg chol., 316mg sod., 32g carb. (4g sugars, 3g fiber), 7g pro. **DIABETIC EXCHANGES:** 2 starch, 1 fat.

PUMPKIN PIE CHEESECAKE

My wife and I agree—this smooth, creamy dessert is a perfect ending to a good meal. Try it in place of traditional pumpkin pie.
—DeWhitt Sizemore, Woodlawn, VA

PREP: 10 MIN. + COOLING
BAKE: 1 HOUR + COOLING
MAKES: 12 SERVINGS

- **1½ cups graham cracker crumbs**
- **1 Tbsp. sugar**
- **5 Tbsp. butter, melted**

FILLING

- **3 pkg. (8 oz. each) cream cheese, softened**
- **1 cup sugar**
- **1 tsp. vanilla extract**
- **3 large eggs, room temperature, lightly beaten**
- **1 cup canned pumpkin**
- **½ tsp. ground cinnamon**
- **¼ tsp. ground nutmeg**
- **¼ tsp. ground allspice**
- **Whipped cream**

1. In a small bowl, combine cracker crumbs and sugar; stir in butter. Press onto the bottom and 2 in. up the side of a greased 9-in. springform pan. Bake at 350° for 5 minutes. Cool on a wire rack.
2. In a bowl, beat cream cheese, sugar and vanilla until smooth. Beat in eggs on low speed just until combined. Combine the pumpkin, cinnamon, nutmeg and allspice. Fold into cheese mixture.
3. Pour into crust. Bake at 350° for 1 hour or until center is almost set. Cool on a wire rack for 10 minutes.
4. Carefully run a knife around edge of pan to loosen; cool 1 hour longer. Refrigerate until completely cooled (center will fall). Remove side of pan just before serving. Garnish with whipped cream.

1 PIECE: 245 cal., 14g fat (8g sat. fat), 87mg chol., 184mg sod., 28g carb. (20g sugars, 1g fiber), 4g pro.

SOURDOUGH DRESSING

We love our traditional Thanksgiving recipes, but sometimes we want to change things up. This sourdough stuffing is a fun twist on an old favorite. Whenever we make it after the big feast, we add a cup or more of leftover cubed turkey.
—Pat Dazis, Charlotte, NC

PREP: 45 MIN. • **BAKE:** 55 MIN.
MAKES: 16 SERVINGS

- **16 cups cubed sourdough bread**
- **¼ cup olive oil, divided**
- **4 garlic cloves, minced, divided**
- **2 medium red onions, chopped**
- **¾ cup chopped roasted sweet red peppers**
- **1 tsp. dried oregano**
- **1 carton (32 oz.) reduced-sodium chicken broth**
- **1 cup cubed cooked turkey, optional**
- **4 oz. Asiago cheese, cut into ½-in. cubes**
- **2 large eggs, lightly beaten**
- **4 green onions, chopped**
- **2 Tbsp. butter**

1. Preheat oven to 350°. Place the bread cubes in a large bowl. Drizzle with 2 Tbsp. oil; toss lightly. Sprinkle with half the garlic; toss to combine. Transfer bread cubes to 2 ungreased 15x10x1-in. baking pans. Bake 20-25 minutes or until lightly browned, turning occasionally. Let cool.
2. Meanwhile, in a large skillet, heat the remaining 2 Tbsp. oil over medium-high heat. Add the red onions; cook and stir for 5-7 minutes or until softened. Add the red peppers, oregano and remaining garlic; cook 1 minute longer. Stir in broth; bring to a boil. Remove from heat.
3. Place toasted bread in large bowl. Stir in broth mixture, turkey if desired, cheese, eggs and green onions. Transfer to a greased 13x9-in. baking dish; dot with butter. Cover and bake for 30 minutes. Uncover; bake 25-30 minutes longer or until golden brown.

¾ CUP: 207 cal., 8g fat (3g sat. fat), 34mg chol., 475mg sod., 24g carb. (4g sugars, 1g fiber), 8g pro. **DIABETIC EXCHANGES:** 1½ starch, 1½ fat, 1 lean meat.

HANUKKAH

CHEESE & RED PEPPER LATKES

These zesty latkes combine three cheeses with a handful of garlic and a colorful burst of red peppers.
—Christine Montalvo, Windsor Heights, IA

PREP: 30 MIN. • **COOK:** 5 MIN./BATCH
MAKES: 3 DOZEN

- **3 large onions, finely chopped**
- **3 medium sweet red peppers, finely chopped**
- **⅓ cup butter, cubed**
- **18 medium garlic cloves, minced, divided**
- **1 Tbsp. celery salt**
- **1 Tbsp. coarsely ground pepper**
- **3 lbs. russet potatoes, peeled and shredded**
- **1½ cups grated Parmesan cheese**
- **1½ cups shredded cheddar cheese**
- **1 cup shredded part-skim mozzarella cheese**
- **1 cup all-purpose flour**
- **¾ cup sour cream**
- **Canola oil for frying**
- **Minced fresh parsley**

1. In a large cast-iron or other heavy skillet, saute onions and red peppers in butter until tender. Add ¼ cup garlic, celery salt and pepper; cook for 1 minute longer.
2. Transfer vegetables to a large bowl. Add the potatoes, cheeses, flour, sour cream and remaining garlic; mix well.
3. Heat ¼ in. of oil in same skillet over medium heat. Working in batches, drop batter by ¼ cupfuls into hot oil. Press lightly to flatten. Fry until golden brown, carefully turning once. Drain on paper towels. Sprinkle with parsley.

3 POTATO PANCAKES: 437 cal., 29g fat (11g sat. fat), 46mg chol., 677mg sod., 33g carb. (5g sugars, 3g fiber), 12g pro.

JEWISH CHOCOLATE CHIP MANDEL BREAD

This cookie recipe has been passed down in my family for four generations. It tastes wonderful with a cup of coffee or hot cocoa.
—Monica Schnapp, Irvine, CA

PREP: 10 MIN. + CHILLING • **BAKE:** 30 MIN.
MAKES: 12 SERVINGS

- **½ cup vegetable oil**
- **½ cup plus 1 Tbsp. sugar, divided**
- **2 large eggs, room temperature**
- **½ tsp. vanilla extract**
- **1½ cups all-purpose flour**
- **½ tsp. baking powder**
- **¼ tsp. salt**
- **½ cup miniature semisweet chocolate chips**

1. Preheat oven to 375°. In a large bowl, beat oil and ½ cup sugar. Add the eggs, 1 at a time, beating well after each addition. Beat in vanilla. Combine the flour, baking powder and salt; gradually beat into oil mixture. Stir in chocolate chips. Cover and refrigerate at least 2 hours.
2. Shape dough into a 12x3-in. rectangle on a parchment-lined baking sheet. Bake until a toothpick inserted in center comes out clean, 20-25 minutes. Cool on pan on a wire rack until firm, 10-12 minutes.
3. Transfer baked rectangle to a cutting board. Using a serrated knife, cut mandel bread crosswise into 1-in. slices. Place on baking sheet, cut side down. Sprinkle with remaining 1 Tbsp. sugar
4. Bake until golden brown, 4-5 minutes on each side. Remove to a wire rack to cool completely. Store between pieces of waxed paper in an airtight container.

1 PIECE: 84 cal., 3g fat (2g sat. fat), 31mg chol., 33mg sod., 14g carb. (13g sugars, 0 fiber), 1g pro.

DID YOU KNOW?

"Kosher" is a Hebrew word that means "fit," as in "fit to eat." Kosher cooking is detailed and can vary based on different Jewish ethnic cultures and branches of Judaism. The recipes presented here are foods that could be included on a traditional Hanukkah menu. But if you adhere to strict kosher dietary guidelines—for example, never combining meat and dairy—we recommend consulting an official guide or source, such as Chabad.org, prior to menu planning.

CHOCOLATE-STUFFED DREIDEL COOKIES

These dreidel cookies are sure to bring smiles this holiday season. Your friends and family will delight in the surprise chocolate filling. Other fun cookie shapes for Hanukkah include menorahs and stars of David.
—*Taste of Home* Test Kitchen

PREP: 15 MIN. + CHILLING
BAKE: 10 MIN./BATCH + COOLING
MAKES: 3 DOZEN

- **1 cup unsalted butter, softened**
- **1 cup sugar**
- **2 large eggs, room temperature**
- **1 Tbsp. vanilla extract**
- **3½ cups all-purpose flour**
- **1 Tbsp. baking powder**
- **½ tsp. salt**
- **6 to 7 milk chocolate candy bars (1.55 oz. each), broken into 2-section pieces**
- **2½ cups vanilla frosting**
- **White and light blue paste food coloring**

1. Cream butter and sugar until light and fluffy, 5-7 minutes. Beat in eggs and vanilla. In another bowl, whisk together flour, baking powder and salt; gradually beat into creamed mixture. Divide dough in half; shape each into a disk. Cover and refrigerate until firm enough to roll, at least 1 hour.
2. Preheat the oven to 350°. On a lightly floured surface, roll each portion of dough to ⅛-in. thickness. Cut with a floured 4-in. dreidel cutter. Place half the cutouts 1 in. apart on ungreased baking sheets; top with candy bar pieces. Top with remaining cutouts, pinching edges to seal.
3. Bake until bottoms are light brown, 10-12 minutes. Remove from pans to wire racks; cool completely.
4. Tint ⅔ cup frosting light blue. Spread remaining white frosting over cookies. Pipe 1 Hebrew letter on each cookie.

1 COOKIE: 236 cal., 11g fat (6g sat. fat), 26mg chol., 123mg sod., 32g carb. (20g sugars, 1g fiber), 2g pro.

CITRUS-HERB ROAST CHICKEN

Here is one of my all-time favorite recipes. The flavorful, juicy chicken combines with fresh herbs, garlic, lemon and onions to form the perfect one-pot meal. I make the gravy right in the pan.
—Megan Fordyce, Fairchance, PA

PREP: 25 MIN. • **BAKE:** 2 HOURS + STANDING
MAKES: 8 SERVINGS

- **6 garlic cloves**
- **1 roasting chicken (6 to 7 lbs.)**
- **3 lbs. baby red potatoes, halved**
- **6 medium carrots, halved lengthwise and cut into 1-in. pieces**
- **4 fresh thyme sprigs**
- **4 fresh dill sprigs**
- **2 fresh rosemary sprigs**
- **1 medium lemon**
- **1 small navel orange**
- **1 tsp. salt**
- **½ tsp. pepper**
- **3 cups chicken broth, warmed**
- **6 green onions, cut into 2-in. pieces**

1. Preheat oven to 350°. Peel and cut garlic into quarters. Place chicken on a cutting board. Tuck wings under chicken. With a sharp paring knife, cut 24 small slits in the breasts, drumsticks and thighs. Insert garlic in slits. Tie the drumsticks together.
2. Place potatoes and carrots in a shallow roasting pan; top with herbs. Place chicken, breast side up, over vegetables and herbs. Cut lemon and orange in half; gently squeeze juices over chicken and vegetables. Place squeezed fruits inside chicken cavity. Sprinkle chicken with salt and pepper. Pour broth around chicken.
3. Roast until a thermometer inserted in thickest part of thigh reads 170°-175°, 2 to 2½ hours, sprinkling green onions over the vegetables during the last 20 minutes. (Cover loosely with foil if chicken browns too quickly.)
4. Remove chicken from oven; tent with foil. Let stand 15 minutes before carving. Discard herbs. If desired, skim fat and thicken pan drippings for gravy. Serve gravy with chicken and vegetables.

7 OZ. COOKED CHICKEN WITH 1¼ CUPS VEGETABLES: 561 cal., 24g fat (7g sat. fat), 136mg chol., 826mg sod., 39g carb. (5g sugars, 5g fiber), 47g pro.

HOMEMADE GELT

Giving chocolate coins to children, and sometimes to teachers, is a long-standing Hanukkah tradition. This homemade version of gelt uses a miniature muffin pan to mold the coins into shape. The sliced almonds add a nice crunch, but the chocolates can be left plain or topped with other ingredients like sprinkles, crushed peppermint candies or finely chopped candied ginger.
—*Taste of Home* Test Kitchen

PREP: 10 MIN. + CHILLING • **MAKES:** 3 DOZEN

- **2 tsp. canola oil**
- **3 (3½ oz. each) dark chocolate candy bars, melted**
- **¼ cup sliced almonds, finely chopped**

Brush miniature muffin cups lightly with oil. Pour about 1 tsp. melted chocolate into each cup and bang on the counter. Sprinkle with almonds. Refrigerate until set. Remove from muffin cups and blot off any excess oil, if needed.

1 PIECE: 42 cal., 3g fat (2g sat. fat), 1mg chol., 0 sod., 5g carb. (4g sugars, 1g fiber), 1g pro.

CHRISTMAS DINNER

BEEF WELLINGTON WITH MADEIRA SAUCE

This impressive yet easy-to-make dish can be made ahead. Just finish when your guests begin to arrive.
—Janaan Cunningham, Greendale, WI

PREP: 45 MIN. + CHILLING
BAKE: 40 MIN. + STANDING
MAKES: 16 SERVINGS

- 1 **beef tenderloin roast (4 to 5 lbs.)**

MADEIRA SAUCE

- 2 **cans (10½ oz. each) condensed beef consomme, undiluted**
- 2 **Tbsp. tomato paste**
- ½ **tsp. beef bouillon granules**
- 2 **Tbsp. butter, softened**
- 2 **Tbsp. all-purpose flour**
- ½ **cup Madeira wine**

FILLING

- 2 **cups chopped fresh mushrooms**
- 4 **shallots, chopped**
- ¼ **lb. sliced deli ham, chopped**
- ¼ **cup minced fresh parsley**
- 1 **pkg. (17.3 oz.) frozen puff pastry sheets, thawed**
- 2 **Tbsp. 2% milk**
- 1 **large egg, lightly beaten, optional**

1. Preheat the oven to 475°. Place the tenderloin in a greased 15x10x1-in. baking pan; fold the ends under tenderloin. Bake, uncovered, for 20-25 minutes or until browned. Cover and refrigerate for at least 2 hours or until chilled.
2. For sauce, in a large saucepan, combine the consomme, tomato paste and bouillon granules. Bring to a boil. Reduce heat; simmer, uncovered, for 20 minutes or until reduced to 2 cups.
3. Combine butter and flour until smooth. Stir into sauce, 1 tsp. at a time. Bring to a boil; cook and stir for 2 minutes or until thickened. Remove from heat; stir in wine.
4. For the filling, in a large skillet, combine mushrooms, shallots, ham and 2 Tbsp. Madeira sauce. Cook over low heat for 10 minutes, stirring occasionally. Stir in the parsley; cook 10 minutes longer or until the liquid has evaporated, stirring occasionally. Set aside.
5. Preheat the oven to 425°. On a lightly floured surface, unfold both puff pastry sheets; moisten short side of 1 sheet with water. Slightly overlap the edge of the remaining sheet over the moistened edge; press edges together. Transfer to an ungreased baking sheet.
6. Spread half of the filling down the center of pastry. Place the tenderloin on the filling. Spread the remaining filling over the top of meat. Bring edges of pastry over the filling and pinch together. Roll to place seam side down. Brush pastry edges with milk; fold edges under meat. If desired, lightly score puff pastry with a sharp knife to form a diamond pattern and brush with beaten egg.
7. Bake, uncovered, until deep golden brown, 40 minutes, covering lightly with foil if needed to prevent overbrowning (meat will be medium-rare). Transfer to a serving platter. Let stand for 15 minutes before slicing. Rewarm Madeira sauce if necessary. Serve with tenderloin.

1 PIECE: 363 cal., 17g fat (5g sat. fat), 56mg chol., 453mg sod., 21g carb. (2g sugars, 3g fiber), 30g pro.

ROASTED GREEN BEANS WITH POMEGRANATE SEEDS

This is one of the simplest dishes to make, and it requires very few ingredients! I made these green beans for the holidays this year and they were a hit.
—Dalya Rubin, Boca Raton, FL

TAKES: 30 MIN. • **MAKES:** 8 SERVINGS

- 2 **lbs. fresh green beans, trimmed**
- 2 **Tbsp. olive oil**
- ¾ **tsp. kosher salt**
- 4 **garlic cloves, minced**
- ¼ **cup pomegranate seeds**

1. Preheat oven to 425°. Place beans in a greased 15x10x1-in. baking pan. Drizzle with oil; sprinkle with salt. Toss to coat. Roast 10 minutes, stirring once.
2. Add garlic to pan. Roast until beans are crisp-tender, 5-7 minutes longer. Sprinkle with pomegranate seeds.

1 SERVING: 70 cal., 4g fat (1g sat. fat), 0 chol., 187mg sod., 9g carb. (4g sugars, 4g fiber), 2g pro. **DIABETIC EXCHANGES:** 1 vegetable, 1 fat.

KALE & BACON SALAD WITH HONEY-HORSERADISH VINAIGRETTE

Totally scrumptious and packed with nutrition, this salad recipe was my response to friends who asked how they could incorporate kale into their diets without sacrificing taste. It is also wonderful made with collard or mustard greens, prepared in the same fashion as the kale, or with a mix of spinach and arugula or watercress greens.
—Elizabeth Warren, Oklahoma City, OK

PREP: 35 MIN. • **MAKES:** 8 SERVINGS

- **10 kale leaves, stems removed, thinly sliced**
- **¼ cup loosely packed basil leaves, thinly sliced**
- **½ cup alfalfa sprouts**
- **4 bacon strips, cooked and crumbled**
- **½ cup crumbled feta cheese**
- **½ medium ripe avocado, peeled and thinly sliced**
- **1 hard-boiled large egg, chopped**
- **1 cup grape tomatoes, chopped**

VINAIGRETTE

- **⅓ cup olive oil**
- **3 Tbsp. lemon juice**
- **2 Tbsp. prepared horseradish**
- **2 Tbsp. honey**
- **1½ tsp. garlic powder**
- **1½ tsp. spicy brown mustard**
- **¼ tsp. crushed red pepper flakes**
- **⅛ tsp. pepper**
- **Dash salt**

1. On a serving platter or individual plates, arrange the kale and basil. Top with the sprouts, bacon, cheese, avocado, egg and tomatoes.
2. In a small bowl, whisk the vinaigrette ingredients. Drizzle over the salad and serve immediately.

1 SERVING: 236 cal., 15g fat (3g sat. fat), 34mg chol., 248mg sod., 21g carb. (6g sugars, 4g fiber), 8g pro.

CHRISTMAS CRANBERRIES

Bourbon adds spark to this holiday standby, packed in a small heavy-duty glass storage container with a tight-fitting lid. Wrap in a vintage tea towel or cloth napkin, cinch with ribbon and adorn with small ornaments.
—Becky Jo Smith, Kettle Falls, WA

PREP: 35 MIN. • **PROCESS:** 15 MIN.
MAKES: 4 HALF-PINTS

- **2 pkg. (12 oz. each) fresh or frozen cranberries, thawed**
- **1½ cups sugar**
- **1 cup orange juice**
- **¼ cup bourbon**
- **3 tsp. vanilla extract**
- **1 tsp. grated orange zest**

1. In a large saucepan, combine the cranberries, sugar, orange juice and bourbon. Bring to a boil. Reduce heat; simmer, uncovered, until berries pop and mixture has thickened, 18-22 minutes.
2. Remove from heat. Stir in vanilla and orange zest. Ladle hot mixture into 4 hot half-pint jars, leaving ¼-in. headspace. Remove any air bubbles and adjust the headspace, if necessary, by adding more hot mixture. Wipe rims. Center the lids on jars; screw on bands until fingertip tight.
3. Place jars into canner with simmering water, ensuring the jars are completely covered with water. Bring water to a boil; process for 15 minutes. Remove jars from canner and cool.

2 TBSP.: 54 cal., 0 fat (0 sat. fat), 0 chol., 0 sod., 13g carb. (11g sugars, 1g fiber), 0 pro.

CHRISTMAS TREATS

BUTTERSCOTCH GINGERBREAD COOKIES

Every time I make these cookies, the spicy aroma takes me back to my childhood when I helped Mom bake and deliver them to our neighbors.
—Kara Cook, Elk Ridge, UT

PREP: 15 MIN. + CHILLING
BAKE: 10 MIN. + COOLING
MAKES: ABOUT 3 DOZEN

- 1 **cup butter, softened**
- 1 **cup packed brown sugar**
- 2 **large eggs, room temperature**
- 3 **cups all-purpose flour**
- 2 **pkg. (3½ oz. each) cook-and-serve butterscotch pudding mix**
- 3 **tsp. ground ginger**
- 1 **tsp. baking powder**
- 1 **tsp. ground cinnamon**

1. In a large bowl, cream the butter and brown sugar until light and fluffy, 5-7 minutes. Beat in the eggs. Combine the flour, pudding mixes, ground ginger, baking powder and cinnamon; gradually add to the creamed mixture and mix well. Cover dough and refrigerate for 1 hour or until it's easy to handle.
2. On a lightly floured surface, roll out dough to ¼-in. thickness. Cut with lightly floured cookie cutters. Place 1 in. apart on ungreased baking sheets.
3. Bake at 350° for 6-8 minutes or until firm. Remove to wire racks to cool. Decorate as desired.

1 COOKIE: 194 cal., 8g fat (5g sat. fat), 38mg chol., 144mg sod., 29g carb. (15g sugars, 1g fiber), 2g pro.

PEPPERMINT BISCOTTI

I make these peppermint biscotti every year for Christmas. The chocolate and crushed candies add a festive look to my annual cookie platter.
—Paula Marchesi, Lenhartsville, PA

PREP: 1 HOUR • **BAKE:** 40 MIN. + COOLING
MAKES: ABOUT 3½ DOZEN

- ¾ **cup butter, softened**
- ¾ **cup sugar**
- 3 **large eggs, room temperature**
- 2 **tsp. peppermint extract**
- 3¼ **cups all-purpose flour**
- 1 **tsp. baking powder**
- ¼ **tsp. salt**
- 1 **cup crushed peppermint candies**

FROSTING

- 2 **cups semisweet chocolate chips**
- 2 **Tbsp. shortening**
- ½ **cup crushed peppermint candies**

1. Preheat oven to 350°. In a large bowl, cream butter and sugar until light and fluffy, 5-7 minutes. Add eggs, 1 at a time, beating well after each addition. Beat in extract. Combine the flour, baking powder and salt; stir in peppermint candy. Gradually add to creamed mixture, beating until blended (dough will be stiff).
2. Divide dough in half. On an ungreased baking sheet, shape each portion into a 12x2½-in. rectangle. Bake 25-30 minutes or until golden brown. Carefully remove to wire racks; cool for 15 minutes. Transfer to a cutting board; cut diagonally with a sharp knife into ½-in. slices. Place cut side down on ungreased baking sheets. Bake 12-15 minutes or until firm. Remove to wire racks to cool.
3. In a microwave-safe bowl, melt the chocolate chips and shortening; stir until smooth. Dip 1 end of each biscotti slice into melted chocolate, allowing excess to drip off; sprinkle with candy. Place on waxed paper; let stand until set. Store in an airtight container.

1 COOKIE: 121 cal., 5g fat (3g sat. fat), 24mg chol., 63mg sod., 17g carb. (8g sugars, 1g fiber), 2g pro.

5i

HOT CHOCOLATE BOMBS

These hot chocolate filled spheres are all the rage! Make them ahead of time as a holiday gift or to have on hand when you have a hot chocolate craving.
—Rashanda Cobbins, Milwaukee, WI

PREP: 45 MIN. + CHILLING + DECORATING
MAKES: 6 CHOCOLATE BOMBS

- **22 oz. semisweet chocolate, such as Baker's Chocolate, finely chopped**
- **½ cup baking cocoa**
- **½ cup nonfat dry milk powder**
- **¼ cup confectioners' sugar**
- **6 Tbsp. vanilla marshmallow bits (not miniature marshmallows)**
- **Optional: sprinkles, colored sanding sugar, melted candy melts**

1. Place chocolate in a microwave-safe bowl. Microwave, uncovered, on high for 1 minute; stir. Microwave, stirring every 30 seconds, until chocolate is melted and smooth, 1-2 minutes longer. Chocolate should not exceed 90°.
2. Add 1 Tbsp. melted chocolate into a silicone sphere-shaped mold (roughly 2½-in. diameter). Brush melted chocolate evenly inside the molds, all the way to the edges, rewarming melted chocolate as needed. Refrigerate molds until chocolate is set, 3-5 minutes. Brush a thin second layer of chocolate in molds. Refrigerate until set, 8-10 minutes. Place remaining melted chocolate into a piping bag fitted with a small round decorating tip; set piping bag aside.
3. Remove chocolate spheres from molds. In a medium bowl, whisk together baking cocoa, milk powder and confectioners' sugar. Place 3 Tbsp. cocoa mixture into half of the chocolate spheres. Top with 1 Tbsp. marshmallow bits.
4. Pipe a thin line of melted chocolate on edges of remaining spheres; carefully adhere to filled halves, pressing lightly to seal, using additional melted chocolate if necessary. If desired, decorate bombs with optional ingredients. Refrigerate until set. Store in a tightly sealed container.
5. To prepare hot chocolate, place a hot chocolate bomb in a mug; add 1 cup warm milk and stir to dissolve.

1 CHOCOLATE BOMB: 619 cal., 34g fat (20g sat. fat), 1mg chol., 31mg sod., 36g carb. (29g sugars, 4g fiber), 10g pro.

CHOCOLATE-CHERRY SANDWICH COOKIES

I make these at Christmastime, but they're special for any holiday or occasion. Chilling the cookies before you dip them in chocolate is important because it firms up the filling.
—Amy Sauerwalt, Columbia, MD

PREP: 35 MIN. + CHILLING
MAKES: 3½ DOZEN

- **4 oz. cream cheese, softened**
- **½ cup confectioners' sugar**
- **½ cup finely chopped maraschino cherries, drained**
- **¼ tsp. almond extract**
- **1 pkg. (12 oz.) vanilla wafers**
- **18 oz. milk chocolate candy coating, melted**
- **Red and white sprinkles or colored sugar**

1. In a small bowl, beat cream cheese and confectioners' sugar until smooth; stir in cherries and extract. Spread 1 tsp. cream cheese mixture on bottoms of each of half of the wafers; cover with the remaining wafers. Refrigerate 1 hour or until filling is firm.
2. Dip sandwiches in candy coating; allow excess to drip off. Place on waxed paper; top with sprinkles or colored sugar. Let stand until set. Store cookies in an airtight container in the refrigerator.

1 SANDWICH COOKIE: 105 cal., 5g fat (3g sat. fat), 4mg chol., 39mg sod., 14g carb. (11g sugars, 0 fiber), 1g pro.

SNOWY PINE CONES

Pull out each goldfish graham and dip it in the soft center to snack on these pine cones. There's nothing more fun or creative on the cookie table this year!
—Betty MacArthur, Portland, OR

PREP: 1¼ HOURS
MAKES: 16 PINE CONE COOKIES

- **8 cups Goldfish fudge brownie grahams (about 24 oz.), divided**
- **1 cup butter, softened**
- **1 cup Nutella**
- **½ cup Biscoff creamy cookie spread**
- **3 cups plus 2 Tbsp. confectioners' sugar, divided**
- **8 pretzel rods, halved**

1. Pulse 1 cup grahams in a food processor until fine crumbs form. In a large bowl, beat butter, Nutella, cookie spread and 3 cups confectioners' sugar until smooth; stir in crumbs.
2. Mold ¼ cup dough around a pretzel rod in a cone shape to within 1 in. of top; place on a waxed paper-lined baking sheet. Starting at the bottom, insert tail ends of Goldfish grahams, flat side up, into dough to resemble a pine cone, trimming tails of fish as needed near the top. Using kitchen scissors, cut off tip of pretzel; place a small amount of dough on top of pretzel. Repeat with the remaining dough and pretzels.
3. Dust pine cones with the remaining confectioners' sugar. Store in an airtight container in the refrigerator.

1 COOKIE: 524 cal., 26g fat (10g sat. fat), 31mg chol., 332mg sod., 70g carb. (49g sugars, 3g fiber), 4g pro.

GNOME COOKIES

Everywhere we went on our trip through Copenhagen, these sprightly, festive folks greeted us. Baking up our simple cookie version helps make our warm memories even cozier.
—James Schend, Pleasant Prairie, WI

PREP: 30 MIN. + CHILLING
BAKE: 10 MIN./BATCH + COOLING
MAKES: 3 DOZEN

- **1 cup butter, softened**
- **1½ cups confectioners' sugar**
- **1 tsp. vanilla extract**
- **½ tsp. almond extract**
- **1 large egg, room temperature**
- **2½ cups all-purpose flour**
- **1 tsp. baking soda**
- **1 tsp. cream of tartar**

DECORATION

- **2 cups red, green or blue candy coating disks**
- **36 miniature marshmallows**
- **1½ cups white candy coating disks**
- **2 cups sweetened shredded coconut**
- **36 Sixlets or other candies**

1. In a large bowl, cream the butter, confectioners' sugar and extracts until light and fluffy, 5-7 minutes. Beat in the egg. Combine the flour, baking soda and cream of tartar; gradually add to creamed mixture and mix well.
2. Divide dough into thirds. Shape each into a ball, then flatten into a disk. Place in a covered freezer container and freeze for 15 minutes or until easy to roll.
3. Preheat the oven to 350°. On a lightly floured surface, roll 1 portion of dough into a 10-in. circle. Cut into 12 wedges. Place wedges 2 in. apart on ungreased baking sheets.
4. Bake until edges are lightly browned, about 10-13 minutes. Cool for 2 minutes. Remove from pans to wire racks to cool completely. Repeat with remaining dough.
5. To decorate, spoon the melted colored candy coating over pointed end of cookies; add a marshmallow to each point for hat. Let stand until set. Spoon melted white candy coating over remaining portion of cookies and sprinkle with coconut. Place a Sixlet for the nose; let stand until set. Store in an airtight container.

1 COOKIE: 234 cal., 13g fat (10g sat. fat), 20mg chol., 115mg sod., 28g carb. (21g sugars, 0 fiber), 1g pro.

SNOWMEN COOKIES

These cute snowmen cookies make great treats for children's parties. Kids are always eager to help decorate.
—Sherri Johnson, Burns, TN

TAKES: 20 MIN. • **MAKES:** 32 COOKIES

- **1 pkg. (16 oz.) Nutter Butter cookies**
- **1¼ lbs. white candy coating, melted**
- **Miniature chocolate chips**
- **M&M's minis**
- **Pretzel sticks, halved**
- **Decorating gel or frosting**

1. Using tongs, dip the cookies in candy coating; allow excess to drip off. Place on waxed paper. Place 2 chocolate chips on 1 end of each cookie for eyes. Place the M&M's minis down middle for buttons and between eyes for nose.
2. For arms, dip ends of 2 pretzel stick halves into coating; attach 1 to each side of snowmen. Let stand until set. Pipe mouth and scarf with gel or frosting.

1 COOKIE: 180 cal., 9g fat (6g sat. fat), 0 chol., 67mg sod., 23g carb. (17g sugars, 1g fiber), 1g pro.

CHOCOLATE-DIPPED BEVERAGE SPOONS

These make cute gifts during the holidays. To set the chocolate quickly, simply chill the dipped spoons in the freezer.
—Marcy Boswell, Menifee, CA

PREP: 45 MIN. + CHILLING • **MAKES:** 2 DOZEN

1 cup milk chocolate chips
3½ tsp. shortening, divided
1 cup white baking chips
24 disposable wooden or plastic spoons
Optional: Coarse sugar or chocolate sprinkles

In a microwave-safe bowl, melt the milk chocolate chips with 2 tsp. shortening; stir until smooth. Repeat with white baking chips and remaining shortening. Dip the spoons into either mixture, tapping the handles on bowl edges to remove excess. Place on a waxed paper-lined baking sheet. Pipe or drizzle milk chocolate over white-dipped spoons and white mixture over milk chocolate-dipped spoons. Use a toothpick or skewer to swirl chocolate. If desired, decorate with coarse sugar or sprinkles. Chill for 5 minutes or until set. Use as stirring spoons for coffee or cocoa.
1 SPOON: 81 cal., 5g fat (3g sat. fat), 3mg chol., 12mg sod., 8g carb. (8g sugars, 0 fiber), 1g pro.

CHEVRON ORNAMENT COOKIES

My crispy, buttery cookies are playful and elegant. It's so much fun to make the chevron pattern in the dough. After it's rolled out, I use ornament and mitten cookie cutters but you can use any shape of your choice.
—Aria Thornton, Milwaukee, WI

PREP: 45 MIN. + FREEZING
BAKE: 10 MIN./BATCH + COOLING
MAKES: ABOUT 2 DOZEN

1½ cups butter, softened
2 cups sugar
2 large eggs, room temperature
2 tsp. vanilla extract
5 cups all-purpose flour
1½ tsp. baking powder
1 tsp. salt
½ tsp. baking soda
⅛ to ¼ tsp. paste food coloring

1. Cream butter and sugar until light and fluffy, 5-7 minutes. Beat in eggs and vanilla. In another bowl, whisk flour, baking powder, salt and baking soda; beat into creamed mixture. Divide the dough in half; add desired food coloring to 1 portion (or different colors to each portion). Shape into two 9x4-in. rectangles that are 1 in. thick; freeze until firm, about 30 minutes.
2. Using a sharp knife, cut rectangles crosswise into ⅛-in. slices. Create 2 new rectangles by stacking alternate-colored dough slices side by side, brushing water between slices so they adhere. Trim off any uneven dough. Roll dough portions between 2 pieces of waxed paper to ½-in. thickness; freeze until firm, about 15 minutes.
3. Preheat oven to 350°. With a sharp knife, cut the rectangles diagonally into ½-in. slices. To form chevron pattern, turn every other slice upside down, brushing water between slices so they adhere. Roll between sheets of waxed paper to ¼-in. thickness.
4. Cut with desired cookie cutters. Place cookies 2 in. apart on ungreased baking sheets. Bake until set, 10-12 minutes. Cool 1-2 minutes before removing from pans to wire racks to cool completely.
1 COOKIE: 269 cal., 12g fat (7g sat. fat), 46mg chol., 253mg sod., 37g carb. (17g sugars, 1g fiber), 3g pro.

ALPHABETICAL INDEX

SUBSTITUTIONS & EQUIVALENTS

EQUIVALENT MEASURES

3 teaspoons	= 1 tablespoon	**16 tablespoons**	= 1 cup
4 tablespoons	= ¼ cup	**2 cups**	= 1 pint
5⅓ tablespoons	= ⅓ cup	**4 cups**	= 1 quart
8 tablespoons	= ½ cup	**4 quarts**	= 1 gallon

FOOD EQUIVALENTS

Macaroni	1 cup (3½ ounces) uncooked	= 2½ cups cooked
Noodles, Medium	3 cups (4 ounces) uncooked	= 4 cups cooked
Popcorn	⅓-½ cup unpopped	= 8 cups popped
Rice, Long Grain	1 cup uncooked	= 3 cups cooked
Rice, Quick-Cooking	1 cup uncooked	= 2 cups cooked
Spaghetti	8 ounces uncooked	= 4 cups cooked

Bread	1 slice	= ¾ cup soft crumbs, ¼ cup fine dry crumbs
Graham Crackers	7 squares	= ½ cup finely crushed
Buttery Round Crackers	12 crackers	= ½ cup finely crushed
Saltine Crackers	14 crackers	= ½ cup finely crushed

Bananas	1 medium	= ⅓ cup mashed
Lemons	1 medium	= 3 tablespoons juice, 2 teaspoons grated zest
Limes	1 medium	= 2 tablespoons juice, 1½ teaspoons grated zest
Oranges	1 medium	= ¼-⅓ cup juice, 4 teaspoons grated zest

Cabbage	1 head = 5 cups shredded	**Green Pepper**	1 large = 1 cup chopped
Carrots	1 pound = 3 cups shredded	**Mushrooms**	½ pound = 3 cups sliced
Celery	1 rib = ½ cup chopped	**Onions**	1 medium = ½ cup chopped
Corn	1 ear fresh = ⅔ cup kernels	**Potatoes**	3 medium = 2 cups cubed

Almonds	1 pound = 3 cups chopped	**Pecan Halves**	1 pound = 4½ cups chopped
Ground Nuts	3¾ ounces = 1 cup	**Walnuts**	1 pound = 3¾ cups chopped

EASY SUBSTITUTIONS

When you need...		Use...
Baking Powder	1 teaspoon	½ teaspoon cream of tartar + ¼ teaspoon baking soda
Buttermilk	1 cup	1 tablespoon lemon juice or vinegar + enough milk to measure 1 cup (let stand 5 minutes before using)
Cornstarch	1 tablespoon	2 tablespoons all-purpose flour
Honey	1 cup	1¼ cups sugar + ¼ cup water
Half-and-Half Cream	1 cup	1 tablespoon melted butter + enough whole milk to measure 1 cup
Onion	1 small, chopped (⅓ cup)	1 teaspoon onion powder or 1 tablespoon dried minced onion
Tomato Juice	1 cup	½ cup tomato sauce + ½ cup water
Tomato Sauce	2 cups	¾ cup tomato paste + 1 cup water
Unsweetened Chocolate	1 square (1 ounce)	3 tablespoons baking cocoa + 1 tablespoon shortening or oil
Whole Milk	1 cup	½ cup evaporated milk + ½ cup water

GET COOKING WITH A WELL-STOCKED KITCHEN

In a perfect world, you plan weekly or even monthly menus and have all the ingredients on hand to make each night's dinner. The reality, however, is that you may not get to think about dinner until you walk through the door.

With a reasonably stocked pantry, refrigerator and freezer, you'll still be able to serve a satisfying meal in short order. Consider these tips:

QUICK-COOKING MEATS—such as boneless chicken breasts, chicken thighs, pork tenderloin, pork chops, ground meats, Italian sausage, sirloin and flank steaks, fish fillets and shrimp—should be stocked in the freezer. Wrap individual pieces and portions, so you can remove only the amount you need. For the quickest defrosting, wrap meats for freezing in small, thin packages.

FROZEN VEGETABLES are a real time-saver. Simply pour out the amount needed—no additional preparation is required.

PASTAS, RICE, RICE MIXES AND COUSCOUS are great staples to have in the pantry—and they generally have a long shelf life. Remember that thinner pastas, such as angel hair, cook faster than thicker pastas, and fresh (refrigerated) pasta cooks faster than dried.

DAIRY PRODUCTS like milk, sour cream, cheeses (shredded, cubed or crumbled), eggs, yogurt, butter and margarine are perishable, so check the use-by date on packages and replace as needed.

CONDIMENTS like ketchup, mustard, mayonnaise, salad dressings, salsa, taco sauce, soy sauce, stir-fry sauce, hot sauce, lemon juice and lime juice add flavor to many dishes. Personalize the list to suit your family's tastes.

FRESH FRUIT AND VEGETABLES can make a satisfying pre-dinner snack. Oranges and apples are not as perishable as bananas. Ready-to-use salad greens are perfect for an instant salad.

DRIED HERBS, SPICES, VINEGARS and seasoning mixes add lots of flavor and keep for months.

PASTA SAUCES, OLIVES, BEANS, broths, canned tomatoes, canned vegetables and canned or dried soups are ideal to have on hand for a quick meal—and many of these items are common recipe ingredients.

GET YOUR FAMILY INTO THE HABIT of posting a grocery list. When an item is used up or is almost gone, just add it to the list for your next shopping trip. This way you're less likely to run completely out of an item, and you'll also save time when writing your grocery list.

MAKE THE MOST OF YOUR TIME EVERY NIGHT

With recipes in hand and the kitchen stocked, you're well on the way to a relaxing family meal. Here are some pointers to help get dinner on the table fast:

PREHEAT THE OVEN OR GRILL before starting on the recipe.

PULL OUT THE REQUIRED INGREDIENTS, mixing tools and cooking tools before beginning any prep work.

USE CONVENIENCE ITEMS whenever possible. Think pre-chopped garlic, onion and peppers, shredded or cubed cheese, seasoning mixes and jarred sauces.

MULTITASK! While the meat is simmering for a main dish, toss a salad together, cook a side dish or start on dessert.

ENCOURAGE HELPERS. Have younger children set the table. Older ones can help with ingredient preparation or can even assemble the recipes themselves.

TAKE CARE OF TWO MEALS IN ONE NIGHT by planning main-dish leftovers or making a double batch of favorite sides.

TRICKS TO TAME HUNGER WHEN IT STRIKES

Are the kids begging for a pre-supper snack? Calm their rumbling tummies with nutritious, not-too-filling noshes.

START WITH A SMALL TOSSED SALAD. Try a ready-to-serve salad mix, and add their favorite salad dressing and a little protein, like cubed cheese or julienned slices of deli meat.

CUT UP AN APPLE and smear a little peanut butter on each slice, or offer other fruits such as seedless grapes, cantaloupe, oranges or bananas. For variety, give kids vanilla yogurt or reduced-fat ranch dressing as a dipper, or combine a little reduced-fat sour cream with a sprinkling of brown sugar. Too busy to cut up the fruit? A fruit snack cup will also do the trick.

DURING THE COLD MONTHS, a small mug of soup with a few oyster crackers on top can really hit the spot.

RAW VEGGIES such as carrots, cucumbers, mushrooms, broccoli and cauliflower are tasty treats, especially when served with a little hummus for dipping. Many of these vegetables can be purchased already cut.

OFFER A SMALL SERVING of cheese and crackers. Look for sliced cheese, and cut the slices into smaller squares to fit the crackers. Choose a cracker that's made from whole wheat, such as an all-natural seven-grain cracker.